Noble
Abstractions

Noble Abstractions

American Liberal Intellectuals and World War II

Frank A. Warren

Ohio State University Press

Columbus

Library of Congress Cataloging-in-Publication Data

Warren, Frank A.
  Noble abstractions : American liberal intellectuals and World War II / Frank A.
Warren.
     p.   cm.
  Includes bibliographical references and index.
  ISBN 0-8142-0814-2 (cloth : alk. paper)
  1. United States—Politics and government—1933–1945.   2. United States—
Military policy—History—20th century.   3. World War, 1939–1945—United
States—Influence.   4. United States—Intellectual life—20th century.
5. Intellectuals—United States—Political activity—History—20th century.
6. Liberalism—United States—History—20th century.   7. Roosevelt, Franklin D.
(Franklin Delano), 1882–1945.   I. Title.
E806.W2713   1999
320.973'09'044—dc21   98-44839
                                                                                          CIP

Type set in Goudy Old Style by G & S Typesetters, Inc.
Printed by Braun-Brumfield, Inc.

9 8 7 6 5 4 3 2 1

For Victoria, Catherine, Charlotte, and Frank

Are we fighting to preserve capitalism, or are we really sincere about the noble abstractions which we have together espoused?

—*The New Republic*, June 5, 1944

Contents

Acknowledgments

Every historian has his or her debts. I would first like to thank the students who helped me as research assistants: Ann Quinn, John Welch, Donald Gordon, and Betty Fowler. Four PSC-CUNY grants through Queens College enabled me to take essential research trips. I would like to thank the librarians at the State Historical Society of Wisconsin, Madison, Wisconsin; the Newberry Library, Chicago, Illinois; the Library of Congress; the Mudd Library at Princeton University; the Sterling and Beinecke Libraries at Yale University; the Schlesinger Library at Radcliffe College; the State University of New York at Stony Brook Library; the New York Public Library; the Tamiment Institute at New York University; the Harry S. Truman Library in Independence, Missouri; the Benjamin S. Rosenthal Library, Queens College (in particular Evelyn Silverman for the efficiency and cheerfulness with which she responded to my many requests); and especially the Bryant Library in Roslyn, New York, where Carol Klotz and later Mary Carroll Moore were most helpful in interlibrary loan, Marcie Zuckerman was master of the microfilm machine before the library bought reliable ones, and Lilly Handelman tracked down whatever strange request I made.

I am indebted to Sara Alpern and Alonzo Hamby for their thoughtful reading of the manuscript and for their helpful suggestions for improvement. I am further indebted to Karie Kirkpatrick for her careful and perceptive copyediting. I want to thank the following people whose computer help enabled me to survive my dinosaur computer and Luddite mentality: Robin Koumis (my son-in-law), Sheila Williams, David Bruce, and Kim Geiger. I also want to thank Francine Kapchan, Lana Yee, and especially Marilyn Harris for their help in the preparation of the final manuscript.

I hope my colleagues at Queens College will forgive me for not naming individually all of those whom I questioned about particular aspects of my work. That I wasn't able to follow up on every suggestion they made reflects the limits of my own capacities and not the generosity of their help. The late Ira Marienhoff shared with me his personal memories of the Union for Democratic Action, and Bernard Bellush and Lewis Coser kindly answered queries I had about the Socialist Party during the war. I discussed with Richard Greenwald, a former undergraduate student of mine and a recent Ph.D. in labor history at New York University, twentieth-century trends in the labor movement.

I am, as so often, most indebted to my colleague and close friend Michael Wreszin. Mike read the first draft of the manuscript, raised important questions, and his comments—both critical and supportive—were tremendously helpful. His own work on Dwight Macdonald shed light on any number of issues that my group of liberals also faced, although often the liberal analyses and answers were quite different from Macdonald's—and certainly the wit and the prose suffered in comparison. But beyond any immediate help with the book, Mike has offered an example of vibrancy in living one's life and political courage in fighting injustice. Ours is a friendship that I count as one of the best things that ever happened to me.

I am sorry that my friend Bill McLoughlin did not live to see the publication of this book. As my dissertation adviser, he first encouraged me to think that I had something important to say. Through the years, he continued to encourage me, and he and Virginia McLoughlin provided a home away from home whenever I was in Providence.

My greatest support continued to come from my wife, Joyce. Her awareness of the snare of abstractions has influenced my thinking. Beyond that I will not be more effusive; I believe she knows what she has meant and means to me. The book is dedicated to my children, Victoria, Catherine, Charlotte, and Frank. Each is very special to me, and I hope that the book may help them understand where their father came from politically. And this is important. For though they share generally my politics, the language that framed my politics is a language that was rooted in the thirties and the war years and has apparently lost its resonance for even those who may agree with many of its policies. Where I came from was right out of the noble liberal aspirations and abstractions. And this is one reason why the writing of this book has been an intensely personal experience. I grew up with parents who during World War II shared many of the attitudes and beliefs that I write about here, often critically. I can still feel the sense of disappointment and betrayal of liberal principles (the principles that provided the basis for the liberal interpretation of World War II) that pervaded our house when Roosevelt's reorganization of the State Department in 1945 included a decidedly conservative group. It is clear from this study that I do not share some of the views that my parents held then (they too modified some of them, though my father retained his faith in the American people—in 1972 he believed that McGovern would somehow defeat Nixon). But seldom a day passes in which I do not think about the goodness of their lives and the richness of their causes—from civil liberties and civil rights to peace vigils; their courage continues to inspire me. The lives they touched and enriched affirmed the bonds of humanity in ways that I am still trying to figure out. They were always in this study, encouraging me to follow my own views.

What I have written here, then, should suggest that this work was motivated by reasons that went beyond intellectual curiosity. My interest in liberalism and radicalism is far deeper than academic interest. It comes out of my personal past, and researching and writing about wartime liberal intellectuals have meant confronting that past on an intellectual and emotional level. My work is not a definitive history of wartime liberalism, but it is my own summing up of its strengths and weaknesses. It is a dialogue with liberalism's own past and with my own past, written, I hope, with a respect for the historical record.

Introduction

When I first started to conceive of this book, liberalism as a political persuasion had begun to fall, but had not yet completely fallen, into the political and intellectual disrepute it now finds itself mired in. Nor had historians begun increasingly to turn their attention to World War II. All of which is to say: this book was a long time in coming. For this I have some regrets. I made some decisions about how I could benefit education in my local community and in my department that may or may not have been wise, but which did delay at various stages the work on this book. This long period of germination, however, has had some benefits; it enabled me to focus on what, when I began, was not my original conception. Thus, the evolution of the book is important to understanding its concerns. After I completed my book on the Socialist Party of the 1930s, and having already written on the liberalism of the 1930s, I decided I wanted to move forward into the 1940s to do a comparative study of the retreat of American intellectuals from socialism and the continued flourishing of socialist ideas among British intellectuals. After beginning my research in American sources and after immersing myself in the writings of the British left during a year in England, I realized that there was far more I wanted to explore about the American liberals than could be dealt with in a comparative study. And although I had familiarized myself with a rich variety of the British writers—from the familiar names of Harold Laski, G. D. H. Cole, and John Strachey to the less familiar ones of Richard Acland and Kenneth Ingram—there was so much within the British left tradition that I did not yet understand that whatever points I had to make by way of comparison and contrast could not sustain a book. Moreover, I was becoming increasingly absorbed in how the American liberal intellectuals interpreted the war and what consequences this had in how they responded to events and political developments.

My scholarly interest has always lain in the area where conceptions of the world and political principles intersected with events, and the kind of political and moral dilemmas the intersections caused for the liberal and socialist left. And so I increasingly turned my attention to the American liberal intellectuals. Reading the liberal press and working through the papers of a number of liberals, I was particularly interested in their interpretation of World War II as a democratic revolution and an international civil war between democracy and fascism. I was equally interested in their continued commitment to Roosevelt and the New Deal, and the political and moral dilemmas created by the difference between their conception of the world and how Roosevelt acted internationally and domestically. And these were not the only dilemmas created by their conception of the war. My reading convinced me that much of liberal thinking involved abstractions that had very little to do with the reality of the war. This did not mean that I thought the liberal interpretation of World War II was unimportant. In fact, I came to believe it was manifestly important in providing the country with an interpretation of America and the war. I also came to believe that it was very important in completing a process, largely begun in the 1930s, whereby a new conception of the United States was taking hold in much of the popular consciousness.

Nevertheless, in terms of what the liberals believed about the world during the war, their interpretations were filled with abstractions—abstractions that created illusions about what *was* and what *would be*. But if the liberal world view was abstract and often illusory, it was also noble. The ideals they held by way of interpreting the war and the United States remain positive ideals, despite conservative and neoconservative efforts to besmirch democratic and egalitarian ideals and social compassion.

Yet, if the book explicitly and implicitly rejects the conservative critique of liberalism, it nonetheless has a critical perspective. The distance between the liberal abstractions and the reality of the war, on one hand, and the distance between those abstractions and liberal performance, on the other hand, has given my study a critical edge. I hope I have not done this with a heavy hand. I have tried to understand and explain, but I have not refrained from judgment, often critical judgment. And anyone who reads to the end will find that my sympathies lie with the democratic socialist left, which gave the war only "critical support." This was the Socialist Party position. The Socialist Party not only refused to support

Roosevelt and his wartime policies—indeed it focused much of its energies on exposing the administration's inequities and failures—but also continued its prewar criticism of the capitalist system, which, it believed, contributed to producing World War II. I have my criticisms of the Socialist Party too, but they are not as severe as some of my judgments on the liberal intellectuals.

I frankly admit that I admire the small band of socialists who attempted to keep alive what I had many years ago called "an alternative vision." From "Torchy" corresponding with the socialist servicemen to the socialist conscientious objectors participating in hunger strike protests against prison conditions, from the ideological Travers Clement to the moralistic Norman Thomas, from Lillian Symes, dying of cancer, but continuing to write her feisty and acerbic column, to McAlister Coleman peeling away the pretentiousness of received opinion with humor and wit, it seemed to me that they created a kind of saving remnant which, juxtaposed with the illusions of the liberal intellectual community, helped to reveal its failures as well as to point toward an alternative politics that the liberals unfortunately ignored.

In arguing that the Socialist Party's analysis of the war and its political perspective offered an alternative politics, I should make clear at the outset that I do not mean that it offered an alternative that promised immediate success. Some critics may object that there was no viable alternative to the liberal support of Roosevelt and the New Deal and that any move to the socialist left would simply have meant further liberal marginalization. But "viable" is one of those tricky words that is too often used to dampen politics that depart from the mainstream. Almost every protest movement that has furthered the cause of economic and social justice was told that its strategies did not offer a viable alternative. What my reading of the history of the liberal intellectuals during World War II suggests is that their goals would have been better served if they had dropped their strategy of building liberal influence within the Democratic Party and devoted their energies to building a democratic left movement detached from the Democratic Party. I do not suggest that these intellectuals could or should have been the organizers of such a movement, but that they should have advocated such a movement and thrown their support to those areas that would have furthered it. There may have been few such areas in existence, but those that were, such as labor opposition to the no-strike pledge or organized opposition to the Japanese-American internment, received little help from the liberals examined here. And the one significant political move that might have been made—a break with Roosevelt to support Norman Thomas in 1944—was rejected out of hand.

But in my critique of the liberal intellectual community, I do not want to be misunderstood. Many years ago, in *The Revolt against Formalism,* Morton White made an extended critique of John Dewey's attempt to solve the question of the "is" and the "ought." But in the end, he said that, despite Dewey's failures, he wished to associate himself with Dewey's efforts rather than with those of his critics like Reinhold Niebuhr and Walter Lippmann. After my critical journey through the liberal terrain, I do not want to associate myself with either the liberal politics or the liberal view of World War II, but I do want to associate myself with—for want of a better word—the liberal "spirit." There is a largeness in aspiration and a caring about humanity that despite my criticisms I continue to find attractive. As I have already said, the aspirations were *noble* and that is important in a world too often filled with a mean-spiritedness that continues to violate them. I am convinced that those aspirations helped motivate what might be called rank-and-file liberals to do in their lives "good deeds," just as the original ideals, as distinguished from the corrupted party bureaucracy, motivated many rank-and-file Communists to do "good deeds." My judgments on the liberal "influentials" and their intellectual supporters is not always as kind, and certainly my judgment of the Communist Party leadership is different from how I view the rank and file. But in the case of the liberal intellectuals, despite my often critical judgments on the abstractions and their consequences, I would not want it to be forgotten that what they were trying to achieve was noble. That I personally find it better expressed in a democratic socialism infused with many traditional liberal principles may help clarify my perspective in this study.

Historians are wont to make large claims for their work, and I certainly do not want to claim my study is less than important. But I have an aversion to historians claiming—or letting their publishers claim—that their works are definitive when they are not. I believe my study tells us a lot about the history of modern liberal intellectuals, but I do not think it is definitive. I would hope that it might inspire others to explore some of the issues I have discussed in greater depth. Certainly, some of the individuals in this study deserve full-length biographies. I would cite particularly Tom Amlie, who is an important figure in this study.

In this study, I refer to "liberal intellectuals," "pro-war liberals," or "the liberal intellectual community." I recognize that there were other liberal intellectuals than those I have considered. Some were pro-war, like many around *The New Leader;* some supported the war with less enthusiasm, like many around *The Progressive.* So I am aware that the scope of the liberals I have considered is not definitive. Yet I would also insist that those I have considered—what might be called the Union for Democratic Action–New Republic–Nation–PM circle—have an importance in terms of the role they played in creating a conception of the war that went beyond liberal circles.

Some readers may object that some of the liberals I have discussed do not fit a theoretical definition of liberalism. This is a problem that I faced in my earlier study of liberalism in the 1930s. My solution then is the same one I have followed here. My approach is not to create an abstract definition of liberal and then see who measured up to it. Rather, it is to look at what was considered the liberal milieu at the time—especially the liberal journals—and to see what the writers there were saying and doing. Thus, someone may say that J. Alvarez Del Vayo was not a liberal but a radical. I don't disagree. But he wrote and functioned within the liberal milieu of *The Nation* and *The Free World.* A friend who read the manuscript raised a similar question about I. F. Stone. Again, I am willing to concede his politics were to the left of most of the people I have considered, but not by much—there was a lot of commonality in beliefs. But, most important, Stone wrote and functioned in the liberal milieu.

The issue of liberalism-radicalism is connected with the issue of Communism and the continuation of the Popular Front. It is an issue I discuss in the first chapter, but because some readers may wonder why I have not spent more time on liberal-Communist relations, a few introductory points are required. Del Vayo has been accused of being a Communist; certainly he was a strong defender of the Soviet Union. I. F. Stone too—most unfairly I believe—has been accused of secretly passing information to the Soviets. In his autobiography, Michael Straight acknowledged that he secretly joined the Communist Party in Great Britain during the Popular Front period. However, Stone's wholesale critique of the business community was a *liberal* staple, not a Communist staple; during the war the Communists drew distinctions between progressive and reactionary business. Straight broke with the Party over the Nazi-Soviet Pact and its post-pact line. His indignation at the Darlan deal was representative of liberal indignation, not of the Communist Party's acceptance of it. And when Stalin recognized the Badoglio government in Italy, Del Vayo proclaimed the dividing line was *fascism* and Badoglio was a fascist. What these examples illustrate is that whatever the relationship these individuals had to the

Communist Party, the claims of the liberal interpretation of the war was the strongest claim in their writings.

The issue of the Popular Front is more complex, but I argue that wartime sympathy for the Soviet Union did not mean the reestablishment of the *political* Popular Front of the late 1930s. There was a continuation of the cultural Popular Front and what might be called the Popular Front sensibility. Certainly liberals and Communists worked together in a political organization like the CIO Political Action Committee (CIO-PAC). But there is a difference between working together through the CIO-PAC to re-elect Roosevelt and taking part — through advocacy and support — in the kind of political Popular Front of the thirties. The U.S. political Popular Front of the 1930s was not the formal alliance that characterized the Spanish or French Popular Front governments. But it did involve on the part of the liberals an acknowledgment that the Communist Party was a progressive political party that deserved respect if not total agreement, and that it was an essential political ally in the struggle against fascism. Even among liberal intellectuals with pro-Russian sympathies during the war no such acknowledgment was made. Instead, liberals disparaged the Communist Party and often viewed it as an impediment to an effective anti-fascist struggle.

It is important to remember that despite the similar language of a "people's war," a "people's peace," and an ideological war of democracy versus fascism, and despite common opposition to John L. Lewis, support for the no-strike pledge, and support for Roosevelt, the liberal conception of the war differed significantly from the Communist Party's conception. The liberal belief that World War II was an ideological war between democracy and fascism was rooted in the concept of a "democratic revolution" which drew clear lines domestically between the business community and the democratic aspirations of "the people." Using similar language of "the people," the Communist concept broadened the people to include the "progressive" segments of the business community and persons and groups of any political stripe that would proclaim their support for the war. Max Lerner, hardly an anti-Communist and a strong defender of the Soviet Union, called Earl Browder's courting of the business community the "unpopular front" and associated it with a policy of home-front appeasement. Speaking for *PM*, Lerner rejected the Communist line as "the abandonment of the struggle for economic mastery and social freedom and equity at home." Abandoning that struggle was "a betrayal of the best

American progressive tradition." One needs to remember that, for the liberals, Mayor Hague was still a fascist; for the Communists he was, because he supported the war, included in the anti-fascist front.[1]

Further, while I criticize the liberal willingness to support restrictions on civil liberties for the ultraright, their position derived from Niebuhr's theory that in times of crisis the balance between liberty and community should fall on the latter. The Communist support of clamping down on opponents was prompted by an undifferentiated desire both to curb any right-wing opposition to Roosevelt and the war and to curb any left opponents. The liberals, as I argue, shunned Norman Thomas because of differences over foreign policy issues, but they did not accuse him, as the Communists did, of being a fascist and demand that he be taken off the air. The liberals opposed the prosecution of the Minneapolis Trotskyists under the Smith Act. The Communist Party supported it. The Communists condemned Walter Reuther as an ally of the "fascist" Lewis. The liberals considered Reuther, a member of the Union for Democratic Action (UDA), as one of the most important of the progressive unionists. In considering the relationship between the liberal intellectual community and the Communist Party it is important to avoid drawing conclusions from parallel arguments. The Communists accused John L. Lewis of aiding the axis by calling the miners out on strike during the war. The liberals, with less hysterical language, made similar criticisms. But the liberal who perhaps wrote the most frequent and the harshest condemnations of Lewis was James Wechsler, one of the leaders of the anti-Communist liberal group at *PM*.

Finally, it is necessary to say a brief word about the words *liberal* and *progressive*. In the 1930s many liberals disliked the term liberal because of its association with mild reformism and preferred to call themselves progressives. Later in the 1948 Wallace campaign, the term progressive became a euphemism for fellow traveling. But in the war years, liberals were not ashamed of the term liberal, and they called their ideas both liberal and progressive. And in the war years, progressive was not a term necessarily associated with the Communist left. The Socialist Party often used the term and spoke frequently of appealing to progressive unionists. In this study I have used the terms interchangeably because I do not think that during World War II liberals drew a line between liberalism and progressivism.

Although it is clear where secondary works have influenced how I viewed an issue, I have tried to support my main arguments from the war-time liberal books, articles, and journals and from the papers of the liberals. With one exception involving the liberal-Communist issue, I have deliberately not placed historiographical debate in the text. Largely, this is because I wanted to avoid the kind of running argument I had with the interpreters of the 1930s Socialist Party in *An Alternative Vision*. I still believe it was essential in that book. I do not believe it is essential in this book. This does not mean that I am not indebted to other scholars who have previously written on wartime liberalism. First in his August 1968 *Historian* article, "Sixty Million Jobs and the People's Revolution," and later in the opening chapters of *Beyond the New Deal* (1973), Alonzo Hamby discussed a number of the issues I consider. The opening chapter of Richard Pells's *The Liberal Mind in a Conservative Age* (1985) also discusses the liberal intellectuals during the war. The work of both authors was helpful in defining the issues, but the main focus of their books was the postwar liberal community. With the exception of the final chapter on the collapse of the wartime liberal community, *Noble Abstractions* focuses entirely on the liberal intellectual experience during the war years. Although some of our judgments differ, I have benefitted greatly from Sara Alpern's 1987 biography of the remarkable Freda Kirchwey.

My book is, then, the story of the pro-war liberal intellectual community's dreams and the reality those dreams confronted. Chapters 1 and 2 explore the dream of a democratic revolution. This was an expansive dream that had both domestic and international dimensions. Chapter 1 establishes the liberal intellectual community and delineates the broad outlines of its shared interpretation of World War II as a democratic revolution. Chapter 2 analyzes the specific ideas the concept of a democratic revolution involved and traces the concept from the high hopes of the early war years to the efforts to sustain the concept in the face of a chastened liberal reform agenda as the war drew to a close.

Chapter 3 analyzes what happened when the liberals' definition of the war confronted the international and domestic actions of the president and the administration in which they had embedded their definition of the war and to which they had given the fullness of their support. The confrontation between liberal hopes and Roosevelt's actions created liberal disillusionment, which had the potential of turning total support to critical support. It was, in large measure, only the figure of Henry Wallace, as representative of liberal hopes and of the "true" New Deal, that prevented this from happening. Chapter 4 details the apotheosis of Wallace as an embodiment and symbol of liberalism's definition of the war.

In the process of supporting a democratic revolution, liberals engaged in an ongoing process of redefining America that had begun in the 1930s. Chapter 5 explores the lengths and limits of that redefinition. But liberals were not engaged only in intellectual efforts to articulate a democratic revolution. In the organization of the UDA, the liberal intellectual community sought to ground their vision in specific political actions. Chapter 6 follows the efforts of the UDA to become politically effective and analyzes the impediments to political effectiveness resulting from its close ties to the Roosevelt administration. Chapter 7 explores a variation on the theme of political effectiveness by examining the political life of Thomas Amlie, a liberal who started out working for the UDA but wound up far more alienated from its politics and from the New Deal milieu than most others in the liberal community.

Total support of World War II did not just place the liberal intellectual community in a position where it needed to make judgments about the Roosevelt administration; it also placed it in a position where it was required to make judgments about the United States' main wartime allies, England and the Soviet Union. Chapter 8 examines the nature of the initial liberal support for Churchill, the limits that were present from the beginning, and the reasons why a narrow limited support gave way to full criticism. It also explores the close relations between the American liberal intellectual community and the British Labour Party, a relationship that did not prevent some liberal illusions about the similarity of the two groups. Chapter 9 analyzes liberal attitudes toward the Soviet Union by attempting to place frequently noted liberal views in the context of wartime views of general foreign policy.

The liberals gave total support to the war. But was there an alternative for liberals, one that would have maintained their support, yet perhaps have placed them in a less awkward intellectual position than supporting an administration that so often acted on assumptions that ran counter to the liberal definition of the war? Chapter 10 explores the alternative of "critical support" offered by the Socialist Party. It discusses the commonality of some of the liberal and Socialist views, but delineates what separated the two groups and prevented wartime cooperation. In the process of analyzing the two groups, it argues that the Socialist view, though open to criticism at points, offered a viable alternative. While this chapter departs from a direct focus on liberalism, it is essential, as noted, to the book's argument that there was a political alternative to the liberal position on the war and on the Roosevelt administration. To explain the Socialist alternative, it is necessary to see how it emerged, and since it emerged out of the internal composition of the Socialist Party, it is necessary to situate the policy by exploring the party's internal dynamics as they pertained to the war issue.

I argue that the liberal intellectual community was a community, that what it agreed upon was more significant than what its members differed over. The final chapter analyzes the breakup of liberal unity as the war came to a close. It is a story of shattered unity, just as much of the early story is a story of shattered dreams. But those dreams were shattered when liberals sought desperately to avoid surrendering them because surrendering them would mean surrendering their very definition of the war. In clinging to much of that definition, the liberals helped leave us with much of the mythology that has gone into the popular versions of the "good war." But they also left themselves with a lot of intellectual baggage from which liberalism has never been able to extricate itself.

1

Defining the War

IN SEPTEMBER 1944, as Freda Kirchwey, the editor of *The Nation*, contemplated the freeing of Paris, she was filled with a mixture of joy at the inevitability of Hitler's defeat and apprehension over the continued inability of the western Allies to recognize the political nature of the war. Churchill's statement that the war had become less ideological was wrong; the American appointment of the conservative diplomat Robert Murphy as political adviser to General Eisenhower indicated that the United States had "only the foggiest idea" of the nature of the war. The French fighting democrats knew what the Churchills and Murphys failed to comprehend: World War II was "a fragment of an unfinished revolution."[1]

If the analysis of the political nature of World War II had been confined to the pen of Kirchwey, it would simply have been a personal political statement of one person's hopes. But it was not so confined. The basis for Kirchwey's mixed emotions was widely shared by the pro-war liberal intellectual community, which played a major role in formulating the ideological rhetoric of World War II. The role was not only a matter of the official propaganda coming out of the Office of War Information (OWI). Headed by a liberal, Elmer Davis, and staffed with many liberals, this organization was of great importance—even though the conflicting interests within the administration prevented it from always being consistent in its liberalism. But beyond the specific role of the OWI, from Franklin D. Roosevelt's Four Freedoms speech, through Henry Wallace's wartime addresses on the Century of the Common Man, to the editorials in *PM*, *The Nation*, *The New Republic*, *Common Sense*, and *The Free World*, and all the way to the music of "The House I Live In" and "The Ballad for Americans," liberal ideology, liberal rhetoric, and liberal assumptions permeated discussion of the war. "Democracy," "freedom," the "common man," the "people," and the "people's revolution" were the words and phrases which, to borrow from Daniel Rodgers, *did* things in defining the meaning and purpose of World War II. Often violated by events, the transcendent words of the liberals served many functions from propaganda to politics, but most of all they offered the country an interpretation of the war and a conception of the world and of the United States that subscribed meaning to the present and future. The vision of a world in which democracy and freedom would become realities for the peoples of the world grew out of the liberal interpretation of the war.[2]

For liberal intellectuals, all this was much more than rhetorical propaganda to keep up morale in the face of the reality of all wars: death and destruction. For liberals, the propaganda war was essential, not as a narrow tactical weapon, but as the deep expression of the meaning of the war. The liberal rhetoric, then, was the articulation of a deeply felt ideology that subscribed a crusading purpose to World War II. A crusade was precisely what the liberal community was engaged in and what has often been ignored in the literature on World War II.[3]

As the contrast has traditionally been drawn, gone was the crusading spirit, the idealistic fervor to make a war "to end all wars," to make a war for nothing less than worldwide "democracy." In its place was the grim and fatalistic realization that Hitler threatened U.S. security and the traditional values of western civilization. In this view, the seriousness of performing a necessary task replaced the passion of a world-transforming crusade. Certainly the liberal community was grim in spirit when the United States entered World War II. Convinced in the early months of the war that there was a distinct possibility of an Allied defeat, liberals warned the nation of the seriousness of the tasks that lay ahead. But the liberals' fear of military defeat was never divorced from their ideological interpretation of the war. In early 1942, J. Alvarez Del Vayo, the last foreign minister in the Republican government of Spain, expressed fear of military defeat and argued that only political warfare based on the conception of World War II as a revolution could result in the bold military and political actions necessary to defeat Hitler. During the same period, *The New Republic* warned that unless the influence of those denying the revolutionary nature of World War II was removed, we would lose the war.[4]

It was with the spirit of the ideological crusader and the frightened citizen that the liberals exposed the footdraggers and chastised the half-hearted; they freely gave military advice and even more freely political advice designed to rouse the nation to the enormity of its task. Even as the defeats of the early months gave way to better military news and the long-range prospects for victory increased, the liberal community grimly warned of the need to avoid early optimism and of the slackness that might come with assumptions of forthcoming victory.[5]

Thus, liberals saw the war in intensely moral and idealistic terms. They viewed it as not simply a war to defend civilization, but as a war to transform the world. As Richard Rovere recognized early in the war, World War II was an "ideological war." A warning against the dangers of ideology becoming dogma, Rovere's article nevertheless pointed to the heart of the liberal community's analysis of the war.[6]

And a community it was. Though not without their tensions and disagreements, liberal intellectuals are best understood as a community. It is important to stress this because there is a great temptation to read back into the wartime experience the kinds of antagonisms and divisions that prevailed in the postwar period. Despite its limited membership, the Union for Democratic Action (UDA) was the political center of the liberal intellectual community. Both Mary McAuliffe, writing from a perspective critical of post–World War II anticommunist liberalism, and William O'Neill, writing from a perspective critical of the Popular Front mentality, have portrayed the UDA's exclusion of Communists from membership as antagonizing a significant body of liberal opinion. It is hard to see how this is the case. McAuliffe claims that the CIO "participated easily" in "such popular-front organizations as the National Citizens Political Action Committee and found little in common with the anti-Communists in the Union for Democratic Action." Since many of the leading members of the UDA were active in, and a number were on the National Board of, the NC-PAC, McAuliffe's distinction makes little sense. O'Neill claims that the "U.D.A.'s anti-Communism made it unpopular so long as America and Russia were allies." Again, this is unconvincing, since Kirchwey, Bruce Bliven, Max Lerner and other liberals sympathetic to the Soviet Union were active members of the UDA.[7]

Part of the tendency to read later divisions back into the wartime experience derives from assuming a greater continuity between the political Popular Front and wartime liberalism than actually existed. Despite significant continuities in the Popular Front theme of democracy versus fascism and in the cultural Popular Front, and despite the renewed sympathy for the Soviet Union during the war, the idea of any quasi-formalized domestic liberal–Communist Party cooperation — a keystone of the Popular Front strategy—had little left-liberal intellectual support during the war. The liberal press ridiculed the sincerity of the Communist Party, even disparagingly questioning its wartime transformation into a political association. In 1944 *The New Republic* called the Communist Party "a pathetic little group of negligible people." Certainly the liberal community stood for cooperation among the variety of antifascists who made up the resistance in the occupied countries in Europe and within De Gaulle's Free French movement, but there was no desire to reforge the kind of liberal-Communist alliance that had characterized the political Popular Front in the United States before it was shattered by the Nazi-Soviet Pact and its aftermath.[8]

In order to understand the wartime liberal attitude toward the Communist Party, it is necessary to review the impact of the Nazi-Soviet Pact on liberal thinking. The Nazi-Soviet Pact destroyed the Popular Front and ex–Popular Front liberals had to reformulate their political thinking. Granville Hicks, Max Lerner, Matthew Josephson, Robert Lynd and other ex-Communists or ex–Popular Front liberals held some discussions on developing a new perspective and a new political group but could not agree on an approach. Ex–Popular Front liberals like Kirchwey and Bliven continued to defend the Popular Front's pro–New Deal political perspective, but they strongly criticized the Communist Party, which in the aftermath of the pact had adopted an anti–New Deal, antiwar line. Liberal distrust of the American Communist Party was rampant from the pact onwards, and the image of the Communist Party in the liberal press was that of a pliant, slightly ridiculous, tool of the Soviet Union.[9]

Even after the German invasion of the Soviet Union in June 1941, the Soviet war effort, the rehabilitation of Stalin by some liberals, and the American Communist Party's all-out support of the war effort, Roosevelt, and the New Deal, the Party was never able to regain liberal trust or to recapture its Popular Front position as a legitimate and essential participant in a liberal-left coalition. It was still perceived as a tool of Moscow, and Moscow was often advised to drop its American Communist Party affiliates who, liberals like Kirchwey and Bliven argued, embarrassed the Soviet Union by their sycophancy and political acrobatics. In minimizing the significance of the Communist Party in 1944, *The New Republic* called it a "nuisance" and "an embarrassment." The liberals made efforts to differentiate their position when it overlapped the Communists' position. In urging the government to commute the sentence of Earl Browder, the Communist Party secretary who had been sentenced to prison in 1941 for using a false passport during the Spanish Civil War, *The Nation* said the government's case was legitimate, only the sentence was too harsh.[10]

The Nation and *The New Republic* tepidly welcomed the transformation of the American Communist Party into a "political association" in 1944, but the move did not erase their distrust of the party or presage an advocacy of including the Communists in a new Popular Front. Liberals ridiculed the Communist Party's efforts to defend "progressive" big business and "to clasp the hand of J. P. Morgan." In commenting on the dissolution of the American Communist Party, *The New Republic* wrote: "In its desire to accord with what it surmises to be Stalin's wishes, the party had recently come out for free enterprise, and had actually scolded the liberals for attacking big business — over the Saudi Arabia Oil deal, for example."[11]

After the dissolution of the Comintern, Lerner did speculate that it had created the possibility of left unity. But he also commented that up to that point the American Communist Party had been "more of a liability than an asset on all the liberal fighting fronts." And a year after this expression of hope for left unity in the fight against fascism, he labeled the "free enterprise" line of the Communist Party as bordering on the "ridiculous" and the Party itself as continuing to be untrustworthy. The closest any of the leading liberal intellectuals came to voicing the need for a Popular Front was an editorial by Kirchwey following the 1944 election. Buoyed by the work of the CIO political action organizations, Kirchwey urged the creation of a permanent political federation of independent liberals and progressives. She spoke of feeling "acutely the need of a Popular Front in America." But the whole idea had none of the 1930s specificity about the components of such a front. She spoke only of "a solid union of progressive forces." And it is important to remember that Kirchwey was still an active and supportive member of the UDA, which opposed the kind of 1930s political Popular Front alliances.[12]

It is worth noting in view of later, postwar developments, when it was assumed that wartime sympathy for the Soviet Union equated with procommunism, that *The Nation, The New Republic,* and *PM* sided with George Counts, Reinhold Niebuhr, and what was called the "right wing" of the American Labor Party (ALP) in their internal fight with the Communist-oriented faction. In 1943 *The New Republic* wrote of the ALP fight that "no progressive could conscientiously remain in a party controlled by the Communists." As the ALP conflict grew, the liberals also criticized some of the tactics of the right wing, but so did Richard Rovere, a member of the right. *The Nation* and *The New Republic,* though not the

UDA, did regret and were critical of the right wing's decision to break away and form a new party—the Liberal Party. But these tactical criticisms, often matched by criticisms of Sidney Hillman (usually a liberal hero) for meddling in the ALP's internal affairs on the side of the left, had nothing to do with a favorable disposition toward the Communist Party. Rather, it had to do with how best to mobilize the liberal and labor vote for Roosevelt in 1944. Kirchwey and Bliven were concerned that the ALP–Liberal Party split was detracting from the main task and feeding the forces of reaction.[13]

What is most striking about the leading liberals during the war, then, is not how they continued old political alliances or foreshadowed later battles, but how they formed an intellectual community of their own. Bliven, editor of *The New Republic*, worked closely with James Loeb, the UDA's executive secretary. When they later parted political company in the aftermath of Henry Wallace's 1946 speech it was the separation, not of two persons who had been fiercely debating issues during the war, but of two comrades in arms. Thomas Amlie, the former representative from Wisconsin, headed UDA's Washington office in the early years of the war, and, in turn, did the major work on *The New Republic*'s 1942 and 1944 supplements designed to defeat isolationism and elect a liberal Congress. And Amlie was also on good terms with Kirchwey and wrote *The Nation*'s 1943 supplement on the postwar economy. Kirchwey hailed the formation of the UDA and gave it continual support. Robert Bendiner, an editor of *The Nation*, published a book on the State Department which the UDA had done much to sponsor. Niebuhr, the chairperson of the UDA, was on the editorial board of and wrote frequently for *The Nation*. And Niebuhr and Louis Fischer of *The Nation* spoke frequently at UDA functions. Lerner was a former contributing editor of *The Nation*, a contributing editor of *The New Republic*, an editorial writer for the liberal newspaper *PM* and a speaker for the UDA. I. F. Stone had a regular column in *The Nation* and *PM*. Michael Straight was the Washington editor of *The New Republic* before he went into the air corps. Although a UDA-sponsored speaking tour for Straight fell through in late 1942, Loeb enthusiastically endorsed him as "the most thrilling speaker that sophisticated New Yorkers have heard in a long time." The overlapping of close ties is not as clear in relation to *Common Sense*, but its editor, Alfred Bingham, had been a founder of the UDA and earlier was a sponsor of Tom Amlie and continued to encourage his UDA work during the war years.[14]

Such close relationships were surprising considering the history of these individuals in the thirties. Although most had supported the New Deal after 1935, they had arrived at this support from different directions, and there existed important differences among them late into the decade. Bliven and Kirchwey had shared similar domestic ideas in the thirties: strong criticism of the early New Deal, support after 1935, and support for the domestic Popular Front. But they had differed strongly over foreign affairs. Kirchwey was an internationalist and a supporter of collective security; Bliven opposed collective security and supported the neutrality legislation (except for Spain) until the Nazi blitzkrieg. Although Niebuhr supported collective security in the late 1930s, he was in the Socialist Party for most of the thirties, and he was a harsh critic of the New Deal and its liberal politics until the end of the decade. Loeb also was in the Socialist Party and was a supporter of Norman Thomas in the 1930s. Loeb had tried working with the Communists on aid to the Spanish Loyalists and had developed a deep distrust of them. His later close ally Bliven never published anything on Spain in *The New Republic* from the anti-Stalinist left. Louis Fischer had been a fellow traveler until the Nazi-Soviet Pact. Lerner and Stone moved from a Marxist-influenced radicalism to support of the New Deal without giving up their socialism; Bingham moved from a non-Marxist radicalism that bitterly attacked the New Deal to offering half-hearted and then full support for it after 1936. Amlie generally followed Bingham's domestic path, but his support for collective security differed greatly from Bingham's anti-interventionism.

Even after the war brought them together, the close relationships were sometimes odd and sometimes strained. Kirchwey liked the clarity of clearly differentiated moral positions; her close associate Niebuhr often appeared to delight in the complex balancing of antagonistic positions. Both Fischer and Stone at times annoyed Kirchwey—Fischer for his prima donna demands and Stone for his occasionally reckless targeting. Yet these minor conflicts or irritants were dwarfed by the many ties that intellectually bound the liberal intellectual community together. All viewed the war in ideological terms. The war, Bingham wrote, is a war of ideas, and his sentiments were expressed throughout the liberal journals. Writing in *The Nation*, Archibald MacLeish argued that World War II was inescapably "a war of ideas." In *PM*, Victor Bernstein worried that U.S. foreign policy resulted in lost battles for ideas. In contrast, in a burst of optimism in the late summer of 1943, *The New Republic* proclaimed that democratic ideas had triumphed over fascist ideas and the only thing left was a "mopping up operation on the enemy—at home and abroad." [15]

The New Republic's triumphant announcement reflected another linkage among liberals: all saw the war as a war in which the future of democracy and progressive reform were at stake. The editors of *The New Republic* proclaimed that they must fight for democracy at home and overseas, and the sociologist Robert Lynd argued that democracy would be lost unless the "internal political battle continued." In addition, although they were often critical of Roosevelt, all saw his presidency as essential to liberalism and viewed the New Deal as the central core of liberalism in action. The New Deal, wrote the editors of *Common Sense* in November 1942, is "the American version of a world-wide revolutionary change." And in March 1944, Bliven described the Roosevelt administration "with all its faults" as one of the "two great centers of dynamic energy in the world today." With varying degrees of intensity, all also stood in opposition to isolationism. All disliked the dollar-a-year mentality and the racist mentality of southern conservatives. All felt that the people representing antiliberal views had, like the isolationists, too much power in the country and especially in the Republican Party, or had, like the dollar-a-year men and the southern conservatives, too much influence in the Democratic Party and the corridors of power in Washington. And all looked toward Henry Wallace as the political leader who best embodied the liberal spirit of the New Deal. Certainly there were differences in emphasis, in tone, and in analysis among the many liberal intellectuals, but what united them was more important than what divided them.[16]

What most united liberal intellectuals was their view of the war. How they interpreted the war's meaning is vital to understanding their passionate concerns as well as their later dilemmas and frustrations. They looked at the world and saw the forces that had given rise to Hitler at work in all countries; the ultranationalism and authoritarian structures, the class-dominated society were not unique to Germany. At the same time, they saw forces resisting fascism: those working to extend democratic rights and civil liberties, those struggling to provide economic rights through labor unions and workers' struggles. Seeing the world in these terms, the liberals were convinced that the future of democracy—a future that lay with "the people"—was at stake. The word *people's* (i.e., people's war, people's peace, people's century) which some have associated with Communist Party terminology was not the property of the Communist Party or reflective of its influence. It was a terminology that stretched through the liberal community to embrace such moderate liberals as Herbert Agar. What was at stake was nothing more than a new world. Declaring themselves in favor of a democratic "new order," the editors of *Common Sense* called for a world that would establish the "Four Freedoms" and a world federation that would formulate war aims that promised freedom for colonial peoples, addressed the issue of segregation and racism at home, and established goals of "human decency and brotherhood."[17]

These themes ran through liberal literature. *Free World,* a journal created in late 1941 to rally the world democratic forces in support of the war, called for a "political war for democracy to counteract the political war of the fascists." *The Nation* and *The New Republic* joined suit. In September 1942 *The Nation* created a specific political section under the editorship of Del Vayo to perform the essential tasks of expanding the public's knowledge of the political war that was being fought in countries throughout the world. Del Vayo's opening statement read: "In starting this section our purpose is simple. We intend to underline the revolutionary character of the war and help develop a political strategy through which the democratic elements in all countries may overcome the forces of reaction and capitulation, and free the peoples of the world from the tragic conflict of fighting under colors not their own. The section will be a weapon in this political war." For the next three years, the Political Warfare section would bring *The Nation's* readers reports and analyses of the struggles for democracy and revolutionary change throughout the world.[18]

The New Republic's views paralleled *The Nation's.* In an attack on "the deadwood at the top," *The New Republic* contrasted the liberals' conception of World War II as a "war for democracy" with the Tory conception of the war as a traditional "war of self-defense against aggression." In such statements, certain themes are repeatedly developed: the need for a war of ideas to accompany the military war and the need to articulate clear war aims. In arguing for the need for a war of ideas and for social change to accompany the military war, Kirchwey wrote in 1944 that we could defeat Hitler by "allied arms," but we could not defeat fascism without "a revolutionary social change in Europe." It was either social change or fascism. MacLeish distinguished between a military victory and a "real victory," by which he meant the triumph over fascist ideas and the Nazi mentality. Fischer said that a victory with the reactionaries entrenched in power would not bring a meaningful peace. Indeed the persistence with which the liberals warned against the dangers of a reactionary peace suggests that they recognized the possibility of a military victory without defeating fascism and destroying its roots. In early 1943 *The New Republic* warned that the war was becoming a war of "anti-Hitler fascists" against "pro-Hitler fascists," and Del Vayo distinguished between a genuine war against fascism and a war simply against those responsible for aggression. To the liberals, the war lost most of its meaning if it was conceived as anything less than a united struggle for the liberation of the common man and for a new world order. Quoting Wendell Willkie, Del Vayo voiced the view that "this war is either a 'grand coalition' of peoples, fighting a common war of liberation, or it is nothing." The editors of *The Nation* wrote that little would be accomplished in the war if we destroyed Hitler and his fellow fascists and left in power his big business "patrons and partners." And in *PM*, Victor Bernstein applied the same terms to Japan: "So long as the Emperor remains, so long as the military and its supporting industrial cliques in Japan stay intact, our ultimate victory in the Far East will prove no victory, but a dreadful armistice that must end in another march of death." [19]

As a war of ideas, the lines were clearly drawn. "Fascism against anti-fascism," wrote Del Vayo, "it's as simple as that." And with such clear lines, there was a double duty: to refuse to cooperate with opportunistic converts from fascism, with those who held fascistic economic and political beliefs, and with all who were less than fully committed to the war; and to purge any of the above from positions where they guided the direction of the war. Added to these themes was the belief that winning the war was not enough; the peace must also be won. Winning the peace meant a future world federation and a democratizing of economic and political life throughout the world. These themes were never separate; they were joined, intertwined, and mutually reinforcing. The articulation of war and peace aims required a belief in freedom and democracy. A propaganda war of ideas flowed from such a commitment. "If the idea of freedom is to win in the end," wrote *Common Sense*, "it must be by means of the only weapon available for the spread of an idea—propaganda." *Free World* printed discussions on "What is Wrong with American Propaganda" that centered on the need for more effective and democratic political propaganda. [20]

These interconnected themes pointed to three basic interpretations of the war, all of which the liberal intellectual community held either intermittently or simultaneously. Some liberals placed more emphasis on one than on the others; some may not have accepted all of the interpretations—it is never absolutely clear because assumed beliefs are sometimes not articulated and the interpretations often overlapped. The first interpretation was that the leadership of the war was not fully committed to democracy and thus the war itself was, so to speak, "up for grabs." On one side stood those who would fight the war for narrow national security goals and seek to restore the pre-war status quo; on the other side stood the liberal and progressive forces determined to create a more peaceful, just, and democratic world. In this interpretation, the war must be *made* democratic. *Common Sense* articulated this view when it argued that a fascist counterrevolution had unleashed the war and placed the democratic forces on the defensive. But the fascist counterrevolution had also clarified the necessity of transforming a defensive war against the counterrevolution into an offensive revolutionary war to extend democracy.[21]

Bliven's statement that the war had begun as a war for the status quo but was being transformed into a genuine war for democracy by the struggles of the people reflected this interpretation of the war. So too did Pearl Buck's 1942 call for the extension of freedom to the whole world. When Bliven asked at the end of 1942 whether the peace was already lost, he was voicing the constant fear of this interpretation of the war: that the war was not being, and would not be, transformed into a democratic war, that the war would remain in the hands of those who sought to maintain the status quo.[22]

A second basic interpretation was very close to the first. It too viewed the war as uprooting the world; fascism may have been seeking to conquer the world, but in reaction it had unleashed movements throughout the world—movements dedicated to the creation of a new democratic world. But whereas the first interpretation emphasized the necessity of transforming the war into a democratic war, the second view saw the democratic movements as already present. What was needed was not so much a transformation of a nondemocratic war into a democratic war, but a marshaling of the democratic movements by a dynamic leadership. Straight's articles in *The New Republic* were shaped by this conception of the war. On one hand stood the forces resisting change; on the other hand stood the unleashed democratic forces for change. Written in breathless prose, his articles amounted to a call for dynamic leadership to seize the initiative. Straight was certain the war constituted a revolution, but not so certain that he didn't feel it necessary to issue a cautionary warning against those who might lead it astray and return the status quo to power. In one article Straight declared that World War II was already a people's war for Russia, that it was partly one for the United States, Great Britain, and China; but that it was necessary for it to become a people's war for India and the other colonies. A genuine revolution had been unleashed; what was required was bold leadership to combat the reactionary forces and to fulfill the promises of the global people's revolution.[23]

Admittedly the differences between these first two interpretations are a matter of emphasis. The first focused more on the necessity of transforming what had begun as a defensive war against aggression into a democratic revolutionary war; the second assumed that the democratic revolutionary forces were already profuse, but that more vigorous and creative leadership was necessary to marshal them into a fully developed and ultimately victorious revolutionary force. But both interpretations wound up positing a struggle between the forces of reaction and compromise seeking to hold back the democratic revolution and the forces of progress seeking to further it.

The third basic interpretation viewed the war as *by nature* a democratic war. At first glance, this may appear the same as the second and, in its focus on the internal struggle between reaction and democratic progress, very similar to both of the other interpretations. However, in its larger claims it risked undercutting both interpretations by assuming that the nature of the war had already been defined. That none of the liberals saw the potential conflict between the two fluid interpretations, whereby the nature of the war was "up for grabs" or required vigorous leadership to make it a democratic revolutionary war, and an interpretation that defined the war as democratic as a starting point is understandable. Since the message of all three interpretations was the necessity of defeating reaction and fascism and to build a democratic world, the intellectual distinctions did not seem to matter.

But there was, nevertheless, a distinction. According to the third interpretation, unlike the first interpretation, it was not a matter of transforming the war into a democratic war; unlike the second it was not a matter of marshaling the latent democratic forces into a cohesive whole. In this third view, it was a matter of recognizing the existing reality, the reality that the war was a civil war—not a civil war to be created, but a civil war that had existed from the beginning.

No one set forth this large claim for the essential revolutionary–civil war nature of World War II more forcefully than Kirchwey in the pages of *The Nation*. In late February 1942, Kirchwey wrote an impassioned attack upon some equally large claims about the war by Henry Luce. Following up on his previous year's call for an "American century," Luce set forth a view of the war in which the opportunities for an American-dominated peace (residually helped by England and China) were given Luce's moral blessing. In Luce's mind, the right of the United States to so lead involved both the nature of the war and his version of American "exceptionalism."

The war, Luce wrote, was "a war against the cleavage of mankind into right and left." Proclaiming the evils of class conflict and the uniqueness of America's freedom from the same, he wrote:

> It is a war against the hidden civil war which, raging throughout the world, weakened the structure of nations until much of their national identity had been lost before Hitler overwhelmed them. . . . It is a war against the politics of unprincipled power, the setting of group against group, of labor against business, business against government, farmers and wage-earners, which turns the rivalries of politics into class war. Because America alone among the nations of the earth was founded on ideas and ideals which transcend class and caste and racial and occupational differences, America alone can provide the pattern for the future. Because America stands for a system wherein many groups, however diverse, are united under a system of laws and faiths that enables them to live peacefully together, American experience is the key to the future.[24]

With zeal, Kirchwey launched her counterattack. Comparing the "Lucite New Order" to the Nazi New Order, she declared that Luce's "cult of American superiority is no whit less revolting and no less unjustified than the Nordic myth that provides the moral sanction for Hitler's brutal aggression." For Kirchwey, Luce's vision of a capitalist world led by the United States and achievable only through American principles was insulting to the anti-Nazi guerrillas, to the concentration camp inmates, and to the Russian soldiers. Luce's myopic vision ignored the Soviet Union and Latin America, revealed an "unconcealed contempt" for Europe, and left only Britain with any role in the postwar world—and even that was "clearly, permanently, below the United States."[25]

Luce, no less than Kirchwey, was an ardent supporter of World War II. But his internationalism, conventionally conservative and deeply rooted in a liberal-conservative interpretation of the uniqueness of American society, clashed sharply with Kirchwey's view of the nature of the war. Only when one probes the societal vision behind Kirchwey's critique does one discover the roots of her differences with Luce. Where Luce proclaimed transcendent ideals that erased class differences and social conflict, Kirchwey placed such differences and conflict at the heart of her social analysis. For Kirchwey, Luce's treatment of our revolutionary ideals "immunized" us against "the ordinary ills of social conflict" and ignored the nature of the "political struggles waged in Washington" and "the industrial struggles waged in Detroit or West Virginia." And then she reached the core of her argument: "More serious still, Mr. Luce's fantasy obscures, by denying, the real meaning of the war itself." Luce was asking his readers to fight against a view of the war as a civil war, but that, for Kirchwey, was precisely what World War II was all about; that was its meaning and nature. And it was a civil war in which we were "*forced to take sides.*" Kirchwey recognized the "mixed" quality of the anti-Hitler side: the "rather nice imperialists and capitalists" coexisting with the "very elements of the left toward whom he directs such specific contempt." For Kirchwey, the civil nature of the war was inescapable:

> For Hitler's war was *first of all* a war waged against the organized political and economic forces of the working class—against trade unions and Socialists and Communists. Hitler's war began as a class war and it is still that, along with several other kinds. It is still a civil war, too. And it is that war which must be won—not by America but by the men and groups in all countries who know what the war is about and on which side they are fighting. One can understand Mr. Luce's dislike of this war in which he is enlisted, but he can't change it around just to suit his preference. Hitler set the terms long ago—sometime back in the twenties.[26]

Week after week, Kirchwey returned to this theme. Whether she was writing on Latin America, the United States, England, or the Soviet Union, World War II as a civil war dominated her analysis. Politics and ideology, not economics, determined international alignments, and to her politics meant democratic or fascist politics. Going beyond the other liberal interpretations, Kirchwey saw the *essence* as democratic. For Kirchwey, it was impossible to deny that the democratic civil war throughout the world was the basic nature of World War II. Kirchwey's contention can, of course, be argued; the case is highly questionable at best. But *The Nation* did not really argue its case; it accepted it—as if the nature of the war was an a priori truth whose existence one could not deny.[27]

If Kirchwey was correct in stating that Luce could not change the terms of the war "to suit his preference," then neither could she. But that is precisely what she did. Out of hatred for fascism and a lot of wishful thinking, she articulated an interpretation of the war that often served as the premise—sometimes the inarticulated premise—of much of liberal thinking about the war. For example, it entered powerfully into the debate over civil liberties during the war. In a 1942 letter to the *Wall Street Journal,* Lerner explained why extreme reactionary newspapers constituted enemies of the war:

> What is the danger that we speak of. It is quite clear that Mr. Moley and we proceed from different premises. . . . Moley may think that the Nazi war

against American [sic] began with Germany's partner, Japan, attacking us on December 7th, 1941. We think that Germany has been making war on America long before Pearl Harbor. We think that one of her war technics had been the attempt to influence, if not to organize, such groups as America First, and to make use of such symbols as Lindbergh and Coughlin. . . . It is from these premises that we conclude that the McCormick-Patterson newspapers are in no essential respect different from the New York *Inquirer.* . . . This brings us . . . to the real issue between Mr. Moley and ourselves—as to whether a "world civil war" is part of the World War. Mr. Moley is . . . right in saying that Congress never declared a world civil war. But Hitler did. Every speech of his about the "Jewish criminal" and "decadent pluto-democracies" is a declaration of it. And he has waged against America not only a military but a civil war.

Kirchwey and Lerner used this conception of the war to battle their wartime critics. For Kirchwey, her critics did not understand what the war was all about because they did not share her definition of World War II as inherently a civil war. Liberals like Bingham of *Common Sense* were more tentative than Kirchwey in defining the nature of the war, but few could entirely escape the attractiveness of her analysis.[28]

What were the attractions? Simply put, her interpretation eliminated the need to debate the war. The issue became the depth of one's conviction, a matter of faith more than reason. If the war was "up for grabs" and required a democratic transformation in order to establish the validity of total support then the matter was consistently open to debate. How much had democracy been extended? Was it enough to grant total support or should one give, as the Socialist Party did in effect, "critical support?" If the war had simply unleashed democratic forces that required guidance, leadership and a united effort, then the issue was still debatable. Were those forces being furthered or stymied? Too many roadblocks put in the way of the democratic forces could lead to a withdrawal of total support, which could lead again to critical support. Was total support even the best way to further the stated democratic aims of the liberal left? Bingham and a few others were not too far removed from critical support, but Kirchwey and the editors of *The New Republic* and Loeb of the UDA were. To them, a critical supporter like Norman Thomas was suspect.

But there was another consequence of Kirchwey's interpretation that went beyond its serving as a moral club against doubting Norman Thomases. If World War II was in essence a democratic revolutionary war, an international civil war between the forces of reaction and progress as Kirchwey claimed, it was also, for her, a war whose democratic revolutionary outcome could not be denied. This aspect of her interpretation—an interpretation that she shared with the liberal community—was masked by the simultaneous belief that the forces of reaction and progress were battling in an undetermined contested terrain. When urging the forces of progress to take the offensive in the battle, when demanding the purging of the forces of reaction from the corridors of Allied power, the liberals portrayed a future of indefinite darkness if fascism and reaction triumphed. But they at the same time also argued that the democratic revolution could not be defeated. It could be temporarily thwarted, but its victory was inevitable. Acknowledging past mistakes in Allied foreign policy and the difficulties that would be certain to occur in the future, Max Lerner declared in the wake of D day: "But, whatever may be our shrinking from the image of the democratic revolutions in Europe, we shall not be able permanently to stop them. We can thwart them for awhile, thus mess things up both for them and for us. But in the end neither we nor the British are of the institutional stuff that can play Metternich successfully with the future, nor maintain a condominium over the world in which we are the grandees of a new Anglo-Saxony."[29]

The previous year the editors of *The New Republic* had expressed similar opinions. Social revolution was following "the tides of war." We were giving the peoples of Europe their freedom, but our policies showed no awareness of the social revolution that had already begun in Europe. We could temporarily halt this revolution against the old order by armed force, but the clear implication was that we could not destroy it. Our only choice was to become part of it, to participate in it and through our power enhance the abilities of the European peoples to fulfill their "popular desires" or to forcefully—and again the implication was, in the face of a hostile people, unsuccessfully—resist it. Later that fall, the editors reiterated the impossibility of stemming the "revolutionary impulses" in Europe indefinitely. Attempted suppression would simply mean more violent revolution in the future; the stability Allied policy sought could only come from "healthy social change."[30]

Most of the paper and ink expended by the liberal intellectual community in attempting to shape the war to their vision was devoted to a nondeterminist version of the democratic revolution. The warnings that only fascist reaction could defeat the democratic revolution, the predictions that attempts to defeat it would produce World War III, and the constant efforts to redirect American and British foreign policy all pointed to a deep concern that the democratic revolution linked to the war might not be fulfilled.

Still, Kirchwey's essentialist interpretation of World War II and the inevitability of its outcome played to a pervasive liberal optimism about the future—an optimism that was often hidden by the dire warnings of the consequences of Allied foreign policy. Few liberals could calmly acknowledge, as T.R.B. did in *The New Republic* in 1943, that the war was only a war against fascism, that "world reformation" was not in the cards, and that the liberals who continued "to think of the war in revolutionary terms" were divorcing themselves from reality. To the vast majority of liberals, a war against fascism had to be a war for world reform. To acknowledge that the outcome of the international civil war would defeat fascism but not bring a democratic revolution contradicted their whole understanding of world events. If T.R.B.'s statement was valid, it would mean defeat. Better to maintain that defeats were only temporary and that ultimately the democratic revolution would occur. This was not an easy thing to do; liberal optimism would be severely tested time and again. Events would produce within the liberal intellectual community deep frustration, anger, and a sense of disappointment and even betrayal. But no criticism growing out of frustration or disappointment was allowed to interfere with the faith in the democratic nature of the war. Indeed the sense of frustration and betrayal was a product of that faith. Having created a progressive definition of the war, having given themselves fully to the war and demanded that others do so too, and finally having made a full political commitment to FDR and the New Deal for embodying the liberal aspirations for a new democratic and progressive world, they had created a predicament that inevitably created the conditions for shattered dreams and illusions. But dreams and illusions die hard.[31]

2

Toward the Democratic Revolution

ON FEBRUARY 4, 1942, Charles Eliot, director of the National Resources Planning Board, delivered an address on "Winning the Peace That Follows" to an audience at the City College of New York. After detailing the board's new bill of rights and its overall goals of full employment, security, and building America, he quoted from a poem by Herman Hagedorn to illustrate the drama and excitement needed to sustain the "offensive action" necessary "to win the peace":

> Help us remember that the high crusade
> Whereon we now embark calls forth the free
> In hosts with spears and flaunting flags arrayed
> Not one dragon's end, one victory,
> One last great war, but to unending war—
> Without—within—'til God's white torch supreme
> Melts the last chain; and the last dungeon door
> Swings slowly wide to the triumphant dream.

The crusading spirit of Hagedorn's poem, a spirit that would melt the chains of insecurity, unemployment, disease, and poverty and replace them with the "triumphant dream" of a new society where full employment, security, and international peace abounded was a spirit that characterized the outpouring of liberal-authored books and articles designed to create a new society in the postwar period.[1]

In his book *Beyond Victory*, liberal congressman from California Jerry Voorhis declared: "it isn't enough to 'make peace'—we have to make peace *work!*" Writing in 1944, Voorhis could anticipate victory in the war and thus emphasize the peace to follow. Other liberal writers publishing in 1942 or even 1943 could not write with the same assurance and had to place greater emphasis on what needed to be done to win the war. Yet it usually turned out that what needed to be done to win the war had a direct applicability to the creation of a different kind of society in the postwar period; whether it was 1942 or 1944, the liberal writers were concerned with both winning the war and winning the peace and inseparably intertwined them in their minds. In 1942 two liberal academics, J. Donald Kingsley and David Petegorsky, expounded on the interconnectedness of military victory and postwar reconstruction: "The choice that confronts us . . . is not . . . between the status quo and the barbarities of totalitarianism. Rather, it is between the extension of democracy and its destruction. We must extend democracy *now* in order to achieve . . . a scheme of rehabilitation."[2]

The talk about "constructing" an order of society or about "problems of reconstruction" reflected the shared liberal belief that an old order was dying and a new order was being born. The expectations were so high that one liberal, the historian Carl Becker, was moved to write a cautionary analysis. In *How New Will the Better World Be?* Becker predicted a postwar world in which nationalism, power politics, and imperialism continued to play a major role in guiding the foreign policy of the major nations. Becker foresaw the expansion of the government's role in the economy and a greater degree of international cooperation, but nothing that resembled a new social order in which "spears and flaunting flags" went forth to melt the last chain and swing open the last dungeon door.[3]

In contrast to the damper Becker placed on the hopes for a genuinely new and better world stood the euphoric liberal rhetoric of societal reconstruction. In its rhetoric and in its spirit, societal reconstruction — the democratic revolution — tolled the end of capitalism and implied the creation of democratic socialism. The language of Freda Kirchwey's rejection of Luce's vision of the American century was the language of class struggle. The "noble abstractions" that the liberals claimed were the purposes of the war were not viewed as compatible with capitalism. And yet, few liberals advocated democratic socialism. The democratic revolution remained a vague and amorphous term that expressed deep discontent with the status quo and deep yearnings for social and economic justice, but which, because of its amorphous quality and because of the liberals' connection with Roosevelt and the New Deal, was compatible with a significantly reformed capitalism.

If on examination and analysis the liberal ideas did not envisage quite as new a world as they imagined and proclaimed, that does not mean that their goals were minimal. It was not that the thought and emotion that the liberals invested in trying to describe what was happening and what must happen in the modern world turned out to produce a mouse instead of an elephant. Rather, it was that without the necessary political force or movement to support their ideas—the kind of a force that the British Labour Party provided for the ideas circulating around "social security" in England—the ideas took on an abstract quality. And when it came to implementing them, the liberals had to choose whether it was worth supporting measures that failed to measure up to their high hopes. In a letter to Selden Rodman, the coeditor with Alfred Bingham of *Common Sense*, Petegorsky, who was one of the chief propagators of the liberal ideas for a new and better world, acknowledged the political failure of the progressives: "What is absolutely clear is that the progressives who had the right ideas were absolutely unable to get them across to the people. . . . We simply have not been able to convert any appreciable number of the unconverted."[4]

The political problem Petegorsky defined was never solved during the war. But liberal ideas for a new world continued to pour forth. There was no absolute agreement among liberal writers, no carefully formulated liberal dogma. But there was a remarkable agreement on the larger outlines. In the first place, there was a general consensus that the new world that was in the process of being created had developed out of a revolutionary situation. In 1941, before the United States entered the war, Max Lerner published *Ideas for the Ice Age,* which was subtitled *Studies in a Revolutionary Era.* What this meant was that there were revolutionary forces in the world, forces that Hitler had capitalized on but were susceptible to other revolutionary solutions.[5]

What were these revolutionary forces or elements? First, there was the disorganization of Europe. The peace settlement after World War I had failed to provide an economic settlement. That failure meant national rivalries and "capitalist collapse." Into the disorganized mess of Europe had stepped the brutal force of Hitler. Politically disorganized Europe was closely related to a second revolutionary force. The economic nation-state was historically outmoded. The inability of any nation-state to achieve economic self-sufficiency led to "international chaos." Once again Hitler's efforts to achieve a forced world economy were reflections of the impossibility of holding to "an anarchic and unplanned economy and still survive."[6]

In Lerner's analysis, Nazism seized on the economic, political and diplomatic failures of the modern world, and on the resulting psychic despair that undercut political democracy. Hitler centralized the economy, destroyed the nation-state, developed the revolutionary concept of total war, and appealed to the irrationality of the discontented. The end result was a revolution, but one that could not be met by traditional responses; it could only be answered by a different kind of revolution—"democratic socialism." The revolutionary forces that created the conditions for democratic socialism were present, but these forces required organizing. It was necessary to compete with Hitler's revolution—in the military war, in the civil war between fascist forces and progressive forces within each country, and finally in the battle between the democrat and the fascist within every individual.[7]

Other analyses of the revolutionary nature of the modern world were formulated along lines similar to Lerner's. In *The Coming Showdown*, Carl Dreher, a former executive engineer, wrote a lengthy study of the development of monopoly capitalism and its breakdown. Published in January 1942, but written before U.S. entrance into the war, *The Coming Showdown* traced the periodic depressions, the laissez-faire response of Hoover, and the inadequacies of the governmental response of the New Deal in addressing the manner in which monopoly capitalism had created economic inequities and economic breakdown. Dreher concluded that the world's economic system had collapsed. Like Lerner, he saw fascism as one example of a collectivist response to this breakdown; also like Lerner, he saw it as brutal and tyrannical form of collectivism. Finally, like Lerner, he felt that fascism needed to be fought by a better form of collectivism—democratic collectivism. Democratic collectivism controlled the machine for the betterment of human beings; fascism chained "ordinary men to the machine for the benefit of the capitalist, the militarist, and the party gangster." Dreher was optimistic enough to believe that the people would prefer the "life and growth" of democratic collectivism to the "death and disintegration" of the fascist variety.[8]

The following year Kingsley and Petegorsky published *Strategy for Democracy*. There was a new factor in their work: the United States was at war. But like Lerner and Dreher, they believed that an economic and political crisis had been reached in the United States and in the rest of the world. Monopoly capitalism threatened political democracy; fascism was an end product of the attempt to save the former by eliminating the latter. Political democracy could only be protected if a new system of domestic and international democratic planning was established.[9]

Even writers who had grown somewhat disenchanted with their earlier more clearly articulated collectivism continued to view the world as engaged in a revolutionary struggle over the nature of collectivism. During the early 1930s Bingham shared with writers like Stuart Chase and George Soule the belief that democratic collectivism was part of a global revolution and that the only choice was whether the United States chose a democratic form of collectivism or a totalitarian form. In the 1930s he was concerned primarily with the economic crisis that was pushing the world in the direction of collectivism. By 1942 Bingham's interests had turned toward the consideration of how political democracy could be extended and what kind of democratic techniques could be developed as alternatives to totalitarianism's coercive techniques of control. He also began to take an interest in scientific management and how it might contribute to democratic techniques, as well as to the kind of "social integration" necessitated by the development of new technology.[10]

If these new interests did not lead him to write with the same emphasis on the breakdown of monopoly capitalism as found in Lerner or Dreher, Bingham nevertheless was motivated by a similar desire to develop, in the midst of revolutionary changes, democratic alternatives to fascist brutality. There remains in Bingham a curious combination of crediting fascism with the development of certain "techniques of economic and administrative management" and expressing a moral revulsion at its "cave-man" brutality, a combination that creates a certain moral ambiguity that at times could lead to perceptiveness and at times to moral insensitivity. In the end, however, Bingham shared with the other writers the belief that the revolution that had spawned fascism could be won by democracy.[11]

Lewis Corey shared with Bingham an interest in democratic economic techniques, but he was equally concerned with the breakdown of monopoly capitalism. Thus he shared with Lerner, Petegorsky, and Kingsley a greater sense of urgency. Under his birth name, Louis Fraina, Corey had been a founder of the American Communist Party. Under controversial circumstances, he had disappeared on a Comintern mission in Mexico. Reappearing in the early 1930s, Corey established a reputation as an important independent Marxist radical. By 1940 he was in the process of rethinking a number of his previous ideas. He was one of the founders and theorists of the UDA, and in 1942 he published *The Unfinished Task*. Corey reported in his introduction that as he was writing it, news arrived of the fall of Singapore—"an omen of black days ahead." He expressed confidence in the Allies' victory, but again one senses the urgency of validating the possibilities of a democratic reconstruction.[12]

Like Lerner, Corey spoke in large terms: the breakdown of the old order, its inability any longer to satisfy human needs, and the need for democratic economic reconstruction. Unlike Lerner, who drew clear distinctions between the Soviet Union and fascist totalitarianism, Corey was worried about both the Communist and fascist totalitarian revolutions. Otherwise, they shared many of the same premises. Monopoly capitalism had strangled the economic system; totalitarianism arose out of the ensuing economic crisis and threatened democracy and freedom. And in order to avoid destructive totalitarian revolution, democracy had to create a new economic order: "Nothing is wrong with democracy, but there is something wrong with many of the economic arrangements within democracy. Democracy came into the world as a revolutionary liberating economic (and political) force; we must renew the force."[13]

There were writers who fall within the liberal camp who were less favorably inclined toward collectivism but who were calling for great changes within the American way of doing business—or at least they considered them great changes. Herbert Agar wrote in favor of a "creative conservatism," although he is better described as a moderate liberal. Agar was chair of the Fight for Freedom Committee, a pro-interventionist organization active before the attack upon Pearl Harbor and the author of *A Time for Greatness* in 1942. He and his brother, William, were the directors of Freedom House during the war, and before he entered the service, Agar wrote a column, "What Are We Fighting For?," for *PM*. More than most liberals, Agar defended the existing social order and was no friend of collectivism. Yet, like other liberals, Agar viewed Nazism as a revolution—a revolution "against civilization." And if he did not call for a new economic order or a democratic revolution to counter the fascist revolution, he did call for economic decisions to be based on ethical and political choices; he did praise the Leon Henderson–Thurman Arnold type of strategic economic planning and much of the New Deal. And he did call for an end to economic selfishness and the development of brotherhood.[14]

Like Agar, James Warburg did not favor a socialist alternative to capitalism. Warburg, a member of a wealthy New York banking family whose political journey had taken him from the Republican Party to support of Roosevelt, then a break, and then back to support of FDR, worked for the Office of War Information (OWI) at the beginning of the war. Caught in the periodic political crossfires that battered the OWI, Warburg, who stood with the liberal faction demanding a greater emphasis on political warfare, was forced out. In 1944 he published *Foreign Policy Begins at Home.* But if Warburg was not, like Lerner and Dreher, looking toward democratic socialist solutions for the United States, he was scathing in his criticism of capitalists. He thought that the selfish actions of capitalists created economic breakdowns and the breeding ground for discontent and revolution.[15]

For Warburg, then, the fascist revolution was a counter- or pseudo-revolution caused when revolt threatened a capitalism that had become "rigid instead of flexible, monopolistic instead of competitive, and hence subject to periods of excessive expansion followed by periods of acute depression." To avoid these crises, which created the conditions both of revolt and of fascism, it was necessary, Warburg claimed, to add economic democracy on to political democracy. We must, he wrote, "harness 'free enterprise' to economic democracy."[16]

The common theme of democratic collectivism as an alternative to fascist totalitarianism permeated the thought of all these liberals, with the possible exception of Agar. The three terms that were constantly projected as the essence of democratic collectivism were *democracy, equality,* and *the common man.*

Bingham's exploration of democratic techniques was one of the more far-ranging attempts to reconcile and thereby to advance collectivism and democracy. He argued that democracy could not be equated with "a form of government" or with "a particular set of political institutions." It was more than each. Bingham proceeded to explore a large variety of techniques designed to integrate the freedom of the individual with the needs of the group or institution. Ranging over traditional democratic techniques such as the ballot, representative assembly, party politics, and constitutions, he attempted to demonstrate where they had broken down, where totalitarianism had stepped in to create the coercive state, and where the traditional democratic techniques required strengthening in order to avoid the totalitarian solution. Bingham believed that democratic management and the creation of economic democracy offered the necessary supplements to the traditional forms of democracy. Making use of ideas associated with scientific management—which started personnel departments that enhanced worker participation, dealt fairly in labor relations, and created manageable decentralized units in the organization—Bingham argued that these policies added up to the "democratic way of life," which he confidently predicted would triumph in the long run.[17]

It was a roseate picture. It foresaw the triumph of economic democracy without any change in property relations. Without accepting the more dire warnings of James Burnham's managerial revolution, Bingham's fellow liberals were more wary of managerial techniques. Some, like Reinhold Niebuhr, did not have Bingham's confidence in human nature. Others, like Lerner, were more concerned with human irrationality. What Bingham's long elucidation of democratic techniques did do in its quixotic way was to emphasize the liberal absorption during the war with the question of how to establish a true democracy to combat fascism.[18]

There were, of course, liberals who were casual in their approach to democracy. If Bingham devoted perhaps an excessive amount of space to technique and included some managerial techniques that were as potentially manipulative as they were democratic, Dreher spent far too little time on democracy compared to the space he devoted to collectivism. He talked of private, competitive, small-scale businesses, of regional planning and the maintenance of local self-government, of the continuation of the right to strike and the formation of farm cooperatives. He spoke of the security of having a job as a form of economic democracy, a typical liberal belief. But when it came to talking about how democratic collectivism was to be achieved or institutionally maintained, he was vague. In discussing how democracy was to "adapt itself to civilization," Dreher wrote, "so it all comes down to the common man, in whom this sentiment of democracy must reside if it is to continue to live at all." Such a truism left unanswered hard questions about the preservation and extension of democracy in face of the fascist threat that Dreher wished to avoid.[19]

Most liberals, however, were more careful than Dreher in their attention to guaranteeing the democratic nature of their brand of collectivism. Corey spelled out a series of measures to ensure that the democratic planning that replaced unplanned capitalism not degenerate into totalitarian planning. TVA-style public corporations, regional decentralization and diversification of industry, and limited strategic—rather than total—planning were among Corey's methods for creating a democratic "free economic order" and not the nightmare of the total state.[20]

Perhaps it was Kingsley and Petegorsky who most strongly voiced the need to link the new social order to the expansion of democracy. If they were less thorough than Corey in discussing new organizational forms of democracy, they were more expansive in attempting to show how existing groups such as labor, or existing policies such as taxes, could be used to both strengthen and expand democracy. "It is clear," they wrote, "that if democracy is to survive it must be given new institutional expression." The creation of these new expressions had to begin immediately. For Kingsley and Petegorsky, the democratic revolution provided the vision around which "the oppressed people" of Europe could rally to overthrow fascism. At home, the democratic revolution would lead to the destruction of the roots of native fascism by giving "the common man . . . a real stake in the continuation of democracy."[21]

Alongside democracy, the second word that was constantly used by liberals to define the nature of the required social change was equality. Kingsley and Petegorsky's proposals for including labor in economic planning and government agencies were designed to give labor "equality." In developing his "techniques of democracy," Bingham spoke of the American tradition of equality of rights and of equality under the law. He noted that political equality depended on universal suffrage and that Americans believed in "equality of opportunity" rather than "equality of income" but that the "philosophers of democracy," particularly Jefferson, "always realized that sharp class distinctions and extremes of wealth and poverty were inimical to democracy."[22]

While more conservative in his defense of western civilization and the existing social order than Petegorsky, Kingsley, and Bingham, Herbert Agar nevertheless placed the "explosive idea of equality" at the center of his argument in A *Time for Greatness.* He gave equality a religious rationale by arguing that all men are "equal *in* God, in the divine spark which gives abiding value to the individual soul." Deeply embedded in the religious and political rhetoric of the western world, equality, said Agar, had nevertheless proved a mirage. But if America would seize the idea and put it in practice it would help democratize the world and provide a fighting creed to combat fascism.[23]

If Agar's religious emphasis and "mystic joy" were not typical of liberal rhetoric—though one should not forget similar emotions in Henry Wallace—the manner in which Agar would use the idea of equality was consistent with liberal thinking. Using the "explosive idea," Agar went on to criticize racial discrimination against African Americans, economic and social discrimination against black and white tenant farmers, and the regional concentration of wealth in the North. In focusing especially on racial discrimination, Agar joined such writers as Lerner, Voorhis, and Pearl

Buck who also addressed the domestic and international patterns of race relations.[24]

Kingsley and Petegorsky also stressed equality. The revolution was to be democratic, and equality, according to them, was central to democracy. The Nazis had chosen "to base their system upon the reactionary principle of privilege," Kingsley and Petegorsky wrote, and the United States needed to counter this with the "progressive" principle of "equality." They linked equality and democracy with social change: "equalitarian democracy must become the cornerstone in any progressive reconstruction." If followed, progressive reconstruction, unlike the status quo or the Nazi alternative, would benefit "the common man."[25]

Liberal books resonated with the rhetoric of the people's century. Linking with Kingsley and Petegorsky on the liberal-left, Agar connected equality and democracy with Wallace's call for "a people's century." Lerner counterposed Henry Luce's "American century" with the "people's century." Associating the New Deal with what Harold Laski called "revolution by consent," Lerner argued that the people in democratic countries could achieve social change nonviolently. On the other hand, the people in undemocratic countries would have to "overthrow their leaders to achieve freedom." Both methods were alternatives to Luce's "new order." Whether it was a people's revolution by consent or violence, it still held the promise of a democratic alternative: "ours must be a people's century. It must involve the leadership not just of America and England, but of a *democratic* America and England." And ultimately it must be "a people's century for all nations." Finally, in *Make This the Last War*, Michael Straight linked "the conditions of world progress" with "the people." Each chapter in one section of the book introduced a theme relating to "the people."[26]

Who were these people? The answer was the third word or phrase that defined the nature of the necessary social change. They were the "common people." They were Henry Wallace's farmers trying to sell their products, workers trying to join unions, and children trying to receive an education. They were the average citizen and soldier, in G. A. Borgese's *Common Cause*, who having been "lifted . . . to supreme heights" were still searching for a "common cause," a mystifyingly vague cause that Borgese spent four hundred elliptical pages of a one-year diary of the war ruminating over and trying to define. Some writers placed an emphasis on labor; others on the group that made up the technical and professional middle class. But when one tries to move beyond the vague generalizations about the people as embodied in "the common man" and to root the concept in specific classes or occupations, it appears that it was an inclusive term characterized more by who was not "the common man" or "the people" (e.g., fascists, monopolists, dollar-a-year men, reactionary politicians, racists, isolationists) than by who was specifically to be included. In short, the "common man" was a term that was evoked both because it expressed the historic struggles for democracy and because World War II was seen as a majoritarian, egalitarian, democratic war against the ranks of privilege and exclusiveness.[27]

The democratic, egalitarian "people's revolution" for the common man was not only to be a revolution with a domestic agenda for the United States; it had international implications as well. There was also a "people's peace" to be won. In *The Peace We Fight For* (1943), Hiram Motherwell, a publicist for the Committee of Economic Development, described a devastated Europe at Armistice Day. It was a Europe where government had broken down, where bands roamed, where the economy was in disarray, and where food was scarce. In short, he foresaw anarchy unless a true reconstruction were to take place. In developing his ideas for reconstruction, Motherwell's proposals, especially in terms of colonial empire and his emphasis on the world peacekeeping function of an Anglo-American union, place him somewhat outside the mainstream of the liberal postwar international plans. But the areas he dealt with—economic reconstruction, imperialism and colonial empires, and world organization–big power relations—were the key areas of liberal concern. And the fact that he saw his plans as creating a "people's peace" and that he evoked the name and spirit of Henry Wallace indicates that he was part of the liberal milieu.[28]

In *Beyond Victory*, Voorhis developed these themes. He laid out plans for the immediate economic reconstruction of Europe, for self-government for India and steps toward self-government in other colonial areas, and for a permanent world organization. Similarly, in *Foreign Policy Begins at Home*, James Warburg argued for a permanent world organization, the dismantling of colonial empires, and the need to follow economic policies that would contribute to European recovery and world prosperity. The latter included the reduction of trade barriers, the breakup of international cartels and monopolies, and the willingness of all powers to accept economic self-determination in Europe. Both Voorhis and Warburg, as well as Motherwell, foresaw continued Big Four cooperation in keeping the peace and argued that such cooperation depended on recognizing the security concerns of all the members of the Big Four—England, France, the United States, and Russia.[29]

The attention given to the postwar world was central to the liberal analysis of the nature of the war. If the war was to fulfill its purposes, if fascism and not just Hitler were to be truly defeated and eradicated, then international relations in the world to follow would have to be different and new. For liberals, this made it imperative that the new relations begin immediately. Just as the domestic people's revolution that would create a new postwar world must begin during the war, so too must the kind of international relations that would create the people's peace, the international equivalent to the people's revolution. Throughout the war, but especially during the first two years of American participation, U.S. liberal intellectuals did not believe that the necessary beginnings of international cooperation were being made. Both *The Nation* and *The New Republic* ran numerous articles on the lack of coordination among the Allies and the need to replace the chaotic individual decisions with a truly unified alliance. Two works that reflect these deep liberal concerns were Kingsley and Petegorsky's *Strategy for Democracy* and Straight's *Make This the Last War*.[30]

Although much of *Strategy for Democracy* was written before the American military involvement, Kingsley and Petegorsky were concerned with the absence of a genuine alliance among democratic forces. By integrating the antifascist forces, such an alliance would make possible "a unified and coordinated military strategy." It would provide the impetus for transforming the Allied military policy of "caution and conservatism" to an offensive strategy. Kingsley and Petegorsky, who acknowledged they were not military strategists, could not resist proposing a series of attacks including ones through Spain and Italy.[31]

In addition, the alliance would create for antifascists "for the first time . . . the psychological offensive." A worldwide antifascist alliance would dispel "the widespread suspicion that we are fighting to destroy Hitler rather than to crush fascism." Neutrals would rally to the Allies; the underground would have "new hope." The alliance would give the impetus to start a "political and ideological offensive." Finally, the alliance for victory in war would lay the foundations "for an enduring and meaningful peace." The unity of the Big Four, which was necessary for peace, would have been created in war: "the institutional, the economic, the psychological basis for international order" would have been laid.[32]

Straight shared Kingsley and Petegorsky's call for a unified military command. Propelled by an urgency even stronger than theirs, Straight, in prose dripping with calls for sacrifice, proclaimed the high purposes of the United Nations. Calling for a proclamation of "moral principles of universal application," and for a world bill of "political and economic rights," Straight urged a world charter that would guarantee all peoples the political rights of the U.S. Bill of Rights as well as "the basic economic and social rights of the affirmative state; the basic collective rights of free association, of full national representation, and of full equality among all peoples, the basic right of all peoples to freedom from exploitation and to full national development."[33]

All of Straight's proposals were designed to bring durable peace. All were based on the assumption that World War II was a war of liberation throughout the world against the forces of fascism and reaction. All were propelled by a sense that the Allies were still inactive and that the American people and soldiers still did not understand the purposes of the war. The purposes for Straight, as for the liberal intellectual community as a whole, were the people's revolution and the people's peace. Writing with his usual excess emotionalism, Straight called on the United States to make the people and the soldiers know that this was "The Last War" and to send our forces into battle with a Battle Hymn of the United Nations: "What are we fighting for? What must we do to win? until the answer sounds above the watch fires of a hundred circling camps, is built in the altar of the evening dews and damps, is read in a righteous spirit by the dim and flaring lamps; that we are fighting a war of liberation and only through liberation can we win!"[34]

Between the rhetoric of liberation, of a democratic people's revolution and of a people's peace, and the creation of anything that would give reality to the high words lay the whole area of specific action. In terms of the war and international relations, Petegorsky, Kingsley, and Straight all placed great emphasis on a unified military command. *The Nation* and *The New Republic* frequently joined in the call. They often attributed military setbacks or delays to the lack of a unified command, as they often did the political misunderstandings and the absence of coordinated political warfare. Many of these calls for unified commands came early in the war, although even toward the end their absence could be hauled out to explain a military or political snafu.[35]

But two things happened as the war progressed to lessen the calls. First, even though liberals saw continued problems over the absence of a second military front to relieve German pressure on the Soviet Union, they also saw greater military cooperation than in the early days of the war. Similarly the series of wartime conferences among the foreign ministers and the heads of state reduced the concern over the lack of political coordination—at least as it pertained to the war effort. The second thing that reduced the call for a unified military command was the changed perspective on the outcome of the war. In the early days of the war there was a great deal of pessimism among liberals about the prospects for victory. With the changed military prospects during 1943 it was harder to argue for a unified military command with the same sense of urgency. Similarly, as the war progressed and as liberal intellectuals developed criticisms of Allied political warfare as it manifested itself in relations with the Free French or the post-Mussolini governments in Italy, it became apparent that the faults the liberals found in Allied political warfare came not from the lack of coordination among the Big Four but from what the liberals perceived as fundamental differences in political outlook which might be narrowed through Big Four diplomacy but which would not be solved by a unified political command.

The end result of these changes was the reduction of the unlimited possibilities that liberals had envisioned earlier. As the United Nations evolved and the first proposals came forth from the wartime conferences for a permanent United Nations, it became apparent to liberals that the range of possible activities was more restricted than Straight had proposed. The liberals still wanted an organization that could further a people's peace, but the emphasis was placed more on a peace that might allow for some later democratic transformation instead of on a peace that was directly part of the people's revolution.

At the same time that the larger dimensions of a people's peace as embodied in a fully democratic world organization were being restricted by the evolution of world events, so too were the larger claims of the domestic branch of the people's revolution. Lerner and some of the other liberals may have thought of themselves as democratic socialists and advocated democratic socialism for Europe, but by 1943 democratic socialism was not the term Lerner used any longer in relation to the United States. Stone was one of the few liberals to use the "s" word as having relevance to American politics. But he was practically alone. Even Dreher's democratic collectivism and Corey's mixed economy served more as silent assumptions than as proclaimed goals in liberal rhetoric as the war advanced toward its conclusion. Just as there were reasons for the curtailment in the calls for a unified military commands, so too were there reasons for the curtailment in some of the more expansive domestic rhetoric.[36]

For one thing, the domestic political outlook during World War II was not promising. The 1942 congressional elections were a severe blow to liberal intellectuals. Much as they might call for the need to take the offensive against the domestic reactionaries, some of their responses took the form of defensively checking reaction. In addition, Roosevelt put reform in mothballs for the duration, and the liberals had a hard time envisaging major social changes coming out of the remnants of the New Deal. The 1944 elections marked a mild upturn in liberal hopes, but everything continued to point to moderate reform as the limit of social change.[37]

How, then, was the dream of a democratic revolution and a people's peace to be sustained? If sweeping political, social, economic, and international changes were not there to sustain the dream, what was? In pursuit of answers, the liberal intellectuals began to focus on the United States and how it would emerge from the war. Their attention was drawn both by military victories and by what seemed possible politically, and they began to fix on the issue of unemployment. If the country faced the prospects of unemployment, depression, and major economic dislocations, then it would not be prepared for either democratic peace or democratic social change. If these bleak economic conditions arose, the liberal intellectuals believed, the United States would most likely turn inward and retreat from the world scene. The consequences of a rebirth of isolationism would be disastrous for the American people and for world peace.[38]

Based on these sentiments, *The Nation, The New Republic, Common Sense,* and *PM* began to pay increasing attention to plans for economic reconversion. *The Nation* and *The New Republic* published supplements on economic reconversion. Both publicized the Keynesian-influenced writings of Alvin Hansen and various other plans for reconversion that were rolling forth from all points along the political spectrum. In *PM,* Lerner and Stone turned their attention to the postwar need to "mobilize for abundance" and to guarantee full employment, and in *Common Sense,* Stuart Chase, Lewis Corey, and Robert Nathan wrote on reconversion plans. The liberal economist Chase also wrote several books about the need for planning in the process of economic reconversion. Liberal politicians like Wallace, Voorhis, and Chester Bowles devoted books, articles, and speeches to advocating a full-employment economy as part of reconversion—not only for its domestic benefits but as essential to the world prosperity required for peace.[39]

The need for economic planning for full employment in the reconversion process had come to substitute for the democratic people's revolution. To put it another way, the liberal intellectuals who continued to believe in and periodically call for a democratic revolution and a people's peace saw the viability of these goals depending on continued U.S. prosperity in the reconversion period. An American depression would create world economic dislocation, which would stimulate the resurgence of fascism. It would place in jeopardy the ambitious British plans for full employment and full social security, whether developed under a Tory government or, as the liberals hoped, under a Labour one. It would make difficult the economic recovery of the Soviet Union, which would increasingly turn inward, search for security through establishing a security belt of border states, and feed its nationalistic tendencies. It would cause Europe to remain in economic disarray, with all the potential for fascism that entailed. It would encourage the colonial powers to hold onto their colonies and thus prevent a democratic free world from being created. Thus a lot rested on U.S. prosperity: it was not only jobs for American workers and returning servicemen; it was the world's future.[40]

In defining the necessary conditions for U.S. prosperity, the key phrase became the "full employment economy." Popularly transformed from Roosevelt's speeches and Wallace's writings into "sixty million jobs," full employment became the sine qua non of progressive social change. But how did liberals propose to achieve full employment in the reconversion process? One way—these were Wallace's chief targets—was to destroy the restrictive practices of monopolies and trade barriers.

Corey and Dreher had addressed both requirements early in the war. Though differing in their solutions, both men had pinpointed the restrictive production practices of monopoly capitalism as the key to its periodic depressions and to its inability to provide a viable economic system. Of the liberals Bingham was the least worried about the monopolistic tendencies of big business. He wrote his friend Tom Amlie that one should not look at monopolies and cartels as the main evils of capitalism. But Bingham's complacency about monopoly and cartels was not shared by most liberal intellectuals. Throughout the war, *The Nation* and *The New Republic* undertook a running battle against the cartels. In the daily press, *PM* joined the attack. Exposés of fascist connections and of restrictive practices were common. Stone especially targeted monopolies and their political allies as the chief culprits in the domestic economic bottlenecks in war production and as the chief enemies of a full-employment economy after the war.[41]

Trade barriers were linked with monopolies in terms of restrictive practices. From left liberals like Kingsley and Petegorsky to moderate liberals like Agar, tariffs and other trade barriers came under attack. Kingsley and Petegorsky viewed the falling of trade barriers as part of the end of imperialism and economic nationalism. Agar, on the other hand, was not interested in large changes in the capitalist system. "What is needed," he wrote, "is a change of mind and heart rather than a change of system." But one of the changes he was willing to accept was the continued lowering of the tariff barriers.[42]

Convinced that the New Deal shot-in-the-arm spending policy required a more systematic and institutionally permanent approach, the liberals around *The Nation* and *The New Republic* called for policies that would draw up budgets ensuring full employment and for agencies to implement the policies. Excited earlier in the war by the National Resources Planning Board's plans and its issuance of a new bill of economic rights, and believing that the board furnished the next creative step beyond the New Deal and toward a genuine democratic revolution, *The Nation, The New Republic,* and *PM* anticipated that it would become part of the political agenda. However, the National Resources Planning Board was eliminated; instead, Congress created a committee under conservative Senator Walter George to examine reconversion. Unlike Sir William Beveridge's plans for full employment and a full social security system, which seemed to point Great Britain in the direction of the ideals enunciated by the National Resources Planning Board, there was no parallel political move on the part of the Roosevelt administration. Still, liberal intellectuals continued to press for a full employment program.[43]

With the struggle over the Murray Full Employment Bill in 1945, the issue of full employment received even more attention. The UDA mobilized for the passage of the bill. *The Nation, The New Republic,* and *PM* gave it strong support, although they felt it did not go far enough. Stone argued that the original plans set forth by James Patton of the National Farmers Union were superior to the inadequate Murray Bill. Eventually, Stone wrote, there would have to be planning for industrial output. However, he viewed the battle over the Murray Bill as of "historic importance" and he supported its passage. Alvin Hansen was more enthusiastic than Stone in his praise of the Murray Bill. He saw in its National Production and Employment Budget the "broad outlines" of the kind of expansion program that Beveridge was advocating in Great Britain.[44]

But whether the Murray Bill was supported with reservations or enthusiastically, the battle over the bill suggests the seriousness with which liberals regarded full employment as absolutely essential for domestic justice and international peace. The people's revolution for a democratic, egalitarian, common-man society and for a people's peace had been reduced in terms of specific political battles to the struggle over full employment. And here lay an ambiguity in liberal thought. The fact that the full employment fight was a struggle to try to assure full employment under capitalism; the fact that advocates of full employment like Warburg, Voorhis, and Bowles were all arguing for a reformed capitalist system and were linking full employment to capitalism, and even in the case of Bowles to the unleashing of free enterprise; the fact that Wallace wrote about economic change in terms of maintaining the reality of the Horatio Alger story, of making free enterprise really "free," and of the role of private capital working with government capital in creating full employment, suggests a dichotomy between the liberal rhetoric of an international civil war and a democratic revolution and the reality of how that civil war played itself out.[45]

In 1942 Kingsley and Petegorsky wrote: "We have discussed . . . what have seemed to us the fundamentals of such a program: the abolition of inequality and special privilege in our economic relationships . . . the equal participation of labor in the formulation and administration of national policy . . . the launching of a dynamic political and ideological offensive against the Axis through the propaganda of the deed as well as of the word and through the elaboration of plans for radical social reconstruction after the war." Few of these goals came to pass, at least not in the form the liberal intellectuals had originally envisaged. The "radical social reconstruction" they had in mind did not seem so radical when it was translated into the liberal politics of World War II. Despite the rhetoric of democratic revolution, the actual concrete economic issues that were supposed to create "the new world a coming," to further "the democratic revolution" or "radical social reconstruction," amounted in practice to reformed capitalism.[46]

In late 1945 the British socialist Harold Laski wrote an article in *The Nation* in which he told his liberal readers that there was "no middle way." Free enterprise and the market economy meant war; socialism and a planned economy meant peace. Laski wrote three months after the Murray Bill was set aside (it would be rehabilitated, watered down, and passed in the next session). Laski may have thought—and possibly some wishful thinking liberals did too—that the Murray Bill pointed toward the kind of planning he was advocating. It was fairer to the spirit behind the Murray Bill, however, to see it as representing the American vision of consumer capitalism motored by Keynesian economics and accompanied by increased security benefits. As visions go one can imagine a lot worse, but it was hardly the forerunner of the people's revolution.[47]

What triumphed, for better or worse, was liberal capitalism. The liberals' own recommendations on planning for reconversion, full employment, and eliminating monopolistic bottlenecks had undoubtedly contributed to that triumph. But it was a far cry from the high, if vague, hopes for a new democratic revolution.

Perhaps it was inevitable that the desperate war situation and the horror of fascism should have produced a political vision high on idealistic goals but minus the power or the ability to implement the goals. But what the liberal intellectuals did was to invest in Roosevelt as the leader and in the New Deal as the administration that represented the progressive forces that could achieve those idealistic goals. Defining World War II in ideological terms that the administration used, but did not share, and believing that the New Deal, with the help of labor and progressives, could create a domestic democratic and international revolution—neither of which was on the administration's agenda—was bound to make the relationship between the liberal intellectual community and the New Deal one that was filled both with illusions and with frustrations.

3

Liberals Confront the New Deal

LESS THAN A month after the United States entered World War II, the Free French forces under Charles De Gaulle liberated Saint Pierre and Miquelon, French islands at the entrance of Newfoundland Bay, from the control of the Vichy government. It might have been anticipated that the U.S. government would welcome this small, but dramatic, effort to displace an Axis-oriented government. Instead, the State Department issued a strongly worded condemnation of De Gaulle's actions.

The outrage in the liberal press was immediate. Freda Kirchwey's January 1942 editorial deserves special attention because it expressed the liberal intellectual community's response to much of U.S. foreign policy during the war. In this editorial one can see Kirchwey's moral indignation as well as the political analysis of the relationship between appeasement and the war effort and between Roosevelt and U.S. foreign policy. Headlined "Mr. Hull Should Resign," the editorial bristled with anger at the State Department. In the worldwide civil war, democratic forces everywhere had waited eagerly for news of strikes at fascism. When at last one had come, the State Department's condemnation had depressed the morale of these struggling democrats. According to this analysis, appeasement did not simply strengthen fascism by giving aid and comfort to the collaborators; it also weakened the fighting spirit of the democratic forces.[1]

Who was to blame for this policy of placating fascism? It is here that Kirchwey's analysis of Roosevelt's role is essential in understanding the views of the liberal intellectual community. Kirchwey made a clear distinction between the president and the State Department. Could Roosevelt have known that the State Department would condemn the Free French? If he did, she proclaimed, he stood disgraced in the eyes of democrats throughout the world; but clearly he did not. The worst that could be said of him was that he continued to tolerate the appeasers and pro-fascists in the State Department. Such tolerance was bad enough, but there was, according to Freda Kirchwey, no way that Roosevelt himself would have outwardly and directly condemned an antifascist action like De Gaulle's.[2]

One does not need to know the details of Roosevelt's interaction with the State Department over the wording of its statement to recognize that Kirchwey had let the president off the hook. Certainly, the policy of recognizing the Vichy government was his, and from this policy flowed the State Department's statement. This separating the good, if excessively tolerant, Roosevelt from the bad State Department was a pattern *The Nation* and *The New Republic* would follow. *Common Sense*, whose attitude toward Roosevelt was not as indulgent, also was disturbed by the State Department's machinations with governments whose leaders collaborated with fascist dictatorships.

Eventually all these journals had to acknowledge that the State Department was not solely responsible for the policy of appeasing fascist collaborators. In the fall of 1943 one of the editors of *The New Republic*, George Soule, wrote that the supporters of Roosevelt had gotten into the habit of viewing him as "a spotless knight-errant of progressivism" and of "blaming subordinates for the actions which they dislike." And in the summer of 1943 *The Nation,* in an editorial criticizing the columnist Ernest Lindley's defense of the State Department's anti-De Gaulle policy, concluded: "It is now all too clear . . . that Mr. Lindley is right when he attributes our French policy to the President and Mr. Hull rather than to any group of subordinates. So much the worse."[3] Nevertheless, liberal intellectuals continued to criticize mainly the State Department for the appeasement policy.

The State Department did not view its policies toward the neutrals in the same light as the liberals did. Its rationale in recognizing pro-fascist governments was based on military strategy: breaking relations with the Vichy government would result in its turning the French Navy over to the Axis and would cause the Vichy government to aid Hitler more overtly. It insisted that the Vichy government was not completely in the fascist camp and that its semi-neutrality was beneficial to the Allies. The same rationale was applied to Spain and Latin America.[4]

The State Department's assessment of the diplomatic and military benefits of its policies fell on the deaf ears of the liberal intellectuals, who felt that in the ideological civil war, the Lavals, Petains, Francos, and Ramirezes had already made their choice; they had chosen the Axis. State

Department appeasement merely enabled such leaders to maintain the pretense of neutrality. As Kirchwey had said, Hitler had forced all to choose sides, and it was better to have collaborationists openly and honestly on the side of the Axis rather than to maintain the hypocrisy of a neutrality that sapped the fighting spirit and morale of the democratic peoples and nations of the world.[5]

Soon after the State Department's condemnation of the Free French, and in the face of its continued recognition of the Vichy government and dismissal of De Gaulle's claim to the leadership of the French people, *The Nation, The New Republic,* and the UDA began to plan a campaign to expose the State Department. The end result was the publication—first as a series of articles in *The Nation* and then as a book—of Robert Bendiner's *The Riddle of the State Department.* The managing editor of *The Nation,* Bendiner portrayed a reactionary State Department which preferred the status quo to democratic change and practiced a pattern of appeasement that dated back to the thirties and the Spanish Civil War.[6]

The status quo politics-as-usual that was found rampant in the State Department was matched by the business-as-usual crowd, which liberals believed was stymieing the war effort throughout the nation's production program. There were four elements, they believed, that impeded full war production: business footdragging over conversion, the pro-business orientation of Jesse Jones and other dollar-a-year production coordinators in Washington, the failure genuinely to include labor in the wartime economic plans, and the ineffectuality of well-intentioned people like Donald Nelson of the War Production Board. And these issues were well covered in the liberal press. I. G. Stone wrote exposés of pro-fascist businesses for *The Nation* as well as other articles on the failure of the business community to give fully to the war effort. Dwight Macdonald did a two-part exposé of Jones and his cronies for *The Nation.* In *The New Republic,* Michael Straight and Bruce Bliven found the business community wanting. Similarly, *PM* found that Jones and the entire business crowd in Washington hindered full production. Editorials and articles abounded on scandals in the rubber industry, on the I. G. Farben connections, on the firing of whistle-blowers, and on the unwillingness of government agencies headed by businessmen to force business compliance.[7]

Once again, Roosevelt's failure, according to liberal intellectuals, was his tolerance of the Jesse Joneses and William Knudsens. The liberals were impatient with Roosevelt's reliance on such men, who did not share the liberals'—and presumably Roosevelt's—ideological interpretation of the war. And their impatience would grow as Roosevelt placated Congress and conservative pressures by gutting the most liberal parts of the New Deal and withdrawing a series of liberal appointments to New Deal agencies or permitting liberals to be fired by government agencies. In addition, there were the liberals—Paul Appleby, Edgar Ansell Mowrer, James Warburg—who resigned from government agencies in protest of the conservative policies being followed.[8]

The fact that Appleby's resignation was from the State Department over its pro-Vichy policy and that Mowrer's and Warburg's were from the Office of War Information, where the liberal intellectuals had high hopes of conducting liberal political warfare, made the exodus of liberals from Washington harder to take. Some of the episodes, such as Malcolm Cowley's withdrawal of his nomination for a position with the OWI and Roy Parmelee's resignation from the Board of Economic Warfare, were designed to protect the agencies from congressional enemies. This served as a reminder of the power of the Dies committee and other reactionary groups in Congress, a reminder that the liberals did not have the political upper hand. The elimination of the National Youth Administration, the Farm Security Administration, and the National Resources Planning Board served as further reminders.

Surveying the cuts in New Deal programs, the loss of liberal appointments, and the influence of the Dies committee, in May 1943 Cowley declared the "end of the New Deal." It is quite remarkable, considering that he could not be completely separated from any of these actions, that Roosevelt escaped with a chastisement for his timidity. The blame was attributed largely to the Dies committee and congressional reactionaries.[9]

The Nation, The New Republic, and the UDA went on the attack with an exposé of Martin Dies. Responding to Dies's attack on the UDA in 1942 and to his investigation of New Deal liberal agencies and appointments, Kirchwey published a supplement on Dies in October 1942, from which *PM* published excerpts. In addition, the UDA sponsored an anti-Dies meeting at which Kirchwey and Bliven of *The New Republic* spoke. Kirchwey edited a pamphlet exposing Dies, the UDA contributed to its circulation, and *The New Republic* participated in the research. These attacks on Dies were the equivalent in domestic affairs to Bendiner's articles and book on the State Department in foreign affairs. Kirchwey's critique took up a familiar liberal position—making a slashing attack on a clear spokesperson for reaction: "Dies is not important as a man or a politician. He is important as a symbol of forces that have mobilized to defeat our hope of a democratic America, a victorious war, and a people's peace. Dies speaks for a reaction that is today engaged in civil war. And he speaks effectively. Dies is not performing a democratic function badly; he is performing an anti-democratic maneuver well. His every move is an act of war. His committee is a camouflaged pillbox in the fascist fight for control of our democracy. It needs to be stormed and overthrown—not reformed." [10]

Roosevelt's motives in placating the Dies committee and the reactionaries in Congress derived from his fear of political disunity during the war; his turning to Jones and Knudsen reflected the conventional wisdom of trying to gain business cooperation by putting business leaders in charge. In either case, as with New Deal foreign policy, there is a distinction between how the New Deal fought the war and what the liberals believed the meaning of the war to be. Roosevelt based his foreign policy and domestic decisions on what he felt was best to protect national security and not on the ideological grounds that liberal intellectuals championed. World War II was not for Roosevelt, as it was for liberal intellectuals, an ideological war for democracy. Roosevelt may have wished for the defeat of reaction at home and abroad, but for him, World War II was not a war whose purpose would be lost if reaction were permitted to remain in power throughout the world.

Nevertheless, for the New Deal, liberal ideology and the liberal interpretation of the war were not without their uses. Building as it did on traditional American values of freedom and democracy, liberal rhetoric was seen as essential to giving a defining purpose to the war for the American people. Roosevelt may even have generally shared these liberal aspirations; his Four Freedoms speech was not simply a cynical device to win political support. But the liberal aspirations that might emerge out of a war being fought on the narrow basis of defeating Germany, Italy, and Japan were one thing; the liberal aspirations that were deeply embedded in every domestic and foreign policy decision—so embedded that they established a kind of moral imperative—were another. And Roosevelt was in no way wedded to the latter.

The liberal intellectuals' acceptance of these publicly proclaimed values as representations of the essence of the Roosevelt administration provided the basis for their willingness to separate Roosevelt from so much of what was going on around him. It divided him from Secretary of State Cordell Hull and the reactionaries in the State Department and from the dollar-a-year men he was so mistakenly relying on. But it was not simply the rhetoric alone that caused the liberal intellectuals to draw these distinctions. When *Common Sense* called the New Deal the "American version of a world-wide revolutionary change," it pointed to its actions: the Good Neighbor Policy and government domestic programs for "the forgotten man." In other words, there was a *liberal* history of Roosevelt which the liberal intellectuals subscribed to and drew on in order to read into the Roosevelt administration their interpretation of the war. Even Stone, one of Roosevelt's severest critics among the liberal intellectuals, wrote that it was clear where Roosevelt's sympathies lay—on the liberal side. The liberals created their own liberal history, but to do so one had to be selective: the Wagner Act, not NRA; efforts to modify the Neutrality Acts in 1939, not support for the application of the Neutrality Acts to Spain from 1936 to 1939.[11]

The critical war years were perhaps not the ideal time for thought, yet a little reflection on the history of the New Deal might have suggested the outer limits of New Deal ideology. Stone perhaps came closest to understanding New Deal history. In January 1944, in noting Roosevelt's own silence on the more controversial parts of the New Deal (the Wagner Act and TVA), Stone pointed out that in the beginning the New Deal had had "a curious combination" of groups behind it. There were the big business-men seeking the relaxation of the antitrust laws, farmers desiring tariff protection, "retail business men who understood the need for government spending," and workers whose organizing thrusts pushed Roosevelt to the left. If Stone had followed through on his analysis he might have arrived at the later historical insights of Stephen Fraser, who in *Labor Will Rule* has argued persuasively that for a brief period in the mid-thirties a com-bination of retail-oriented businessmen and labor leaders came together to push a high-wage economy rationalized by government regulation and a well-organized but disciplined labor movement and spurred when nec-essary by government spending—a kind of Keynesian-driven consumer capitalism.[12]

If this was the outer left limits of New Deal thinking in the 1930s, and if Roosevelt's commitment to it was as ambiguous, as tentative and as driven by political concerns as were all his commitments, how unlikely that the war years would bring about a more consistent left movement on his part. And yet, without always putting it in these terms, this is what the liberal intellectuals—by distinguishing between Roosevelt's motives and those of the State Department, his business-oriented administration as-sociates, and all of the conservative forces surrounding Congress—were hoping and demanding.

As *The New Republic* summed up domestic and international conditions at the end of 1942, the editors saw that the struggle on both fronts between the progressive forces and the forces of reaction had become a double fight: the first between Roosevelt and all "the primitive forces in American life"—the Republican machine, the radio and press, the reactionary industrialists, the appeasers and isolationists; the second between the liberal and reactionary forces within the Democratic Party. In the latter fight, it was the "planning mentality of the War Production Board" versus the "dollar-a-year mentality," "the Wallace-Perkins group" versus "the State Department group," those "who mean democracy" versus those "who use it as a convenient slogan." This battle, the editors said, would not be easy. It meant defending the New Deal's "constructive achievements" against its outside enemies, and fighting "to maintain and extend" it against its inside "pretended friends, but actual betrayers." It meant supporting "a vigorous prosecution of the war" in contrast both to defeatist sentiments and to the "tired titans who fashion world policy." Roosevelt had to "insist that the war is not one between nations, but between principles."[13]

This interesting editorial contains most of the liberal intellectuals' claims about Roosevelt. In both battles in the "double fight," Roosevelt was viewed as at heart on the liberal side. In the first battle, which might be considered a battle against the Republican-isolationist right, it assumed that Roosevelt was the torchbearer of liberalism. In the second battle, it was considered possible that Roosevelt would capitulate to the conservative and reactionary forces within his administration. In this view of Roosevelt, he was a vacillating liberal, perhaps too weak to stand up against conservative pressure—unless the progressives mobilized. The progressives, in the latter case, would be fighting to keep Roosevelt's liberal soul on course and prevent it from collapsing under the weight of conservative pressure. Both interpretations create the possibility of a good deal of criticism directed at Roosevelt, but both assume that he was, at heart, "one of us."

Because the liberal press was so filled with criticisms, because a liberal like Alfred Bingham could write from Germany in the fall of 1944 that he had no hope about what Roosevelt would do and the only reason he was voting for him was that he might put Chester Bowles in charge of the reconversion program, because there was so much liberal disillusionment with Roosevelt, it is important to recognize that as upset as the liberal intellectuals became they could never erase the idea that he was on their side. To the liberals, then, there were many Roosevelts, but all wound up in the same camp. There was the Roosevelt who after his victory in 1944 was, according to *The New Republic,* free "to act for the pages of history." And what was he free to do? Essentially fulfill the liberal agenda: discard Mayor Hague, judge Franco on his own merits without having to worry about the Catholic vote, and fight vigorously against the poll tax and for "full justice" for African Americans. No longer having to prove to conservative Democrats and Republicans that he was a friend of free enterprise, he could attack monopolies and extend social security. One could argue that this was simply a liberal "wish list." But one would not have drawn up such a list without assuming that at some deep level Roosevelt shared these goals.[14]

For *The Nation,* there was also the Roosevelt who deserved support because of "his record"; he had demonstrated sympathy "toward popular distress and aspiration" and had shown a "willingness to experiment" in seeking solutions. And the journal viewed Roosevelt as sharing liberal goals for the postwar domestic economy: "Mr. Roosevelt . . . believes that it is the major responsibility of government to take the steps necessary to bring about full employment, the full utilization of natural resources, and full social security. We shall see more social planning, not less, in the next term of Franklin D. Roosevelt."[15]

But there was also the Roosevelt who had to be reminded that the New Deal was larger than himself, that he was as much a product of social forces and movement as their creator. When Roosevelt proposed setting aside "Dr. New Deal" for "Dr. Win the War," on his return from Teheran in December 1943, *The New Republic* sought to remind its readers that the New Deal was not a "slogan" that one could turn off and on. Rather it was "a conception of government" with a "social direction." It was "a program for social action." Insofar as the New Deal was a slogan, the words were unimportant, but "as a fact and as an aspiration" it was "essential." In making his proposal to mothball the New Deal, Roosevelt assumed "he had created the New Deal" and that he could "drop it and move on to fresh fields and pastures new . . . [but] the New Deal is bigger than the man whom history will regard as its creator."[16]

In one sense, this Roosevelt was cut down to size. He was warned that the New Deal could go on without him, that it transcended him. But in another sense, as its embodiment, he was associated with its liberal dynamic. What he was really being warned about was not to abandon the liberal movement that he had helped to create, not to desert the progressive forces for whom he had been a catalyst. In the very act of cutting

Roosevelt down to size, the editors had assured his place in the liberal pantheon.

In the end, the many Roosevelts rested securely on liberal ground. It was from this ground that the liberals, even when they were forced to acknowledge that a policy they opposed derived from Roosevelt as well as from the tired titans who fashioned world policy, either explicitly or implicitly distinguished between the two. When Sumner Welles, once a liberal anathema but as the war progressed increasingly respected, was forced to resign from the State Department, *The Nation* commented, "chalk up a victory for Cordell Hull and a loss for the Administration." [17]

The result of the fundamental distinction between Roosevelt and the reactionary groups within his own administration was that no wartime decision that contradicted or betrayed the liberal rhetoric and principles was fully attributed to Roosevelt himself. The most direct criticism was somehow deflected. Roosevelt often was portrayed as vacillating in the face of pressure, as surrendering to conservative forces and groups, as unwilling to face the serious nature of domestic and international problems, but no matter how tarnished he emerged from his and his associates' actions and inactions, somehow his fundamental liberalism remained intact.

It is hard to say where this faith in Roosevelt derived from. One might legitimately say it was created when the liberal legislation of 1935 presented Roosevelt as a bold initiator standing in sharp contrast to the passive conservatism of his opponents, but even in moments of criticism, liberals had never completely written Roosevelt off. At one such moment in the summer of 1935, *The Nation* had written that Roosevelt was not being true to the "best" within him. For liberal intellectuals, that "best" was validated in the liberal turn in 1935. In the late 1930s, those most antithetical to liberal beliefs—corporate leaders, racists, anti-Semites, right-wing Republicans—all hated Roosevelt. The liberal image of Roosevelt grew further during this period as much because of his enemies as because of his own actions. With the liberal consensus over foreign policy that developed in the aftermath of the spring 1941 Nazi blitzkrieg, the image further solidified. By 1942 it was firmly in place.[18]

This view, however, was difficult to maintain. The distance between the liberal intellectuals' interpretation of the war and the actions of Roosevelt and his administration was too difficult to ignore. The result was sometimes liberal anger, sometimes liberal bitterness—and always liberal discouragement and frustration. The State Department's attack on the Free French over the invasion of St. Pierre and Miquelon was a first signal.

No policy was more designed to produce these emotions than the policy toward the Vichy government. And no issue brought these matters to a head more than the Darlan deal.

Even before U.S. entrance into World War II, a large body of liberal opinion was urging Roosevelt to break diplomatic relations with the Vichy government. In the summer of 1941, the UDA and other groups petitioned Roosevelt to make the break. The St. Pierre and Miquelon episode had furnished one more example of the corrupt nature of U.S. policy toward France: we condemned our friends and were cozy with our pro-fascist enemies.[19]

When Roosevelt made the choice of an American invasion in Northwest Africa in November 1942, he chose a plan that involved diplomatic and military complications. Since the landing was to take place in an area held by the Vichy government, Roosevelt faced both the likelihood of French military resistance and the disruption of U.S. relations with the recognized government of France. From the beginning of the war Roosevelt had worried that the Vichy government would directly join the Axis and bring with it the remains of the French navy. Continued French military neutrality was a priority. Faced already with this delicate diplomatic situation, the United States was disappointed when the initial North African landing met considerable resistance. At this stage, Robert Murphy, the President's special envoy to Vichy France, and General Mark Clark, with the endorsement of General Eisenhower, negotiated a deal with Admiral Darlan, the commander of the Vichy military forces in North Africa. The agreement exchanged the military neutrality of the French armies in North Africa for the Allied recognition of Darlan as the head of political affairs in French North Africa. Although motivated by the military timetable of a quick capture of Tunis and by the easily understood desire to save American lives, the deal was bound to have political repercussions. A prominent Nazi sympathizer and known anti-Semite, Darlan had aided Rommel's North African campaign and had been in charge of the anti-Jewish laws and the jailing of political prisoners in North Africa.[20]

The Darlan deal was announced on November 12, 1942. Because of the public outcry, Roosevelt felt impelled to make a public pronouncement endorsing Eisenhower's decision, but emphasizing that it was a temporary situation and was done exclusively for military expediency. Roosevelt's assurances and explanations satisfied most writers and political leaders. Important persons inside the U.S. and British governments opposed it, but the sustained public outcry—an outcry to which Roosevelt was apparently very sensitive—came from the liberal intellectual community. Outside anti-Stalinist radical circles, the only continual voices of protest rose from the *Nation–New Republic*–UDA circle of liberals. Even *PM*, or at least key *PM* editors, accepted Roosevelt's military rationalization and his assurance that the arrangement would be only temporary. *PM*'s willingness to accept a policy that countered its own definition of the war outraged liberals like Michael Straight, and Straight's outrage was characteristic of the liberal intellectual community.[21]

The New Republic initially voiced concerns over the political implications of the agreement. To make the deal, the United States had shunted aside the Free French and "snubbed General De Gaulle." Saying that they did not object to collaborating with the Darlans of the world "on military terms," the editors argued that there was a difference between a "military bargain" and a "political partnership." Whatever the possible military necessity in having Darlan bring the French officers over to the Allied side, it would be unfair to have the deal become a precedent for establishing "sunshine patriots" like Darlan as the future political leaders of France. While Darlan had been competing with Pierre Laval to do Hitler's bidding, De Gaulle and the Free French had been conducting the struggle against them. "If we really do mean friendship and comradeship with the murderers of labor, the despisers of reason, the betrayers of liberty," they wrote, then "what sort of war is this that we are part of?"[22]

The next week *The New Republic* returned to the appeasement theme. Faced with State Department and Roosevelt chiding of "self-appointed pundits" and politically motivated critics of the American second-front efforts, it conceded that "the temporary acceptance of Admiral Darlan, after so much previous intrigue, was probably a wise move." But, the editors went on, if the issue was strictly a military matter then "they would apologize and say nothing more." But the issue was not strictly military; the problem was not the Darlan deal as an isolated military deal, but the Darlan deal as a pattern of appeasement and its political implications. The military benefits of the "opportunistic" policy might look persuasive now, they wrote, but it "must inevitably influence the nature of the peace that follows." Despite the lives saved by the "purchase of appeasement," millions of lives were going to be lost in the war. And if the peace was lost by the wartime compromises and deals, then we would have caused lives to be lost in vain. Roosevelt declared that Darlan's political power was temporary, they continued, but how was one to know. Right now, Darlan held political power, which set a precedent that seemed to the editors part of "a deliberate policy" by the State and War Departments for dealing with the semi-fascists rather than with the underground and with what the two regarded as "all the 'slush about a people's war.'"[23]

In *The Nation*, Kirchwey responded with even more passion. She labeled Darlan "America's first Quisling." In an editorial that combined *The Nation*'s critique of State Department appeasement with an enunciation of how the deal "betrayed the democratic nature of the war," Kirchwey wrote: "Prostitutes are used but seldom loved. Even less frequently are they honored. . . . We should have done without [his favors] — even if lives were to be lost and military advantages forfeited as a consequence. . . . For the United States has only one claim on the allegiance of the peoples of the world: an honest and courageous democratic policy. We can't afford new ventures in double-dealing or in reactionary diplomacy even in the interests of military gains. The price is too high."[24]

It is easy to criticize Kirchwey's seeming casualness about the loss of American lives. But if one accepted her interpretation of the war it was not a cold-blooded disregard for human life. For Kirchwey and the liberal community, a nonideological war, a war that would leave in place the economic forces and pro-fascist opportunists who only abandoned ship when their side began to lose, would not only mark a defeat for democracy but fail to maintain the peace. More dictators, more wars would quickly follow. Only an unambiguous political and military war against fascism would assure its permanent defeat. In this sense, additional casualties in 1942 were worth preventing far more casualties in a soon-to-follow World War III.

Two things are striking about the liberal intellectuals' response to the Darlan deal. First, it is obvious that they were unaware of the extent to which the deal bypassed the State Department and was a direct Roosevelt initiative. They were aware — I. F. Stone briefly noted his political background — that Robert Murphy had played a role as the president's special representative. But a lot of their response focused on the State Department. *The New Republic* connected the policy with the continued State Department appeasement of Franco. Kirchwey viewed it as part of a pattern that included the appeasement of Franco, the consideration of the House of Savoy as the basis of a future Italian government, and the apparent negotiations between Archduke Otto von Hapsburg and the State Department for a "Free Austria" battalion. Although he could accept the military expediency argument for the Darlan deal, Alexander Uhl in *PM* recited the same litany of appeasement: Vichy, Franco, and the Hapsburgs.

It was a litany—with new additions—that Uhl and other liberals would frequently repeat throughout the war.[25]

A second thing that stands out in the liberal response to the Darlan deal is the distance between Roosevelt's premises and those of the liberal intellectuals. According to James McGregor Burns, Samuel Rosenman had never seen Roosevelt more affected by political criticism than he was as a result of the Darlan deal. But the impact apparently did not result from Roosevelt feeling he had somehow betrayed the liberal interpretation of the war. In September 1942, Roosevelt had issued a specific directive to his special envoy Robert Murphy in which he said that the United States did not contemplate any change in the French civil administration. Earlier, in 1940, Roosevelt had told his ambassador to Vichy France, Admiral William Leahy, to gain the confidence of Petain and Darlan, who controlled the French fleet. It is clear that Roosevelt was motivated by military and geopolitical considerations and not by the ideological and moral concerns of the liberals.[26]

Although the liberal intellectuals focused much of their criticism of the Darlan deal on the State Department, Roosevelt did not escape completely unscathed. In the midst of her agonizing over the Darlan deal, Kirchwey defined the difference between "two themes of political behavior." On one hand, there was the "quarterback" or "opportunist" theory; on the other hand, there was the theory that insisted on the "importance of a thought-out consistent political line." The first she associated with the president; it pointed to a Europe of future "Quisling governments." The latter represented the liberals' interpretation of the war. In this revealing editorial, there was little attempt to hide Roosevelt behind the skirts of the State Department. Kirchwey focused her criticism on Roosevelt, his lack of political foresight and the inadequacies of his rationalizations. If carried to its logical outcome, such frankness over the difference between Roosevelt's opportunistic conception of political and military decisions and the liberal intellectuals' belief that principled decisions needed to be made in light of the ideological nature of the war should have led to a serious reconsideration of the liberals' relationship to the Roosevelt administration. But despite their growing frustration and disappointment, liberal intellectuals were reluctant to push their criticisms to the logical outcome.[27]

The liberal ability to evade any serious break with Roosevelt was not the result of his changing his French policy following the Darlan deal. After Darlan's assassination on December 24, 1942, the United States turned to General Henri-Honoré Giraud, who had escaped from a German

prison camp earlier in 1942. Giraud was not implicated in the French surrender and Vichy collaborationism, but he was on better terms with the
Vichyites and less inclined than De Gaulle to clean the house of collaborators in French North Africa. And he had remained aloof from De Gaulle's
Free French, a factor that raised him in the eyes of those in the U.S. government who were particularly hostile to the prickly De Gaulle. As American and British efforts to bring together Giraud and De Gaulle were beginning, the State Department compounded liberal antagonism to its French
policy by importing from Argentina Marcel Peyrouton to hold a civilian
office in the French North African government. Peyrouton, although anti-
Laval, was a notorious Vichyite, a symbol for the liberals of French surrender and collaboration. He, together with the French military commander
in Morocco, General Nogues, and a series of other Vichyites were clear
indications to the liberals that although Darlan was dead, Darlanism was
still in power—and with the blessing of the State Department.[28]

Liberal journals published editorials and articles condemning the Peyrouton appointment. The UDA held a meeting at which Paul Appleby,
who had recently resigned from the State Department in protest; Reinhold
Niebuhr; and Quincy Howe spoke critically of the U.S. North African
policy. The UDA also sponsored a March 31, 1943, meeting on the meaning of the Peyrouton episode at New York's Town Hall. This time it was
Edgar Ansel Mowrer, recently resigned from the OWI, who spoke, along
with Niebuhr, Max Lerner, and Johannes Steel.[29]

At the January 1943 Casablanca meeting between Roosevelt and
Churchill a hastily devised arrangement brought Giraud and De Gaulle
together. Ultimately De Gaulle froze Giraud out of the French Committee of National Liberation and removed him as commander in chief. Despite continued criticism of State Department appeasement, the liberals
were pleased with the larger role De Gaulle was playing. Known Vichyites were purged, and some prominent officials were put on trial. The liberals were aware of De Gaulle's conservative, nationalistic background. But
the ideological diversity of the committee, which included Socialists and
Communists; De Gaulle's role in carrying on the fight against Hitler; and
especially his willingness to purge the ex-fascist collaborationists all made
him the symbol of the liberal intellectuals' interpretation of the war: fascism versus antifascism.[30]

If internal developments within the French Committee for National
Liberation and in areas where De Gaulle had power were positives for the
liberals, the Roosevelt administration's policy continued to be a source of

frustration and bitterness. Every step toward the U.S. government's acceptance of De Gaulle seemed agonizingly slow and designed to frustrate the
leader of the Free French. The United States continued to refuse to endorse De Gaulle even after Giraud's efforts to unite the French antifascists
had proved ineffectual. Once De Gaulle had assumed sole leadership of the
National Liberation Committee and demonstrated his ability to unite the
French antifascist forces, the United States refused to recognize the National Committee as the provisional government of France. On the eve
of the Allied invasion of Normandy, Roosevelt grudgingly recognized the
committee as the de facto civil administration of France. Roosevelt's role
in this long process was displeasing to the liberal intellectuals, but the root
of the problem, according to their analysis, lay in the reactionary politics
of the pro-Vichy appeasement crowd in the State Department. Roosevelt
was once more the tolerator, not the author, of what was felt to be a disastrous policy. He could not escape liberal criticism, but because of the distinction a serious break with Roosevelt was avoided.[31]

Reaction to the Darlan deal had focused on the dangers of collaboration with French fascists. The events following Mussolini's dismissal from
office in July 1943 raised similar issues for Italy. King Victor Emmanuel
asked Pietro Badoglio to become prime minister, a combination that was
immediately distasteful for the liberal intellectuals: the king had cooperated with Mussolini, and Badoglio had led the invasion of Ethiopia and
been a leading military official in Mussolini's government. The fact that
Roosevelt's dismissal of the liberal concerns about relying on yesterday's
fascists as meaningless did not help matters. On September 8, 1943, as the
Allied invasion of Italy was beginning, the Badoglio government surrendered. Once more the issue of military expediency versus the ideological
nature of the war was drawn.[32]

In the months preceding the Italian surrender, Gaetano Salvemini and
Count Sforza, the two Italian exiles who published most frequently in the
liberal press, had been warning of the dangers of a peace between the Allies and, as Salvemini put it, the fascists without Mussolini. Neither Sforza
nor Salvemini could forgive Badoglio's participation in Mussolini's government. Both saw Allied recognition as undercutting the democrats in Italy
and abroad who favored the republic. Like the American liberals whom
they so deeply influenced, both men viewed the war as an antifascist crusade. They favored a peace which did not punish the oppressed Italian
people but which thoroughly cleansed Italy of fascism and its supporters.
On that account alone Badoglio was found wanting.[33]

To the liberals, the quasi recognition of Badoglio ran counter to the Allied policy of unconditional surrender which had been announced at the Big Three conference in Casablanca in January 1943. The policy stated that the Axis military defeat had to be accompanied by the destruction of the fascist system and ideology. The liberals began protesting even before the surrender and the quasi recognition of the Badoglio government. The UDA released a statement signed by a number of prominent liberals and labor leaders. Declaring that the policy of unconditional surrender would be betrayed by a policy of "fascists . . . for sale," the UDA expressed their concern about the rumors that the king, Badoglio, and other former members of Mussolini's government were being considered "as possible collaborators with the allied cause." To deal with these "Darlans," the statement said, would betray the "total war against fascism." There could be "no compromise between fascism and democracy, between fascists and democrats." [34]

The New Republic repeated the UDA's point that any dealings with any government recently converted from fascism or with "the fascist hyena in the sheep's-clothing of the monarchy" would be to betray the policy of unconditional surrender. It expressed deep concern that this betrayal would take place unless "the American people" demanded adherence to the policy of unconditional surrender. The State Department had already made distinctions between Italian fascism and the House of Savoy, and it was to be expected that they might make distinctions between "Mussolini and politer forms of fascism, a category that would include Badoglio." *The New Republic* ended by calling on Roosevelt to wipe the slate clean of fascists and the monarchy, to hold to the policy of unconditional surrender, and then to let the Italian people decide.[35]

When the Badoglio government was recognized as a cobelligerent, it furnished further proof the U.S. government was willing to do business with recently sanitized fascists. Coming as it did on the heels of the Darlan deal, this quasi recognition of Badoglio was just one more bitter reminder to Salvemini and his American friends that their democratic civil war was losing, that far from abetting the democratic revolution, the U.S. government was using Badoglio "to stave off revolution." Once more military and geopolitical considerations and not the ideological and moral concerns of the liberals had prevailed. Once more the friends of freedom and democracy had been betrayed in their own house. Once more the heads of the Allied governments had failed to understand the revolutionary nature of the international civil war. Once more the State Department appeasers and the British Tories with their monarchist and elitist sympathies had won. A few months later, when Stalin—regrettably siding with Roosevelt and Churchill and placing his own pragmatic concerns above the needs of the people's war—recognized the Badoglio government, it only added to the liberals' chagrin.[36]

By October, Churchill was urging all Italians to support the Badoglio government. Badoglio had indicated that after the fall of Rome he would extend "political participation." The State Department had indicated it would let Count Sforza return (England would continue to deny his return). These small signs of a future enlargement of government were unimpressive to *The Nation*. "So long as the campaign to sell the House of Savoy continues," it wrote, "we cannot regard these swallows as signs that the democratic summer has arrived."[37]

For the liberal intellectuals nothing really seemed to improve the Italian situation. In March 1944 in a move *The Nation* described as pleasing everyone but the "democrats," the Soviet Union went one better than the United States and Great Britain by giving full diplomatic recognition to the Badoglio government. In the summer of 1944, when Rome fell and the king abdicated in favor of his son (seen as a minor improvement), and especially when Badoglio was forced out and replaced by Ivanoe Bonomi, a liberal statesman, there was a brief upturn in liberal hopes for Italy. The liberals' hope that the Bonomi government would be a prelude to a true democratization of Italy turned out to be false. The continued influence of U.S. military occupation authorities held in check the revolutionary impulses in northern Italy. The Allied policy of "stability and order" rather than democratic change continued to hold sway. The entire U.S. policy toward Italy, like its policy toward France, had been a failure as far as furthering the "democratic revolution" and "the people's peace." The State Department appeasers and reactionaries had prevailed.[38]

The liberal intellectual image of Roosevelt in terms of his Italian policy was again that of the tolerator. In this case, he had refused or been unable to stand up to the State Department appeasers, the military expediency proponents in the War Department, and especially Churchill. Roosevelt did not come off well. But, by again diverting the major responsibility onto his subordinates or onto Churchill, the liberals had prevented the kind of confrontation that could spell a political break.[39]

The U.S. policy toward Spain was also a major concern for the American liberal community. With the historic background of Franco's triumph over the Republic in 1939 always in mind, the liberals viewed U.S. policy as a test case of the democratic commitment of the administration. Uhl portrayed American policies toward Franco and Vichy France as betraying the people's war. "Either we're fighting a people's war against Fascism—which means that a Fascist France and a Fascist Spain have no place in the peace that is to come out of this 'people's revolution,'" he wrote, "or we're fighting a Capt. Joe Patterson's war—which means that the peace will be a whole series of deals and 'practical' arrangements that won't solve anything." No issue proved a bigger disappointment. The liberals saw Franco as an essential part of the Axis. His supplies to Germany, his Blue Legion fighting on the Russian front, his influence in Latin America, where, according to the liberals, he was the key figure in the fascist conspiracy, all indicated the important contributions he made to Hitler's cause. At the same time, the liberals also believed his hold on the Spanish people was precarious. Del Vayo wrote frequent articles on how the democratic aspirations of the Spanish people were being held down by Franco's terror. And his terroristic government, in turn, was only able to keep power because of the support it was given by Great Britain and the United States.[40]

Just as they had with Vichy France, the liberal intellectuals urged the government to break diplomatic relations with Franco's Spain. The UDA sent calls for a break to the State Department. Kirchwey organized a mass rally in support of democratic Spain in early 1945, and *The Nation*, *The New Republic*, and *PM* had frequent editorials and articles exposing Franco's ties with the Axis and with South American fascists. Del Vayo was convinced that if the United States broke diplomatic relations with Franco and recognized the Republican government that the Spanish people could free themselves from Franco. Despite periodic rumors that predicted an imminent break, none came. The liberals could take some satisfaction at the refusal to admit Spain to the United Nations. But on the larger issue of breaking with Spain and embedding the ideological line between the fascist countries and the antifascist countries in the war itself, the liberal intellectuals' efforts again came to nought.[41]

Again, the policy was attributed mainly to the State Department. Though not knowing that at the conclusion of the Spanish Civil War Roosevelt had expressed his regrets to Ambassador Bowers for not having lifted the embargo on Loyalist Spain, the liberals subscribed to the belief that there was a difference between Roosevelt and the "appeasement crowd" in the State Department when it came to Spain—otherwise why ask him to clean house of the appeasers. However, even if there were a difference, the same decisions based on military expediency still prevailed; a "neutral"

Spain was apparently considered more militarily advantageous than the possibility of Spain entering the war on the Axis side or the prospects of a renewal of the Spanish revolution.[42] For liberal intellectuals, Spain was vital for itself. It was also vital for its link to Latin American fascism. And in the case of the latter, the liberals found that the State Department had a great predilection for appeasement. Early in the war, the pattern was set. In reporting the outcome of a conference in Rio de Janiero in early 1942, Sumner Welles, the under secretary of state, hailed the new cooperative spirit and hemispheric unity. He expressed the opinion that the new relationship between the Latin American countries and the United States depended on the joint understanding against any nation interfering in the internal affairs of another nation. Welles went on to criticize "certain individuals and groups" who had urged the United States to cooperate only with Latin American governments and groups favoring "revolutionary democracy." He compared this proposal with Hitler's five-year-old policy of "picking puppet governments."[43]

Reacting as if Welles's criticisms were directed specifically at *The Nation*, Kirchwey defended its position on Latin America. What *The Nation* was proposing, she said, was not sending troops to Argentina to remove Castillo but removing our financial support of pro-Axis dictators and supporting the democratic forces throughout Latin America. If we did, she said confidently, the Latin American democrats could take care of their own dictators. And she concluded: "We would realize that our natural— and only—allies are those people, in office and out, who are committed to the democratic cause; and we would not let the bogy of 'interference' or the tyranny of protocol prevent intimate collaboration with them. . . . I wonder whether Mr. Welles has ever realized that the policy he has pursued of supporting pro-Axis dictatorships in Latin America is itself a policy of picking puppet governments? The only difference between our strategy and Hitler's is that the puppets we pick are Hitler's—not ours."[44]

Germany presented a somewhat different case from that of France, Italy, or Spain. With no Darlan or Badoglio in a geographic position to make deals, with the policy of unconditional surrender apparently in place, and with increased military coordination, if not always agreement, among the Big Three, it seemed to the liberals that there might exist in Germany a real chance to destroy the whole structure of fascism in Germany. Yet Roosevelt continued to disappoint. According to the liberals, Roosevelt's failure to spell out more clearly his conception of the future of Germany resulted in hindering a democratic revolution there.[45]

What most of the liberal intellectuals sought for Germany's future involved a delicate balancing act. Most liberals argued consistently against Vansittartism. Lord Vansittart was the former English Permanent Secretary of State for Foreign Affairs. In his wartime speeches and writings he set forth the theory that Germans were inherently aggressive and authoritarian and that a punitive Carthaginian peace was required in order to prevent future German aggression. His views gained enough popularity so that the term *Vansittartism* was commonly used to characterize proposals that would punish all Germans. According to its liberal critics, Vansittartism, by failing to distinguish between the German democrats and the Nazis and their big business and military supporters, offered no incentive for the German democrats to resist Hitler or to rebel against his government. To the liberals, Vansittartism was a racist theory that missed the hierarchical class nature of German society and ignored the courageous struggle of the German underground. Only a peace that offered a place for a democratic Germany within a democratic Europe could inspire the democratic underground during the war or serve as a basis for rebuilding a democratic Germany after the war.[46]

The writings of the German émigré Paul Hagen most forcefully articulated these parts of the liberal analysis. In *Will Germany Crack?* and in articles and letters to the editor, Hagen argued that there was a democratic Germany, one that was being held down by Hitler's terror. Proposed peace plans that would leave Germany economically and politically prostrate, he argued, would extend the war by killing off any chance of a democratic revolution within Germany and would set the stage for an angry and embittered resurgence of German fascism. Nazism needed to be severely purged, he believed, and Germans needed to be reeducated in democracy by German democrats. But in the postwar period Germany needed to be permitted to reenter the political and economic life of Europe. The UDA and its leaders, Reinhold Niebuhr and James Loeb, strongly supported Hagen's work with the German underground through the American Friends of German Freedom. They defended Hagen against unfair charges in *The New Leader* that he was a secret Communist.[47]

In his own writings, Niebuhr joined Hagen in opposing Vansittartism, which, he believed, rested on faulty racist grounds. Somewhat more than Hagen, he stressed what he called the "political immaturity" of the Germans, but he agreed with Hagen in opposing a Carthaginian peace. Hagen's analysis of Germany and Germany's future drew frequent support. The critique of Vansittartism, the distinction between German democrats and German Nazis, and the need to offer a peace permitting a democratic Germany to function in the world community of nations were staples in the liberal press. Editorials in *The Nation*, *The New Republic*, *Common Sense*, and *Christianity and Crisis* often reflected the kind of anti-Vansittartism and the kind of peace terms found in Hagen's writings. But if most liberals were anti-Vansittart, there were some who were attracted to Vansittartist thinking. The statements and activities (organizing the League for the Prevention of World War III) of Rex Stout, the mystery novelist and chairperson of the Writers' War Board, went beyond anti-Nazism to seemingly condemn all Germans and all German culture. Sidney Hertzberg, who edited *Common Sense* in 1944, criticized Stout and then gathered opinions from the intellectual community. From the response, it was clear that many, but by no means all, writers felt, as Hertzberg did, that Stout was using his position as the head of the Writers' War Board to propagate a Vansittartist interpretation of German history and Vansittartist peace terms — both of which they opposed. When confronted with an anti-Vansittartist Hagen–Niebuhr-inspired manifesto for a postwar democratic Germany, Lerner attempted to avoid taking sides. Although he said he "lean[ed] . . . strongly to the manifesto," he did not think you could reduce Vansittartism "to a simple animal bloodthirstiness." In 1944 most liberals were not prepared to concede this much to Vansittart.[48]

If most liberals wished to avoid a punitive peace, they were equally insistent that Germany be thoroughly denazified. Not only must Hitler and his closest collaborators be punished, but so must the industrialists and the military leaders who had permitted him to rise and who had fueled his war machine. A clear line needed to be drawn between the German democrats and the total structure of Nazism, and the latter required total demolition. Both aspects were necessary in developing the war aims for Germany; only such a differentiation between democrats and democratic institutions, on one hand, and fascists and fascism's institutional structures, on the other hand, and only the complete destruction of the latter, could make possible a democratic Germany.[49]

As the full horror of the Holocaust became known and as the failure of any concrete signs of democratic revolt became more evident, it was harder to argue Hagen's case for the hidden German democratic allies, and the temptation to adopt a Vansittartist conception of communal guilt became harder to resist. Liberals became more defensive about what might be perceived as a "soft" peace; *The Nation* still insisted that the issue was not a hard peace versus a soft peace, but a peace that was hard on the political, military, and industrialist classes that had supported Hitler and Nazism, and especially hard on the war criminals, but not hard in the sense of punishing all Germans equally.[50]

In late 1944 Lerner took aim at the liberals who were overly concerned with the possibility of a draconian peace that would return Germany to a pastoral state. He accused them of treating the Germans as "misunderstood children" who "behave worse when they are unfed and embittered." Because of this belief, Lerner said, liberals thought Americans had "to raise living standards, integrate the economy, create democracy and wipe out bitterness." Further, liberals believed that German democracy was waiting to rise out of the "fascist ashes" and that therefore the problem was "less to prevent a renascence of German strength than to unify Europe and restore a healthy, functioning European economy." Lerner named the English writer H. N. Brailsford and the American journalist Dorothy Thompson as liberal culprits, but he could have named Hagen or, at this stage, Albert Guerard, who reviewed frequently in *The Nation* and *The New Republic*. Or he could have named the editors of *Common Sense, The Nation,* or *The New Republic*. Even though none was altogether guilty of Lerner's caricature of their thought processes, they all had written analyses that were the objects of his criticism.[51]

All of these writers, Lerner continued, were frightened of saddling Germany with too hard a peace. But that was no longer the problem; there was no danger of a Carthaginian peace. The danger was that those powerful forces that had appeased fascism were trying to prevent "a thoroughgoing uprooting of fascist power in Europe." For Lerner, Henry Morgenthau's plan to dismantle German industry was not motivated by "sheer vindictiveness." Rather it was a product of the internal struggle in Washington to check the War and State Department's plans for rehabilitating German industry and the "economic caste" that had supported Hitler: "The real danger is not that of a vindictive settlement but of an indecisive settlement—one that leaves in control in Germany the very same forces of industrial power and racist bigotry that handed Germany over to Hitler in the first instance. The danger is not that Germany *will* be mangled, but that fascism in Germany *will not* be mangled."[52]

Although he rejected the Morgenthau plan as technologically unfeasible and damaging to Europe's economy, he also ruled out what he saw as the liberal nostrum: the democratic revolution and reeducation of Germany from within. Any "democratic revolutionary potential," he wrote, "is negligible." There was no hope of transforming the German economy from within; it would have to be done by the Big Three. They would have to impose a form of collectivism: state socialism, state capitalism, or cartel capitalism—whichever they could agree upon.[53]

The editors of *The New Republic* were not as ready as Lerner to give up the analysis they had developed during the war. They chided Lerner for his confidence in declaring that the democratic revolutionary potential was negligible. Even if it was, there was no reason to believe "that Germans, given the right conditioning, will ultimately be any more incapable of self-government than other Europeans." The "decisive defeat" in the war would begin to provide the right conditioning; it would be "educational" to Germany. The editors favored a hard peace for the Nazis and their industrialist supporters. But they also believed that the goals of denazification, economic change, and reeducation could not come from exclusively "military measures or by intervention from the outside." They depended on releasing "the energies and freedom of those Germans whom the Nazis have persecuted—in other words, whatever German democratic forces there may be."[54]

The contention that internal democratic forces still held the key to a successful outcome of the war with Germany was picked up by Heinz Eulau two months later. A professor of political science at Columbia University, Eulau had become one of *The New Republic*'s assistant editors during the war. Eulau accepted Kirchwey's premise that World War II was "a revolutionary war." For him, revolution meant socialism, and he was confident that the German defeat would create "a revolutionary situation." The "intensity of fascist rule" would arouse an "intense antifascism" and he already saw signs of mass resistance reemerging as military defeat neared. The only thing that could stop the revolution and socialism was foreign intervention—in this case Allied intervention—to prevent it. Eulau reminded Lerner that those who denied "the possibility of democracy in Europe are the most anxious to prevent a German revolution."[55]

The defeat of Germany was intensely satisfying to liberal intellectuals, but the proposed postwar treatments of Germany circulating in the Roosevelt administration caused concern. Although most liberals had stuck to their initial analysis in drawing a distinction between a Vansittartist punishment and a thorough denazification, and between German democrats and the entire Nazi support structure, not all had stuck to it. Contemplating the German nation in 1945, the former anti-Vansittartist Guerard wrote, "I deeply regret that Vansittart is right." But even those who stuck to their anti-Vansittart distinctions could not be as optimistic as Eulau about a German revolution.[56]

The real problem for the liberals, however, lay not with any of their differing analyses of Germany's future but in the lack of any clear democratic signals from the Roosevelt administration. In this, they saw a reflection of the problem all along. The administration's willingness to collaborate with pro-fascists like Darlan in North Africa or Badoglio in Italy sent a message that the problem was Hitler the person and not the entire fascist system. The failure of the U.S. government to spell out a role for the German underground in a future democratic Germany or even to fully use émigré German antifascists in the Allied propaganda work reflected the problem. So did Churchill's comments that the war was a war against aggression—a position that ran counter to the liberals' idea of an ideological civil war and suggested that the only problem was that Hitler did not stay at home. With little U.S. or Allied encouragement for a German revolt, much less for a German revolution, and few administration signs that the German resistance would be the backbone of a democratic Germany, the Roosevelt administration again failed the liberal test of democratic policy. In this sense, the administration's indicators of an "easy" peace that would not radically disturb the economic and social structure served to betray the liberal intellectuals' international civil war as much as the administration's talk of a draconian peace—the Morgenthau plan—in which Germany would be returned to a preindustrial agrarian society.

In each case, U.S. policy in relation to France, Italy, Spain, Latin America, and Germany had presented the liberal intellectuals with a moral, ideological, and political problem. Should they condemn ideologically an administration to which they were committed politically? Their criticisms had, at times, drawn forth testy responses on the part of the administration and of Roosevelt himself. When this happened, liberals sought to explain the difference between their friendly criticisms (those made by liberals committed to a total war) and the damaging criticisms of the neoisolationists and others less committed to the war effort. These periodic reassurances, however, did not solve their dilemma, a dilemma generated out of their deep disappointment and frustration with an administration that did not act on the liberal intellectuals' premises about the war. The only way to avoid the political break with Roosevelt, a break that they occasionally referred to but which they were obviously desirous not to occur, was to divert the major focus of their criticism from Roosevelt to the

State Department or, depending on the particular issue, to Churchill. In that way, they could keep the integrity of their moral and ideological critique without breaking with the erring knight.[57]

When one turns to domestic issues that raised analogous moral and ideological questions, the manner in which they were handled suggests a related pattern. The majority of liberal intellectuals did not pursue the critical dimension of the issues to the point where it might mean reexamining not only their relations with the administration but their analysis of the war. In the case of domestic issues, it was not so much that they diverted their critique to other departments, but that they refused to make a full critique and, in one case, turned a negative into a positive. This refusal to confront the full moral dimensions of crucial issues can be illustrated by briefly examining five issues: (1) the internment of Japanese Americans, (2) civil liberties, (3) the policy toward Jewish refugees, (4) civil rights, and (5) the dropping of the atomic bomb.

Reading through the articles and editorials in the liberal press on the internment of Japanese Americans, with their frequent strong condemnations of the administration's policy, one might easily conclude that the liberal intellectuals' overall support for Roosevelt was strictly verbal—a ritualistic form of praise before undertaking a critical assault. But when analyzed closely, the support is what is fundamental; the criticisms are far from ritualistic—they are genuine and heartfelt—but they exist within the context of a relationship that had no option of a break or even of "critical support." Many liberal intellectuals believed that the internment of Japanese Americans was wrong. Niebuhr and Bingham condemned the policy, Kirchwey opened *The Nation* to Carey McWilliams and other critical writers, and *The New Republic* and *PM* printed occasional critical articles and comments. But few liberal writers confronted the full dimension of the violation of civil liberties. What is remarkable is the complacency of the liberals' favorable response to the American Civil Liberties Union's 1942 positive report on the state of civil liberties in the United States when one hundred thousand Japanese Americans were being interned in the largest wholesale violation of civil liberties in American wartime history.[58]

The major thrust of most of the critical articles and editorials in the liberal press was on the conditions in the internment camps and not on the fundamental violation of civil liberties. There was a great temptation among liberals to view the camps as "unfortunate necessities." The

Japanese American Citizens League, an organization that sought better conditions in the camps but cooperated with the authorities in accepting the fact of internment, received liberal praise. The liberals made little effort to distinguish between the radical Japanese Americans who opposed such cooperation and similarly disposed Japanese-American nationalists who supported the Japanese side. It was not *The Nation* and *The New Republic*, despite the numerous articles critical of conditions in the camps, that raised the fundamental civil liberties issue. That was left to some—not all—civil libertarians within the ACLU, to critical supporters of the war like Norman Thomas, and to assorted pacifists and political radicals who opposed the war.[59]

In one area of civil liberties, most of the liberal intellectual community turned a threat to civil liberties into a positive good: *The Nation, The New Republic* and *PM* called for suppressing the fascist press. Kirchwey also discussed the possible suppression of fascism's "fellow travelers"—the McCormick, Hearst, and Patterson papers. The latter needed to be watched and exposed constantly, and "the moment they skid across the thin line that divides their doctrine from open treason they should face the full blast of the law." Fascist techniques had been used in the occupied countries and the American people were no "wiser or better fortified" than "our brothers in countries that today are captive units in the fascist world." One needed to act while there still was time: "tolerance, democratic safeguards, trust in public enlightenment—these happy peace-time techniques have demonstrated their inadequacy."[60]

Two months before Kirchwey wrote this editorial, Niebuhr set forth a philosophical rationale for suppression of civil liberties in wartime. In discussing liberty and community as essential to democracy, Niebuhr argued that "any community in a time of crisis will tend to preserve its unity; it will use coercion as a last resort." He acknowledged that too much coercion could lead to a "vicious circle of repression which ends in tyranny." But, he concluded, "it is silly to assume moderate restrictions inevitably end in dictatorship. Communities may, like individuals, face emergencies and diseases which need not be fatal. To be sick in bed does not doom the patient to stay there until he dies. Coercive means of unity are analogous to the doctor's medication and stimulants. The constant use of stimulants will not restore a weak heart, but neither will its momentary use necessarily prove fatal." Since Niebuhr's analysis of liberty and democracy was developed within the framework of a discussion of the absolutist and relativist positions on civil liberties, it was clear that he was laying the philosophic framework for a "moderate" amount of suppression of the domestic threat to community unity: the fascist press.[61]

Kirchwey's "curb the fascist press" editorial set off a running exchange of letters over whether "words were triggers." Roger Baldwin and Arthur Garfield Hays wrote to defend the traditional civil liberties position of the rights of free speech even for one's enemies argued against the idea that one should punish words because they were triggers. The editors and most of the readers defended Kirchwey's views. Even private letters to Kirchwey from Norman Thomas and John Haynes Holmes asking her to reconsider her position did not dissuade her. Believing that the United States was in a war to the death with fascism, that fascism constituted a worldwide conspiracy against democracy, that one should not tolerate those who, if in power, would destroy civil liberties, and that fascism had immense powers of corruption, she held to her position. Holmes warned her that everything she said would come back to haunt her side—the liberal and left side—but she would not budge. There was no prosecution of a known or suspected fascist—including the dubious conspiracy charges against twenty-nine fascists in January 1943—that Kirchwey, and also the editors of *The New Republic* and *PM*, did not support. Holmes would, of course, prove correct in his prediction, but in the ideological civil war that absorbed the liberal community during World War II, the traditional civil liberties position of the liberal community seemed, to many liberal intellectuals, outmoded. If anything, the criticism of people like Kirchwey was that the Justice Department was not being vigilant enough.[62]

In contrast to the rights of free speech, the domestic issue that brought the liberals closest to a direct break with Roosevelt was his refugee policy. Unlike *The New Leader*, which wrote maudlin editorials on Hull's humanitarianism and continued to trust Roosevelt to do his best by manipulating within the quota system, *The Nation, The New Republic,* and *PM* realized that there was something essentially wrong with both U.S. policy and the administration of the policy. In *The Nation* and *The New Republic,* Varian Fry, who had done secret rescue work in Europe in 1940–41 for the Emergency Relief Committee, wrote on the "massacre of the Jews" and the pervasive anti-Semitism of the U.S. consuls in Europe. In *PM*, Lerner, Stone, and Victor Bernstein called attention to the plight of the Jews and the inadequate response of the Roosevelt administration. Kirchwey was especially eloquent in expressing the horrors confronting European Jewry and the paltry efforts of the United States to aid the Jewish refugees. She exposed the roadblocks that U.S. policy placed in the way of increasing the number of Jewish refugees. Roosevelt did not escape these pointed critiques. Still, he was usually faulted only for his toleration of the State Department's insensitivity. From Cordell Hull through the crucial second-level officials like Breckinridge Long, the State Department was again the chief recipient of liberal criticism.[63]

The question here is not the sincerity of the liberals' concerns for the Japanese Americans or the Jewish refugees. There was a strong case to be made for better treatment within the camps, and the liberals made it sincerely and often eloquently. There were strong grounds for condemning the State Department from top to bottom for its insensitive cruelties to the Jewish refugees. The issue here, however, is how much the liberals would allow the president's delinquencies in—and his ultimate responsibility for—these areas to interfere with their all-out support of the war or their opinion that Roosevelt represented the hopes and aspirations of the democratic peoples of the world. Roosevelt was, Bliven wrote in announcing his vote as early as January 1944, "more than any other American who could possibly become President . . . in tune with the fundamental currents that are sweeping through the world." In the end, despite individual criticisms over a broad range of issues, there would be no fundamental interference.[64]

Given the great concern throughout the liberal intellectual community for civil rights for African Americans, and given, as I will argue in a later chapter, that liberal intellectuals contributed to a redefinition of America in pluralistic terms, it may seem unfair to argue that they pulled their punches on civil rights. And in terms of publicizing the issue it is unfair. *Common Sense, The Nation, The New Republic,* and *PM* frequently condemned racial discrimination as the greatest blot on American democracy. They opened their pages to Pearl Buck and Lillian Smith to write critical articles on American attitudes toward African Americans and other non-whites. Without always referring to the Double-V campaign (the campaign to fight fascism at home and abroad), the liberal intellectuals gave support to the issues involved in the campaign. They endorsed an integrated work force; they attacked the poll tax; they condemned the racist structure of southern society. There were frequent exposés of notorious southern racist politicians—the Rankins, Talmadges, Bilbos, and Coxes. They printed articles, especially in regard to black soldiers, on the humiliating conditions in the South. They supported the strengthening and extension of the Fair Employment Practices Commission and condemned congressional efforts to reduce its scope. If they did not push for immediate desegregation of the armed forces, they urged a beginning, and

The Nation published an article on the Winfred Lynn case challenging the constitutionality of the draft into a segregated army. When the Detroit race riots occurred, the liberals pointed to the social and economic conditions that bred racism. Editorials and articles were published arguing that in order to fulfill its principles and to win the allegiance of African Americans, the United States needed to eliminate racism and segregation. In all these and on other specific issues, it was an impressive performance. And yet there was something missing: any sustained organized action.[65]

The UDA did participate in petition drives organized by the March on Washington, but there was no real sustained effort on the part of the liberal press to keep the March on Washington Movement going in terms of its initial direct action orientation. Liberal intellectuals protested the execution of Odell Waller, a black sharecropper who had shot in self-defense the owner of his land, but there were no marches or demonstrations that paralleled the Scottsboro case or even matched the protest in the Angelo Herndon case. It is true that in both those earlier cases it was the Communist Party that was involved in much of the direct action. And even more than the liberal intellectual community, the Communist Party had put direct action on civil rights away for the duration. Still, given the amount of time devoted to the issue of civil rights and the amount of space given to urging progressives to organize, one could have expected to find greater organizational action on the part of the liberal intellectual community; one could have expected a willingness to support, if not to organize, greater civil rights direct action. But there were no liberal calls for civil disobedience or mass marches, and one suspects that given their total commitment to the war and their attitude to less than all-out support for the war they would have been uncomfortable—if not directly opposed to—such direct action.[66]

Certainly this was the prevailing liberal attitude towards labor when John L. Lewis led the Mine Workers Union out on strike during the war. Liberal intellectuals acknowledged the existence of real grievances, but they could not tolerate Lewis's interference with the war effort. They interpreted his actions as reflecting power drives and his opposition to the war. The liberal intellectual press was consistently pro-labor during the war; it supported the rights of unions to organize, the need for full labor participation in government agencies, and the need for labor to be deeply involved in politics. But the liberals also supported the no-strike pledge; in most cases they supported holding the line on wage increases. And they did not completely rule out the Labor Draft. The labor voice they wanted to hear was in the ballot box, not on the picket line. Lobbying Congress and using the "bully pulpit" of the liberal press was one thing, but direct action that would lead into confrontations with the administration was another.[67]

The connection between the Democratic Party and the structure of racism was another area of civil rights that was not pursued fully. Liberal intellectuals did attack southern Democratic racist politicians and looked forward to a future realignment of parties into more consistent liberal and conservative positions. Nevertheless, when Norman Thomas tried to suggest that the connection between Senator Eugene Cox of Georgia and the Democratic Party was more than accidental and tried to make a connection between the southern segregationists and Roosevelt and the Democratic Party, the liberals resisted the analysis. Thomas was trying to demonstrate the merits of independent third party politics, but the liberals drew a line between themselves and Thomas. It was a line based on differing conceptions of the war. If Cox had a close organic connection with the Democratic Party, if he was not an anachronistic aberration, but central to its structure and success, what might this say about the chosen vehicle for fighting a democratic war?[68]

There is a final issue: the dropping of the atomic bomb. *The Christian Century* opposed it. Selden Rodman had moral criticisms, and Niebuhr discussed the moral issues. But what is striking about the liberal discussion of the atom bomb in *The Nation, The New Republic, PM,* and in the papers of the UDA is how it revolved almost exclusively around the future control and use of the bomb. Moral issues were occasionally discussed but were usually dealt with by pointing to the saving of lives that would have been lost in the prolongation of the war. Sometimes, as in the case of Lerner's discussion of the use of technologically brutal instruments of war, they were dealt with by distinguishing between the sadistic motives of Hitler and the Allies' desire to quickly end the war. But the context of the moral discussions was always on the future. The destructiveness of the atomic bomb did not give the pro-war liberal community pause to question the decision; it did lend encouragement to pressing hard for an international organization that would prevent future destructive wars.[69]

One of the reasons why moral considerations slid so easily into future considerations was because pro-war liberals went beyond regarding the dropping of the bombs as an unfortunate necessity; as Paul Boller has shown, *The Nation, The New Republic,* and *PM* all saw it as a positive good—a good that would shorten the war and contribute to unconditional surrender and the elimination of the Japanese emperor and the entire im-

perial system. Such a positive attitude was compatible with the stark recognition that the dropping of the atomic bombs had ushered in a new
world. In this sense, they did not treat it as just a larger weapon, and they
did foresee that the bomb had future implications beyond merely ending
the war. This led the liberals to emphasize how to assure that the peaceful
use of atomic energy prevailed over future military use, which in turn led
to a focus on the international civilian control of atomic energy. Obviously, this was a weighty and important issue, and there was much to be
said for this focus in terms of undercutting the idea of a permanent atomic
monopoly and in trying to prevent an atomic arms race. Yet, given the
liberal concerns for the *future*, there was a glaring, if not unexpected, short-
changing of any serious discussion of the moral issues.

It was not as if the moral issue of bombing had not been debated previously. In brief discussions earlier in the war, *The Nation* and *The New
Republic* had both rejected the moral arguments that were being made
against saturation bombing. On the other hand, Bingham had argued that
in our saturation bombing of cities we were adopting fascist tactics in our
efforts to defeat fascism. Given these admittedly brief earlier moral arguments over the mass bombing, one would have expected the liberals to
have had a lengthier moral debate over the dropping of the atom bomb.
Instead, it was the religious leaders and pacifist antiwar people who raised
the moral issue. Since Harry Truman ordered the bomb dropped, one cannot say that the lack of moral consideration—much less moral reservations—throughout the liberal intellectual community can be attributed to
their commitment to Roosevelt. However, the residual pattern of thought,
the refusal to fully confront issues that brought into question the liberal
interpretation of the war, played a role in the disregard of the moral issues
surrounding the dropping of the atom bomb.[70]

The years 1942 and 1943 had been bad ones for the liberals. The Darlan
and Badoglio deals abroad were paralleled by a series of liberal domestic
defeats: the Dies committee–induced purges, the failure of the anti–poll
tax bill and the soldiers vote bill, and the 1942 congressional elections. Big
business continued to dominate war production and to carry great weight
in political decisions. The year 1944 also started out badly, with Roosevelt's announcement that he was shelving the New Deal for the duration.
But then there was an upturn in liberal prospects—at least on the surface. Two important events raised liberal spirits: internationally, the Allied invasion of France created a second front that presaged the end of the
war and fascism; and domestically, the CIO-Political Action Committee

(PAC) began functioning with the strong support of liberals in and out of government. Created in 1943 in the wake of the Republican congressional resurgence in the 1942 elections, the PAC offered a liberal-labor alliance, a liberal program, and the kind of practical organizational activism that could mobilize the "common people."

If mid-summer brought an uncommon mood of optimism to the liberal community, it was for only a brief moment. It would soon become clear that Henry Wallace, the personal symbol of the liberals' interpretation of the war, was in serious political trouble in his efforts to regain the renomination for vice president. Roosevelt's refusal to publicly endorse Wallace and his opening the nomination to the convention floor signaled that the conservative anti-Wallace forces within the Democratic Party had prevailed.[71]

In the end, liberal pressure on Roosevelt to keep Wallace was to no avail. Battered by southern threats of a revolt if Wallace was nominated and by labor's threat to sit out the election if the South's favorite, James Byrnes, was chosen, Roosevelt chose the safe middle ground of Harry Truman. In the end, disheartened as they were, the liberals did not follow through on their threats to break with the Roosevelt administration. Whether they would have done so if they had been fully aware of Roosevelt's role in the dropping of Wallace and of the tacit approval given to the decision by Sidney Hillman, the head of the PAC, is impossible to say.[72]

With a president who tolerated and practiced a foreign policy that ran counter to the liberals'—and they believed his own—interpretation of World War II, with a congress filled with reactionaries and a president who had mothballed reform in the face of their opposition, and with the man who was viewed as embodying the liberal interpretation of the war unceremoniously dropped from the ticket, the time might have appeared ripe for a liberal reconsideration of both their politics and their interpretation of the war. In an Open Letter published in *Socialist Call*, Norman Thomas invited liberals to support the Socialist Party now that the one genuine liberal within the New Deal hierarchy had been rejected by his own party. Niebuhr, UDA's chair, answered Thomas. Repudiating Thomas's utopianism, he reminded his readers of Thomas's prewar pacifism; and he urged liberals to continue the struggle within the Democratic Party. Wendell Willkie too was rejected as a possible alternative; personally, he might be a liberal, but the controlling forces in the Republican Party remained conservative. Sidney Hertzberg, editing *Common Sense* while Bingham and Rodman were in the service, voted to support Thomas at a meeting of the editorial board, but the rest of the editors outvoted him, and *Common Sense* endorsed Roosevelt. *The Nation* and *The New Republic* endorsed Roosevelt on the basis of his domestic concerns, his ability to see the country through the war, his understanding of world events, and because he was far better than Dewey, who was tied to a conservative party with a strong isolationist wing.[73]

Of course, this begged the question: Roosevelt might be liberal, but if he had been forced to dump Wallace, who then were the controlling forces within the Democratic Party? Time and again, Roosevelt had been forced to capitulate or had been defeated by the reactionary wing of his party—a wing whose saving grace for liberal intellectuals, despite its racism and economic conservatism, was its internationalist inclinations. Certainly it was not the liberals who controlled the Democratic Party. They could help mobilize the vote for Roosevelt, but they had little influence throughout the war in the corridors of power. Their interpretation of the war had not prevailed. Their democratic agenda received no priority. And yet they remained totally committed to the support of the war and, despite intense flurries of specific criticisms, fully committed to Roosevelt.

At Roosevelt's death, Bliven wrote of the president who had been so frustrating to the liberal intellectual community that "he was one of the greatest leaders who ever lived." And Kirchwey declared he was a "symbol . . . for a whole struggling generation, their hope of security and freedom, of release from intolerable oppression." But she also saw that the progressives had grown overly dependent on Roosevelt and that his death might mean "the coming of age of the progressive political forces in America." But Kirchwey herself had done little to free the progressives of their dependence. Along with the rest of the liberal intellectual community, she had refused to consider that their interpretation of the war might have been better furthered by a less than total support of the war and of Roosevelt. Along with the liberal intellectual community, she had rejected the opportunity to break with Roosevelt in 1944. Shrewd politician that he was, Roosevelt sensed that the liberals, out of choice or circumstance, had no place else to go. He had them, as Lyndon Johnson would graphically put it, "in his back pocket." They could squirm, but the manner in which they defined the war and how they defined Roosevelt's role in giving meaning to the war, left them no escape.[74]

4

The Apotheosis of Henry Wallace

NO PERSON played a greater role in providing the liberal meaning to the war than Henry Wallace. In the process he became a liberal icon, a symbol of liberal aspirations and hopes.

That Henry Wallace should have become the liberal icon during the war years is not without its ironies. If history could have been frozen in 1934, Wallace would not have been included in the pantheon of genuine liberal New Dealers. As secretary of agriculture, he had defended the Agricultural Adjustment Act (AAA) against liberal and radical criticism of its harsh impact on tenant farmers. His bureaucratic answers to the criticisms of Norman Thomas and his support for the AAA purge of those who criticized its contracts did nothing to win liberal and leftist support for Wallace. At most, he was seen as a decent but weak person who would not stand up to the conservative farming interests.[1]

Some of the post-1936 work of the Agriculture Department and the Farm Security Administration helped rehabilitate Wallace's liberal reputation. But by the start of World War II he had hardly gained the full confidence of the liberal intellectual community. At the beginning of 1942, I. F. Stone wrote that Wallace, now head of the Supply Priorities and Allocations Board (SPAB) and the Economic Warfare Board, never had the "courage . . . equal of his vision." He had done a number of good things as secretary of agriculture, but he had "in a showdown knuckled under to the packers and the milk trust and the big agricultural interests." Stone's image was of a weak Wallace who would do nothing to change the big business domination of SPAB or the State Department domination of the Economic Warfare Board. Potentially Wallace could have reformed both, but he was not "a fighter."[2]

Other liberal intellectuals may not have shared Stone's harsh judgment, but there was nothing in the liberal press in the first months of 1942 that combated the idea that Wallace was well-meaning but ineffectual. But within a few months of Stone's critique, Wallace was about to take steps that would propel him into the role of the leading administration spokesperson for the liberal interpretation of the war. On May 8, 1942, Wallace spoke before the Free World Association, an organization founded in 1941 to win public support for the Allied cause. Its journal, *Free World*, trumpeted the internationalism of those seeking a permanent and cooperative United Nations in the postwar world. Coming at a most opportune time, Wallace's speech reverberated throughout the liberal intellectual world. The war news was still generally bad; the transformation to a full war economy was still sluggish. Liberals were deeply disturbed by the role of appeasers in the State Department: the memories of St. Pierre and Miquelon were still on the liberals' minds. The status quo in Great Britain and the United States still appeared to be in control. And on top of everything else, as far as liberals were concerned, the American public was still not fully aware of the total commitment that would be necessary to win the war. To awaken the American people there had to be, according to the liberals, clearly articulated war aims that demanded political and economic changes.

In this context of grim liberal pessimism, Wallace's speech appeared to indicate that at last the Roosevelt administration had fully embraced the liberal interpretation of the war, that, through Wallace, Roosevelt was expressing the administration's war aims. The speech thus transformed Wallace into the political touchstone for liberal views. Henceforth, he would symbolize liberal aspirations and hopes during the war. This hero-forming process is of great importance in understanding liberals during the war. With Wallace as the defining touchstone of New Deal war aims, it was possible to withstand the series of assaults by the State Department appeasers against the liberal interpretation of the war. In the midst of the Darlan deal or the Badoglio episode, one could always fall back on the distinction between Roosevelt and the State Department because it could be assumed that Wallace—not Cordell Hull—stood for Roosevelt's fundamental goals, the goals he too often betrayed and whose opponents he too often tolerated, but the goals that, if liberals and labor were to organize more effectively, might yet be fulfilled. Wallace, then, came to symbolize the heritage of the progressive New Deal of the 1930s and the hopes for a new world of security and peace in the postwar years.[3]

It is important to explore Wallace's speech in order to understand its impact on the liberal imagination. The first chord to which liberals responded was Wallace's direct challenge to Henry Luce's imperialist and elitist vision of an "American century." Noting the arrogance and the status quo assumptions of Luce's vision, Wallace boldly proclaimed that the next century would be the century of the "common man." In every country, it would be the improvements in the people's education, in the people's work skills and material well-being, and in the people's political rights that would mark the world to come. These were historical developments, they were the aims of the war, and they were what fascism sought to destroy. The measure of success would henceforth lie not in a country's power to dominate, but in how well it satisfied its people's political and economic well-being.[4]

To usher out the world of privilege and usher in the century of the common man, Wallace presented an international vision. Where Luce's internationalism was posited on sustaining and extending the national power of the United States, Wallace spoke for the internationalism of a world organization. The cooperation of the Allies in war would be followed by a cooperative world order in which aggressive nationalisms, like fascism, would be controlled. To win the war it was necessary to channel the aspirations of the people into a united war effort. Like the liberal intellectuals, Wallace emphasized both the necessity of a fully functioning military and war economy and the harnessing of the democratic spirit of the people to a vision of a people's war and a people's peace. The latter could not be achieved by offering a future status-quo world; it could only be achieved by revolutionary changes. It was the liberal interpretation of World War II as an international civil war in which, in country after country, the forces of democracy and progress were pitted against the forces of autocracy and reaction.[5]

In terms of what liberals had been saying about the nature of the war in the early months of 1942, there was nothing new in this part of Wallace's analysis or vision. What was so exhilarating and what gave it such great force in the liberal community was the position of vice presidency from which Wallace spoke combined with the prevailing liberal gloom about the war effort and about the administration's commitment to the liberals' war aims. The ability to focus on just those parts of Wallace's speech that paralleled the liberal interpretation gave the speech its potency among liberals, but closer attention to other notes in his speech might have resulted in it not striking so responsive a chord.

There was, for example, the religious—specifically Christian—overtones to the speech. Associating democracy with the Old and New Testament and with Christ's message, Wallace projected a religious vision of American society. He linked the Allied cause with God's cause and Hitler's cause with Satan's cause in language that most secular liberals and many Niebuhrian religious liberals would normally have found bothersome. He ended on the most traditionally overblown conclusion: that the Allies could not lose because God was on their side.[6]

The same roseate vision characterized Wallace's version of history. The democratic principles of Christianity had been fulfilled in the American Revolution and the U.S. Constitution; the Civil War had eliminated the aberration of slavery. Successive revolutions—the American, the French, and the Russian—had, despite some excesses, extended democracy. It was the nineteenth-century historian George Bancroft's vision of an unfolding democracy transplanted to the twentieth century and ready to include the Communist and the capitalist worlds in a mutual extension of political and economic democracy. And all under God.[7]

It was not that Wallace was unaware of injustice and oppression throughout history. Indeed, his speech was punctuated with frequent references to fascism's efforts to continue those wrongs that existed and to perpetuate new ones of its own. Rather, the problem was that Wallace's version of history fell back simplistically on an unfolding progress—of democratic progress under God's aegis. In the ecumenical spirit of World War II, in an atmosphere in which Wallace's sentimental religiosity was treated respectfully even by liberals who felt religion had shackled people's minds for centuries and that organized religion too often was linked to political reaction—in such an atmosphere the intellectual problems created by Wallace's speech dissolved in the spirit of wartime cooperative unity. What matter that Wallace's volunteerist arguments for the need to fully mobilize the peoples of the world for victory were undercut by the inevitability of victory for a people with God on their side. It was enough that he had projected into the gloomy atmosphere of war news and business-as-usual in Washington an interpretation of the war that reinforced the liberals' own. Wallace had broken the spell of gloom and had offered hope to the besieged liberal community.

Freda Kirchwey's editorial covering the Free World Association dinner at which Wallace spoke and a meeting of the UDA was entitled "The People's Revolution." Wallace's speech, said Kirchwey, was "the boldest analysis of the meaning of the war to come from any high official of this country." He had declared that the "people's revolution is on the march" and that it was both the domestic and international fascist and reactionary forces that sought to stop the drive of "the common people toward wider education, better control of the tools of production, greater power through their own organization." It was the people's revolution versus the fascist revolution, which, of course, was what Kirchwey had been arguing right along. *The New Republic* had equally lavish praise and republished selections from the speech, as did *PM*.[8]

It was clear that Wallace had offered a beacon of hope to the liberal intellectual community. His voice was evidence that their voice held a high governmental position. After his speech, there would be no repeats of Stone's concerns with Wallace's lack of backbone; if anything, in the administrative battles that would follow, Wallace was portrayed as courageous, principled and fighting.

Even Wallace's religion was viewed positively. In March 1943 Wallace made a speech at the Conference on Christian Bases of World Order. In it, he discussed three philosophies: fascism, Marxism, and the "democratic Christian philosophy." The first two believed in war. Fascism believed in the war of the "single master race" to subjugate the world; Marxism believed in class warfare to create a classless society. But the democratic Christian philosophy denied that "man was made for war." Instead it "asserts boldly that ultimate peace is inevitable, that all men are brothers, and that God is their father."[9]

Having labeled the third philosophy the democratic Christian philosophy, Wallace immediately turned ecumenical. The democratic philosophy, he said, "pervades the hearts and minds not only of those who live by the Christian religion, both Protestant and Catholic, but of those who draw their inspiration from Mohammedanism, Judaism, Hinduism, Confucianism, and other faiths." All these faiths, he continued, preached "the doctrine of the dignity of each individual soul, the doctrine that God intended man to be a good neighbor to his fellow man, and the doctrine of the essential unity of the entire world." Wallace went on to discuss the conflict between the Antichrist of fascism and the Christian conception of responsibility. Pointing out that Christ urged that we "feed the hungry, clothe the naked, comfort the sick," he labeled the Good Neighbor Policy "a Christian policy" and urged that the policy be extended in the postwar world, when the United States should work to create a domestic policy of full employment and thereby help raise the world's standard of living. There was nothing unique about Wallace's version of the Social Gospel. The need to be tolerant toward Russia, to lend China and India "a helping hand," and "to put God's earth more completely at the service of all mankind" all flowed from his religious liberalism. It was traditional and standard fare of those who proclaimed their patriotism and their religious responsibility: "I believe in the democratic doctrine — the religion based on the social message of the prophets, the heart insight of Christ, and the wisdom of the men who drew up the constitution of the United States and adopted the Bill of Rights. By tradition and by structure we believe that it is possible to reconcile the freedom and rights of the individual with the duties required of us by the general welfare." [10]

While there was nothing unique about Wallace's views as they were expressed here, there was something unique about the liberal indulgence of his religiosity. *The Nation* described the speech as "bold, simple, and utterly disinterested." As for its "religious overtones," they "usually sound like a politician's set phrases," but they "held no hint of hypocrisy, for Wallace is genuinely religious." His analysis of the three philosophies "might not satisfy the political philosopher," but it was "basically sound and easily understood by the ordinary person." The fact that *The Nation* never looked to religious sincerity as something to be viewed positively for those on the right or even for ordinary politicians suggests that it had created a separate category for Wallace. Similarly, for a person who lectured the "children of light" on the naïveté of their premises about democracy, Reinhold Niebuhr was strangely silent on Henry Wallace. There is no evidence in his published records that Niebuhr held Wallace's sentimental Christianity up to the same standards that he did others'. [11]

Indeed, there is a murkiness about Wallace's entire social philosophy that was never addressed by the liberal community. Sometimes he sounded like the liberal intellectual community calling for a democratic revolution; other times the stress he placed on making free enterprise work made him sound more conservative than his liberal applauders. Sometimes he sounded as if he were reviving Woodrow Wilson's New Freedom in his emphasis on using the government to restore free competition, to give the small businessman a chance; at other times he seemed to speak for a kind of government-business planning that was reminiscent of Theodore Roosevelt's New Nationalism. He praised the Soviet Union abroad and also praised the American philosophy of "individual opportunity." He wrote that "Horatio Alger is not dead in America and never will be" at the same time he was calling for new directions in the U.S. economy. Sometimes his emphasis on the new democracy of the common man seemed to duplicate the liberal emphasis on ordinary workers and farmers; sometimes it seemed so inclusive that literally everyone was included: "In the new democracy, there will be a place for everyone—the worker, the farmer, the business man, the housewife, the doctor, the salesman, the teacher, the student, the store clerk, the taxi driver, the preacher, the engineer—all the millions who make up our modern world." One can argue that beneath these seemingly different emphases and approaches there was an essential consistency, that all Wallace was asking for was a fusion of "individual initiative and enterprise, and governmental responsibility for the general welfare." But that in itself is such a general statement that it permits a number of approaches to the fusion—all of which, at one time or another, Wallace sounded as if he were embracing.[12]

Whatever social philosophy Wallace had—or did not have—he offered a beacon of hope to the liberal intellectual community throughout the war. The wrenching break he had with parts of that community in 1946 would be so painful precisely because he had come to stand for so much to them. If it became clearer that Wallace by no means spoke for Roosevelt, it could still be imagined that he spoke for the best of the New Deal and for what Roosevelt would be if liberals were more successful in defeating his reactionary Republican and Democratic opponents.

On issue after issue, Wallace and the liberal community embraced each other. Traveling to Latin America, he supported the liberal aspirations for the South American labor movement and the poor peasants. Speaking against racism and urging the defeat of the poll tax, Wallace backed the liberal integrationist viewpoint. Struggling against Jesse Jones in the managing of war production, he spoke for the liberals against big business domination. Addressing a Soviet-American Friendship rally in November 1942, he thrilled *PM* with a reaffirmation of his common man theme and his vision of postwar international cooperation and prosperity. Wallace, John Lewis exclaimed, had proved "the pen is mightier than the sword." He had offered "a blueprint on the kind of world and the kind of human understanding" that demonstrated the purpose behind the recently launched African campaign. In the "indivisible" war, the African campaign promised military victory, while Wallace "points the way to the victory of ideas and ideals." And speaking before the American Labor Party in the spring of 1943, he presented liberals with his vision of an economy with jobs for all.[13]

Wallace's articulation of a liberal agenda on domestic and foreign policy led to fights within the administration, and the liberals rallied to Wallace's side. In late 1942, Stone warned that there was an anti-Wallace plot by the Jesse Jones faction over the Board of Economic Warfare (BEW), a battle that would go on through the first half of 1943. While it was progressing, both *The Nation* and *The New Republic* would frequently praise Wallace. In January 1943 *The Nation* called Wallace an idealist but added—probably to refute conservative criticism of his idealistic impracticality—that he was an idealist with common sense. He understood the dangers of unemployment in the postwar period and the need to eliminate economic barriers and expand productive capacity. Three months later, *The New Republic*'s T.R.B. assured readers that Wallace's idealism had a "great influence on Roosevelt's independent mind."[14]

While Jones and his allies were trying to stymie Wallace's ideas on the economy, the State Department, according to *The New Republic*, was trying to "cut Wallace out of the peace." It was the battle between those supporting the status quo and those recognizing the need for social change—the same battle that he was fighting with Jones. At first the liberals reported Wallace was winning. In January *The Nation* reported that Wallace had "slugged it out" with Jones and won. In early July Stone again reported that Wallace had triumphed over Jones. The issues involved control over imports by the Jones-headed Reconstruction Finance Corporation or the Wallace-headed BEW and a congressional effort that would have stripped the BEW of its final say in strategic purchases and given Jones a veto on them. When Wallace and Jones engaged in a public criticism of each other, *The Nation* believed that Wallace was the winner "on the solid basis of the facts." But it also realized that Wallace had a big battle on his hands. It urged that anyone interested in an "all-out war effort" organize support for Wallace through their "progressive groups, patriotic organizations, and trade unions." In *The New Republic*, Helen Fuller endorsed Wallace's charge that Jones was obstructing the war effort. And in the summer of 1943 *PM* printed a series of sympathetic articles on Wallace and even more critical articles on Jones. In an Open Letter to Jesse Jones in early July, Victor Bernstein wrote that Wallace was for the "little fellow" and Jones was "mostly for Jones."[15]

Two weeks after the liberals' mid-summer show of support for Wallace, Roosevelt abolished the BEW and created a new board with Leo Crowley as its head. "Mr. Wallace Walks the Plank" announced the discouraged editors of *The New Republic*. It was the most "disheartening" news since the Spanish Civil War. The Jones cabal had gotten Wallace and would now look ahead to replacing Wallace as vice president in 1944. In one of its periodic threats to cease support for Roosevelt, *The New Republic* said that liberals could not "put all their eggs in one basket" and be subject to the whims of someone "playing power politics" and unable to fire his friend Jones.[16]

The editors of *The Nation* reported that Roosevelt had killed the BEW and turned "its functions over to a reactionary henchman of Mr. Jones." By rewarding his political opponents, Roosevelt's "guiding directive" was "political appeasement." And in a spirited attack on Roosevelt's action, Stone compared Roosevelt's verbal slaps at Wallace and Jones followed by his abolition of the BEW to his "plague on both their houses" speech during the 1937 Little Steel strike. In 1937 Roosevelt had equated the steel magnates who vigorously opposed the New Deal with the labor movement, which had worked so hard for his reelection in 1936. Now, in 1943, he had again "run out on his friends" by a "craven tactic." In 1937 his actions had driven John L. Lewis out of the "progressive ranks" and turned him into a "dark menace." In 1943 they would probably cost Wallace the vice presidency in 1944. Wallace had followed Thurman Arnold and Leon Henderson as "sacrifices to the right." Roosevelt had "created the New Deal" but appeared to be "intent on destroying it." Like the editors of *The New Republic*, Stone wound up by suggesting that liberals, in the face of Roosevelt's international and domestic appeasement, should start looking to new leadership.[17]

Other liberals followed Stone's lead in talking of a reassessment of their relation with Roosevelt. In *PM*, John P. Lewis discussed whether Wallace should resign. Although he came to no conclusions, Lewis did declare that Wallace was the only candidate liberals could support for the vice presidency in 1944. Max Lerner rejected any notion that Wallace should resign. He labeled Roosevelt's rebuke to Wallace "appeasement" and said that progressives should have no "illusions" about Roosevelt. Progressives, he said, needed to realize that the New Deal lay with them, with a few in Congress, with a larger group of administrators, and, most of all, "in the plain people all over the country." Yet he insisted that as long as the war continued, Roosevelt's reelection was essential to progressives. But "the kind of President" he would be depended on the fight against reaction, and that fight—the fight to make Roosevelt a New Deal leader again—depended on Wallace's renomination and reelection. He was "more than ever a symbol of what the New Deal can become."[18]

Less than a month after his public rebuke by Roosevelt, Wallace spoke at a large labor meeting in Detroit. In an address that developed his frequent themes of international cooperation, the century of the common man, and a policy of full production, Wallace made one of his most moving statements. With the recent Detroit race riots in the audience's mind, Wallace began a litany: "We cannot fight to crush Nazi brutality abroad and condone race riots at home. . . . We cannot plead for equality of opportunity for peoples everywhere and overlook the denial of the right to vote for millions of our own people. . . . We cannot offer the blueprints and the skills to rebuild the bombed-out cities of other lands and stymie the rebuilding of our own cities. Slums have no place in America. We cannot assist in binding the wounds of a war-stricken world and fail to safeguard the health of our own people."[19]

In a collection of Wallace's speeches in 1944, Russell Lord wrote that with his Detroit speech the liberal and radical press began to make Wallace "a hero and martyr." The speech may have helped make Wallace a martyr, but he was already a hero—and had been since his "century of the common man" speech in 1942. But the Detroit speech certainly furthered the liberals' heroic image of Wallace. *The New Republic* called it his "finest speech" and one of the best in America in many years. It acknowledged that Roosevelt was still "the leader of the democratic forces" in the United States and the world, but warned that "disheartened" liberals, looking at Roosevelt's swing to the right, might stay home and cost him the election in 1944. Roosevelt needed to remember that liberalism was not a "luxury." Praising Wallace's refusal to "pull punches on the race issue," *The Nation* declared that he still spoke for "the authentic voice of the New Deal." It believed that labor needed to demonstrate its strength in order to keep Wallace on the ticket in 1944, but that there were positive signs that Roosevelt wanted him. On the ticket, Wallace would be a signal to labor that the progressive New Deal was not dead. Similarly, in *PM* Lerner praised Wallace's willingness to speak out, to refuse to be "an opportunist or a trimmer." Again, what was at stake for Lerner was Wallace's future as vice president and the future of the New Deal. For Lerner, the two were interconnected: Wallace's candidacy was "a symbol of the crucial issue—whether the liberals of America can knit their forces together, and insist on retaining the New Deal in Roosevelt's hands, and making Roosevelt himself once more a militant New Dealer."[20]

During the remainder of 1943 and the first half of 1944, there were frequent references to Wallace's successes. Comparing a Hull speech to one by Wallace, *The New Republic* contrasted Hull's status-quo world of political stability with Wallace's world of democracy and "dynamic social change." Wallace, it said, recognized the revolutionary forces in the world and understood that it was only a matter of whether it was going to be a violent or a peaceful revolution. In recognizing this truth, Wallace spoke for the "democratic revolution," for "the social change stirring among every people in the world, seeking its outlet in new democratic freedoms." His West Coast trip in early 1944 was reported to have gone well. Defending Wallace against the conservative press's criticism of his attacks on "American fascists" and "Wall St. stooges," James Wechsler praised "the sense of urgency" in Wallace's speeches. In May, Lord reported that Wallace's speeches attacking the barrier of race, creed, and color separating humans, had "gained enormously in reach and effectiveness." Wallace, Lord said, had achieved a deserved reputation throughout the world "not only as a good man but as a great man." Wallace carried the liberal message of Soviet-American friendship. He portrayed a Russian people, leadership, government, and industry growing toward a full democracy. His reports on his trip to Russia in the early summer of 1944—a trip that would later haunt his career—were effusive enough to camouflage, as some liberal intellectuals were prone to do, the repressiveness of Stalinism. On his trip to China he was praised for his efforts to bring together the warring political factions in China and for his condemnation of imperialism. His reports on the two trips were described by *The New Republic* as "thrilling."[21]

In May the newly formed New York Liberal Party endorsed a Roosevelt–Wallace ticket. Louis Fischer nominated Wallace as the embodiment of the "spirit and principles" of the Liberal Party. He was, said Fischer, in support of an international organization of peace and against imperialism and power alliances. He was an antifascist and stood for the extension of democracy. Even while nominating Wallace, Fischer expressed fears that he might be dropped from the Democratic Party ticket.[22]

By July with the convention only a couple of weeks away, the rumors of moves to dump Wallace grew stronger. Liberal intellectuals redoubled their efforts. The UDA's top leaders wrote in support of Wallace. James Loeb, the executive secretary, wrote to Robert Hannegan, the chairman of the Democratic National Committee, that "political realism" needed to take into account "rank-and-file support." The temptation to seek a compromise candidate to keep party harmony could easily prove self-defeating; Wallace's standing with "professional politicians" might be low, but "his stature has risen steadily in the minds and hearts of the 'common man'—the voter." And, as chair of the UDA, Niebuhr telegraphed Wallace that his nomination was "absolutely essential" to victory. Niebuhr wrote Roosevelt that both "political principles" and practicality dictated Wallace's renomination. With the military side of the war preoccupying Roosevelt, Niebuhr wrote, Wallace had "come . . . to be regarded as the spokesman of the average citizen, the common man." And then, in a paragraph that demonstrates that Niebuhr shared the liberal image of Wallace and of what Wallace meant, he continued: "the average citizen, the rank-and-file voter working on the farms and in the industrial centers of the nation, refuses to believe that the New Deal is dead, that it was a political fad or mere passing strategy. The common man believes that the New Deal lives, in Henry Wallace, as it lives in your own practical idealism and deepest instincts. He believes indeed, and we of the Union for Democratic Action believe with him, that the New Deal must continue to live, if the war is to be truly won." [23]

In *The New Republic,* T.R.B. said that dumping Wallace for a conservative would mean that domestically it made little difference whether the Democrats or Republicans won. The editors urged Roosevelt to remember that "morality and expediency" pointed to Wallace. It was also important for Roosevelt to remember his own place "in history." For, they said, Wallace in the cabinet would be like "a white stone marking our possible way out of the forest when the war is over. To discard him now will make the future seem disproportionately darker." And citing every poll and survey, Kirchwey declared that "the people want Wallace." The "back-room boys" opposed him as the last "important symbol of reform in the Roosevelt Administration." But a victory for them would run a risk for Roosevelt; while most liberals and labor people would still vote for him, many progressives, already "alienated . . . by his concessions to the big-business crowd at home and by his ambiguous foreign policy," could stay home.[24]

Stone, who criticized Wallace as weak in 1942, had changed his mind by 1944. No one was better able to carry out "the New Deal tradition" than Wallace, Stone wrote at the beginning of July. Two weeks later, in an article entitled "Henry Wallace — a Great American," Stone reviewed his career. Noting Wallace's compromises at the time of the Agriculture Department purge in 1935, Stone wrote that Wallace, like Roosevelt, had broadened his social awareness during his tenure in Washington. Again, like Roosevelt, he was not "a revolutionist, but a democratic leader trying within the limits of political possibility to correct the economic evils of our society and to help the underprivileged." He held out hope for "peaceful and gradual reform in our society." He recognized the dangers of unemployment in the postwar period and sought "governmental and private action" to achieve security. Stone predicted that in the likelihood of a postwar crisis, Wallace "would acquit himself with greatness," and in closing, Stone proclaimed: "Few people understand the problems of our society and of the world so well, and few have his broad humanity, his tolerance, his concern for people, few that genuine personal saintliness that is Wallace's. I think we may count our country fortunate in having in a single generation two leaders of the stature and vision of Franklin D. Roosevelt and Henry A. Wallace." [25]

When he wrote these words, Stone, who had for weeks been reporting the plots against Wallace, was confident that Wallace would win the renomination. He said that Roosevelt wanted Wallace and "Wallace it will be." A week later, Wallace was defeated. The backroom boys had won. Only the CIO-PAC had been really organized to fight for Wallace, Kirchwey reported. But at least the defeat had clarified matters; it had drawn the line between the progressives and reactionaries. The "battle of Chicago" had "opened up a new phase of an old war." [26]

The editors of The New Republic were also urging the progressives to organize for the coming struggle ahead. Chicago had been a defeat, but the Wallace forces had shown strength enough to force the choice of a liberal Truman over one of the southern conservatives. In the process of analyzing the developments at the convention and the prospects for liberals and labor in the months ahead, however, the editors revealed how much Wallace had become a myth. Wallace, who had always insisted that he stood for government-business cooperation and sought to make free enterprise really free, was portrayed as being as far left as the British Labour Party. The editors asked the readers to compare Wallace with "any of the major leaders" of the Labour Party:

> Wallace stands up against any of them in his international liberalism and realism, his conviction about the need for genuine socialization of the instruments on which economic democracy depends, his militancy in the people's cause. No one so far to the progressive left has ever so sweepingly received the approval of the large mass of people in American history, nor ever come so close to breaking the hold of the professional politicians. In short, the people were not fighting a rearguard action under Wallace's banner. They were fighting a vanguard action. They were beaten. But in their defeat there were the conditions of a future victory. [27]

Having called forth the progressives to do battle, the liberals watched the election of 1944 unfold. Even in the wake of his rejection for the vice presidency in 1944, Wallace represented the liberal cause. Refusing to engage in recriminations, which he and the liberals felt might hurt the war effort and the larger cause of liberalism, Wallace campaigned vigorously for Roosevelt, carrying the liberal message of labor, civil rights, democracy, and the people's war and peace across the country. In turn, his enthusiastic campaigning was appreciated by the liberal intellectuals. He was continuing the fight for a "liberal, constructive Democratic Party," *The New Republic* reported. And Kirchwey wrote that the Democratic Party regulars were passive in the campaign; only Wallace and Ickes were talking and writing.[28]

The next big fight would come at the very end of 1944 when Roosevelt nominated Wallace to be secretary of commerce. It would intensify in January and early February of 1945 as Jesse Jones, who had been discharged by Roosevelt as head of the Reconstruction Finance Corporation at the same time that Wallace's appointment had been announced, attempted to block the nomination. Once more it was Wallace versus Jones in a dramatic battle that engaged the emotions of the liberal intellectual community. "There is a tremendous furor over Wallace's appointment as Secretary of Commerce," wrote Chester Bowles to Alfred Bingham in Germany. Wallace's ideas on full production, Bowles reported, were hysterically attacked by the Republicans and southern Democrats.[29]

The liberals rallied to Wallace's full production agenda. It was, for them, the essential element in a fair and secure economy in the postwar period and in establishing the basis for a fair and secure peace. Jesse Jones, Lerner said, was a symbol of a world of "stock exchange quotations and the 'soundness' of investment," while Wallace symbolized a world where hope lay in "the fellowship of men and the partnership of nations." A U.S. economy bogged down in unemployment and limited production would produce a world of want, and the result would be nationalism, the resurrection of fascism, and war. As we have seen, by 1945 full employment had come to be the heart of the democratic revolution—or what was left of it. The issue in the new Jones–Wallace fight, Stone kept reiterating, was full employment. Settling the issue, he wrote, would "decide whether we shall have an expanding economy after the war or a restricted economy operated by dog-in-the-manger monopolists at the expense of a wide margin of joblessness and misery." In carrying on the fight for a government-stimulated full employment economy, Wallace was, for liberals, continuing to hold the banner for the democratic revolution and the century of the common man.[30]

If only Wallace could be confirmed, good things would happen. Stone wrote that it would mean less imperialism and a better economic deal for the workers of Latin America. No longer associating Wallace with British socialism, *The New Republic* wrote that Wallace only proposed to supplement free enterprise with government public works when necessary. He simply sought to expand trade, maintain good wages for workers and good farm prices for farmers, and create a full employment economy. His were "compensatory economics" and the only criticism of them was that they were not radical enough. His confirmation would mean the Commerce Department would be run for the people and not for the rich monopolists. Those fighting him were the same people fighting Roosevelt and the New Deal. Stone said that the progressives' battle for Wallace was only equaled by their battle for a "stable United Nations peace." And Tom Amlie wrote William Evjue, the editor of the *Madison Capitol Times*, that the old progressive businessman James McGill reported that in Washington it was considered the most important battle since the Supreme Court fight of 1937.[31]

With such high stakes, the liberals organized behind Wallace. Howard Y. Williams of the UDA was particularly active in organizing support for Wallace throughout the Midwest. In late January the UDA sponsored a testimonial dinner in New York at which Niebuhr, Eleanor Roosevelt, and Walter Reuther offered tributes. Later, a pamphlet of the tributes with a foreword from President Roosevelt was published. In late February the UDA combined a New York City rally for Wallace's confirmation as secretary of commerce with a rally for full employment. Highly laudatory speeches were delivered by the economic adviser Leon Henderson, the labor leader Emil Rieve, Congresswoman Chase Woodhouse from Connecticut, the former assistant director of the Board of Economic Warfare, liberal businessman Morris Rosenthal, and the New York civic leader and civil rights advocate Channing Tobias. As speech after speech extolled his ideas on full employment and his vision, Wallace, who was given to religious metaphors, might reasonably have interpreted the dinner as the anointing of the saint who had toiled for so long and hard during the war in the liberal vineyards. Even without pressing the religious metaphor, the celebration was such that Wallace ceased to be simply a liberal crusader; he was a symbol of the entire liberal cause. The symbiotic relationship between the liberals' and Wallace's view of the war had so developed that, to use John William Ward's phrase about Andrew Jackson, Wallace had become the symbol of the liberal age.[32]

In 1947 Paul Sifton, who had worked for James Patton's Farmers Union and for the UDA during the struggle for the Full Employment Bills of 1945 and 1946, published a book entitled *Public Men In and Out of Office* in which he devoted a chapter to Wallace. Despite not having a wide circu-

lation, the chapter is important for an understanding of the liberal perception of Wallace at this time. Sifton started the chapter by describing the
day Wallace came to testify on his nomination before the Senate Commerce Committee, a "clear and cold" January 25, 1945, when oil and coal
shortages had created a "chill" in "thousands of homes." The war news was
good, but the fighting remained intense. There was hope for an early victory, but, Sifton went on, "there was fear, too, and a wild fierce hope, fear
of peace itself and the unemployment that it would bring; hope that somehow the trick of transition from full employment for war to full employment for peace could be turned, that 'freedom from want' would not become as sour on the tongue as 'safe for democracy' had become twenty-five
years before."[33]

Contrasting Jesse Jones's appearance ("an aged bad-tempered banker . . .
who avoided contact with the Common People") with Wallace's appearance before the Senate Commerce Committee, Sifton continued: "A tall,
gangling man, hatless, wearing a topcoat and carrying a briefcase, appeared
in the big side doorway through which the Common People had come into
the room. He was alone. He came in fast, at an easy gate. Handclaps,
cheers, whistles, cowboy and rebel yells started at the instant he came
through the door and grew in volume as he passed through the crowd,
down between the press tables to the witness chair and table."[34]

Sifton now shifted to a baseball metaphor. This was a bases-loaded situation in which a smart pitcher does not wind up, and "Henry A. Wallace
[was] a smart pitcher . . . in the Iowa bush league, in the national league,
in the international league." He was "facing a committee determined to
cut him down to size and bury him as so many had tried to do for twelve
years." There was also the Wallace grin—"that damned boyish apologetic
grin of a friendly farmer in town for the day, prices up, and the missus
getting a new dress at the dry goods store." According to Sifton, although
the committee was "bored and impatient" during Wallace's five-hour presentation of Roosevelt's economic bill of rights, "the Common People in
the back seats and most of the Press" understood and "[ate] it up." They
listened "as intently as a crowd at an Iowa-Nebraska football game, breaking in with applause again and again." In presenting Wallace's testimony
as drawing a line for the country's future between Jesse Jones's big business
vision and Wallace's "little business – sixty million jobs" vision, Sifton had
created a mixture of Bob Feller (another Iowa farm boy mowing down
hitters), St. George coming to slay the dragon of privilege, and Jimmy
Stewart in *Mr. Smith Goes to Washington*.[35]

Reviewing the ascendancy of Wallace as the leader of the progressive forces in America, Sifton declared that by the spring of 1945, he was "the undisputed progressive leader in the U.S.A." In 1940, Sifton wrote, Eleanor Roosevelt had gone to the Democratic convention and "by sheer force of character" convinced the delegates "that Franklin D. Roosevelt insisted on Wallace." Having set aside the New Deal because of the war in Europe, Roosevelt "wanted Wallace as life insurance for the New Deal." Only he had "the mental breadth and moral stamina" to "hold the imagination and hot loyalty of many peoples around the world." Wallace, then, was "Roosevelt's pledge to his own conscience." Roosevelt had already decided to purchase business cooperation in a war-mobilized economy, but after the war "the march of progressivism would be resumed" and "Wallace was the best man . . . to lead that march." In 1944 Roosevelt had listened to anti–New Dealers and anti-Wallaceites, but in the fall campaign, he had witnessed Wallace's resurrection:

> A conscience-stricken Roosevelt watched the political corpse rise from the scene of the assassination stronger than ever before, transformed into a political power in his own right, carrying with him the charm of a superman, whom no political bullet or poison could harm. FDR saw this walking miracle go up and down the country like a Johnny Appleseed in seven-league boots, campaigning months on end for the man who had abandoned him, winning back the support of millions of progressives who had been outraged by the job done at Chicago. The cold anger of FDR's dismissal of Jesse Jones is a gauge of his remorse over the "sacrifice" of Wallace.[36]

Sifton's Henry Wallace was larger than life, a symbol in an ideological war. Throughout his account, some of it reasonable and some less than accurate, Sifton always came back to two aspects of Wallace: his connection with the *people* and his economic expertise. In a few startling paragraphs that dramatically link Wallace with "the people," Sifton began by denying that Wallace was "a sap" or a "moon calf" as his political opponents caricatured him:

> This label of sap may turn out to have been his greatest political asset. Remembering the label and feeling a helplessness in the maze of modern life, listening to his words of hope and cheer mixed with hard facts and Old Testament anger against the exploiters, millions of Americans have felt kinship, sympathy, new hope, and a fierce partisanship crossing party and sectional lines. As the eternal sap who makes good, the hick who tells off the city slickers, the political corpse who won't stay buried, the shy, smiling man with the hair that won't stay combed, the one politician who talks jobs, food, land,

airplanes, patents, monopolies, freight rate discriminations, decent housing, and the world-wide brotherhood of man, Wallace adds up for millions in
this and other nations to the average man's dream of what he himself might
be and say and do. Wallace's very awkwardness, his breaking of the rules of
the political game, his ability to do things the hard way and the wrong way
and get away with it, are assets in that they seem to many to make him, but
for the grace of God, themselves. Actually Wallace comes pretty close to being an intellectual aristocrat. . . . Wallace wears his learning as carelessly as
Roosevelt, an economic aristocrat, wore his campaign caps. . . . Wallace is the
first great man of the coming American Renaissance. His interests are broader
than Da Vinci's, as the horizons of today's world are broader than Da Vinci's.
His patron is the People, as Da Vinci's was the Duke of Milan.[37]

Sifton's Wallace, like the Lincoln of *The Lonesome Train*—Earl Robinson's musical narration of Lincoln's funeral train—was a mythic figure;
to adapt the words to Wallace: "You couldn't quite tell where the people
left off and where Henry Wallace began." But if Sifton's mythic Wallace
transported him beyond even the typical liberal effusions, it drew from the
same conceptions of Wallace and the same analysis of the domestic and
international forces. In his crusade for liberalism during the war Wallace
was always part human and part symbol.

Like so many myths, Wallace's was sustained partly by truth and partly
by fiction. Sifton's story of the confirmation hearing, for example, conve-
niently left out the fact that Wallace's confirmation was achieved by a
compromise whereby certain lending functions were removed from the
Commerce Department. It was not quite St. George who slew the dragon;
Roosevelt's negotiated deal played a role. Because Wallace was so often
hemmed in during the war and did not have the power to move in any
meaningful direction toward his stated goals, the myth was largely sustained by words and speeches. Occasionally there would be a moment of
triumphant vindication, as in his victory over Jones in winning confirmation. Then the liberal intellectual community and Wallace could celebrate
their joint efforts and their joint victories. But mostly it was the words
expressed in the struggle for liberal goals, not the triumph of those goals,
that won a place for Wallace in the heart of liberal intellectuals.[38]

Toward the conclusion of World War II there was an outpouring of
books dealing with the future of the U.S. economy. Wallace's *Sixty Million
Jobs*, published in 1945, was his statement of what the United States
needed to do in order for the capitalist system to provide abundance, peace

and freedom. Presumably it detailed the kind of revolutionary changes that the liberal intellectuals believed he was calling for in 1942. When examined, however, the programs it urged, and the assumptions behind those programs, point toward a greater shared prosperity under capitalism and not toward any radical transformation of capitalism. Indeed, Wallace's argument begins by saying that to win the war, the government needed to assume domination of the economy, but to win the peace Americans have "to get rid of this government domination." In Wallace's plans, government still had an important, positive role to play. He clearly was not an advocate of a planned economy, however, and in international affairs he sought free trade at every opportunity.[39]

Wallace's economic thinking was in line with many of the Keynesian-oriented ideas circulating in liberal circles. In terms of health care, it also appears to have been influenced by the British Beveridge Plan. Advocating a full employment economy, Wallace saw the government playing a role in stimulating investment, in adjusting credit to the rate of inflation, and in freeing the economy of monopolistic practices. A degree of planning was required; his programs required governmental-business-labor cooperation. Based on a high-wage, full employment economy in which certain social services such as health and social security had become universal, the plan required government assessment of unemployment rates and government actions to stimulate the economy if employment fell below certain levels. But such stimulation was to be directed toward stimulating private industry, with only a minimum of direct governmental intervention. Juxtaposed against the business-as-usual schemes of corporate leaders, the free market theories of Friedrich Hayek and intellectuals like John Chamberlain who were coming under Hayek's influence, or even against the more business-oriented and less social service – oriented plans for government-business cooperation that were emerging from Bernard Baruch and the Committee for Economic Development, Wallace's plan may have taken on a radical hue. But in fact it was in the liberal mainstream, a vision of a high-wage, full employment capitalism in which business, labor, and the government sought mutually beneficial programs. Expanded into areas like health care, it was based on the kind of thinking Sidney Hillman and progressive capitalists like Edward Filene had developed in the 1920s. As Steven Fraser has shown, this thinking, in which a strong labor movement and government stimulation played important roles, had struggled to prevail within the New Deal in the mid-1930s. It had appeared to prevail in the period between 1935 and 1937, only to suffer setbacks in the late 1930s and during the war years when William Knudsen, not Hillman, had dominated wartime economic thinking. Now it was emerging out of the war years.[40]

Formulated with different emphases by different writers, as has been discussed earlier, full employment capitalism proved attractive to some liberals because it offered greater economic and social justice without major changes in the ownership of property. But it also proved attractive to some liberals because, as we have seen, the high hopes of a democratic revolution had by 1945 not been matched in reality, and a modified vision of what could ostensibly amount to a democratic revolution was needed. Like the liberal advocates of economic planning in the early 1930s, the wartime liberals were wont to combine high calls for revolutionary changes and a people's revolution with programs that, on examination, were reformist. This does not make them bad programs; indeed, looking at the continuing and deepening economic and social problems facing the nation today, one longs for some of their boldness. What it does suggest, however, is that when Wallace spoke for revolutionary change in 1942, what he had in mind was a democratized modified capitalism. The liberals' rhetoric of a democratic revolution had implied more than that, and calls from many liberals for a democratic socialist Europe gave liberals a more radical domestic image. But there was always a vagueness about the "democratic revolution," a phrase that castigated many capitalist practices while it avoided any direct proclamation of socialism. In the end—partly because that is what came to be seen as all that was possible and partly because their calls for a democratic revolution had never been directly linked with democratic socialism—the liberals, like Wallace, and despite what their conservative opponents said, opted for a modified capitalism. It was the promise of a truly democratized capitalism and not the vision of socialist America that Wallace and the liberal intellectuals finally opted for.[41]

In formulating their idea of a democratic revolution, liberals had used the rhetoric of "the people" and of "the common man." If these terms meant anything, if Wallace was engaged in something more than creating categories that contributed to his political analysis, then the meaning of these terms requires exploring. In exploring them, one is also exploring the meaning of the American experience.

5

The Meaning of America

IN THEIR CHAPTER on the Sacco and Vanzetti case in *After the Fact*. James Davidson and Mark Lytle ask, how did a payroll murder trial of two previously obscure Italian immigrants became a national cause célèbre? Why did the Boston Brahmin establishment quake, and why were Sacco and Vanzetti's defenders so impassioned? Davidson and Lytle argue that more was at stake than the guilt or innocence of Sacco and Vanzetti, that the case drew forth such deep emotions because it involved a struggle over two views of America. Was the United States to be defined as a white Anglo-Saxon Protestant country in which the values of the Protestant ethic and the business community prevailed? Or were Americans to include in their conception of themselves and their nation a variety of religions, nationalities, races, ideologies, and sets of values, some of which offered alternatives to those of the business community?[1]

The view of America as Protestant and middle-class had predominated in the nineteenth century. Of course, rival value systems and rival visions of America were present, and I have no wish to support a monolithic, consensus version of American culture. But the manner in which so many debates were framed ("we" could assimilate the Irish, the freed African Americans, the "new immigrants," or "we" could not) suggests how deeply embedded this vision was. Its hegemony is indicated by how frequently Progressive reformers shared its assumptions. The cultural pluralists like Randolph Bourne and Horace Kallen were always a minority in a majority of assimilationists, melting pot theorists, and outright "bar-the-gates" racists. In the 1920s, when so many alienated American intellectuals and writers engaged in an extended critique of the Protestant middle-class culture, their quarrel assumed that Protestant ethic – business community values did define the United States. That was what they objected to; that was what was so stifling and deadening to creativity.

In the depression years, a different type of alienated criticism developed. Social, economic, and political critiques of American capitalism abounded. A literature focusing on exploitation and injustice developed in fiction and nonfiction. The conditions under which industrial workers, tenant farmers, immigrants, and African Americans lived their lives engaged the attention of the American liberal and radical intellectual community. Using what William Stott has aptly labeled the "documentary" style, writers set out to expose the facts of injustice and exploitation and to present them in such a way that they would move the audience intellectually and emotionally and stir it to action. The documentary style had been common among Progressive reformers, with their strong belief that if the public were given the "facts," then the particular injustice being exposed would be rectified. In the thirties the documentary style expanded its range of concerns and arranged the facts even more dramatically in order to reach the social conscience of the American people.[2]

The documentary style fit the mood of social protest, and the thirties fostered a vast literature of angry and concerned protest. One can find it everywhere: in the stark photographs of sharecroppers, in the paintings and murals of industrial workers, in proletarian novels, and in many of the social and economic articles in *The Nation, The New Republic,* and *Common Sense.* Liberalism was radicalized; the elder spokesperson of liberalism, John Dewey, wrote in 1935 that a liberalism that wasn't radical was irrelevant.[3] In the process of developing a radical critique and exposing the terrible injustices that capitalism had created, groups of Americans—African Americans, immigrants, sharecroppers, workers, poor women and children—were beginning to be seen as actors in the American experience.

As many writers have pointed out, the protest literature of the thirties was intensely nationalist—even when the authors of the work considered themselves internationalists. The writer Harvey Swados once noted how many book titles of the thirties contained the word *America.* The historical studies of the Works Progress Administration writers and the endeavors of the WPA in art, music, and theatre demonstrated how American themes and the search for an American style characterized much of the cultural work of the thirties. Writers went "on the road" in order to discover or rediscover America or searched out ignored aspects of American life in order to demonstrate the particularities of American humor, folklore, and customs.[4]

The original motivation for much of this effort was a desire to change social and economic conditions: reform or radical transformation of American capitalism was the initial driving force behind much of the "rediscovery of America." However, in the process of searching for the "underside" of American society, for those shunned and deprived by the workings of American capitalism, the liberal and radical writers were formulating a different vision of America. Instead of a Protestant middle-class America, it was an America of many classes and groups. African Americans, poor Americans, Italian, Jewish, and Slavic Americans were all part of it. It was a United States with a variety of cultures, of mores, of traditions. Small-town America was no longer the stultifying conformist place of Hamlin Garland, and even small-city America consisted of a far greater variety of cultures than Sinclair Lewis's *Main Street*. The literature of the 1930s projected a rich, variegated American experience. As William Stott has written, American intellectuals in the 1930s set out to reform America and wound up celebrating it.[5]

The tension between these two perspectives or impulses—reform and celebration—was part of the Popular Front. More than a narrow political strategy for checking fascism, the Popular Front involved an entire way of looking at the American experience. On one hand, the Popular Front had a reformist thrust: in its commitment to the workers and the union movement; its dedication to the deprived; its belief that the New Deal was trying to change the lives of that "one-third of the nation"; its division of the world between fascists and reactionaries and between democrats and "the people"; and its efforts to aid the people domestically and, through aid to the Spanish Republic, internationally. This aspect of the Popular Front involved an America in which there continued to be a multitude of injustices to be fought. On the other hand, the Popular Front celebrated the American experience. It admired not the alienated intellectuals of the 1920s but the socially engaged people of the 1930s. The New Deal was celebrated as the latest expression of a long tradition of American reform. The Communist Party slogan, "Communism Is Twentieth-Century Americanism," was itself only the most extreme example of this mood of celebration. For liberals, the European ideological experience had placed American democracy in a better light. Even while continuing to rationalize the Moscow Trials, Popular Front liberals argued that the lack of political outlets in the Soviet Union had increased their own appreciation for American democracy. When Granville Hicks left the Communist Party he turned not surprisingly—if one had been paying attention to the rehabilitation of small-town America in the eyes of the intellectuals—to local small-town democracy in the Berkshires.[6]

There was, then, in the Popular Front period a tension between its reformist impulse and its celebratory impulse. "Balance" perhaps is a better way of looking at it than tension because tension implies an incompatibility. From a historical distance, there may have been an incompatibility, but to the liberals living in the late 1930s the two impulses were intertwined. Because they cared so much for their version of America—for its variegated population—the barriers that held its people back needed to be destroyed. Privilege needed to be removed so that the richness of American democracy could triumph. With the coming of World War II, whatever latent tension that existed between the two sides vanished; the liberals' total support for the war meant both celebrating America and fighting for the inclusion of all peoples into American society. For liberals, that was what the war was all about.

Discussing the emergence of this celebratory literature of what he calls "unity in diversity," Stott has written that most of the documentary books of the 1940–42 years "celebrated America and its people's great diversity and greater unity." Stott connects the "unity-in-diversity-as-strength theme" with the celebration of the meaning of America when he cites Eleanor Roosevelt and Frances Macgregor's *This Is America* (1942) answer to Goebbels and Hitler: America's diverse races and religions were its strength.[7]

In exploring what the stock liberal phrases of democracy, freedom, the common man, and the people meant for the liberal intellectual community during World War II, it becomes clear that part of its vision of democracy pointed toward this pluralistic version, a variety of national, racial, and religious groups with their own customs and traditions contributing to a rich and variegated larger American culture. And part of the meaning of the common man was just those groups—African-Americans, migrants, sharecroppers, industrial workers—who entered into this redefinition of the American experience. But it was not simply the poor and the workers; the common man was not equivalent to the working class or the poor or the oppressed. The common people included most of the members of the recently reenvisioned small-town America: the honest small businessman, the local newspaper editor, the farmers, the clerks and the soda jerks. The vision of the common people derived not so much from a class analysis as from an inclusive Jacksonian vision of honest workers. Corporate

leaders, reactionary politicians, semi-fascist and outright fascist dema-
gogues, and southern racists were excluded. Almost everyone else was eli-
gible to be members of the democracy of the common man.[8]

This liberal view of democracy suggested a form of cultural pluralism.
But it also suggested a common American culture. That common culture
was often formulated in accordance with the democratic ideals represented
in the Declaration of Independence and supposedly in the U.S. Constitution. Liberals had high praise for Gunnar Myrdal's *An American Dilemma*
(1944). As recent studies have shown, Myrdal's work was deeply rooted in
the wartime experience, and its formulation was influenced by his own
efforts to render the war's meaning. In developing his critique of racism
and the entire segregation system, Myrdal focused on their incompatibility
with American democratic ideals. The conscience of Americans, he believed, was torn by the discrepancy between racist practices and democratic ideals. Myrdal believed that the democratic ideals were rooted in
the Declaration of Independence and Constitution and were shared by all
Americans. Optimistically, he had confidence that this creed would win out
and that practice would be brought into conformity with ideals. Because
he saw the solution to racism in the ideals of the American creed—an already existing common democracy—Myrdal saw no need to formulate a
newer, pluralistic vision of America. Indeed, he shunned interpretations
of African-American culture that stressed its continuity with its African
roots. African-American assimilation into a democratic common culture
and the victory of this cultural heritage over racist practices in the struggle
for the conscience of white America would end the "American dilemma."[9]

Myrdal's focus on the internal American dilemma struck a responsive
chord in the liberal intellectual community. Even before the publication
of his book, the idea of a conflict between the ideals of American democracy and racist practices was common among liberals and served as a basis
for much of their critique of the South's segregated institutions. In reviewing Carey McWilliams's *Brothers under the Skin* for *The New Republic* in
early 1943, George Mayberry noted that McWilliams based his analysis
on two Americas—one liberal and democratic, the other bigoted and authoritarian. Thus, Myrdal's idea of a basic American creed connected with
the war between democratic and fascist values, and it was compatible with
both celebrating and criticizing America. Reviewing Myrdal's book for
The New Republic, the black writer Saunders Redding expressed this battle
within the American soul: "Either the American creed must prevail and
the world sustain its hope in democracy, or the American deed must pre-

vail and the faith in human goodness be destroyed. There is nothing else to choose. *The American Negro problem is a problem in the heart of America.*" Writing two years earlier, Pearl Buck expressed an analogous belief in the inner conflict. In *American Unity and Asia*, she declared that the American suffered from "a split personality": "He is two distinct Americans. One of him is a benevolent, liberty-loving, just man. The other one of him is a creature who may or may not be benevolent but who is certainly undemocratic in his race attitudes, and who, on this subject, throws justice and human equality to the winds as completely as any Fascist. . . . The split personality which is America is found not in separate individuals but in most of the individuals of our nation. We are divided in our individual structure."[10]

Many liberal intellectuals did not accept Redding's or Buck's idea of a conflict within the individual American soul literally. To do so would have been to blur the clear lines between the democratic liberals crusading for racial justice and the racist reactionaries whose support for segregation betrayed American democratic ideals. Still, as a metaphor that caught both what was to be celebrated in the American experience and what was to be criticized and condemned in American behavior and institutions, the idea of an inner struggle was attractive. Langston Hughes did not express the dilemma in terms of the individual, as Smith and Redding had, but his words summarize the twin thrusts of celebration and criticism that had found their theoretical formulation in Myrdal's massive work. In a collection of essays by black writers entitled *What the Negro Wants*, Hughes wrote:

> Yet America is a land where, in spite of its defects, I can write this article. Here the voice of democracy is still heard—Wallace, Willkie, Agar, Pearl Buck, Lillian Smith. America is a land where the poll tax still holds in the South—but opposition to the poll tax grows daily. America is a land where lynchers are not yet caught—but Bundists are put in jail, and majority opinion condemns the Klan. America is a land where the best of all democracies has been achieved for some people—but in Georgia, Roland Hayes, a world-famous singer, is beaten for being colored and nobody is jailed—nor can Mr. Hayes vote in the State where he was born. Yet America is a country where Roland Hayes *can* come from a log cabin to wealth and fame—in spite of the segment that still wishes to maltreat him physically and spiritually, famous though he is.[11]

Myrdal's assimilationism and his positive reception by the American liberal intellectual community should suggest that the contemporary distinction between a commonly shared democratic culture to which all groups need assimilate and a pluralistic conception of democratic culture in which all groups maintain the richness of their cultures was not at all clear in wartime America. The language of pluralism can be found coinciding with the language of a common culture; Myrdal's assimilationism was accepted without rejecting pluralism. The statement of the Common Council for American Unity, the parent organization for the journal *Common Ground*, reflected both the need for unity based on a common democratic faith and the need to honor the cultural traditions of different groups. The council stated its purpose:

> To help create among the American people the unity and mutual understanding resulting from a common citizenship, a common belief in democracy and the ideals of liberty, the placing of the common good before the interests of any group, and the acceptance, in fact as well as in law, of all citizens, whatever their national or racial origins, as equal partners in American society. To further an appreciation of what each group has contributed to America, to uphold the freedom to be different and to encourage the growth of an American culture which will be truly representative of all elements that make up the American people. To overcome intolerance and discrimination because of foreign birth or descent, race or nationality. To help the foreignborn and their children solve their special problems of adjustment, know and value their particular cultural heritage, and share fully and constructively in American life.[12]

Common Ground's own articles often used the metaphor of a shared unity of values, but at other times they used images closely related to the symphonic image associated with the cultural pluralist Horace Kallen. Writing as a cultural pluralist, Edward E. Grusd posed the question: "On the other hand, is it possible that despite the forced assimilation, which through the generations tends to standardize the American type of thought, custom, and even food and appearance, the standardization can be defeated, so that the rich social tapestry now being woven by Americans of French, German, Italian, Russian, Irish, Jewish, and Negro origin, and all the others, will not degenerate into a monotonous pattern?" While Grusd was worried about the dangers of a common culture becoming standardized and forcing a conformist assimilation, elsewhere liberals worried that pluralism might become the basis for ethnic chauvinism. In 1944 Louis Adamic published *A Nation of Nations*, in which he contrasted two views of American history. In one view, the United States was "an Anglo-Saxon country with a White-Protestant-Anglo-Saxon civilization struggling to preserve itself against infiltration and adulteration by other civilizations brought here by Negroes and hordes of 'foreigners.'" In the other view, the United States was "a blend of cultures from many lands, woven of threads from many corners of the world." Adamic believed that in the past the telling of American history had too often been based on the first view, and he consciously set out to tell the story of the various immigrant groups from a perspective that reflected their diversity and the diverse nature of the United States. If his chapters too often read like roll calls of prominent immigrants from each group, and if his statements about the positive attributes of specific immigrant groups occasionally resembled the flip side of Jacob Riis's 1890 statements about the negative attributes of specific immigrant groups, Adamic's book, nevertheless, was an attempt to see the strength of the United States as resting on its pluralism and "stubborn creative differences."[13]

Although his emphasis was on different "essential faiths" and not on one "essential faith," Adamic did see the "greatness" of the United States as deriving both from "the variegated texture of its makeup" and from its idea of government—"that all men are created equal and have a voice in how they are governed." In this way, Adamic introduced a common culture—democracy's ideals—into his tribute to variegation. However, this was not enough for the reviewers—both young historians—in *The Nation* and *The New Republic*. In *The Nation*, Edward Saveth not only criticized Adamic's focus on prominent individuals but also accused the work of encouraging "minority chauvinisms," which, he said, were "as dangerous as the notion of Anglo-Saxon superiority." In *The New Republic*, Eric Goldman had praise for Adamic's attempt to show the diversity of American culture, but, like Saveth, criticized him for encouraging "minority chauvinisms."[14]

For liberal intellectuals there were the dangers of a standardized assimilation to a unified common culture and the dangers of ethnic chauvinism in a diversified pluralistic culture. But for the most part, they were able to keep the twin visions in balance. The liberal intellectual community could be culturally pluralistic, as Grusd was in insisting on the value of a variety of different cultural traditions, or it could be assimilationist, as when it accepted Myrdal's argument—without feeling the two conflicted. And this was because both approaches grew out of a vision of "the people," who shared common ideals and yet were different.

The term *democracy* conjured up the image of this multidimensional common man; it also involved the strong belief in the tradition of political democracy. Voting rights, rights of public assembly, citizen participation in local government—all these were in principle present in the United States and all were under siege by fascism throughout the world. Where absent in practice, as the result of the poll tax and other discriminatory devices, full rectification was required if genuine democracy was to flourish and the democratic nations were to triumph. But the forms and practices of political democracy were not enough. For liberals, political democracy needed to be extended into economic areas. Economic democracy was required to fulfill and guarantee political democracy. The distinction between the two had been commonplace in liberal intellectual circles in the 1930s and had led frequently to apologetics for Stalin and the Soviet Union, where economic democracy was believed to be present. If, at the end of the thirties, it was less clear that the Soviet Union had achieved economic democracy, the belief that political democracy needed to be expanded to include economic democracy still operated in liberal circles.[15]

Translated into wartime possibilities, the idea of economic democracy meant the right of workers to join unions, the extension of social benefits to American workers, and through unions, the increased role of the worker in economic planning and control of company operations. In the business-government sphere, it meant greater governmental control of business and greater regulation of business practices for the public good. Economic democracy involved neither socialism nor greater governmental ownership, although these were not incompatible with it. It was not a system but both an extension of workers' rights and benefits and a decline in business domination and control great enough to create a shift in power relations. In this sense, economic democracy was an essential part of a revolution—the people's revolution—that was designed to increase the political and economic rights of the common man.[16]

As with what might be called the ethnic component of democracy, the political and economic dimensions of democracy could also lead to demands for reforms or reasons for celebration. The denial of African-American voting rights, segregation throughout the South, the growth of corporate power, the role of the House Un-American Activities Committee, all pointed to the denial of democracy and the subsequent need for social reform. The existence of democratic ideals and a tradition of democratic reforms were grounds for celebrating democracy's strength in the face of fascism's assaults. The same was true abroad—only there the celebratory reasons were fewer, and the reasons for change (imperialism, suppression of workers in Latin America, strength of fascist groups throughout Europe) were more. Once more the formulation of the American experience around the terminology of democracy, the common man, and freedom pointed toward the concept of World War II as an international civil war.

If the term *democracy* had economic connotations, the terms *freedom* and *liberty* had to be protected against their traditional economic interpretations. For liberals, freedom definitely did not mean laissez-faire, and liberty definitely did not mean the right to do whatever one wished with one's property. For the liberal intellectual community, the unfettered freedom or liberty of business meant the destruction of other freedoms and thus the end of true democracy. For liberals, freedom consisted first of all of civil liberties and civil rights—freedom of speech, of assembly, of religion. But it also had an economic dimension. As articulated in Roosevelt's Four Freedoms, freedom also meant freedom from want, from starvation and poverty; it meant having the economic security to enable one to enjoy political and civil rights. To ensure this kind of economic freedom, the older definition based on individualistic property rights required modification. For liberals, that older kind of economic freedom became, in the real world, excessive economic power over others' lives and monumental greed and selfishness in one's own. Thus, the extension of New Deal control of business had extended the real freedom of the people, and its further extension would mean enlarging true freedom.[17]

Internationally, a United Nations would have a similar effect. Freed from want and fear, freed to enjoy their political rights, and to follow their religious beliefs, to speak for their social causes, the peoples of the United States and the world would enjoy their freedom. Again, the definition of freedom pointed toward the liberals' interpretation of World War II: the battleground of freedom was the world; its enemies held far too much political and economic power.[18]

The attempt to define the meaning of the words democracy, freedom, and the people so as to give validity to one's cause was not new to World War II. The term *common man* was more recent, but not without precedents. In attempting to define the terms and to interpret their meanings, liberals drew on previous attempts and developed concepts and nuances of their own. In the end, the ability of Henry Wallace to elicit such a response from liberal intellectuals resulted from his embracing their conceptions and from his ability to dramatize their vision of America and the world. An America in which people of different nationalities, races, and religions respected each other's different traditions and yet embraced a common democratic culture; an America in which the traditional forms of democracy had been rendered universal in practice and in which the idea of democracy had been extended to include economic concepts empowering working people; an America in which the benefits would fall evenly to rural, small-town, and urban common people, a term loosely defined to mean the simple, honest, hard-working people across the working and middle classes; an America in which genuine freedom from economic want had replaced the spurious and selfish freedom to unilaterally use one's property for one's own benefit—these ideas came together to provide the liberal intellectual community with its own definition of the American experience. It is a definition that has had long-range consequences in creating a self-definition for Americans who share little in common with the social concerns of the World War II American liberals. But whatever the later effects, during World War II the liberal intellectual community offered a powerful reading of the American experience that reverberated beyond the community itself.

When Paul Robeson sang his rendition of "The Ballad of America" and "The House I Live In," he roused the emotions of liberals within the audience precisely because the words matched their vision of the American experience and because Robeson performing seemed to confirm the reality of the vision. My argument does not claim that liberal intellectuals believed Robeson's egalitarian and democratic vision described the literal reality of contemporary American life. Rather, the claim is that in its definition of the essence of historical and contemporary America, this reading of the American experience fostered the celebratory side of the liberal vision. And in the context of wartime America, the celebratory side functioned to mythologize the American people, with consequences for liberal social and self-understanding.

> The House I Live In, my neighbors white and black,
> the people who just came here and from generations back.
> The House that we call freedom, the home of liberty
> and the right to speak my mind out,
> that's America to me. . . .
> The people that I meet.
> The house, the church, the school house,
> the home of liberty,
> but especially the people
> that's America to me.

Here was the liberal image of America and its war: the people's—all races and religions—fight for freedom, the culmination of a long upward struggle for democracy and liberty.[19]

Though liberals would be loathe to admit it and certainly did not mean it to have such consequences, this vision, these stirring words, blurred reality. Not only was an entire race barred in one section of the country from this vision of America, but few neighborhoods anywhere were integrated. And members of another race were placed in internment camps with relatively little protest from the liberal community and with support from the Communist left, with whom Robeson was close. The words spoke of the right to speak one's mind, but the liberal intellectual community had helped to create a theoretical framework for curtailing free speech in wartime and was actively campaigning for the curtailment of freedom of the press. And the Communist left's record on civil liberties was disgraceful. Perhaps most important, by portraying an optimistic view of the historical struggle for freedom and democracy in the United States, this view of the American experience implicitly denied the tragic nature of much of American history. Finally, moving though it was, the vision served as a hindrance to self-scrutiny on the part of the liberal intellectual community.[20]

On one level, the gap between the idealized version and reality is no worse—and, given the nature of its vision, better in its goals—than the usual gap between rhetoric and reality in war. Indeed, if the vision could have been taken just as a goal, just as a spur to the reformist impulse, the benefits would have been largely positive. But precisely because this vision was not simply a goal but a reading of the American experience, the gap between rhetoric and reality is more important.

Convinced that they spoke for the people, the liberals too often did not ask themselves if their own practices lived up to their vision of a pluralistic diversified America. *The New Republic* and *The Nation* published frequent articles and editorials on civil rights, but leading African-American organizational spokesmen like Walter White of the NAACP, Lester Granger of the Urban League, and A. Philip Randolph of the Brotherhood of Sleeping Car Porters rarely, if ever, published in either journal. The person who wrote most regularly on race issues in the South for *The New Republic* was Thomas Sancton, a white. Sancton's pieces were often very good, and the point here is not to suggest that the liberal press was uniquely guilty for its lack of a diversified staff. But the liberal reading of the American experience encouraged a celebratory posture toward the diverse "people" that allowed rhetoric to pass for reality.

In 1942 Katrina McCormick, who was helping Alfred Bingham and Selden Rodman with *Common Sense*, wrote to Rodman:

Now for the Negro problem—our own Negro problem. I thought Powell's piece was good. But I suppose not good enough. I have been thinking a lot about the Negro question in relation to us liberals with magazines. It seems to me that we, the liberals, do an awful lot of talking about the Negro problem in our parlors and whenever the question is hot—and God knows it's plenty hot now—we shout about it in print for a spell and then we forget it again. That is until somebody has another pole [sic] tax party. The point is that the New Republic and the Nation don't carry it any further than that, and it has occurred to me that perhaps COMMON SENSE should do something permanent. Have a Negro staff writer or some such. Never *forget* the problem. I realize that it would be hard to work out. That it would have to be carefully studied. This is obviously only the kernel of an idea, but would you and Hilda think about it, and then we can talk it over when I come next.

Rodman and Bingham apparently did not give McCormick's suggestion about hiring a "Negro staff writer" a great deal of thought. Bingham wrote McCormick that he had seen her letter and was "impressed with . . . [her] idea of pushing ahead with the Negro issue." But, he went on, he felt there were not enough pages in *Common Sense* to have "a regular feature on Negro problems." He noted that Rodman was planning to publish in the next issue a group of letters from Negro soldiers, and he acknowledged that the subject needed "to be followed up frequently." Thus a suggestion for a small act of integration was brushed aside, and *Common Sense* did not have, no more than *The Nation* or *The New Republic* did, a staff that matched its integrated vision of America.[21]

McCormick's reference to poll tax parties is revealing. Important lobbying acts in themselves, they can also serve as a symbolic boundary for liberal activism on civil rights. Petition drives against the poll tax or for desegregation of the armed forces, public exposés of racism, lobbying— these were the ways in which liberals sought to eliminate racism during the war. The liberals wrote sympathetically of Randolph's March on Washington Movement, and they certainly never criticized it or tried to undermine it, as the Communists did; but they never placed their full weight behind its difficult efforts to organize for what Randolph called "Non-Violent Good Will Direct Action" in the South. Randolph's ideas were on a far smaller scale than later forms of direct action, and they were nearly impossible to organize during the war. It is not fair to say that the liberals were not activists; they were—as described above. The problem was that by not helping to organize forms of direct action, they too often replaced action with words. Shortly after the end of the war, Alexander Pekelis wrote an article for *The New Republic* about combating racism: "The answer to hatred and oppression is not mere debate, or legislation alone, or half-hearted pressure. Once again, the history of labor affords a lesson: debate *plus* pressure, legislation *plus* picketing, individual protection *plus* group action offer the only chance of success." [22]

Pekelis's words could serve as a complimentary *and* critical epitaph for liberal activities on behalf of civil rights during the war. There was debate, efforts at legislation, and more than half-hearted pressure. But there was no liberal organizing or picketing or group pressure, no "good will non-violent direct action" to speak of. Liberals contributed to the pioneering efforts of the thirties to redefine the American experience in terms of a diversified definition of Americans, but during the war they did not adequately further the pioneering efforts at direct action techniques that might have helped turn that definition into a reality.

Was the same lack of African-American staff members in the liberal press true for women? On the surface, the answer is "no." Freda Kirchwey edited *The Nation* and the book review editor was Margaret Marshall. Anna Louise Strong, Pearl Buck, and Lillian Smith all published in *The Nation*, Diana Trilling wrote regular reviews of literature, and Kate Mitchell wrote frequent reviews of books on the Far East. In *The New Republic*, Helen Fuller published a regular column on domestic issues, and Agnes Smedley and Helen Mears frequently reviewed books on the Far East. Pearl Buck and Freda Utley, until she became too conservative, published in *Common Sense*, and, as noted above, Katrina McCormick helped with its publication. Both *The Nation* and *The New Republic* published several articles by women pertaining to war work and problems women faced on the home front. Yet when one probes more deeply, the picture is not quite so diverse. Diana Trilling was not the only woman reviewer of literature, but she was the only regular reviewer. There were far more women book reviewers than women writers of feature articles. In both *The Nation* and *The New Republic* the most frequent women reviewers reviewed books on the Far East: Smedley, Mitchell, Mears, and Betty Graham. The only regular women writers of feature articles or editorials were Kirchwey in *The Nation* and Fuller in *The New Republic*. Kirchwey's co-editors and influential writers — Reinhold Niebuhr, Robert Bendiner, Louis Fischer, J. Alvarez Del Vayo — were all male, as were the chief editors of *The New Republic*. The true issue, however, was not as much the lack of true diversity as the absence of any real imaginative and questioning thinking about the conditions of women in American society. The liberal pluralistic vision of the American experience focused on classes, nationalities, and races, but tended to mute gender. This can be seen in the liberal opposition to the Equal Rights Amendment.[23]

There were legitimate concerns on the part of labor and working women in the conservative political climate of the war years that the Equal Rights Amendment might work against protective labor legislation for women. The fact that the Republican Party gave the strongest political support to the ERA tended to arouse suspicions about the nature of the support for the amendment. Yet there was something cavalier and automatic about the manner in which liberals and liberal organizations dismissed the ERA without any debate. The opposition to the ERA was not confined to the male liberals but was shared by Kirchwey, whose attitude was consistent with the majority of women New Dealers of the thirties who viewed it as threatening to working women. When both the Democratic and Republican parties endorsed the ERA in 1944, liberals mounted a campaign against it. The National Farmers' Union passed an anti-ERA resolution, which it forwarded to the UDA for endorsement. The UDA, whose leadership was practically all male, supported the resolution without taking time for any serious discussion or debate. *The Nation* and *The New Republic* editorialized against the stand of the Republicans and Democrats. Almost the only time Wallace was criticized was for his endorsement of the ERA. Although the amendment failed to pass the Congress in 1945, Truman endorsed it that spring, and in *The New Republic* T.R.B. warned its liberal opponents that they had "better get busy." [24]

The fact that the liberal intellectual community was impeccable in its support of equal pay for equal work, that its press published sensitive articles on the problems of women war workers and made favorable references to new household and domestic arrangements, indicates that liberals were not blind to important women's issues. But the speed with which they made the ERA a non-debatable issue suggests that they had their own definition of women's issues that they guarded carefully. The absence of true debate also suggests that liberal interest in women's issues was never in the forefront — important, yes, but vitally important, no.

In June 1944 Olga Robinson, a California reader of *Common Sense*, wrote to Stuart Chase, who had recently reviewed Bingham's *The Practice of Idealism*. In his book, Bingham had written of five contemporary revolutions. Declaring that Chase could treat the letter "as the ranting of a female feminist, and let it go at that," Robinson expressed her need to "speak out." Bingham, she said, should have written about a sixth revolution:

> He "plumb forgot" the revolution of the women. Isn't it a turning around in our lives leaving our homes for the factory, the motor bus, the army and the farm? And doesn't that make it a change for everybody in the home, and so in the world? . . . Then there is the matter of the Equal Rights Amendment. Why is labor afraid of it, and why are all the congressmen afraid of labor, on this matter? As giving the suffrage to women was about the only democratic thing that came out of the war to make the world safe for democracy, even so glaring an injustice as the denial of equality of legal status to women, will not even that come out of this holocaust? . . . can you not persuade the editor to say a word for this supreme revolution of them all?

Bingham in *Common Sense,* and also Freda Kirchwey in *The Nation* and Bruce Bliven in *The New Republic,* said a lot about revolution and a significant amount about women, but they never linked the two organically because they never saw gender in the same way as they saw class, race, and nationality.[25]

There is a certain irony in all this. What I have been suggesting is that the liberal intellectual community made an important contribution in redefining the American experience. But because it too readily accepted the *words* of that redefinition for the reality, it did not scrutinize its own practices sufficiently; it did not contribute significantly to putting into practice tactics and strategies that might further its diversified vision; and it did not bother to seriously reformulate its analytical categories to include a new look at gender. What this points to is a significant disparity between liberal words and deeds. And this is ironic because there was nothing more central to liberal thought during the war years than the need to match word and deed, rhetoric and reality.

The idea of an international civil war was intended to close the distance between democratic ideals and the actual conditions of people's lives. In February 1943 Kirchwey wrote one of her frequent analyses of Roosevelt, after he had just promised total victory over the Axis and the elimination of the Quislings and Lavals of the world from political power. Kirchwey welcomed Roosevelt's promises of complete victory over "the whole fascist conspiracy." She paid tribute to the sincerity of his "antipathy for fascism" and "his desire to supplant tyranny with freedom." Roosevelt had reminded the world of "the meaning of the war," and his words deserved dissemination in occupied Europe — as well as in the State Department. But, she continued, there were hostile reactionary forces attempting to thwart Roosevelt, and there was his own confident nonchalance, which assumed there would be solutions to the political problem of fascism even if we cooperated with "near-fascists" in military victory. The president's words, she said, were only a pledge and must not be taken for reality; to do the latter "would be to betray the last, best hope of a democratic future." It was time for the president to take action against the Francos and against the "reactionary elements" in the United States, including the State Department. Roosevelt's compromises with these antidemocratic forces, she went on, had helped to sabotage "his expressed aims." "Wishes and promises" were not enough; only "courageous and uncompromising policy" would do.[26]

Here, Kirchwey held Roosevelt to his rhetorical standard: he needed to match word and deed. But the liberals too often took their own words for more than a pledge; whether they were defining the war or projecting their "people's" version of the American experience, rhetoric and reality became entangled. As a result of the confusion, badly needed liberal self-criticism failed to take place. We have seen how this lack of self-criticism affected the liberals' practices and ideas about African Americans and women. But it also affected the liberals' attitude toward the New Deal.

With his tragic sense of history and his capacity to understand the irrationalities of human behavior, no one was better prepared philosophically to offer the necessary self-criticism than Niebuhr. In *The Children of Light and the Children of Darkness*, Niebuhr did engage in liberal self-criticism. He criticized liberalism, with its enlightened rationality, for having blissfully ignored the darker irrational forces that bred fascism. He criticized many of the liberal internationalists for not understanding the depth of nationalism and the drive for power. This was a point he made frequently in articles and reviews in which he seemed to engage in a balancing act of criticizing unadorned advocates of realpolitik for a lack of idealism and idealistic advocates of world government for their lack of realism. Overall, Niebuhr believed liberal thought was characterized by an excessively optimistic faith in human nature. Believing that evil resulted from bad institutions and was not rooted in human nature, liberals, according to Niebuhr, built their institutions on weak soil. Democracy was a necessity, not because it represented the highest attainment of man's reason, but because man's irrationality necessitated it. "Man's capacity for justice," he wrote in a famous passage, "makes democracy possible; but man's inclination to injustice makes democracy necessary." No one seemed better prepared to penetrate the gap between the liberal interpretation of the war and the liberal vision of the American experience ("The actual behavior of the nations is cynical. But the creed of liberal civilization is sentimental"); as the national chairperson of the UDA and a highly respected figure in the liberal community, no one seemed better able or in a better position to point the liberal intellectual community toward an intense self-scrutiny.[27]

But in the end Niebuhr was prepared to demand neither of himself nor of others the kind of self-scrutiny that might interfere with the basic liberal interpretation of the war and especially with the course of liberal political commitment to the Roosevelt administration. Any scrutiny of the Roosevelt administration's practice, and any self-scrutiny of the liberal relation to it and of the liberal interpretation of the war and the American experience, pointed in the direction of critical support for the war, a serious break with the Roosevelt administration, a more tragic rendition of the American experience, and a reformulation of the meaning of World War II. But Niebuhr was no more prepared than Kirchwey, Bliven, Max Lerner, or James Loeb to engage in such genuine self-criticism. Instead he offered philosophical rationalizations for curtailing free speech, and he served as the heavy gun in rejecting Norman Thomas's overtures for liberal support in 1944. The organization he chaired, the UDA, reflected the common liberal frustration during the war, but it engaged, like *The Nation* and *The New Republic*, in the same deflecting of criticism on to the State Department, and the same refusal to give anything less than total support to the war even when U.S. policy at home and abroad undercut what it believed the war was all about. Most of all, the UDA refused to break with the Roosevelt administration. In fact, much of its work was designed to win friends and influence in high administrative places.

6

The UDA in Action

FROM LATE 1940 into the spring of 1941, a group of liberals and ex-Socialists were planning a new committee dedicated to conducting a struggle for democracy at home and abroad. James Loeb, Reinhold Niebuhr, Freda Kirchwey, Lewis Corey, Alfred Bingham, and Alfred Baker Lewis, among others were active in formulating a statement on domestic and foreign policy that would be used to launch the new organization. The Union for Democratic Action (UDA) was formed in April 1941 and formalized at a conference the first week of May.[1]

In the words of Niebuhr, its chair, and Kirchwey, its treasurer, the UDA was designed "to express the thought and the will of all those progressive forces in our nation who believe that the struggle for democracy at home and the fight against the foreign foes of democracy is essentially one struggle on two fronts." Although leading liberals like Kirchwey were among the founders, much of the impetus came from the ex-Socialists. Niebuhr; Loeb, its initial executive secretary and later national director; Murray Gross, its original secretary; and Franz Daniel, one of the original co-chairmen, had been important members of the Socialist Party during the 1930s. So had Jack Altman, Albert Sprague Coolidge, Francis Henson, Alfred Baker Lewis, and Paul Porter—all of whom were either members of the executive board or the sponsoring committee of the UDA.[2]

In A Program for Americans, its statement of its principles and program, the UDA proclaimed that the defeatists who predicted the triumph of the total state were "false prophets." The program defined two dangers: the external danger of Germany and the internal danger of an unfulfilled democracy disappearing at home. Neither military victory nor internal democratic reform alone, it said, would defeat fascism. Therefore, in a new program of "democratic action" the UDA called for whatever political, economic, and military means were necessary to defeat the fascist aggressors externally and for the extension of democracy within the United States as a way to defeat fascism internally: "Liberals and democrats must recognize that basic economic and new social arrangements are necessary if democracy is to survive and grow. Socialists and other radicals, naturally excluding communists, must recognize that if the changes and new arrangements are not made in a form that promotes democracy they can only lead to the tyranny of the Total State." In the 1930s, the UDA declared, "our greater economic resources and our sturdier democracy" and "the emergency measures of the New Deal" had checked the dangers of native fascism. Now, however, it was necessary to "go beyond emergency measures to *fundamental economic reconstruction*."[3]

The fundamental economic reconstruction program required democratic planning—not fascist "despotic planning"—to achieve full production. Such planning did not require total control, but it did require strategic controls. In perhaps its most radical proposal, the UDA wrote: "Among the strategic controls for democratic planning are *socialization of the great banks, a measure of government investment, and transformation of monopoly corporations into public service corporations with democratic administration by management AND labor unions*." The UDA platform ended with an affirmation of democracy: "Democracy was born as a revolutionary force; it must again become such a force."[4]

The UDA program largely reflected the ideas that Corey, a member of the organizing committee, had been working on. Loeb wrote a correspondent that the UDA was distinguishable from all other all-out-aid-to-the-Allies organizations and committees by its emphasis on the domestic fight for democracy. But it was not simply its emphasis on domestic issues that was striking; it was that its initial statement pointed beyond New Deal emergency measures, beyond the specifics of piecemeal reform, in order to argue for the necessity of new economic arrangements.[5]

There is another aspect of the UDA that gave it a semiradical dimension. While it was created by well-known intellectual and labor activists, and while its conferences tried to include influential individuals, it also had a grassroots dimension. In the fall of 1941 it began a "School for Democratic Action" in New York City in which a series of prominent intellectuals including Corey, Kirchwey, Loeb, Niebuhr, and George Counts engaged in lecture-discussion-question sessions with the audience. In addition, the UDA arranged for street-corner meetings with their own speakers. Often planned on the corners of New York City where isolationists were holding their meetings indoors, they were designed to counter isolationist and pro-fascist sentiment and to garner support for an increased U.S. commitment to the Allies. Ira Marienhoff, a City College student at the time, remembered speaking at UDA street corner rallies throughout New York City in the fall of 1941.[6] The U.S. entrance in the war brought an end to the rallies, and the School for Democratic Action only lasted the first fall.

One other feature of the UDA's origins is important, although its relevance can be overestimated. The organization was founded in the period of the Nazi-Soviet Pact. In its platform the UDA distinguished democratic forms of radicalism from the Communist commitment to the total state, and its membership excluded Communists as well as fascists. A number of its early statements warned against the Party's peace drives and cautioned against confusing labor's rights with Communist-manipulated strikes in the defense industries. When Hitler attacked the Soviet Union, the UDA urged aid to the Soviet Union but warned that it was still necessary to guard against Communist infiltration of liberal groups. It is easy to read cold war liberalism back into these earlier disputes, and clearly the antagonisms of the 1950s are not unrelated to earlier controversies. However, the UDA position in 1941 is best interpreted against the background of the late 1930s: the Moscow Trials and especially the Nazi-Soviet Pact.[7]

The UDA maintained its exclusionary membership; Loeb always argued when the issue came up that Communists should not be members of liberal organizations. But in the midst of the war against fascism and Nazism, this exclusionary position had little meaning. The UDA sponsored lectures by writers (Johannes Steel, Alexander Kuh, and Max Lerner) who were sympathetic to the Soviet Union. And Kirchwey, Bruce Bliven, and others who looked positively on Stalin's role in international affairs were important members of the UDA. Its leaders, including Loeb, participated in the National Citizens Political Action Committee (NC-PAC), a nonexclusionary Popular Front–style political organization. Although Loeb, Lerner, Kirchwey, and Bliven had differences with the Communist elements in the NC-PAC, the Communist issue did not cause clear divisions within the UDA until late in the war. It was not until the end of the war and the open ruptures within the liberal community over U.S.-Soviet relations that the UDA's original exclusionary position became a major issue.

The resistance shown by a number of UDA members to Niebuhr's 1946 *Life* article on postwar Germany criticizing the Soviet Union—Niebuhr was accused of having fascist sympathies—indicates that those with sympathy for the Soviet Union that went beyond wartime respect were active in the UDA throughout the war. Nathalie Panek's discovery in 1946 on a UDA organizing trip to the West that a number of West Coast UDA members were fellow travelers also suggests that the UDA's exclusionary position during the war was not a rigid one.[8]

What was central to the evolution of the UDA during the war years was that its quasi-radical domestic program and its quasi-grassroots dimension were lost during the war. Dinners, off-the-record conferences, and lectures—all with influential political or intellectual figures—became its standard organizational operation. When the United States entered the war, foreign policy issues became far more prominent than domestic ones. Recognizing that a new stage had been reached and new initiatives were required, the UDA called a conference for December 21, 1941, to work out a tentative program that was to be ratified at a later conference in January. The attendees at the December conference read like a "who's who" of American liberalism. Although much of the organization's program remained the same, there was a subtle, yet significant, difference in the thrust of its rationale. Whereas the initial UDA platform had talked of "outworn capitalist economic relations" and had called for going beyond the New Deal's emergency measures, for "fundamental economic reconstruction," for "new arrangements," and for the "socialization of the great banks," the UDA now said that it sought a domestic policy "to preserve and extend the social securities of the past decade." In this way, the quasi-radical phraseology of the initial platform was replaced by a liberal phraseology built on the extension of New Deal liberalism.[9]

The series of statements prepared at the January conference were characteristic of liberal intellectual thinking during the war: the need for an offensive war strategy, the need to end State Department appeasement, a larger role for labor in war production, the need to plan for the eventual transition to peace, and the elimination of "all aspects of racial and religious persecution and discrimination." To achieve this last goal, the UDA called for an end to segregation in the armed forces, the passage of the Federal Anti-Lynching Law, the abolition of the poll tax and the "Democratic White Primary," and a federal investigation of white officers of black regiments and of personnel managers in large companies with defense contracts.[10]

In its statement on civil liberties the UDA proclaimed the importance of protecting civil liberties, defended free speech on philosophical and functional grounds, and praised the federal government for its commit-ment to civil liberties. It pledged that as an organization it would "help maintain an atmosphere of vigorous political and economic democracy"— the necessary "climate of opinion" that best guaranteed civil liberties. At the same time, the UDA argued that "incidental liberties" could be re-stricted in "times of grave emergency." And it concluded on an ambiguous note: "In war time an efficiently functioning democracy will not allow or-ganized efforts to propagate ideas *harmful* to its cause. It *will* allow the free play of individual opinion." [11]

In its last statement, on "national morale," the UDA expressed its be-lief that a true national morale required that the "whole people, and labor in particular . . . be taken into the responsibility of government. . . . all citizens must be enrolled in behalf of the victory effort in every town and hamlet in America." This statement is important because it was based on the same conception of democracy and the common man that Henry Wallace would proclaim a few months later to the cheers of the UDA and its liberal supporters. The "most important," the UDA statement read, "is a vision of a new world to which plain people of all humanity can dedicate themselves unsparingly." [12]

These statements serve as a guide to UDA thinking. Ratified January 1942, they remained central to its core. It is little wonder that *The Nation* hailed the UDA as part of the democratic revolution and wrote that it promised "to be a mass organization 'left of center.'" It was, it wrote, "no disparagement of the Administration to point out the necessity of con-certed pressure from this direction." The journal saw the UDA functioning as "the democratic conscience of a country at war and the inspiration of the peace to come." But the UDA's conscience, like *The Nation*'s, separated the president from the State Department. The UDA "heartily commended Roosevelt's call for democratic unity," while condemning the State De-partment's consistent appeasement. [13]

While the liberal journals might be judged on how forcefully they con-tinued to set forth their reform agendas, the UDA, as an activist organiza-tion, was determined to mobilize behind these ideas. That this was how it conceived its role can be seen in 1942 when Loeb wrote Eduard Heimann that the entire executive board had rejected a proposal by board member John Childs to transform the UDA into a research organization and had reasserted the UDA's role as both a research and activist organization. A former teacher of romance languages at Townsend Harris High School in

New York, and described by a former UDA street speaker as a "long drink of water," Loeb, as the UDA executive secretary, worked assiduously to see that the UDA continued to play an activist role.[14]

But how activist was the UDA? In the area of civil liberties, it did criticize the government's trial of the Minneapolis Trotskyists. But such prominent UDA members as Niebuhr, Kirchwey, and Bliven supported the restriction of the fascist press, and Kirchwey and Bliven went further in including reactionary isolationist critics of the New Deal as among those abetting the fascist cause and thus as possibly subject to press curtailment. Although individual members of the UDA such as Niebuhr and Bingham joined with John Dewey, Norman Thomas, Oswald Garrison Villard, and a number of socialists and pacifists in a letter of protest to Roosevelt for the executive order interning Japanese Americans, as far as I have been able to determine, the UDA as an organization never addressed the issue. Its silence suggests far more acquiescence in, than disagreement with, the decision among the organization's members.[15]

In race relations, the UDA campaigned against the poll tax and for the desegregation of the armed forces, and on at least one occasion it helped the March on Washington Movement. But there is no indication that it urged A. Philip Randolph's March on Washington Movement to pursue a highly activist strategy during the war. Although it maintained friendly relations with Randolph, Walter White of the NAACP, and Lester Granger of the Urban League, none of the leading officers of the UDA were black. And the UDA did not engage in any significant grassroots organizing in the African-American community.[16]

On the issue of aliens, the UDA joined with other liberal groups in demanding a revised refugee policy, and it constantly urged the greater use of antifascist refugees in formulating political propaganda. On domestic issues the UDA held conferences on inflation and taxation; it helped publicize the Standard Oil–I.G. Farben connections and the business bottlenecks to full war production. It was quick to defend labor's rights and it constantly sought good relations with the labor movement. But like the labor movement itself, the UDA looked to Washington for enlightened leadership on economic policy and labor legislation. It was sometimes disappointed in Washington's positions on labor, but it never threw its support toward labor militancy during the war. And it never mobilized a total organizational effort behind any economic policy until the Full Employment campaign of 1945.[17]

In foreign affairs, the UDA contributed to the continued critique of the State Department. It protested what it believed was the State Department's semi-recognition of Tibor Eckhardt's Free Hungary Movement. Eckhardt, the prewar leader of the Independent Party of Small Farmers of Hungary, was viewed by Niebuhr as a spokesperson for the reactionary groups in Hungary who wished to retain power if Hitler lost the war; as such, if the State Department recognized his Free Hungary Movement, it would be an affront to real democrats in Hungary. In addition, many prominent UDA members signed letters to Roosevelt urging a diplomatic break with the Vichy government. Most of this kind of activity consisted of "open letters" and press releases. It brought publicity to the UDA and constituted a form of pressure on the administration, but it did not fulfill the UDA's self-image as an activist organization.[18]

Dissatisfied with the UDA's role as mere conscience or inspiration, its leaders attempted to make it a more activist organization. For example, the UDA played a leading role in the anti–State Department campaign that resulted in the publication of Robert Bendiner's *The Riddle of the State Department.* The opening of an office in Washington and the appointment of ex-Congressman Tom Amlie as the UDA director there was also part of the effort to make the UDA more politically effective. It was believed that Amlie, with his Washington contacts, would help the UDA gain influence in Washington, and one consequence of this would be a redirection of State Department policy. Amlie's "Win-the-War" supplement for *The New Republic,* a joint UDA–*New Republic* project, was designed particularly to defeat members of Congress who had a long isolationist, pro-appeasement record.

When the Dies committee struck back at the UDA with charges of Communist leanings, the UDA joined with *The Nation* to expose the sleazy operations of the committee. Although the Dies committee's attack scared off contributors, which eventually led to the closing of the Washington office, in the short run it gave the UDA political publicity. In statements demanding an appearance before the Dies committee and clarifying its own activities (including its attitude toward the Communist Party), the UDA linked the Dies committee with isolationism and fascist sympathies, thus contributing to political efforts to dislodge the appeasers of fascism from elected office and government posts.[19]

Yet to a great extent the UDA's anti-appeasement campaign against the State Department and Congress was largely one of press releases and luncheons where small groups of liberals listened to speakers like Max Lerner or Louis Fischer. Amlie provided useful campaign literature for congressional candidates, and, in a few instances, his efforts may have helped secure a victory. But his Washington office neither brought the UDA into the inner circle of policy makers nor became the basis for the creation of a powerful pressure group.

Efforts continued to be made to expand the organization. Amlie and the field director for the UDA, Howard Y. Williams, visited the UDA branches and potential areas for new branches. Efforts to expand nationally would meet with some success the following year. In 1943 branches were organized in St. Louis, Los Angeles, Portland, and Seattle. But internal problems and political setbacks kept occurring. The publication of one UDA pamphlet was delayed as the contributing writers wrangled over issues and wording. Pledges and contributions dried up after the Dies committee attacks, and the 1942 elections turned out to be a debacle as the Republicans gained nine senate seats and forty-four congressional seats. The leading senate progressive, George Norris of Nebraska, was defeated for reelection.[20]

Following the elections, the UDA helped organize a dinner for Senator Norris. Kirchwey used the occasion not only to honor the defeated liberal but to announce the creation of a new Washington-based political organization headed by Norris. The elections had been the country's "political Dunkirk—a shock which will rekindle the fighting faith of the progressive forces." And no one was better suited to lead these forces than Norris. Predicting the victory of the progressive forces if they were roused "to fight together and to fight hard," Kirchwey summoned Norris "to lead us in the greatest battle of his career."[21]

The idea of involving Norris may have been germinating in Kirchwey's mind before the elections, but the outcome forced liberal intellectuals, already well aware of the precarious status of the international war, to recognize that they were losing the domestic war. Liberal rhetoric became more dramatic after the Democratic congressional losses, and labor people were scared. Attending a Congress of Industrial Organizations (CIO) convention in Boston in late November, James Loeb found labor leaders clamoring for political action.[22]

After discussions in Boston with such labor leaders as John Brophy and Walter Reuther, Loeb helped the UDA initiate a liberal-labor conference in Pittsburgh on December 13 in order to prepare for the 1944 elections. At the conference, participants from the UDA, CIO, National Farmers Union, and Free World Association reported glumly on the political prospects in their states. Strategy and tactics were discussed, with the vast majority arguing for the need to work within the progressive wing of the Democratic Party. Throughout the discussions, a sense of urgency prevailed. Given the need to register in 1943 to vote the following year, it was believed that the next ten months might determine the "political fate of the country." [23]

Following the Pittsburgh conference, Loeb, Kirchwey, Bliven, and other UDA members attempted to involve Norris in the political work decided on at the conference. They believed that a national labor-farmer-liberal organization (labeled the Norris Committee) would "completely change the political trends in America." The early weeks of 1943 were devoted to attempting to win labor support for the Norris Committee. The American Federation of Labor (AFL) rejected the idea, the CIO dragged its feet, and ultimately Philip Murray rejected the plan. The UDA dropped the idea of the Norris Committee for fear of "widening differences" within the labor movement. In early February, the CIO, the AFL, the Railroad Brotherhoods, and the National Farmers Union announced an agreement "to come together on legislative matters." In announcing the agreement to UDA board members, Loeb indicated that this eliminated "all relationships with the UDA or with independent liberals." The UDA was left with the "slight satisfaction of having been the catalytic agent which accomplished this much." According to Loeb, the arrangement could be a "real step in advance" if it was implemented well; meanwhile the UDA hoped it would lead to "a more concrete and all inclusive arrangement." [24]

As far as labor was concerned, the agreement did lead to a more concrete development: the creation of the CIO-Political Action Committee (CIO-PAC) by Sidney Hillman in the summer of 1943. Not the combined liberal-labor committee the UDA had originally envisaged, it nevertheless was an important development in terms of increasing labor political activity and creating a labor program for the 1944 election. *The Nation* and *The New Republic* ran favorable articles on most of the CIO-PAC's activities and defended it against its critics. Loeb wrote positively of the CIO-PAC's organizing endeavors in the summer of 1943. The CIO-PAC was to play a vital role in the 1944 election, but in 1943 the UDA was well aware that it fell short of the UDA's goal of involving more independents and liberals in political action. Looking back at the year's activity at the end of 1943, the UDA could claim that its work in attempting to generate political activity "inspired more healthy political discussion than any other event of the past year," but the breakdown in developing a national political organization was an immense disappointment to Loeb. [25]

Although the efforts to develop a national political organization and domestic issues—such as defending the forty-hour week and modifying the Little Steel Formula—engaged the UDA's attention in 1943, foreign policy remained predominant. The delayed pamphlet on foreign policy, written by Eduard Heimann, was finally published. Meetings were held and statements released condemning the Hapsburg Foreign Legion's becoming part of the American army, the Peyrouton appointment in North Africa, and the recognition of the Badoglio government in Italy.[26]

A political organization of liberals that *would* play an important role in the reelection of Roosevelt was created in 1944. With Sidney Hillman again serving as the driving force, the CIO-PAC organized the NC-PAC. The UDA, which had originally proposed the founding of a new organization connected with labor but appealing to liberals and independents, was well represented in the NC-PAC. Loeb and Kirchwey served on the national executive board of the NC-PAC, and Bliven, Lerner, Niebuhr, and Mortimer Hays were all members. Bliven, Kirchwey, and Lerner later became vice chairs. Even before the creation of the NC-PAC, the UDA was preparing to play an important role in the election. In early spring, the UDA and *The New Republic* prepared another special supplement on the congressional record, and Amlie was again brought in to work on the congressional voting data. But the main generator of liberal involvement was the newly created NC-PAC.[27]

Just as the efforts geared to the fall election were getting under way, the question of Wallace's renomination as vice president arose. As chair of the UDA, Niebuhr wrote to Roosevelt expressing confidence that the majority of Americans wanted to keep the president and the vice president in office. Linking Roosevelt and Wallace as protectors "of the rights" and of the average American citizen, Niebuhr called on Roosevelt to make "an unequivocal declaration" of his support for Wallace. The unequivocal declaration, of course, never came. The UDA liberals shared with the entire liberal intellectual community a sense of betrayal. Writing to Claire Sifton, the wife of the editor of the UDA *Newsletter* and part of the UDA Washington office, Loeb expressed the sense of being betrayed and abandoned:

> Are you and Paul as discouraged as I feel today? I think the President has let us down badly once more. Having no place else to go at the moment politically, we are quite helpless but certainly we shall not forget this retreat when we plan our post-election strategy. If Wallace wins now, it will be a great triumph but the chances are certainly against him. Last night I kept thinking of all the good New Dealers and liberals who might be brought together to

create something of a movement in this country if they could be fired with any real independent enthusiasm: Wallace, Willkie, Milo Perkins, Henderson, etc. etc. You and Paul and Pat Jackson know most of these people well. I would very much appreciate your opinion. Is there any chance that after this election these people will declare their independence and throw themselves into some movement? I am not speaking in any institutional terms, because it does not have to be the UDA. But we cannot keep on retreating and retreating and retreating without at least a little guerilla action behind the enemy's lines.[28]

Even before the Wallace debacle, there were signs that Loeb and the UDA leaders were not pleased with Roosevelt's political direction. In February 1944 Loeb and Niebuhr had made a gesture to political independence in separate letters to *The New Republic*. Loeb wrote that it was unclear whether Roosevelt would run as the "fighting progressive" of 1936 or the 1943 "defender of Jesse Jones and Cordell Hull against Henry Wallace and Sumner Welles." He advised "independent liberals" to "wait until the alternatives present themselves before announcing their final choice."[29] Niebuhr's letter declared that the South's revolt against the New Deal had "well-nigh destroyed the usefulness of the Democratic administration as an instrument of progressive politics." In retrospect, the southern Democratic-Republican alliance demonstrated Roosevelt's earlier achievements in making the divided Democratic Party "a genuine instrument of liberalism"; but now Roosevelt's strategy for achieving this was "played out," and a reelected Roosevelt would most likely produce "a very tired and ambiguous New Deal" in his fourth term with the certainty of "a period of terrible reaction in '48." Despite "apprehensions" over Roosevelt, Niebuhr saw the need to support the Democrats if the Republicans nominated an isolationist and a domestic reactionary. He ended, as had Loeb, by advising progressives to concentrate on the congressional elections.[30]

Although these two letters suggest a degree of political independence on the part of the leaders of the UDA, it is important to recognize that both were written from the point of view that politics, as Loeb put it, was "a science of alternatives." As long as one ruled out third-party alternatives, as both did, then one was left with a situation that, given the nature of the Republican Party, inevitably pointed toward Roosevelt. This was clear by July 1944 when Loeb, in "A Letter to Wendell Willkie," wrote that the isolationist forces and the domestic reactionaries within the Republican Party had produced a situation where "the present administration offers the best hope for America in the next fateful years."[31]

Even if Loeb was not happy with Roosevelt after the dropping of Wallace, he had nevertheless concluded that the immediate fate of progressivism depended on Roosevelt. Writing in mid-August on the fall elections prospects, Loeb wrote: "Let the liberal optimist read the Republican platform carefully, analyze the forces behind the Dewey-Bricker ticket, and then imagine for one black moment what American progressives would face if Franklin D. Roosevelt were out of the picture!" In the long run, Loeb saw promising signs in the fight that liberals and labor made for Wallace at the Chicago convention. They had come together and would be organizing together "for 1944 and after."[32]

Loeb's letter to Claire Sifton had raised the possibility of new political departures after the election. But the proposal to explore postelection alternatives lacked any sharp edge; it is unclear whether Loeb had in mind real independent political action or—as was more likely, given the UDA's history—a more effective liberal pressure group on the Democratic Party. The same lack of any serious consideration of third-party possibilities characterized other verbal gestures of political independence. In July 1943 *The Nation* criticized a regional CIO conference led by Hillman for its "ill timed" rejection of "the idea of a third party"; Kirchwey recognized that this committed the labor unions to Roosevelt a year in advance and thus strengthened the administration's existing practice of conciliating "the reactionary wing" of the Democratic Party. But if Freda Kirchwey had been serious about third-party possibilities in 1943, she would have had to have begun calling for and organizing for one. Despite her criticisms of Roosevelt, she was not prepared to do this.

The same was true of Lerner. In July 1943 Lerner criticized Philip Murray for combining the creation of the CIO-PAC with an announcement that he opposed a third party in 1944. Although Lerner believed that the major effort for the next few years would be the fight within the Democratic Party to make it a truly progressive party, he said that labor could not be "firm while shutting the door against alternative political choice. In political life not to have an 'or else' is to be powerless." With Willkie's defeat in the Republican primary in Wisconsin, all debate and ambiguities were over for Lerner and the *PM* editors. Simply put: "Roosevelt Must Run Again." What Lerner and the other editors failed to say in this endorsement of Roosevelt was that they had eliminated the "or else," which Lerner had previously said was so important for labor. Without any "or else" coming from the liberal community, it was all the easier for Roosevelt to drop Wallace three months later.[33]

As it was, the UDA's political attention in the fall of 1944 was on the reelection of the very person who had apparently betrayed Wallace and the liberal cause. In working to assure Roosevelt's victory in 1944, the UDA worked closely with NC-PAC.[34] However, if the UDA and the liberal intellectuals had known more about Hillman's equivocal role in Roosevelt's dropping of Wallace, they might have had greater doubts about his PACs. They already had reservations but again no immediate alternative. Even before the election, there were indications that UDA-oriented liberals were not entirely happy with the overall direction of the NC-PAC. In July, following a meeting with Hillman, Loeb expressed concern to Morris Cooke over Cooke's hesitation about joining the executive committee of the NC-PAC. Loeb indicated that there was a need for people with an "independent position" like Cooke to participate. He said that he, Kirchwey, James McGill, and James Patton all believed in the necessity of the executive committee having independence in policy making. Apparently Loeb was concerned about Hillman and the CIO unions dominating all policy decisions.[35]

Following the election, Loeb sent a letter to Philip Murray and Sidney Hillman in which he indicated that he, Kirchwey, and J. King Gordon of *The Nation;* Bliven and George Soule of *The New Republic;* and Max Lerner and John Lewis of *PM* had held a lengthy discussion on the steps progressives needed to take to "strengthen the liberal forces of the country for the crucial political and legislative fights ahead." He indicated that all three publications were prepared to support his position. Loeb's letter paid high tribute to the CIO-PAC's work in the election campaign. The CIO-PAC, he claimed, was probably the difference "between victory and defeat," and it was "a significant milestone in the history of the American labor movement." However, Loeb went on, he and his associates believed that more was required to broaden the base of liberal support. They called for the creation of "national progressive federations" organized "on the broadest scale possible." Moreover, the task following the election was no longer a "campaign job" but a long-range effort necessitating careful programmatic planning. With a backhanded swipe at Hillman's fait accompli creation of the NC-PAC, Loeb wrote: "We believe that every effort should be made to include every possible progressive group and individual, and that the most important of these groups and individuals should be approached before, not after, the federation is established." Loeb ended by calling for a "small, off-the-record conference" of these most important persons.[36]

In a letter written the following day to Eleanor Roosevelt, Loeb requested a meeting for his group with her and Wallace to discuss questions raised in the letter to Murray and Hillman: it was the most "opportune moment . . . for the organization of progressive opinion in this country." While the president's triumph was a result of his personal prestige and "the magnificent job which labor and non-labor forces accomplished," future legislative and political battles needed "more organization and strength" than before; thus it was necessary to bring "all the forces together." Hillman, however, at a meeting the previous night, had said: "We have found the formula and let's keep it." Hillman believed that "NC-PAC should continue as part of the whole PAC operation." Loeb disagreed.[37]

Kirchwey and Bliven lent their editorial support to the position outlined in Loeb's letters. Although they praised the efforts of the CIO-PAC and NC-PAC in the past election, both believed there were inherent limitations to a labor-controlled organization's appeal to liberals and independents. Both favored continuing strong ties with the labor movement, but both believed that a national progressive federation would hold out greater promise for the long-range struggles facing progressives. In a postelection analysis, Loeb expressed his belief that "non-labor progressives" needed to develop their own leadership and program in order to reverse the foreign policy and domestic retreat of the New Deal.[38]

Early in 1945, Loeb, along with James Patton of the National Farmers' Union, made an extended effort to articulate a strategy for progressives. In doing so, they revealed just how much of an independent course Loeb was prepared to consider. Published in *The New Republic*, "The Challenge to Progressives" was based on the assumption that progressives were entering the "post-Roosevelt era." Up to 1944, progressives had had the magic name of Roosevelt on the ballot every four years. In the next four years, they said, Roosevelt could contribute to progressivism, but much of his ability would depend on the "wisdom" of the progressives' strategy and the "organizational vigor" with which they supported the strategy.[39]

Loeb and Patton believed that progressives had begun to come together in the 1944 electoral campaign for Roosevelt. But now they wanted to know, "where do we go from here?" What Loeb and Patton proposed was to chart a "flexible" course. There was a need to develop an inspiring program that would address "the magnitude of the foreign and domestic problems." This required "something fundamental, sweeping and bold." They cited as an example the "full employment bill" proposed by the National

Farmers' Union in the summer of 1944. While the bill would not solve all the economic and social problems facing the country, it illustrated the "bold planning" that progressivism required.[40]

The next task was to develop a political strategy for implementing a bold progressive program, a task that required an understanding of the liberal relationship with the New Deal. During its first stage, from 1933 to 1937, the New Deal had addressed the depression with "great imagination and social vision." Because the alternatives to the New Deal were "impossible," liberals had not believed that it was "essential to form any cohesive, organized political force to continue the New Deal." During this period, liberals entered government, and labor made great advances; the "natural" result was that progressives came to "feel a complete dependence on Mr. Roosevelt and his administration, even to the extent at times of losing their own political independence." But 1937 marked a dividing line. In that year Roosevelt, understanding the forces that threatened war, had shifted to policies encouraging national unity: the "quarantine the aggressors" of 1937 was accompanied by a drive to balance the budget and the "plague-on-both-your houses" statement during the Little Steel strike. By 1940 Roosevelt had brought the Republicans Henry Stimson and Frank Knox into the cabinet. Loeb and Patton did not say that Roosevelt was wrong to have changed the direction of the New Deal, but they did believe that the conservative opposition was not content with the concessions and would continue to demand more.[41]

Thus during the war, "political retrogression" had taken place on the part of the New Deal, and the progressives "were at no time able to assert their independence" in the face of this retrogression. This inability derived not only from the absence of any "feasible political alternative" but also from the progressives' own stake in the war against fascism. Like Roosevelt in his struggle against isolationism, they were forced "to seek and accept allies who had little or nothing in common with a democratic domestic program."[42]

With the war almost over and postwar plans being developed, Roosevelt, Loeb and Patton said, faced two alternatives: he could either fight for a progressive agenda based on planning and full employment; or, he could continue his wartime policy of concessions to the Right. It was likely he would do a little of both. In either case, the course for liberals was clear: "Progressives . . . [must] make their own decision, and that decision must be for the first of the two alternatives, namely a fight for an overall progressive program, both in foreign and domestic policy. In other words, the progressives must make a liberal declaration of independence." Loeb and Patton quickly declared that independence did not mean opposition to Roosevelt. Labor and liberals should give him their support in fights against the "reactionary opposition." But if he "continued concessions to the Right," progressives needed to form a "responsible and constructive" opposition that would force Roosevelt "to appease progressivism" instead of "reaction."[43]

Assuring the readers that their declaration of independence was not "made in the spirit of 'infantile leftism' or sectarianism or a reversion to purism," Loeb and Patton argued that it was based on the difference between wartime, where conservative governments could successfully conduct wars, and the postwar world, where future peace depended on avoiding "mass unemployment and economic chaos." In this context, if the "price" of congressional passage of legislation creating a world organization was Roosevelt's acceptance of the economic philosophy of Jesse Jones and Will Clayton, then "American progressives must be prepared to insist the price is too high."[44]

In analyzing the composition of progressivism, Loeb and Patton spotlighted the "great mass" of "have-not" farmers, labor, the independent middle-class, and the returning men and women veterans. As a result of the depression, the New Deal had brought together labor, farmers, and the middle class "without any cohesive organization at all." What was needed now was to bring these groups and the organizations they had developed (National Farmers' Union, CIO-PAC, independent and non-partisan committees from the last election) into some kind of cohesive organizational pattern. Reforming the Democratic Party would be difficult, but Loeb and Patton saw promise in the unsuccessful fight for Wallace at the Chicago convention. In any case, the only way for the Democrats to win without Roosevelt was "to become unmistakably the party of progress."[45]

According to Loeb and Patton, this was the next fight for progressives: to make the Democratic Party a progressive "instrument." To do so required great effort by all the progressive groups at all levels and in all regions, including bringing every national, regional, state, and local organization into a national progressive federation. Here, then, was "the challenge to progressives." Failure would mean "division, depression and another war"; success would mean "a peoples' peace in the USA and throughout the world." "Within and among peoples' groups," Loeb and Patton concluded, "modern man must cooperate or die."[46]

All this was heady stuff for the UDA: talk of a liberal declaration of independence, the threat of possible opposition to Roosevelt, and the dramatic victory-or-death ending. But given the past history of the UDA, what did its director's declaration of independence really mean? Certainly, Loeb — and especially Patton, whose organization had shown more independent gestures in its history — should be taken seriously. Even though they were not prepared to break politically with Roosevelt after the dumping of Wallace, there is no reason to doubt that by 1945 they had become frustrated by Roosevelt's compromises with reaction and that they believed that further compromises in the postwar period would be economically and politically disastrous. But several things suggest that the militancy of their challenge did not mean they were truly prepared to move out of the New Deal orbit.

First, there was the statement that Roosevelt had not necessarily been wrong in adopting the policy of wartime concessions to the Right. If he was not wrong, then what did the UDA's criticisms of his concessions to the Right mean? And if he was wrong, why not say it here, at the very moment when they were laying the foundations for a greater independent course — unless one did not want to burn all the bridges?

Second, there are the assurances that opposition to Roosevelt was only a potential future course. More important, by automatically rejecting a third-party alternative and opting for reforming the Democratic Party, Loeb and Patton had cut themselves off from any real threat to desert the New Deal in the foreseeable future. But most important, as far as the UDA was concerned, was the fact that its orientation and activities did not significantly change in 1945. There was no renewed effort to make it into a grassroots organization or to look at tactics that went beyond lobbying. In short, the call on the part of Loeb, Patton, Kirchwey, and Bliven for a national progressive federation was a call for a more effective pressure group organization rather than an organization truly independent of the Roosevelt administration.

This is clear if we look at the essence of the debate over the NC-PAC. In 1944 the issue was essentially whether the NC-PAC would have a broader appeal if it were more organizationally independent of the CIO-PAC. By 1945 the issue of foreign policy toward the Soviet Union and whether liberals should be part of a united front with Communists began to enter more directly into the discussion of the NC-PAC. These issues were heightened in 1946 when Wallace challenged Truman's foreign policy. As the arguments over Wallace, the Soviet Union, and Communists continued, the hopes of broadening the NC-PAC lessened. Its final death would be part of the birth of cold war divisions among liberals. What is interesting, however, is that despite ostensible differences over the nature of the NC-PAC, neither Hillman and his allies nor Loeb and his allies ever conceived of it as a truly grassroots mass organization. Hillman did use it as a vehicle to mobilize the labor and liberal vote, but he and his temporary allies at the time—the Communist Party–oriented unions and the American Labor Party in New York—were content to use it mainly as a vehicle to gain power and influence in the top Democratic Party councils. Loeb and his UDA allies, including the newly formed Liberal Party in New York, spoke of broadening the NC-PAC, but they saw broadening essentially in terms of attracting key influentials—those with entreé into the same Democratic Party councils. Both sides in 1944–45 were equally committed to Roosevelt, Wallace, and similar domestic programs.

At best, in their imaginative mobilizing of voters in 1944 the CIO-PAC and the NC-PAC appeared to resemble a mass movement with deep roots in the community. But Joseph Gaer, whose *The First Round* described the CIO-PAC's program and role in 1944, was wrong when he said that the heart of the CIO-PAC was in Kalamazoo and not in Hillman's and Murray's national offices. The CIO-PAC was a creature of Hillman; its program was developed by his advisers, and its politics reflected those of Hillman and his allies. Analogously, the UDA demonstrated in 1945 that it had the ability to organize a major political effort behind the Murray Full Employment Bill. But it was an effort that depended largely on organizing pressure groups and influential spokespersons to publicly endorse and lobby for the bill. The UDA did this systematically and energetically, but it was never— despite all the congressional testimonies, lobbying, and public releases— able to transform the campaign into a grassroots mass movement.[47]

The year 1945 did witness new efforts on the part of the UDA to expand its role. The highly successful testimonial dinner for Wallace at the beginning of the year brought in the funds to expand its activities. Following this dinner, the UDA organized the Fight for Wallace and Full Employment Rally at New York's Town Hall. At the same time, the UDA decided to move its national headquarters to Washington, partly, as Loeb explained, to be closer to the center of policy making and partly to escape New York's internecine political wars. Less than two months after this flurry of UDA activity, the Senate defeated the nomination of liberal-supported Aubrey Williams to be director of Rural Electrification, and in April the liberal community received the news of Roosevelt's death.[48]

In the early stages of the war the UDA had focused on foreign policy. With the formation of the CIO-PAC in 1943 and NC-PAC in 1944 and with the Allied invasion of Europe signaling eventual victory, attention shifted to domestic political developments and the transformation from a war to a peace economy. By 1945, with the outcome of the war no longer in doubt, the UDA was ready to turn its attention to the major economic goal of the liberal intellectual community: full employment. But 1945 was also a year in which major foreign policy issues confronted the community. The UDA generally supported the Yalta agreements, without endorsing all the specifics. It campaigned hard for congressional approval of the Bretton Woods agreement and fully endorsed Dumbarton Oaks. In the emerging liberal differences over U.S. foreign policy toward the Soviet Union, the UDA sought a middle ground; it refused to apologize for Soviet intransigence and failure to live up to the Yalta agreements, but, at the same time, it urged a cooperative attitude to achieve friendlier U.S.-Soviet relations. As these relations began to deteriorate the UDA found it harder to hold to the middle ground, but late in 1945 it was still urging a general peace conference to attempt to reach mutual accords. And it combined criticism of the Soviet policy of excluding the West from the Polish peace terms with criticism of the United States for excluding the Soviet Union from the Japanese peace agreements.[49]

Despite its renewed attention to foreign policy, the major UDA political effort in 1945 was the effort to pass the Murray Full Employment Bill. A letter from UDA member Howard Y. Williams to his wife gives a sense of the organization's focus on the bill. Describing a talk by Loeb, Williams said that the postwar fight against fascism had to be fought "on the economic level." He was afraid that people would choose "security" over "freedom" ("you cannot eat freedom") if these were the only two choices. "That is one reason why the UDA is putting so much stress now on the Full Employment Act of 1945. If we can pass this Murray Bill it will mean everything for America and the world."[50]

The UDA's political campaign for the Murray Bill in Washington was largely in the hands of Paul Sifton, the editor of the *Newsletter* and director of its Washington branch. Sifton, whose flamboyant and populist-style rhetoric would eventually lead to irreconcilable differences with Loeb, enthusiastically devoted himself to the full employment campaign. He bombarded Loeb with almost daily accounts of developments—warnings of compromises that would destroy the heart of the legislation; suggestions for contacts and speakers; and reports of meetings with Murray, Robert Wagner, Representative George Outland, and other key legislators. Eager to use the campaign for the bill to strengthen the UDA, Loeb in turn sought Sifton's aid in attaining influential politicians, including President Truman, to speak on the full employment campaign at UDA functions.[51]

The failure to pass the original Full Employment Bill in 1945 was followed by a renewed effort in late 1945 and 1946. Although Truman was willing to compromise on some of the original provisions, and although the UDA was not happy with all of the compromises, there was enough left in the bill, according to Sifton and Loeb, to merit support. As the fight continued into 1946, Truman's efforts on behalf of the bill impressed the UDA enough to enable it to believe that he was carrying on the legacy of the New Deal. There were moments in 1945–46 when the UDA criticized Truman's foreign policy, for example, U.S. engagement in the Chinese civil war and the postwar policy of the American Military Government in Germany. But the UDA clearly did not see the dissolution of the U.S.-Soviet wartime cooperation as resulting from Truman's foreign policy, and it began to urge the liberal community to support a policy more critical of the Soviet Union. In late 1945, the UDA still viewed the emerging conflict between the Soviet Union and the West in terms of "mistrust." In mid-1946, it urged "mutual agreements" with the Soviet Union, and although it rejected those who saw Russia as the center of "virtue," it opposed those who hated and feared the Soviet Union so much that they supported "every policy which widens the gulf between Russia and the West." But the UDA labeled the Soviet policy in the East "imperialist" and contrasted the realism of its position on the Soviet Union with the "romantic liberalism" of too many American liberals.[52]

The falling out of wartime liberal allies will receive more attention later in this study. Here, it is only necessary to indicate that in 1946 the Win-the-Peace Conference, the Wallace Madison Square Garden speech, developments in Eastern Europe, and the issue of any united front with Communists began to rip the liberal intellectual community apart. Kirchwey, Bliven, and Lerner, all of whom in 1944 had supported Loeb's efforts to broaden the NC-PAC and to make it more independent of the CIO-PAC and from any Communist Party members of the NC-PAC, now felt Loeb and the UDA had become too hostile to the Soviet Union and any united front efforts. Loeb, in turn, felt his previous erstwhile allies had, in their attitude toward the Soviet Union, surrendered many of their liberal principles. By the middle of 1946 Loeb was already envisaging a new liberal organization—an organization more clearly disassociated from any lingering popular frontism. By the end of 1946 plans for the new organization were being developed; and in January 1947 the Americans for Democratic Action (ADA) was founded.

Like the UDA it was organized with wide support from the labor movement and from liberal intellectuals. The ADA, however, had prominent New Dealers as members: Eleanor Roosevelt, Leon Henderson, and Wilson Wyatt. Like the UDA, the ADA was officially created at a conference; but whereas the UDA had initially at least had a quasi-grassroots element, the ADA was solely the product of a conference of influentials. The evolution of the UDA—with its shunning of third-party initiatives; its wartime fealty to Roosevelt, despite his State Department, his domestic surrenders of liberalism, and his betrayal of Wallace; its efforts to attract support from influential figures, whether they be Henry Wallace or Eleanor Roosevelt— inevitably pointed in the direction of trying to obtain for the liberal intellectual community the insider role in politics. Loeb, Niebuhr, and the other founders may have envisaged a creative role for independent liberalism, and in "The Challenge to Progressives," Loeb may have considered the need for a more independent liberalism, but the UDA was never independent. It was always tied, by emotion and by analyses developed through the lens of the liberal interpretation of the war, to the Roosevelt administration. Writing to Loeb that the liberals were "blindly hitched to the FDR symbol" and that the UDA was "too full of big names and not active common people," a young UDA organizer, Bill Dodds, tried to raise the issues of the liberals' connection with Roosevelt and the UDA's absence of "grassroots power." Loeb's reply was cursory; he advised Dodds to read Koestler's *The Commissar and the Yogi*.[53]

From Loeb and the UDA in the Roosevelt war years to Arthur Schlesinger Jr. and the ADA in the Kennedy years, there is a direct line that perceived effective liberal action as deriving from a closeness to the seats of power. It was not a temptation unknown to other liberals during the war. *The Nation* and *The New Republic* cultivated Wallace, and Bingham drew on his friendship with Chester Bowles to try to give *Common Sense* a larger voice in Washington. It was a trend that can be traced back historically to *The New Republic* intellectuals' circling, in Charles Forcey's metaphor, like moths around the fire of Theodore Roosevelt and later Woodrow Wilson. In the thirties some liberals were drawn to the fire of Franklin Roosevelt; others were more or equally attracted to that generated by Stalin. In the war years, the UDA and the liberal intellectual community in general circled around the flame of FDR and Wallace, criticizing the

State Department here, chastising FDR's betrayal of Wallace there. But never could they remove themselves from the glow of the fire; never could they consistently envisage a break.[54]

One prominent UDA member and activist who shared some of the UDA thinking on attracting key influentials did, however, slowly come to at least a hazy recognition of the problem. While James Loeb went from being the national director of the UDA to being the national director of the ADA, and then ambassador to Peru, Tom Amlie went from the UDA to a variety of unsatisfactory jobs and ended his career scraping out a meager living with little or no political influence. It is to Amlie's failed career and the insights it afforded him that we now turn.

7

Tom Amlie

THE POLITICAL activity of Tom Amlie during the war illustrates how hard it was for a left liberal to function effectively in those years. Photographs of the portly Amlie make him look as if he would have been comfortable in the environment of Sinclair Lewis's Zenith City. Instead, his entire career made the Babbitts of his state of Wisconsin uncomfortable. A lawyer, elected public official, political activist, and intellectual, Amlie had first won prominence as one of the left congressmen elected in the early 1930s. He had intellectual ties to Alfred Bingham, who in the early 1930s developed a non-Marxian radical critique of capitalism and endeavored to achieve a democratic socialist state through the creation of a national farmer-labor party. In 1924 he had been the district chairman of Robert LaFollette's presidential campaign, and he was first elected to Congress in 1931 as a progressive Republican but was defeated a year later. In 1934 he won reelection to Congress on the new Progressive Party ticket in Wisconsin. At the same time, he served as chairman of two thirties organizations designed to begin a new third-party movement—the Farmer Labor Political Federation and the New American Commonwealth Federation—which Bingham had helped to found. Thus Amlie was comfortable with third-party politics and found himself sympathetic to Bingham's farmer-labor style radicalism. In turn, Bingham saw Amlie as one of the most promising young politicians on the national scene.[1]

In speeches and writings in the early thirties, Amlie condemned an outmoded capitalist system, criticized Roosevelt's New Deal as a vain attempt to save capitalism, and called for a system based on production for use. His 1933 address to the Chicago convention of the United Conference for Progressive Action on the "collapse of capitalism" was possibly the most radical speech delivered by a U.S. congressman. In a nationally broadcast speech in August 1935 he described the New Deal as "charity capitalism." Such speeches and his third-party efforts gained Amlie a reputation as a courageous and outspoken political leader in liberal and left circles and as a dangerous radical among conservatives and traditional politicians. Like Bingham and other liberal-left critics of the New Deal, Amlie found himself supporting the New Deal in 1936 after the attempt to build a national farmer-labor party had failed. In the post-1936 period he associated himself with the thinking of Mordecai Ezekiel and other advocates of a government-induced full employment policy.[2]

In 1937 and 1938 Amlie was a co-sponsor of the Industrial Expansion Bill, which called for a planned economy to achieve full employment. Defeated in 1938 in the Progressive Party senatorial primary, Amlie was nominated by Roosevelt to serve on the Interstate Commerce Commission (ICC). Several New Deal friends encouraged him to accept the nomination, and despite concerns about the prospects of securing congressional approval, Amlie allowed his name to be presented. It soon became clear that Amlie's reputation as a radical or at least as a militant liberal made his confirmation doubtful. Rather than place Roosevelt in a position of either suffering a political rebuff or having to ask Amlie to step aside, Amlie withdrew his name.[3]

By this time Amlie, unlike many of his Progressive Party associates, was fully supportive of the New Deal. Although he had more reservations about Roosevelt himself than most liberal intellectuals, he tended to blame conservative opponents rather than Roosevelt for the failure to follow a consistent full employment policy. As the debates over foreign policy mounted, Amlie endorsed collective security and criticized isolationism. His brother Hans had been a commander in the Abraham Lincoln Brigade, and the Spanish Civil War emphasized for Amlie the need to check fascism. When war broke out in the fall of 1939 and the debate over foreign policy within liberal circles intensified, Amlie's ties with the LaFollettes were severed. He led the internationalist faction within the Progressive Party, which tried to unite with the Democrats.[4]

Despite his outspoken support of and work for the New Deal, Amlie received scant reward. He was appointed special assistant U.S. attorney to work on some land cases in Wisconsin, but his radical past apparently made any prominent position an impossibility. In 1941 he resigned from the Justice Department in order to enter a special congressional race in Wisconsin to fill a seat whose incumbent had died. Despite knowing that his prospects for victory were dim because of the traditional Republican majority and the split among the Progressives, Amlie felt it important to carry the New Deal banner. He also preferred the active political role of congressman. When he was indeed defeated, Amlie—needing an income for his large family—applied for his former job with the land commission. He was told by Thurman Arnold, who was in charge of the division within the Justice Department, that he wanted to rehire him but that Attorney General Francis Biddle believed that Amlie's run for Congress appeared to have violated the Hatch Act. Once more the visibility of Amlie's political activity had closed a door to an administrative appointment.[5]

Biddle's rejection of Amlie initiated a pattern that continued throughout the war and into the postwar years. Amlie and his friends wrote letters to New Deal officials and Roosevelt advisers requesting that Amlie be considered for some kind of position in the New Deal. Later the requests were repeated in the Truman administration. But nothing, not even a minor position, was forthcoming. Word repeatedly reached Amlie through his friends that he politically was still too hot and too controversial. The fact that the friends pushing for him were such liberals as Aubrey Williams, Howard Y. Williams, and later Howard McMurray probably did little to allay any cautious administrator's concerns about Amlie's politics.[6]

Throughout his troubles in finding steady work in and out of the New Deal, Amlie made a distinction between the New Dealers and the "administration men": the New Dealers were the committed liberals who had a social vision; the administration men were the traditional politicians and political appointees who had no genuine interest in social reform. Like most liberal intellectuals, Amlie associated Roosevelt with the New Dealers, but he also believed that he was surrounded by administration men, who, along with the dollar-a-year businessmen, prevented the necessary social change. In this sense, Amlie believed Roosevelt's desire for national unity stood in the way. "The Honest-to-God New Dealers" needed organization, but Roosevelt had failed to take the lead. Like most liberal intellectuals, Amlie also criticized the State Department and held it largely responsible for the lack of a consistent antifascist foreign policy.

As the domestic conservative trend grew and as his own prospects for governmental employment dimmed, Amlie grew increasingly embittered. By the end of the war he had come to view many of the New Dealers themselves as careerists who were more interested in their own jobs than in the cause of social reform. Looking back in 1945, he viewed the congressional elections of 1938 as the end of the New Dealers—"the honest and courageous people." After that "the young punks from the University of Wisconsin" whose formula for success was "going along" had flocked to Washington. Years later, an even more bitter Amlie would write his old friend Aubrey Williams about the post-1938 "smart operators." They considered themselves as liberal as Williams but "smart enough to survive." They were what their mutual friend Norman Kuehne called "shit birds." [7]

But in early 1942 Amile was still hopeful. Early that year, James Loeb contacted him about becoming the head of the newly opened Washington office of the Union for Democratic Action. The UDA was anxious to make contact with New Deal officials and to gain more influence in government circles, and thanks to his years in Washington, Amlie knew many government people. He was eager for action, and he quickly accepted the position. It was also expected that Amlie's midwestern roots and his contacts in the labor movement would prove beneficial in expanding the UDA nationally. [8]

At this stage, Amlie was enthusiastic about the UDA He saw it as the kind of activist-intellectual organization that was essential to spreading the reform message. He was interested both in the necessity of planning for the future and in using a variety of techniques (polls, published materials, publicity) to win immediate influence and political elections. He spoke of reaching the "opinion" setters, or, as he later called them, "the captains of the hundreds." By this he did not mean the powerful and moneyed few but rather the one hundred or so thinking and reading people in each voting district. If one could reach them, Amlie was convinced, one could then win a larger following among the people. Amlie believed the UDA was suited for the task of reaching these crucial people, and he set about making contacts. [9]

Howard Y. Williams, an old friend from the farmer-labor movements of the 1930s, was hired to do field work for the UDA. From Williams, Amlie received frequent reports of political activity and developments in the Midwest. Amlie took a UDA-sponsored organizational trip to the Midwest himself and wrote long letters to Loeb detailing the political prospects. In particular, he maintained an interest in the complex politics of his home state of Wisconsin, where he spent a good deal of energy trying to convince the editor of the *Madison Capitol Times,* William Evjue, to throw his weight within the Progressive Party into a Democratic-Progressive alliance. Evjue was sympathetic but came to feel that the administration in Washington was only interested in the Progressive Party at election times;

it was happy to haul out committees like the Norris–La Guardia committee in 1940, to win independent voters, but then it forgot about the members after the election. It was a sentiment that Amlie would later come to
share.[10]

From February to November 1942, Amlie's biggest project was his work
on a "Win-the-War Congress" supplement for *The New Republic*. This project was a joint UDA–*New Republic* endeavor, but since it was being published by *The New Republic*, its editor, Bruce Bliven, had the final say on
its orientation. The supplement was designed to show the voting records
of the fifty congressmen who had most consistently opposed Roosevelt's
foreign policy. The UDA would then use the supplement or material from
it as campaign literature in these congressional districts. Initially, Amlie
had larger ambitions for the supplement. He envisaged a longer supplement with more commentary to accompany the voting charts. He believed
that longer commentaries explaining the weaknesses of the anti–New
Deal congressmen would make the supplement more effective as campaign
literature. He also saw it as dealing with a larger variety of issues pointing
toward postwar America. According to Amlie, Bliven and Dan Mebane
(also from *The New Republic*) were more interested in reaching their readers (whom Amlie felt were already convinced) than in reaching the key
opinion makers in the voting districts. He also felt that they viewed the
supplement as being geared only to the immediate election and not to a
future reformed America. Conflicts developed between Amlie and Bliven,
and Amlie was forced to reduce the supplement's scope. Although he conceded that Bliven may have been correct in practical terms, he was still
frustrated in not being able to use the supplement for the educational goals
he imagined it could have fulfilled.[11]

What upset Amlie more than his friends during his work on the supplement was the casual attitude of the Democratic Party toward the 1942
elections. Many of the Democrats challenging incumbent Republicans had
received no campaign literature from the National Democratic Headquarters. Amlie tried to induce the headquarters to distribute the supplement
but found little receptivity. Amlie and the UDA were left to provide these
candidates with what literature they had.[12]

It was not even the neutrality of the party headquarters that was so
upsetting; it was the hostility. It became clear that the Democratic Party
was not pleased by the controversies caused by the publication of the supplement. The Republicans charged that the publication interjected partisan politics into the wartime unity and accused the UDA of trying to
polarize the country by dragging out old isolationist/internationalist issues

when both parties were supporting the war. It was clear to Amlie that there were influential members of the Democratic Party who shared this perspective and were willing to go along with a suspension of genuinely contested elections. These status-quo Democrats wanted a toned-down campaign in which, it was hoped, the existing Democratic majority would prevail without polarizing any issues. In turn, Amlie and the UDA felt that the Republican nonpartisan line was a sham and that within congressional districts the Republicans were engaging in highly partisan attacks on the New Deal. Without strong counterattacks they believed the Republicans would win. Despite his efforts at providing Democratic candidates with important campaign material from *The New Republic* supplement, Amlie was shunted aside by the Democratic Party. Except for the UDA and the candidates themselves, no one appreciated Amlie's efforts.[13]

The controversial nature of *The New Republic* supplement increased when the Dies committee started its investigation of the UDA. Angered by the supplement and UDA attacks on incumbent prewar isolationists, the *Chicago Tribune* and other archconservative Republicans accused the UDA of being a Communist-dominated organization. Loeb and Amlie fought the charges, but it became clear to Amlie that the Democratic Party leadership was distancing itself from the supplement because of the UDA's controversial nature. It was not that the Democratic Party leadership actually believed the UDA was Communist controlled, but in a political atmosphere in which consensus was sought and in which the New Deal had already capitulated to its conservative critics by withdrawing liberals' names from nomination and tolerating the discharge of liberals under attack from the Dies committee, it was not surprising that the New Deal distanced itself from anything touching the UDA. Knowing that his own withdrawal from the ICC nomination in 1939 had been in part due to Roosevelt's timidity in the face of conservative opposition, Amlie was convinced that these later signs were an indication of what was wrong with American liberalism: in the face of concerted attacks it ran.[14]

Therefore, Amlie was not surprised that the UDA's sources of funds in Washington dried up following the Dies committee attacks. People who had pledged money to begin the UDA's Washington office walked away from their commitments. The UDA was forced to close the office after the November elections and to let Amlie go—owing him several thousand dollars of back salary.[15]

The experience in the 1942 election had left Amlie bitter at the Democratic Party and the fair-weather supporters of the UDA. His experience with the labor movement in the months following the congressional elections would increase his bitterness. In 1942 Amlie had been invited to the Pittsburgh conference of labor and liberals following the debacle of the 1942 elections. As we have seen in the last chapter, an effort was made by Loeb, Kirchwey, and others to convince labor to enter a liberal-left organization to be headed by George Norris, but after dillydallying with the liberals, Philip Murray had torpedoed the idea.[16]

Amlie and other liberals saw the hand of the Communist faction within the CIO in Murray's decision. But they, especially Amlie, also saw it as symptomatic of labor's general behavior. In Amlie's mind, labor was interested only in the immediate; politically, this meant the next election, and then only if it were fast approaching. Amlie felt labor had been delinquent in its use of the *The New Republic* supplement. It had let matters drift to the last moment and then found it could not recover lost political ground. In rejecting the Norris committee, labor, according to Amlie, was repeating its mistakes and revealing that it was interested only in organizations that it controlled. He summed up his bitterness at the Communists and the shortsightedness of labor leaders in a letter to his friend Jim McGill:

> You remember Phil Murray putting his hand on George Norris' shoulder and saying "You lead the way George." George was willing to lead but Murray and the others dropped away. Such an organization could have rallied the support of important groups that will be quietly knifing what this organization [CIO-PAC] is trying to do. The argument made to Murray was that labor must not have anything to do with any organization that labor does not completely control. The accurate way of putting it would have been that the CIO must not have anything to do with politics unless certain elements within the CIO are in a position to control it.[17]

With a large family of young children, Amlie was again out of work. He spent time at home in Wisconsin, and he traveled to Washington to try to link on to government work somewhere. Ideally, he wanted to be politically active; he saw himself as a kind of political-intellectual publicist. He was only able to keep going because James McGill, a wealthy Indiana businessman whose political activity stretched back to William Jennings Bryan and who had most recently been the treasurer of the Norris–La Guardia committee in the 1940 Roosevelt campaign, put him on a small retainer.

In 1943 Amlie was hired by Freda Kirchwey to edit a special *Nation* supplement on national planning and a postwar full employment economy. With full employment increasingly becoming central to the liberal vision of a new postwar world, Amlie's would be an important statement of what needed to be done to achieve the liberal vision. Having formulated his economic ideas out of a combination of Populist antimonopoly ideas and the Keynesian government-induced full employment ideas associated with Ezekiel, Amlie welcomed an assignment where he could express his belief in the need for government planning, Keynesian pump priming and job creation, and legislation attacking monopolies and monopolistic practices. However, Amlie's old friend Bingham, having moved closer to a policy centering on government, progressive business, and labor, felt Amlie was too rooted in the small business, antimonopoly mentality. People like Bingham and Chester Bowles saw "progressive" businessmen around the Committee for Economic Development (CED) as sources of enlightened economic thinking. Amlie, on the other hand, viewed the CED types as simply "fronts" for the monopolists. Amlie's antibusiness rhetoric was more in line with the thinking of Kirchwey and I. F. Stone at *The Nation*.[18]

Amlie's supplement appeared in *The Nation* in November 1943. He opened it with the prediction of a postwar depression unless a full employment plan was developed. He went on to a forceful attack on the business community's "holy war" to restore free enterprise by exposing its use of advertising and media control. He attacked the fallaciousness of the business attack on bureaucracy and the spuriousness of business's propaganda that "labor must be reasonable," that a balanced budget was required for postwar prosperity, and that the business community should be left to make all investment decisions. Using Thorstein Veblen, Amlie exposed the one-sidedness of business's definitions of private property. Attacking the CED "as an innocents' club for the National Association of Manufacturers and the United States Chamber of Commerce," he argued that claims that business required larger financial returns on "risk capital" served only to further swell corporate profits.[19]

According to Amlie, a business-controlled postwar transition would mean freezing in monopoly capital and freezing out "the little fellow." Small business wouldn't "have a chance." It would also mean eventual depression, because private spending could not maintain the expected postwar economy. The present-day economy required government investment to achieve full employment. Sounding much like his fellow liberals, including Henry Wallace, in insisting that government investment would spur true free enterprise, Amlie drew a glowing picture of the economic possibilities of government investment in full employment.[20]

Amlie approved of many areas for government investment—housing, replanning—and even building new cities. He believed that the security needs demonstrated in the Beveridge Plan in Great Britain could be achieved in the United States by a plan for the payment of $100 a month to all unemployed persons. This plan, however, as Amlie conceived it, would only exist as part of a general societal plan for full employment and a public works/youth training program along the lines of the Civilian Conservation Corps and National Youth Administration. Everything was dependent on a full employment program.[21]

With a return to the businessman's free enterprise pointing the way toward unemployment, depression, and world chaos, Amlie saw only Communism or Keynesianism as the alternatives. He could justify the first as "eminently justified" in Russia, but he felt it was unnecessary to pay such a high price in countries "with long traditions of democracy." Keynes had shown that "it may be possible to by-pass the question of socializing the means of production by socializing the purposes of production."[22]

In trying to develop a program of political action to further his version of the Keynesian alternative, Amlie did not place much importance on Roosevelt and certainly did not romanticize his past New Deal accomplishments. He described him as a "realistic conservative" who had opted in his first term to stabilize "the economic system at a low level" rather than opt for a program of full employment. During the war, Roosevelt's concessions to big business raised the question of whether he could provide the necessary leadership for a full employment program. If reelected, he might reduce unemployment minimally, but it made little difference who was president, since, according to Amlie, either a Republican or a Democratic president would be more liberal than the likely Congress. Moreover, Roosevelt's ideas for world peace—as well as Wallace's proposals for world reconstruction—depended on full employment. Without full employment, Roosevelt's ideas were "politically unrealistic," and Wallace's ideas were economically impossible.[23]

The real battle, then, lay with Congress. There was still time to elect delegates (in non-poll tax states) to the Democratic National Convention who were committed to writing a platform for full employment and carrying the fight into the congressional campaigns. "If the issues could be posed in the 1944 campaign," Amlie wrote, "it would be clear from then on that economic democracy was the alternative to economic monopoly. In an understanding of this fact lies the hope of an eventual revolution by consent." The last phrase was Harold Laski's, and it brought his argument full circle. Amlie had started an earlier section with a quotation from Laski ("either political democracy must be the master of economic monopoly or economic monopoly will be the master of political democracy") and had developed both a Laski-style attack on the business community and a Laski-style plea for a politics that clearly posed the alternatives.[24]

Amlie was proud of the supplement, and apparently Kirchwey was pleased too. But he wasn't fully satisfied. Too much had not been developed; parts of the section on the implications of a full employment economy had been cut. He would be further disappointed when his efforts to expand his ideas into a book came to nought. One editor, Amlie concluded, was "an ardent Communist" who rejected his manuscript on ideological grounds. Another supportive editor was fired in the midst of negotiations. The fates seemed to be against him. But Amlie understood that it was not simply fate or "bad breaks." He realized that the liberals were not as committed to far-reaching changes as he was. When he was first hired by the UDA he spoke of it as desiring to make the same kind of changes as Laski was advocating in England. By 1943 and 1944, he tended to speak of himself as alone in advocating sweeping changes, while the New Dealers sought Roosevelt's reelection only in order to secure their jobs, the labor movement focused only on the day-to-day issues, and the UDA liberals—partly through lack of funds and partly through lack of will—were content to concentrate only on preserving the New Deal.[25]

It was not that Amlie was prepared to break with the New Deal. He still praised its foreign policy and contrasted it with what he called the Vatican-oriented pro-fascists in the State Department. (He loved to quote Lincoln Steffens's comment to Robert LaFollette that it would be good if someone burned down the whole State Department.) And he was eager to help in Roosevelt's reelection. In 1944 he was able to actively participate in the campaign. He served on the executive committee of the NC-PAC, and he was able find work as a staff member of the CIO-PAC during the 1944 campaign.[26]

Amlie, like the liberal intellectual community in general, was pleased when the CIO was willing to move toward a joint effort with liberals through the creation of the umbrella NC-PAC, which would concentrate on the liberal community, and the CIO-PAC, which would focus its efforts on labor. Still, the creation of the two organizations did not allay all of Amlie's concerns. He was still not certain if they would permit focusing on developments and ideas that stretched beyond the 1944 elections.

As it turned out, they largely did not, and Amlie found his CIO-PAC work repeating his 1942 efforts in a similar UDA-sponsored supplement for *The New Republic* in 1944. Accompanied by an impeccably liberal platform, the 1944 supplement, "A Congress to Win the War and the Peace," presented charts of congressional votes on key issues. Amlie believed the accumulating of voting statistics and disseminating them into the hands of candidates and opinion makers was eminently useful work. "A Congress to Win the War and the Peace" reflected his efforts in this direction. The results were at least marginally better than in 1942. Then, Amlie could only claim that the Democratic defeats would have been worse without the supplement as campaign literature. In 1944, the Democrats could claim advances. Many of the most notorious isolationists and reactionaries had been defeated. Still, in analyzing the victory, Amlie saw few liberal victories and a failure to break the Republican-southern Democratic stranglehold on New Deal reform. He was all the more convinced that labor had to look beyond the immediate and to build for the future.[27]

Again Amlie would be disappointed. His work with the CIO-PAC ended with the election. He had hoped to develop his voting analysis into a book, but again publishers were dubious. No labor organization would sponsor his work on a firm enough basis that would assure its success. He was still in debt and still dependent on McGill for financial support. In long letters to his friends, he poured out his political and personal frustration. The letters traced every setback to his political career, his financial woes, the enemies he made, and his ideas for economic planning, ideas that he felt had never received their due. At one stage, his wife urged him to stop living in the past; no one had a "vital interest" in it, and she did. not want him trying "to re-hash the last ten years." The constant repetition of events—even to recipients who were already familiar with them from previous letters—suggests a person tormented by the apparent dead end that his career had struck. His inability to find permanent, useful work with either the New Deal or any labor organization confirmed his belief that the New Deal, labor, and liberals were all "trimmers." The failure to generate enough interest in his proposed book to give him the financial resources to complete it only made him feel that the political climate was not receptive to bold liberal ideas.[28]

In 1945 another supplement to *The Nation*, this one on the postwar economy, was proposed. Amlie spent considerable time developing his ideas. He was particularly anxious to include a discussion of Beveridge's work because he believed that Beveridge had laid the foundations for a future program for the United States. By this time, ideas about a postwar full employment economy were in circulation, and Wallace's phrase of sixty million jobs was being tossed around in liberal circles. Fully committed to the full employment approach, Amlie was nevertheless dismissive of Wallace's book, which he found general and lacking in program. In his letters he belittled Wallace's *Reader's Digest* article, published in 1945, that purported to answer the laissez-faire economics of Friedrich Hayek and John Chamberlain. Amlie believed that Wallace accepted Hayek's premises and wound up supporting Hayek's essential position. Amlie told his friends that the *Digest's* roving editor, William Hard, had really written Wallace's article in order for Wallace to win favor with the business community.[29]

Amlie's less than reverential tone about Wallace probably did nothing to help him in his negotiations with *The Nation* about the supplement. Work proceeded for a while, but *The Nation's* managing editor, J. King Gordon, finally jettisoned the entire project. Amlie was left with a partially written supplement, which again he wished to develop into a book. The cycle continued—there were proposals, negotiations, raised and then dashed hopes. In the end, there was intense personal discouragement.

Even as he reviewed ad nauseam his personal setbacks and the discouraging domestic political climate, Amlie's mind was restless. While many liberal intellectuals were still basking in the aura of a U.S.-Soviet friendship, Amlie was predicting a breakdown of the alliance and the confrontation of rival imperialisms. In his proposed *Nation* supplement in early 1945, Amlie had wished to include an analysis of foreign policy and its relation to domestic issues. Up to this point Amlie's career had concentrated on domestic issues; foreign policy had been important but secondary. He had supported Loyalist Spain and collective security in the late 1930s and, as we have seen, broken with the progressive isolationists to support Roosevelt's foreign policy after the outbreak of war in Europe. He had been firmly antifascist, but perhaps because he believed monopoly capitalism rendered real democracy meaningless, he was less inclined to use the liberal intellectual community's rhetoric during World War II. But he shared with the liberal community the belief that if economic, social, and political change did not occur throughout the world, the war would have been fought in vain. When he turned to concentrate on foreign policy, it was just this concern—how rival imperialisms could destroy a new democratic Europe—that engaged his attention.[30]

In formulating his foreign policy ideas, Amlie hardly satisfied any of his fellow liberals. He was more skeptical of Russian motives than *The Nation—*

New Republic editors, and he was more skeptical of American motives than the leaders of the UDA. Instead of formulating a Wilsonian vision of independent democratic nations throughout the world like Louis Fischer, he was willing to concede spheres of influence to the two major powers. But he was unwilling to concede a total division of Europe in which the United States and the Soviet Union confronted each other with armed might. The dropping of the atom bomb only confirmed his fears of a Europe divided between the superpowers.[31]

Throughout the spring and fall of 1945, Amlie offered a democratically federated socialist Europe as the only alternative to a capitalist-Communist domination and the only hope of avoiding war. Theoretically, this proposal was consistent with many of the ideas circulating in the UDA, and Amlie urged Loeb and then Niebuhr himself to support the idea of a Niebuhr-led European trip to articulate and win support for this view. However, if a democratically federated socialist Europe was impossible, as it appeared to be, the leaders of the UDA were willing to settle for a democratic capitalist nonfederated Europe—that is, to support much of U.S. foreign policy. In contrast, in his own way, Amlie had developed a "third camp" position.[32]

Amlie would maintain his unique "third camp" position as he became increasingly isolated from most of his old liberal associates. His position was unique in that it combined an acceptance of realpolitik in foreign policy and the need for spheres of influence along with a critique of both the United States and the Soviet Union for trying to impose their own systems on the peoples of Europe. From this perspective, Amlie would criticize UDA and later ADA liberals for their excessive anti-Communism, their support of the Truman Doctrine, and their endorsement of an increasingly militarized U.S. foreign policy in general. When he saw that Arthur Schlesinger Jr.—"the boy wonder from Harvard"—was the main speaker at ADA meetings on foreign policy, he knew ADA would endorse Truman's policies of helping any country that was against the Soviet Union. Amlie wrote in 1947 and 1948 that he supported Wallace's foreign policy ideas, but at the same time he criticized the Wallace Progressive Party for being dominated by Communists and fellow travelers and Wallace himself for waffling about Communism, the nature of the Soviet Union, and Soviet foreign policy. The isolation from the liberal intellectual community that Amlie increasingly felt in the war years increased in the postwar years. There was no intellectual home for Amlie.[33]

Amlie had no political home either. He was defeated in primary races for the Wisconsin Supreme Court in 1949 and for the House of Representatives in 1958. Each time he ran his radical past was dragged up. He continued into the 1950s trying to publish his book on political voting. No one was interested. James McGill died in 1948, and with his death went the loss of his financial support. His own law practice was meager. He was dependent on his wife's job and on the income from renting houses to University of Wisconsin students.

Judged from one perspective, Amlie's life was a failure. Although he could claim that the roots of the 1946 Murray Full Employment Bill lay in the unsuccessful Industrial Expansion Bills of 1937 and 1938, his own harsh judgment on the importance of the Murray Bill would indicate that little or no legislation derived from his ideas or activities. At various times he described the Murray Bill as "the worst kind of eye wash," as a fake, and as a "pious wish if not a pious fraud." "It is high time," he once wrote Kirchwey, "that we quit talking about free enterprise and got away from the rubbish of the Murray Full Employment Bill and a lot of similar yuck coming from the some of the so-called spokesmen for current political liberalism in the United States."[34]

Although his political life was a succession of defeats after the mid-thirties, of all the activist liberals of the war years Amlie probably came closest to understanding where liberalism went wrong. But in crediting Amlie's insights I have no wish to offer an idealized picture of the man or his work. He had some remarkable qualities. He was vain enough to want some credit or acknowledgment for what he considered his political accomplishments, but he never fought for the public credit he deserved for the 1942 supplement; and he was willing to submerge his ego for the good of the cause. He had the courage to recommend a political outcast like ex-Congressman John Bernard for government work when his own efforts for placement could only be hurt by his association with a congressman who had been blackballed for his radical politics. Despite his own political troubles, he never compromised when it came to opposing McCarthyism, and his outspokenness in the face of political vulnerability puts to shame the compromising and scurrying postures of many of the "New York intellectuals" on the Committee for Cultural Freedom.[35]

But Amlie was far from a perfect man. Even though his close friends like McGill and the two Williamses remained loyal and sympathetic, he must have bored lesser correspondents with the constant repetition of his political life and woes. He could be politically quixotic, as when he recommended in 1948 that Wallace take over the Socialist Party. Amlie may have suffered in his frequent unsuccessful sojourns to Washington, but he could be indifferent to his exhausted wife, who tended the large family at home, and he apparently had an affair with one of his Washington–New York friends while his wife counted pennies in Madison. His attitude toward women was uncomprehending: he wrote his son that his daughter-in-law's placing her career on a par with her husband's was "absurd." His own social sentiments in terms of a shared abundance were praiseworthy, but he never seems to have done any serious thinking on how to ensure the democratic national planning he favored would continue to be democratic. Although his efforts to reach the important "opinion makers" were positive in terms of democratic thinking compared to the efforts of the UDA and other liberals to win the ear of Washington influentials (while celebrating "the people"), he never pursued systematically ideas on how to extend democracy.[36]

In short, Tom Amlie was a personally flawed political person who never had the time and money, but also never had the patience or temperament, to develop his ideas beyond their elementary stage. Yet he sensed—if only on a gut level—that problems among the liberal community were greater than liberal intellectuals were willing to concede. He genuinely recognized what other liberals recognized only verbally: that one could not rely on Roosevelt and that the president's professed intentions meant little when compared to his actions. He recognized that the problem of liberals in achieving their goals went beyond dollar-a-year men and conservative politicians; it was rooted in the structure of monopoly capitalism. Amlie was no more willing than his fellow liberals to break with Roosevelt and only marginally more willing to openly criticize capitalism during the war. Still, unlike his fellow liberals, Amlie had the insight to see that Roosevelt's wartime concessions to the Right were not solely the product of wartime exigencies, that his record in the 1930s was more ambiguous than what was being projected in the liberal press. And he had the good sense not to celebrate Roosevelt—or Wallace.

Others—like Loeb, Kirchwey, and Bliven—paid lip service to the idea that a successful liberal movement could not be based on one person, but too often they acted as if it could—or as if gaining the ear of influential politicians constituted political power. Most of all, what Amlie sensed was that the liberals' problems lay not simply with the power of their oppo-

nents but also with themselves. Although Reinhold Niebuhr has supposedly given us the deep analysis of mankind's drives to power, it was the
intellectually cruder Amlie (who, in contrast to Niebuhr's pessimism, considered himself an optimist) who said that the liberals themselves had capitulated to the "insider" power game, that they had trimmed their goals
and programs to the needs of the administration, that they had too often
placed their career needs or their desire to remain "inside" above principles
and programs, and that they had failed to develop the roots to sustain their
politics.

It is possible, of course, to read Amlie's life and work in another way —
that he was not that different from the rest of the liberal intellectual community. One can point to both his and the liberal intellectuals' criticism of
Roosevelt's foreign policy and domestic concessions, to his and the liberal
intellectuals' refusal to break with Roosevelt, and to their continued belief
that his intentions were, at heart, liberal. One can argue that his ideas on
full employment were in the mainstream of the liberal intellectual community, and his Keynesianism was not that different from the ideas associated with Wallace, Alvin Hansen, or the UDA. If one were to read Amlie's
work and career in this way, one would see his criticisms of Wallace as
being motivated by the attention Wallace received from his fellow liberals
in contrast to Amlie's own inability to win liberal and labor support for his
writing projects. And one would see his criticism of his fellow liberals as
deriving from this same sense of personal alienation and isolation. One
could even read his critique of the liberal insider game as deriving from his
own inability to achieve an insider role in government.

I would not argue that this way of reading Amlie is completely wrong.
I do not want to exaggerate his differences from his fellow liberal intellectuals nor to deny that his own belief that his views differed significantly
from theirs derived in part from his grievances. And yet, when all this is
granted, there remains the fact that the wartime experience had caused
Amlie to reexamine his earlier views of Roosevelt and to conclude by 1943
that Roosevelt historically was a "realistic conservative" whose compromises with the Right might have already destroyed his ability to provide
the needed leadership for social and economic change and whose reelection was relatively unimportant. Such judgments stood in contrast to the
more common picture of Roosevelt as a genuine liberal who had unfortunately felt it necessary to make too many concessions to the Right but who
remained capable, with better liberal organizing behind him, to provide
the needed leadership, and whose reelection was vitally important. There

is a charade-like quality about the liberal declarations or threatened declarations of independence from Roosevelt. There is genuineness about Amlie's more pessimistic conclusions. And although there were rhetorical exaggerations in Amlie's belief that he was more radical than his fellow liberals, there was truth that differences existed. Despite what they believed was an unfortunate watering down of the original bill, most liberals felt the Murray Full Employment Act, which was finally passed in 1946, was a significant step forward. More interested in substance than symbols, Amlie believed that, given the existence of monopoly capitalism, it was insignificant.

But it is not really the differences in opinion over Roosevelt or over the full employment bill that separate Amlie from most of the liberal intellectuals. Rather, what is significant is his growing understanding of the liberal insider game. Having helped formulate a liberal declaration of independence from Roosevelt in early 1945 (but not when there was a concrete reason and a concrete opportunity in 1944), Loeb had argued for more independence and for wider liberal organizing. Two years later he was one of the main activists in creating a liberal organization that was larger but organizationally no different from the UDA — the Americans for Democratic Action — and guiding it on a path where it repeated the liberal wartime experience: criticizing Truman but never breaking fully with him. Even after the efforts to dump Truman by many members of the ADA in 1948, the same members came scurrying back to him before election time. They continued to play the insider game that Amlie had come to understand had caused liberals to live under the illusion that they had real influence and power. Amlie's own solution to the problem of liberal power — the one hundred opinion makers — may have been inadequate, but at least it pointed outward from Washington and at least it avoided the seductive celebratory rhetoric that often mistook ideals for reality. That this flawed and imperfect man should have lived his last years in political exile may not be tragic, but it speaks to the sadness of the wartime (and postwar) liberal political experience.

8

The Mark of a Tory, the Hopes for Labour

DURING World War II, American liberal intellectuals had a special relationship with Great Britain, and with its Labour Party in particular. An exploration of that relationship, which begins with liberal attitudes toward Churchill, moves to liberal connections with the Labour Party, and ends with a comparison of the direction in which American liberals and the British left were moving during the war, sheds light on the intellectual milieu of the American liberal intellectual community.

The year 1940 was a desperate one for Great Britain. German air attacks, the evacuation of Dunkirk, and the Nazi blitzkrieg in Europe seemed to preview an all-out attack on Great Britain. But when Churchill replaced Neville Chamberlain as prime minister in May, he rallied the spirit of the British people. As American liberals watched in admiration at Britain's refusal to break in the face of the German air bombardment, a new sympathetic response developed throughout most of the liberal intellectual community. Already reeling from the fall of France, Holland, Belgium, Denmark, and Norway in early 1940, American liberals recognized England's crucial role in the war. British surrender would ensure Hitler's triumph.[1]

Even before the tense years of 1940–41, at least since the outbreak of the war in the fall of 1939, Americans had slowly begun to modify their attitudes toward Great Britain. This modification paralleled the decline of liberal isolationism, which in the 1930s had created an image of Great Britain as "Perfidious Albion," a duplicitous country bent on manipulating

the United States into protecting British economic and diplomatic interests. Many American liberals believed, as Quincy Howe had written in
1937, that "England expects every American to do his duty" for the
empire.[2]

British foreign policy in the 1930s reinforced this American public image of Great Britain. Liberal isolationists and liberal advocates of collective
security agreed that British foreign policy seemed bent on appeasing fascism. Britain's solicitude for Franco and Mussolini while they were in the
process of strangling Spanish democracy and Chamberlain's outright appeasement of Hitler at Munich cast British foreign policy as reactionary, if
not semifascist, in its orientation. The final straw for the liberals was the
policy's apparent influence on the U.S. State Department.

With the coming of World War II in Europe, this negative picture was
modified. Liberal advocates of collective security made distinctions between British and German imperialism. The distinctions were based on
the *totality* of Nazi control and the absolute destruction of all forms of opposition under the German system. The distinction did not portray the
British Empire in a positive light, but it did draw a clear moral distinction
between the degrees of evil.

When Churchill replaced Chamberlain, the American liberal supporters of all-out aid viewed the move positively. Despite Churchill's support
for the empire and his Tory background, he, unlike Chamberlain, was seen
as a sincere antifascist. In the period of intense Nazi bombardment and the
threat to British independence, Churchill spoke eloquently for the struggle
against fascism. Yet his defense of the British Empire and his association
with the Tory Party made American liberals' attitude toward his government problematic. He clearly had not adopted the liberal interpretation of
the war. He had brought Labour people into the government, but he had
not fully purged the Tory appeasers. He had addressed the dangers of Hitler
and Nazism, but he had not connected the cause of the British colonies
with the war against fascism. Nor did he follow liberals in linking the
struggle against fascism with the promotion of democracy and freedom
throughout the world; he was not even willing to apply the Atlantic Charter beyond Europe. In the moment of crisis when Churchill assumed leadership, these liberal reservations were muffled. But they would become very
clear as the war progressed.[3]

Despite Churchill's lack of enthusiasm for the liberal view of the war
in general and for changes within the British Empire in particular, liberal
support for Great Britain was not simply a matter of the lesser evil. In its

initial organizational statement, the UDA, for one, had made this clear. Churchill's Great Britain, it declared, because it was based on democratic institutions and because it had incorporated the British Labour Party into the governing structure, offered positive possibilities. The admiration for Churchill, the man, during this early period was in keeping with liberal praise for Allied leaders, whether they be Roosevelt, Stalin, De Gaulle, or, in the early stages of the war, Chiang Kai-shek and Madame Chiang. It is fair to say that liberals viewed the entire Allied leadership through the prism of their interpretation of the war. Through that prism Churchill was criticized but also praised for his leadership when the cause was in jeopardy.[4]

This mixture of liberal praise and liberal reservations can be found in Reinhold Niebuhr's review of Phillip Guedalla's 1941 biography of Churchill with Niebuhr's tribute to Churchill's leadership during Britain's "gravest crisis." According to Niebuhr, Churchill had demonstrated "his superb embodiment of the fortitude of the British people in this dark hour." This tribute to Churchill would continue throughout all liberal criticism and can be found in even his severest British critics, such as Harold Laski.[5]

But Niebuhr was not content simply to praise Churchill. He also saw in his "political realism" the source of his "greatness." Churchill, he believed, had understood the nature of Hitler when too many of the British relied on the "dreams of island security" and the hope of "beguiling Hitler with nice bourgeois bargains." Churchill had also argued for an alliance with the Soviet Union at a time when the Tories were still trying to "come to terms with Hitler at the expense of Russia." His advocacy of a Soviet alliance, in turn, had led him "to proclaim solidarity" with the Soviet Union after it was invaded by Hitler. Niebuhr also saw Churchill as an imperialist whose imperialism was not based on the economic "class interests." He was motivated by "The pride and prestige of empire" and was not an "economic man," which allowed him to understand "the danger of a man and movement which defied the typical bourgeois calculations of his contemporaries."[6]

On the negative side, according to Niebuhr, lay Churchill's lack of understanding of domestic economics and politics. His focus was almost entirely international; despite his "'democratic' toryism," he didn't understand the domestic changes that had occurred between the wars. There were problems with his international perspective as well. His political realism, especially in his views on India, reflected cynicism and prevented Britain from changing its policy in India. His domestic and international deficiencies made Niebuhr apprehensive about his "possible contributions to the problems of post-war reconstruction, both economic and international."[7]

In *The New Republic* in 1942, Max Lerner expressed some of the same themes as Niebuhr and added a few more critical notes. In his article, entitled "The Pilgrimage of Winston Churchill," Lerner paid similar tribute to Churchill's dynamic personal qualities and analyzed in a similar fashion his non-economically motivated imperialism. But he criticized Churchill's administration of war production, his appointments, his impatience with criticism, his failure to understand the political nature of modern warfare, his failure to use the "dynamic of democracy" in regard to India, and his failure to democratize the army. Lerner worried most of all about Churchill's failure to mention the Soviet Union in the "plans for Allied war coordination, or in his picture of the post-war world," which revealed his balance-of-power approach to world politics. Churchill had the insight to turn to the Soviet Union in the struggle against Hitler, but there was now the danger that he would seek some balance to a successful Russia in the postwar period. An "Anglo-American condominium," Lerner wrote, "is no answer to the winning of either the war or the peace." We have to extend "the democratic reach" to include all the anti-Nazi peoples in a partnership. "When Churchill has understood that," he concluded, "he will have completed his pilgrimage."[8] Despite this criticism, Lerner acknowledged that even Britain's left parliamentary critics would be "horrified" if their "sporadic sniping" led to Churchill's resignation.

Even with the partial revamping of Churchill's image in the liberal press, the problems of the empire and of fulfilling the liberal war aims would not disappear. Thus, throughout the months following U.S. entrance into the war—when the war news was still bad and the idea that military success required the transformation of the war into a democratic war was at its highest—liberals increasingly questioned Churchill's understanding of the nature of the war. In February 1942 Freda Kirchwey strongly voiced the sentiments of the liberals who believed that Churchill's inability "to understand the nature of this war" was standing in the way of military success. Kirchwey reviewed the series of military defeats, particularly in the Far East, that clearly showed the Allies were losing the war. Faced with critical questions at home, Churchill had demanded confidence and "cited the unity of the Russians as a model for Englishmen." But this was "a thoroughly disingenuous solution":

The unity of the Russians is grounded in their faith in the tough, realistic, fighting qualities of their leaders. It is not for Mr. Churchill to hold up Russian unity as an example for the British people, but rather for the British people to point to Russian leadership as an example for Mr. Churchill and his government. The Russian army in retreat burned not only bridges but houses, factories, dams, and standing crops; the British signed the terms of their surrender in Singapore in an undamaged Ford assembly plant and, so far as is known, turned over the vast facilities of their Far Eastern base intact save for the inevitable destruction from the war itself. The British people are not demanding victories of their leadership; they are demanding leadership.[9]

All this, Kirchwey believed, pointed to Churchill's inability to understand the nature of the war. While he was free of his predecessors' "commercial fears," he was still "an old-fashioned British imperialist." As such, he was "unversed in the complex political and social struggle that forms the center of the Nazi drive for world dominion." To fulfill the democratic nature of the war, Kirchwey suggested, Churchill needed to change his policy toward India, a policy that had jailed Nehru three days before the Japanese attack on Pearl Harbor and that had created a "sullen, unhappy colony." Churchill needed to recognize that freedom was a "weapon, not a prize for good behavior." At home, Churchill needed to make more dramatic changes in government personnel. She suggested bringing Sir Stafford Cripps into the Cabinet as a step in constructing a Churchill-led Cabinet that "would put new heart into the British people and into democrats everywhere."[10]

The continued bad war news from the Far East caused liberals to support British movement toward Indian independence. Liberals argued that the Indians had no love for Japan but that British control caused them not to fully appreciate the dangers of fascism. Only if they could be enlisted in a democratic cause, a cause incompatible with the empire—at least in the long run—would the Indians fight wholeheartedly on the Allied side. The failure of the Churchill government to take the necessary steps was interpreted as reflecting the continued inability on the part of Churchill and the Tories to understand the nature and goals of the war.[11]

In March 1942 Churchill appointed Sir Stafford Cripps to undertake a mission to India to win India's cooperation in the war. It was greeted by the liberals as a positive step. *The Nation* welcomed the appointment but wrote that it would be more hopeful if there were greater signs of responsible leadership on the part of the Indians. Gandhi, the journal said, acted as if it were important for the British "to confess past crimes" and not "to resist Japanese aggression"; the Indian leadership was forgetting that "the immediate reason for defending India is not to save the British Empire but to save India itself from new conquest and worse exploitation." The Cripps mission was not an altruistic mission to save India, however; it would not have been undertaken if the defeat of India would not have threatened the entire British war effort and, with it, the British Empire. At heart, *The Nation* knew this, but by attributing so many of the difficulties of the Cripps mission to the Indian leadership, it was placing much of the blame onto the colonized if the mission should fail. Nor was *The New Republic* right in believing that Cripps had great latitude in his talks. With so much liberal confusion at the beginning of the mission, it is little wonder that it should have resulted in so much internal liberal sniping.[12]

As the negotiations between Cripps and the Congress Party were unfolding, *The Nation* and *The New Republic* endorsed the Cripps proposals. According to *The Nation*, the Cripps plan increased Indian self-government during the war and promised dominion status after the war with the right of secession. *The New Republic* was optimistic about the possibilities for the success of the mission and said that the American people were insisting on its success. And in *PM*, Herbert Agar dismissed the Indian Congress's criticisms of the Cripps plan, a plan which he defended as "fair."[13]

As the negotiations were reaching their climax, Kirchwey declared that India had reached her "zero hour." The problems that would be created by complete independence in wartime were, she said, insurmountable, and the Cripps plan offered the necessary wartime balance of freedom and "stable administrative processes." Again, she placed the major responsibility on the Indian leadership to accept the proposals that she had previously endorsed. Gandhi, she said, "clothed in his impenetrable faith in non-violence," had "retired from the field." It was up to people like Jawaharlal Nehru and Maulana Azad, who represented the Indian National Congress at the Cripps negotiations, to show "a sense of responsibility" that transcended India and the British Empire. Like *The New Republic*, Kirchwey believed that Cripps had "an almost completely free hand in the negotiations" and that any remaining areas of difference could be successfully negotiated.[14]

In a remarkable passage that revealed that condescension toward India was not confined to Churchill and the Foreign Office, Kirchwey wrote:

> Whether it provides enough freedom to stir the Indians to strong resistance is not so certain. Drugged by years of pacifist teaching, obsessed with their age-

long animosity toward Britain, the people of India must fully believe in the future that is held before them if they are to fight as they must. The longer the negotiations, the sharper the bargaining, the less will be the chance of winning their support for the terrible struggle that lies ahead. Only prompt vigorous, confident leadership will work the necessary miracle in the minds and emotions of the powerful, sluggish Indian population.[15]

Negotiations between Cripps and the Indian Congress Party were complicated. Issues of India's postwar status and, even more, of its wartime status were discussed. Ultimately the negotiations broke down and Cripps returned to England without achieving the aims of the mission. The liberal press greeted the breakdown with expressions of regret. Although it acknowledged that the British offers probably came two years too late, *The Nation* reiterated its support for the plan and criticized the Indian leaders, who, it said, insisted "they must have full responsibility or none at all." Although *The Nation* stated that it was no time for "recriminations and attempts to fix the blame" for the failure of the Cripps mission, it was clear that the journal thought the various Indian groups had been unreasonable. *The New Republic* called the breakdown of the talks one of the "greatest disasters" of the United Nations. With Japan at the gates of India, the two sides were haggling over issues that *The New Republic* thought could readily be compromised.[16]

When the Cripps mission was first announced, an Indian writer, Krishnalal Shridharani, had written in *The Nation* that Cripps had "undertaken what would appear to be a hopeless task" because the promise of independence after the war without a set date would likely not satisfy the Indians. But, Shridharani conjectured, it was likely that Cripps had brought "more radical proposals" than Churchill had publicly acknowledged. Otherwise, he said, Cripps "would hardly have gone." It was precisely around this issue that the liberals' attempt to fix the responsibility for the mission's failure revolved. Few of the liberals were prepared to conclude that there was an irreconcilable gap between the British proposals and valid Indian concerns. The blame for the failure, then, ultimately had to rest either with the irresponsibility of the Indian leaders or with British diplomacy. Louis Fischer, an associate editor of *The Nation*, visited India after the failure of the mission and affixed the blame on the Churchill government. Fischer had already criticized the British government for imprisoning Gandhi and Nehru and for its unwillingness to talk to Gandhi, who, he argued, was anti-Japanese and pro-Chinese and would be more conciliatory if given the opportunity to communicate with the Allied leadership.[17]

The failure of the Cripps mission, according to Fischer, lay with the

Churchill government's betrayal of Cripps. Despite the difficulties of the issues involved, Fischer said, the two sides were close to a compromise. According to Fischer, Cripps had promised the Indians a real national government, but after the offer was made, the British government had pulled the rug from under Cripps. Thus, in Fischer's mind, it seemed that the British had no intention of giving the Indians substantive control over their own defense but, rather, intended to assign them minor administrative tasks.[18]

At this stage—when the British were responding to Gandhi's nonviolence campaign with jailings and violence (Tory parliament members would cheer reports of the massacre of Indians)—Kirchwey was prepared to accept Fischer's explanation. Although she still believed that the fault did not lie entirely with the British, she endorsed Fischer's "terrible story." Kirchwey's support did not satisfy Fischer. What did it mean, he asked in a personal letter to Kirchwey, to call the Indian Nationalist leaders "more intransigent than they should have been" in light of Fischer's demonstration that Congress was attempting an agreement with Cripps and was "within an inch of a defense formula"? Kirchwey's reply focused on Gandhi: "My honest belief is that Gandhi should not have launched the civil disobedience campaign even after the breakdown of the negotiations. He should have gone on trying stubbornly and patiently to reach some sort of an agreement, and he should have refused to do anything which could precipitate civil disorder in the midst of the war. . . . None of this excuses the British. I think intransigence on both sides is inexcusable at a time like this."[19]

It is doubtful that Kirchwey's reply satisfied Fischer, since, without repudiating Fischer's version, she soon provided space for his critics. In mid-November Graham Spry wrote an article in *The Nation* in which he denied that the British had ever offered the Congress Party negotiators a national government. The reasons for the failure, Spry said, lay not with the British but inside the Congress Party. And two weeks later Kingsley Martin of the British *New Statesman and Nation* wrote to disagree with Fischer that an offer for a national government had ever been made.[20]

An angry Fischer demanded space for an article to reply to Spry and Martin and threatened to resign from *The Nation* if he did not get it. Kirchwey acquiesced, telling Fischer that she didn't want to lose him as an editor, but she criticized his imperious demands. In his reply, Fischer reviewed the negotiations and reiterated his belief that Cripps had offered the Indians a national government but had been forced by the British government to withdraw the offer. If Cripps wished to locate the problem,

Fischer wrote, all he had to do was to look at 10 Downing Street. Churchill had recently made his famous declaration that he had not become prime minister "to preside over the liquidation of the British Empire" and that "we mean to hold our own." That, wrote Fischer, was "really why Cripps failed."[21]

Writing first in *The New Republic* and later publishing a book, *Subject India*, H. N. Brailsford, the British correspondent for *The New Republic*, offered an explanation that had certain parallels with Fischer's but which did not depend on either Cripps's having made an offer of a national government or on the British government's having withdrawn it. Conceding that Cripps had publicly used the phrase "national government," Brailsford said that he was satisfied from his inquiries that the British War Department "never intended to concede anything that could fairly be called a 'National Government.'" Despite this important difference from Fischer's analysis, the two were in agreement on key points. Both agreed that the major issues on which the negotiations floundered involved the present and not the postwar arrangements. In addition, both placed an important emphasis on the defense responsibilities that would be given to India. The first effort to define these responsibilities offered a variety of nonmilitary duties including "stationary, printing and forms for the Army." "Imagine," wrote Brailsford, "Nehru in his first broadcast as Defense Minister rousing a liberated people to a delirium of warlike enthusiasm" with a list of those responsibilities.[22]

Later efforts slightly broadened the proposals for an Indian defense minister's responsibilities. But the British, Brailsford wrote, never offered the kind of responsibilities that would permit the Indian defense minister to organize a Home Guard or raise an army. There was nothing, as the Indian leaders said, that would make the Indian people "have and feel their responsibility" in the conduct of a war that could "only be fought on a popular basis": "Even in this crisis the British government did not trust the Indian people, did not mean to arm it and did not intend that it should defend its own country, as the Chinese had defended theirs." In Brailsford's analysis, the mission did not fail because London negated Cripps's original proposal. Although Brailsford did not say it, the liberals had been wrong. They had based their analysis of the possibility of the mission's success either on the flexibility or latitude granted to Cripps or on the existence of more radical proposals than had been publicly announced. According to Brailsford, neither was the case: in the face of a dire military crisis it had been the British who were too intransigent and inflexible in their approach.[23]

The important issue here is not whether Fischer's "betrayal" thesis or Brailsford's "rigid formulaic" theory was correct, but what the theories pointed to in terms of the liberal attitude toward Great Britain. Both theories supported fixing the responsibility on Churchill—something Kirchwey at this early stage of the war was not prepared to do. This is revealed in another exchange with Fischer later in 1942.

In mid-October 1942 Kirchwey published an editorial criticizing *Life* magazine's "Open Letter" to the people of England. Kirchwey blasted *Life*'s use of the phrases "your side" and "our side" and the implication that "your side" was motivated solely by "a selfish devotion to the idea of empire" and "our side" by "a passion for freedom for everybody." *Life* forgot, Kirchwey said, that Great Britain was willing to fight alone before there even was an "our side" and that it was willing "to accept more social change and to sacrifice more social privileges" than the United States. And she concluded with the passage that raised Fischer's ire: "And meanwhile the British people needn't worry. We'll keep on fighting along with them in spite of *Life*'s ultimatum. And we'll fight for the empire, too, since the empire includes not only India but the great self-governing dominions, and the islands of the Caribbean, and Malta. . . . We can't spare the British Empire; everybody knows that, really; even Mr. Luce."[24]

At the beginning of the war Kirchwey had reminded Luce that the antifascist alliance involved a democratic international civil war that included labor and the left. Now she was reminding him that it included the British Empire. No adherent of Luce's politics, but appalled by what he saw as the implications of Kirchwey's remarks, Fischer fired off a letter that was published in *The Nation* two weeks later:

> I am quite startled by the last paragraph. . . . You cannot mean—can you?—that we are fighting for the British Empire. We are fighting to keep the territories of the British Empire out of Axis hands. But where are our war aims (freedom) if we wish to keep the British Empire intact? I thought Sumner Welles said, "The period of Empire is ended." The task of keeping British Empire territory out of Axis hands would have been facilitated in Burma . . . if stupid imperialist policy had not prevailed. The defense of India would be easier for us if Churchillism were abandoned. I think we *can* spare the British Empire. It is obstructing victory. British imperialists are responsible for England's conservative conduct of the war.[25]

Kirchwey replied that after the war "relationships between nations" might be reorganized, but that during the war it was "self-evident" that we were "fighting for the life of the British Empire as well as our own life."

The empire was "a fact"; it was "slightly frayed around the edges but still fairly substantial." We couldn't "write it out of existence" while we were fighting by its side around the world. Kirchwey denied that the empire was solely a matter of territory. It involved "the bond of mutual responsibility." She asked Fischer if he would prefer that she call the empire the Commonwealth which she described as "the only working system of collective security" at the outset of the war.[26]

Although she acknowledged that the empire did not always work well, Kirchwey said it would be "foolish" to think one could eliminate the contradictions in the midst of the war. And then in a remarkable passage that unintentionally could have been used to undercut much of her domestic political criticism during the war, Kirchwey wrote:

> *Life,* when it lectured the British people about "your side" and "our side," was talking dangerous and almost treasonable nonsense. "Our side" includes the British Empire, just as it includes China and Russia and the guerrillas in Serbia and the Fighting French in Syria and Equatorial Africa. Our side— America included—is riddled with contradictions, sins against freedom, treason to the democratic spirit. Oppression, race prejudice, autocratic rule are no monopoly of the British Empire; it harbors less of these than many of the rest of us. We can't draw our skirts aside and wait till injustice is ended and empire reconstructed into brotherhood. We have a war to fight. And our side has to be united in all our faults and virtues or we shall face defeat together. So Americans can ill afford to mutter threats about refusing to fight if the British don't "move to our side." They are already on our side, and they were there long before we were, if you'll forgive the paradox.[27]

Kirchwey's article served well as an answer to Luce's nonsense and hypocrisy. But in the process her reply ran the risk of embracing all those supporting the war—a position she did not really believe. There was never a *Nation* editorial that embraced the contradictions of Jesse Jones's and Will Clayton's support for the war. And this was because Kirchwey saw them as impediments to the war effort and to the liberal interpretation of the war for freedom. But this was precisely Fischer's point on the British Empire. It was clear he was talking about the colonial empire, not the dominion nations, and that his concern lay in the seeming contradiction between Kirchwey's apparent inclusion of the empire in the goals of the war.

The differences between Kirchwey and Fischer indicate a different emphasis on social change during the war. The tenor of *The Nation's* editorials reveals that its principled belief in Indian independence was a secondary consideration compared to the pragmatic issue of the military outcome of the war. Because the loss of the war would mean the victory of fascism and the death of democracy, Kirchwey could believe that her position was compatible with the liberal intellectuals' interpretation of the war. And she had the support of most of the British left who, like Orwell, saw Gandhi's nonviolent wartime crusade against British rule as threatening to bring about a system far worse than British imperialism. And she had the support of the American left too. Niebuhr, a friend of Cripps, along with the rest of the UDA leadership, shared Kirchwey's reservations about immediate independence, her annoyance with the intransigence of the Congress Party, and her opposition to Gandhi's nonviolent campaign. In a letter to Anthony Wayne Smith in 1944, James Loeb said that he and Niebuhr favored Indian freedom but believed that the failure of the Hindus and Muslims to reach an understanding meant that advocating freedom during the war would mean "advocating a policy that might, in all reality, mean complete chaos in India at this time." Both *The New Republic* and *PM* criticized Gandhi's civil disobedience campaign. *The Nation* criticized the British response to the latter, but the campaign itself was seen as disruptive to the war effort. On the other hand, Fischer believed that Indian independence would fulfill the democratic nature of the war. For Fischer, more than the principle of independence was involved. He also believed that not only Nehru but Gandhi as well were antifascists who could be brought fully to the Allied side if genuine steps toward independence were begun.[28]

Despite these alternative views, the differences that had developed between Kirchwey and Fischer did not reach a breaking point because there was more common ground than the dispute might suggest. As the war proceeded and the debate over the Cripps mission faded (though Fischer periodically defended his "betrayal" thesis), the liberal community, Kirchwey and Fischer included, devoted their efforts to trying to persuade Churchill to make new efforts to win Indian cooperation. Disagreements over whether India could be granted independence during the war persisted, as did differences over the wisdom of Gandhi's nonviolent campaign. But all were united in condemning the British coercive response to the nonviolent campaign and to the continued jailing of Gandhi, Nehru, and other Indian leaders. Certainly by 1944 all agreed with Lerner that the British needed to take the "bold stroke" of releasing Nehru.[29]

Other areas of Churchill's foreign policy, however, were beginning to absorb liberal attention in 1943. The liberals criticized British toleration, solicitude, and "kind words" for Franco. They were especially critical of the British role in the recognition of Badoglio and in later Allied relations with the Badoglio government. *The Nation* and *The New Republic* were convinced that the motive behind British foreign policy was the fear of popular democratic revolutionary forces.[30]

Liberal intellectuals were also concerned about the British policy toward the Soviet Union. On one hand, they sometimes praised Churchill's understanding that the Soviet Union was a major force that had to be dealt with. In 1943 *The New Republic* commented that Churchill had demonstrated the ability to work with the Soviet Union "with or without the United States." Niebuhr thought at one time that Great Britain, because it was closer geographically and because it shared with the Soviet Union a common interest in Europe, might serve as a mediator between the Soviet Union and the United States. But at the same time the liberals feared that Churchill was concerned primarily with developing counterweights to Soviet influence in Europe. They feared that two Europes would develop: a Soviet sphere and an anti-Soviet sphere.[31]

Occasionally British policy was praised. Its recognition of Tito's Partisans and ultimately its shift away from the Polish government-in-exile drew praise. But the fear that Britain's ultimate goals were antirevolutionary was seemingly confirmed by the British suppression of the Greek revolution. Churchill's antiradical statements, in which he had labeled the Greek EAM Trotskyist, and his subsequent coercive actions were condemned by the liberal community. *The New Republic* wrote that Churchill's policy in Greece which had led to the killing of innocent women and children was "ignoble," and his defense of the policy in the House of Commons was "not only the weakest but the most shameful of his whole career." He had almost destroyed his reputation "as the spokesman for bulldog British courage in the darkest days of the blitz." It was clear, the journal said, that his true motive was to prevent a truly independent Greek government and to keep Greece within the British "orbit." Churchill stood, it said, for "an extremely narrow" conception of democracy, and "his devotion to conservative capitalism and to the British Empire" was "strong and all-inclusive." The entire Greek episode represented "Churchill's path": "power politics, imperialism, spheres of influence and more and more war."[32]

Behind the liberal criticism of Churchill's actions toward Spain, Italy, and Greece lay an overall concern about the difference between the liberal interpretation of the war and Churchill's own. In commenting on his proposals for "a condominium of power among the great nations which were winning the war," *The New Republic* asked: "Will it really be a war of liberation? Or will it be merely one to establish and maintain the political status quo? Will there be world-wide democratic control of, and room for change within, the invincible combination which will have to be formed to repel future aggression? To put it bluntly, are you fighting to preserve the British Empire, and are we fighting to preserve capitalism, or are we really sincere about the noble abstractions which we have together espoused?"[33]

While Churchill's statement about not presiding over the loss of the British Empire may have confirmed the liberals' original analysis of Churchill as an imperialist, later statements in which he indicated that the British were not concerned with the internal nature of governments and that the British had no quarrel with fascism as long as it stayed home convinced the liberals that Churchill was more than an imperialist. He was a conservative who did not share in any way the liberal definition of the international civil war. In March 1944 *The Nation* wrote that Churchill was "unwilling to recognize the revolutionary implications of the war or to encourage the revolutionary forces it set in motion." Churchill's suggestions for Germany indicated a spheres-of-influence approach, and he had made clear that he did not believe that the Atlantic Charter applied to Germany. In Italy he stood for Badoglio and the king and "snubbed the Italian democrats." While Churchill's tribute to Tito was "welcome," he failed to understand that energies the Partisans unleashed in Yugoslavia could be released in Italy with a different policy. Three months later *The Nation* repeated a similar indictment of Churchill. In short, Churchill represented a barrier to liberal war aims.[34]

Again, the issue of the Soviet Union was important here. The liberals were convinced that Churchill stood in the way not only of communist revolution but of all revolution and of all the necessary political and economic changes that were necessary in Europe. He stood for an old Europe of spheres of influence. But the liberals were forced to recognize that this also meant that one way or another Churchill had to deal with the Soviet Union. When it became clear that Churchill and Stalin were dealing with Europe on the basis of respective spheres of influence, this was not something that would please the liberals, who stood, at least in principle, for a new cooperative diplomacy. At the same time, they believed that it was a direction that would inevitably be taken by both sides if the United States did not interject itself more forcefully into the fulfillment of the democratic aims of the war.

Churchill, then, stood as the symbol of the old diplomacy and as a barrier to the democratic revolution. One could sense as the war progressed toward Allied victory that liberal intellectuals were becoming more impatient with the British wartime unity government and with the political truce. Eager for social change at home and abroad, the American liberals also viewed Churchill as a major opponent of economic change within England. Yet they were forced to acknowledge that Churchill was prepared to go further in the direction of planning, greater social security and more government intervention in the economy than the Roosevelt administration was.[35]

Thus, on domestic matters, Churchill was viewed both positively, for example when his economic policies were being contrasted to the lack of direction in U.S. postwar planning, and negatively, for example when he seemed to be opposed to the full social security ideas associated with the Beveridge Plan. But the American liberal criticisms of his domestic leadership paled beside their condemnations of his Italian, Spanish, and Greek policies and his general foreign policy statements. Thus, there had been a turnaround in the liberal attitude toward Churchill. The liberals had begun the war praising Churchill's understanding of Hitler and fascism and viewing his brand of imperialism as more benign than economically driven imperialism; on the other hand, they had believed his domestic leadership was weak and his understanding of economic problems and policy poor. At the end of the war they were still critical of his economic policy but praised it in comparison with that of the United States. But his imperialism was no longer viewed as benign; the United States was being urged to "counter Churchill's . . . logic of imperialism."[36]

At the moment of D day in June 1944, Harold Laski wrote that he looked at Churchill as a "great Englishman" and not "as the leader of the Tories." But otherwise Laski and the American liberal press portrayed him as the leader of the Tories, whose reactionary policies stood in the way of the democratic revolution and the liberal war aims. For the liberals he was, as the UDA had said in 1941 of Great Britain itself, more than a lesser evil. But he had also been less than an ideal embodiment of the liberal interpretation of the war. By the end of the war, except for an occasional tribute to his early leadership, the liberals left no ambiguity. In his opposition to

European social democracy, he bore, wrote Lerner, "the mark of the Tory." And so the liberals encouraged and then cheered his defeat in 1945 as the defeat of the embodiment of all that their interpretation of the war opposed.[37]

The growing negative criticism of Churchill as the war went on did not mean any lessening of the American liberal intellectuals' interest in developments in Great Britain. They maintained a deep interest in developments in Great Britain in general and in the British left in particular. The liberals looked to the Labour Party to represent their interpretation of the war. Contacts between the American liberals and Great Britain, especially with the Labour Party, were frequent during the war. Kirchwey, Niebuhr, and Keith Hutchinson from *The Nation* all visited England during the war and reported on political and economic developments. Bruce Bliven and George Soule did the same for *The New Republic*. All the liberal journals published articles on Great Britain from writers on the British left. *Common Sense* published a regular London letter from Stephen Spender. H. N. Brailsford was *The New Republic*'s British correspondent. Michael Young, Jennie Lee, Patricia Strauss, Aneurin Bevan, R. H. S. Crossman, Raymond Postgate, Kingsley Martin, and K. Zilliacus all published in *The New Republic*, Young and Lee frequently. Tom Wintringham, a militant British left writer on military matters, published frequently in *The Nation*. So did Laski. Vernon Bartlett wrote a series of articles for *The Nation* and toward the end of the war Aylmar Vallance reported regularly on developments in England. Michael Foot and Patricia Strauss also contributed *Nation* articles.

The UDA was active in trying to build contacts between American liberals and the British left. The organization sponsored tours by the British Labourites Josiah Wedgwood and Jennie Lee in 1941, and Loeb was in contact with Lee, the wife of Aneurin Bevan, throughout the war. Early in the war, the UDA attempted to arrange for a British trade union delegation to tour the United States. In 1942 the UDA held a dinner for Kingsley Martin, the editor of *The New Statesman and Nation*, and in 1946 the UDA was able to get the Labour parliamentary leader Patrick Gordon-Walker for a speaking tour. During the war, the UDA solicited greetings from Herbert Morrison and other prominent British Labour Party officials at important UDA events. At the end of the war, when she was attempting to help Austria's hungry, Lee turned to the UDA for support. And after the war the UDA lobbied hard for the British loan.[38]

Liberal contacts were also built on personal friendships. Niebuhr was a friend of Cripps's, and the purpose of Niebuhr's visit to England during the war was, in part, to extend his personal contacts in order to deepen the connection between American liberals and the British left. Lerner was a good friend and wartime correspondent of Laski's. On a trip to England, Alfred Bingham's and Chester Bowles's good friend William Benton debated Laski on the future of capitalism. Other contacts were less personal but very important. Tom Amlie associated his own intellectual endeavors with Laski's "revolution by consent" and believed in 1942 that the UDA was trying to take the country in the direction indicated by Laski's ideas. Beveridge's plans for social security in Great Britain were picked up by American liberals. Amlie, among others, associated the Beveridge Plan with the kind of planning that needed to be done in the United States. *The Nation* and *The New Republic* published respectful articles and editorials on the Beveridge Plan as they tried to move the United States toward postwar planning.[39]

On both sides of the Atlantic, there was a belief that more connections between American and British liberalism needed to be developed. In a plea for world cooperation among liberal forces, Michael Straight stressed the interconnectedness of British and American liberalism. Describing the British reaction to the Darlan deal, Wintringham argued for linking the American and British anti-Darlan efforts. "If the link is made," he wrote, "the American and British peoples may cease to fight an imperial war for the reestablishment of empires, and may begin to wage the people's war for which Europe is hungrily waiting." The Free World Association did have branches in various countries, but the hopes for any organizational linkage between the American and British left remained hopes. Perhaps the war made this inevitable. What it meant, however, was that American liberals had to look to the British Labour Party to steer Great Britain toward the liberal war goals. And here lay a problem: American liberals were concerned that the British Labour Party's participation in the wartime unity government, while correct, did not encourage the necessary changes in Tory philosophy.[40]

American liberals responded positively to the Labour Party's ideological statements at its annual conferences. But as they watched the performance of the unity government they were worried that the Labourites were hemmed in and forced to accede to Churchill's policy rather than helping to reshape it. In the fall of 1942 Lerner wondered if "the urgencies of national cohesion and party truce have not destroyed the British Labor Party as an independent and critical force." The demotion of Cripps from the War Cabinet to minister of air craft production in late 1942 did nothing to assuage liberal worries. Commenting on Cripps's demotion in a letter to Kirchwey, Fischer wrote, "Stalin shoots his rivals, Winston eats them."[41]

In England, Sir Richard Acland had come to believe that the Labour Party had been co-opted too much by the Tories and that the unity government stood in the way of the necessary social changes. A religious socialist, Acland developed a political organization, Commonwealth, that sought to break the electoral agreement of the Tories and Labour. Challenging unity candidates in some of the parliamentary by-elections in 1942, Commonwealth won several seats and appeared to offer the liberal-left an alternative to Tory-Labour bipartisanship. Commonwealth developed a socialist program to be begun during the war and wrote a democratic foreign-policy statement calling for independence for India under United Nations auspices. Commonwealth was able to attract a number of independent radicals, like Tom Wintringham and, initially, the novelist J. B. Priestly.[42]

Because the rhetoric and goals of Commonwealth were close to the democratic revolution idea of the American liberal intellectuals, one might have expected that it would have gained a great deal of support in the liberal community. American liberals did give it a respectful hearing. *The Nation* published Wintringham's articles on Commonwealth. Acland corresponded with Loeb and sent him material on Commonwealth's views and organization. But Commonwealth was unable to win any wide endorsement. Despite the parallels in democratic rhetoric and in some programmatic areas between Commonwealth and the American liberal intellectual community, that community did not embrace Commonwealth, mainly because its personal contacts with the British Labour Party did not endorse it. Jennie Lee, a semi-independent Labourite in her own right, wrote in *The New Republic* about the limitations of Commonwealth. In the end, the American liberals' real connections were with the Labour Party. Believing political, economic, and social change needed to come out of the labor movement and seeing Labour, despite its present governmental role, as an organized force for these changes in Great Britain, American liberals were willing to accept the party's decision to support a unity coalition for the duration. Like Laski in England, they were often critical of the coalition's limitations for social change; but, again like Laski, they were not willing to support new third parties in England (or in the United States) even if, like Commonwealth, the party embraced ideas closer to their own than the unity government. As the war progressed, the American liberals chafed increasingly at the electoral truce in Great Britain; so did the British Labour writers who wrote in the liberal press. Freed from its governmental ties, Labour was able to campaign in 1945 on a socialist program. The liberals welcomed the program and the outcome.[43]

If one accepted the American liberals' own description of where they were headed; if one accepted that the American liberal democratic revolution and the British Labour democratic socialist revolution were parallels; if one accepted Amlie's connection of the UDA with the ideas of Laski; and if one saw the close connections, like those of the UDA with the British Labour Party, reflecting parallel directions, then one might conclude that the British Labour Party and its American liberal intellectual supporters were moving in the same direction. But this was hardly the case. With the Labour Party constrained by its governmental ties, American liberal intellectuals might appear to have been to the left of the British Labour Party. However, the democratic antibusiness rhetoric of the American liberals, for all its talk about the need for revolutionary changes, was not moving toward or advocating socialism. It was not antisocialist and, in fact, looked positively on the development of socialism in England and Europe, but socialism was not what the UDA was advocating for the United States.

In the United States, the liberal intellectual community was no longer proposing *new* economic arrangements. We have seen this with the evolution of the UDA, and it can be seen in any comparison between what *The Nation, The New Republic,* and *Common Sense* were advocating in the early or even mid-thirties and what they were pushing during the war years. Instead of calling for new economic arrangements, the liberal intellectuals were building on the reformed capitalism of the New Deal. The economic writings of the liberal community were largely efforts to carry Keynesian economics forward, to place them on a permanent basis, and to enable capitalism to offer fuller social programs along the lines of the Beveridge Plan. One can call the ideas and plans bold, or say they were politically realistic, but one should not confuse the militant rhetoric of the American liberals with the kind of socialist advocacy and debate that was taking place among the Labour Party intellectuals in England during the war.[44]

If the direction of the two groups differed, there was still a good deal of commonality. The writings of Laski are important for the light they throw on both the differences and the commonalities. Like the American liberal intellectuals, Laski was an all-out supporter of the war. Similarly, he believed the war was a two-front war. Not only was it necessary to defeat the Axis militarily; it was also necessary to extend democracy within all nations of the world. It was for Laski, as it was for Kirchwey, Lerner, Loeb, and Bliven, an international civil war. And like the American liberals, Laski believed that defeating Hitler without destroying the conditions that created fascism in Germany and elsewhere would mean ultimate defeat in the war against fascism and the beginning of a new war.[45]

Laski also had views similar to the American liberals on Churchill, on the wartime unity government, on the dangers of monopoly capitalism, and on the need for democratic collectivism. There was another judgment that Laski and many—though not all—American liberals shared: admiration for the Soviet Union. For them, the heroic Soviet resistance indicated the progressive nature of the Soviet system; no government that did not represent the people or was based completely on involuntary coercion could have produced such a dramatic show of popular unity and courage. As much as Laski defended democracy against dictatorship and criticized the excesses of Stalin's rule in brutally suppressing opposition, he always had a rationale—the insecurity of the Soviet Union in the face of a hostile world.[46]

Yet without unnecessarily qualifying the important parallels, it is important to probe the differences between Laski and the British left, on one hand, and American liberalism, on the other, because the differences tell us much about the direction of American liberal thought. What is important about Laski's views in relation to the British left is that they were set forth in the context of a debate over socialism. His fellow socialist E. F. M. Durbin disagreed with Laski on the Soviet Union and on a centralized socialist state, but both were attempting to point Great Britain on the road to socialism. In the United States, Lewis Corey shared many of Durbin's concerns, but his work was part of a move away from socialism. Although Corey's *The Unfinished Task* and Laski's *Reflections on the Revolution of Our Time* had a common target in monopoly capitalism, Corey, largely out of a fear of Communist totalitarianism, which Laski did not share, spoke for a mixed economy and against a "monopoly of economic power in the state." In his attack on the socialists who saw "government ownership as the open-sesame of all good things," Corey clearly set himself apart from traditional socialism. In the United States most of the talk of socialism was confined to the antiwar radicals of Dwight Macdonald's *Politics* or to the American Socialist Party. The UDA was not talking socialism; neither was

The New Republic or *The Nation*, except for an occasional word about it from I. F. Stone. Nor were the most influential labor leaders or any of the New Dealers.[47]

In Great Britain, socialism was on the agenda, and the debates taking place were within that context. Like Laski and Durbin, G. D. H. Cole and Francis Williams differed seriously over the nature of the Soviet Union, but both were discussing the future of socialism. And Laski and Cole had different ideas about economic planning under socialism, but they were trying to direct the country toward socialism.[48]

One might suspect that at least initially some of the UDA liberals and possibly Kirchwey, Bliven, and certainly Lerner believed their ideas on full production and prosperity for the people would require some form of socialism. But if they did, that belief was buried in the rhetoric of a people's government and the century of the common man — vague terms when it came to planning an economic system. It is not accidental that the American liberals repeatedly used the phrase "the people." It was vaguer, more inclusive, and more compatible with a variety of economic systems than terms like "class" or even "the masses." On the other hand, throughout *Reflections on the Revolution of Our Time*, Laski used the word "masses" — a reflection not only of his stronger Marxist bent but of the fact that he was writing from within the framework of a socialist tradition.

For all its awareness of the need for more structural economic change, the American liberal intellectual community was headed in the opposite direction. The efforts of left intellectuals in the early 1930s to forge a synthesis of radicalism and liberalism had given way to Popular Front – New Deal reformism after 1935. Bingham's non-Marxist radicalism became New Deal reformism; so did Niebuhr's left-wing socialism. There was an outpouring of liberal books in the late 1930s that amounted to a defense of American democracy, pluralism, and piecemeal reform. The Communist Party's Popular Front line, which was patently created by the Comintern for diplomatic reasons, expressed a mood that permeated almost the entire liberal and left ranks; the danger of fascism had created a psychological mood that unconsciously set limits on social change. The Socialists who left the Socialist Party in the late 1930s and began to work to create the UDA in 1940 initially broke with the party over its foreign policy. But many of them — young militants in the early 1930s — had become deeply concerned by the party's alienation from the main currents of liberal reform: the labor movement and the New Deal. Still ostensibly socialists, it was easier once they were outside the Socialist Party to find a niche in the labor movement or in the New Deal and to join the consensus around the "politics of the possible."[49]

Since Corey was the real formulator of the UDA's original statement of principles, we can see that what he and the UDA meant even in their early, more radical stage by "new economic arrangements" was some form of a mixed economy and not traditional socialism. It had some of the anticapitalist rhetoric, and it involved some of the types of reforms that went beyond traditional capitalist economic arrangements and beyond the liberal pattern of government regulatory agencies. Given a populist-oriented movement as a political base, these reforms might have been carried into an indigenous, democratic form of radicalism. Corey himself was interested in third-party politics and was involved with A. Philip Randolph's efforts to form a new party after the war. But without that base, and with the liberal wartime attachment to the New Deal, it was not Corey's agenda that set the parameters of the debate. It may be that his efforts to develop a "functional democracy" offer creative thinking about a post-Marxian socialism. But in *The Unfinished Task*, Corey muted the socialist vocabulary so that it appears, as in other liberal writing, in only the vaguest and most qualified way. And in the milieu in which the New Deal defined the agenda, his work, whatever his intentions, reinforced the move away from socialism.[50]

Not so with Laski. His *Reflections on the Revolution of Our Time* was a conscious effort to forward democratic socialism. Laski was convinced that the next few years posed an immediate crisis. The war years were both an opportune and an essential time to begin the shift to socialism; if the shift had not begun by the war's end, he wrote, private motives and selfishness would return to the forefront. The end result would be a return to monopoly capitalism, economic failure, and the resurgence of fascism. If a socialist revolution by democratic consent were to take place, then the time was now.[51]

There were major political problems in Laski's formulation. Implicitly, he was calling for a Labour Party break with the Churchill government; otherwise, how could he even believe that it was possible to begin a socialist revolution during the war? Yet he never explicitly called for such a break in *Reflections*. He left the reader with an understanding of why Churchill was ideologically wedded to the old capitalist-imperialist system and why the situation was so critical in terms of the necessity of starting to move toward socialism—without providing a political strategy. It was clear that, unlike the American liberals with their commitment to Roosevelt and their belief that they could pressure him in their direction, Laski had no faith that the unity government could achieve his goals, nor that those who shared his ideas could successfully pressure it to do so. Thus, he was left with what amounted to an abstract call for a democratic socialist revolution.

What is most important here, however, is that Laski's formulations, however abstract in terms of an analysis of specific political forces, was based on the possibility of socialism. Despite the genuine talk of building a new world and making a democratic revolution, the direction of the UDA and the American liberal intellectuals in terms of the United States was away from socialism. To put it another way: antibusiness rhetoric, not pro-socialist rhetoric, permeated liberal journals; American liberals developed an antibusiness critique that amounted to a critique of unfettered capitalism. They did not develop a socialist solution.

The triumph of the British Labour Party in 1945 was greeted with enthusiasm by American liberals. *The New Republic* declared that Great Britain was about to engage in a "vast experiment" and predicted important changes in foreign and domestic policy. *The Nation* called it a "bloodless revolution"—a "revolution by ballot"—and compared it to the revolutions of 1688 and 1832. In *PM*, Alexander Uhl saw it ushering in the "era of the Common man." The UDA sought to build up support for the Labour Party. Some American liberals, however, were disappointed in Labour's first steps toward economic change and with its failure to reverse immediately the Tory foreign policy. Stone wrote that Foreign Minister Ernest Bevin had betrayed "the hopes placed in Labor by the people of Britain and by progressive opinion the world over." To combat this view of the Labour Party, the UDA arranged a speaking tour for Patrick Gordon-Walker. Walker explained the Labour Party's progress toward achieving the security goals of the Beveridge Report and toward transforming the capitalist base of the British economy. His foreign policy speeches attempted to show the liberal direction in which the Labour Party was moving, slowly but surely. The UDA was especially active in rallying flagging liberal support when the Labour Party leadership's position on an independent Jewish state in Palestine threatened to reduce its support among American liberals. Thus, the UDA served as a publicist for the first steps toward British socialism while it maintained its ties to New Deal liberal reformism at home.[52]

In 1945–46 the UDA took a further step to bring together the American liberal community and the British Labour Party. Loeb initiated a search for a person to represent the UDA in England. At first the UDA chose William Duffy, but illness forced him to reject the position. It then chose David Williams, who had been a Rhodes scholar and was teaching at Ohio State. In June 1946 Williams moved to England, where he began to develop connections with the Labour Party and to send information to Loeb about developments in Great Britain. Soon he was publishing a newsletter, the *London Letter*, which was sent to the UDA and later its successor, the Americans for Democratic Action (ADA), until 1951. Williams's efforts to build up American liberal influence among British socialists and to explain and popularize the developments in the British Labour Party for American liberals in the postwar years take us out of the range of this study. But an interesting episode took place in late 1946 and 1947 that sheds light on the differences between the American liberals and the British Labour Party.[53]

By late 1946 the UDA had taken the liberal lead in criticizing the foreign policy ideas of Henry Wallace. While opposed to certain aspects of Truman's foreign policy, the UDA nevertheless supported the major features of Truman's policy against Wallace's critique. Once a liberal hero of the UDA, Wallace had fallen into disgrace. He was now pictured as confused, naïve, and dangerous. Loeb believed that not only were Wallace's foreign policy ideas wrong, not only was he naïve in his views of the Soviet Union and the American Communist Party, but that in the process of expressing his ideas he was damaging the cause of American liberalism. Loeb and the UDA—soon to be the ADA—were anxious that the British Labour Party not confuse Wallace's ideas with those of American liberalism and not give Wallace any support. When in late 1946 the left-wing *Tribune* group within the Labour Party issued a statement criticizing both American and Soviet policy and advocating that Great Britain not align itself with either country, Loeb quickly wrote Williams urging him to take steps to undo the danger he believed would result from the statement. Loeb believed that the American public would interpret—indeed he appeared to have interpreted it this way himself—the statement as an endorsement of Wallace and that this was clearly dangerous: it would damage the cause of the British Labour Party in the United States and it would also lend prestige to Wallace. Williams rushed a reply to Loeb in which he sought to explain the differences between the *Tribune*'s left neutralist foreign policy and that of Wallace. Lee wrote a letter that criticized Wallace's views on the Soviet Union and sought to disassociate the ideas of her group, the *Tribune* group, from those of Wallace.[54]

Despite the friendliness of Lee and Loeb, and despite the connections Williams established between the British Labour Party and the UDA, a basic misunderstanding was involved. Believing that American liberals and British socialism shared parallel interests, Loeb, in this case, treated the *Tribune* group as if it should function as an appendage of American liberalism. Because he believed that the UDA and American liberals shared a commonality with the Labour Party, Loeb assumed that a faction of the Labour Party opposing foreign policy supported by the UDA must necessarily be operating from the same principles and beliefs as the pro-Wallace American liberals and leftists that he and the UDA were trying to combat. Thus it was necessary to mount a counterattack. The anti-Communist "social democratic" *New Leader* apparently shared this feeling because it fired off an anti-Wallace blast in a telegram to Bevin. If the anti-Wallace people misunderstood the nature of the *Tribune's* critique of American policy, those more sympathetic to Wallace did too. While he understood some of the assumptions of the *Tribune* group, Lerner nevertheless interpreted their perspective as much closer to Wallace's than it actually was.[55]

The *Tribune* group was seeking to keep Great Britain on a socialist track, and it believed that both American capitalism and Soviet socialism were impediments to that course. But American liberal intellectuals were narrowing the options internationally as they had narrowed them domestically. Unwilling in the war years to establish a third way in opposition to New Deal reformism and to capitalism, and unwilling in the postwar years to seek a third way between American and Soviet foreign policy, the UDA/ADA wound up supporting the New Deal in one case and Truman's foreign policy in the other. It never understood the socialist milieu in which the debates on the British left took place, or, if it did understand them, it never saw that the socialist goal required autonomy on the part of the Labour Party. Ultimately, in the postwar years, the UDA viewpoint prevailed. The neutralist Keep Left faction in the British Labour Party faded by 1950; after the rounds of nationalization, socialism—as distinct from nationalization—as a force within the British Labour Party faded. Although the Labour Party retained a socialist rhetoric and a mass base that was willing to entertain socialist ideas, there was little to distinguish between the long-range vision of the British Labour Party and American liberalism in terms of a vital socialism that could become a third force.[56]

9

The Soviet Union Revisited

IN MAY 1945 Louis Fischer resigned from the editorial board of *The Nation* in protest over its biased reporting and analysis of world events. The journal, he said, had developed a line; there were now "sacred cows." Fischer believed that it had become "very much like a party organ: its opinions appear to be determined by loyalties to organized groups and to governments rather than to principle. *The Nation* is playing politics; that distorts its policies."[1]

Although Fischer's original letter of resignation had not designated *The Nation*'s views on the Soviet Union as the point of issue, Freda Kirchwey's reply indicated that it was differing perspectives on the Soviet Union and its policies that had caused the break. Noting that Fischer had frequently in person chastised *The Nation* for indulging Soviet "bad behavior" and ignoring its suppression of "small, weak states," Kirchwey defended the independence of *The Nation*'s views: "We say what we believe. What we believe is very different from what Mr. Fischer believes."[2]

In defending *The Nation*'s views on the Soviet Union, Kirchwey argued that Russian policy was not imperialist but derived rather from security concerns. It could become dangerous, but "only if Russia decides that the other major powers are plotting against it and takes steps, unilateral and aggressive steps, to offset the threat of a new anti-Soviet alliance." If Soviet foreign policy, for Kirchwey, derived from security concerns, it nevertheless remained at heart an antifascist foreign policy: "With all its arrogance and its open contempt for diplomatic procedure, Russia is carrying through an anti-fascist policy. . . . The western Allies plainly fear that the revolutionary changes certain to follow a clear victory of the anti-fascist forces in

Europe—and the Far East as well—would endanger their control, economic as well as political. Indeed, this is the heart of the matter. Russia can afford to ally itself with the forces of change; it can afford to wipe out the remnants of Fascism and pre-fascist feudalism. Because Russia is not defending a crumbling status quo."[3]

Having the Russian gauntlet laid down explicitly before him by Kirchwey, Fischer was quick to pick it up. Fischer noted that he had grievances against *The Nation* other than its analysis of Soviet affairs; but clearly the Soviet Union was the key issue, and Fischer used Kirchwey's reply to his resignation to vindicate his charges. Acknowledging that Great Britain and the United States had followed bad policies in Spain, Greece, India, and Italy, Fischer denied that these policies were creating the threat of a war with the Soviet Union. That threat, Fischer said, was created by Russia's "expansion in Eastern and Central Europe." For this, all the major powers had a share of the blame, but *The Nation,* according to Fischer, refused to grant this and adopted a double standard whereby England and the United States were "the devils" and Stalin, "though he misbehaves on occasions, is the archangel."[4]

Fischer documented the double standard by pointing out that all imperialists have "pleaded security as their motive." *The Nation* accepted the Russian "security" rationale, one incapable of proof, whereas it had not accepted similar rationales by Germany, Italy, or Japan. Bristling with indignation at Kirchwey's antifascist defense of Soviet policy, Fischer rattled off a list of Soviet actions to illustrate that "antifascist" was a blatant misnomer for Soviet foreign policy: the original partition of Poland with Hitler; Stalin's annexation of eastern Poland in violation of the Atlantic Charter; "the purging of democratic, antifascist, and peasant groups in Poland, Romania, Bulgaria, and Yugoslavia"; its toleration of King Michael in Romania; and its "coddling" of captured Nazi generals in Moscow. Fischer had resigned, he declared in conclusion, because he "did not want to give even the appearance of responsibility" for the "partial . . . presentation of world affairs," and Kirchwey's reply had, to his mind, "prove[d] my point."[5]

Fischer's resignation was not an isolated incident. A few months earlier, in a review of Max Lerner's *Public Journal* in *The New Republic,* Granville Hicks had accused Lerner of having a double standard and of supporting Soviet totalitarianism. Almost at the same time, Varian Fry, who had written frequently on French affairs for *The New Republic,* resigned from its editorial board for reasons similar to Fischer's. Although Fischer's resignation drew greater attention, both resignations set off exchanges in the letters columns of both liberal journals. Clearly, as the war reached its end, the antifascist cause that had held so many American liberals together, as it had held the Allies together, was losing its unifying power. The ties that bound were becoming unraveled.[6]

In the midst of *The Nation* debate, Reinhold Niebuhr wrote a letter in which he stated that he was closer to Kirchwey's views on the Soviet Union than he was to Fischer's, although he warned liberals against romanticizing the Soviet government. That the "realist" Niebuhr should associate himself with the supposedly "idealist" Kirchwey suggests that the issue of foreign policy among American liberals and their views on Soviet foreign policy require further exploration.[7]

It is not enough to write a litany of liberal apologetics for Stalin. There were plenty of apologetics, and whether they took the form of Maurice Hindus's and Lerner's sentimentalization of "Russian people" and the Russian army, J. Alvarez Del Vayo's romanticization of the revolutionary developments in Eastern Europe, or Frederick L. Schuman's "realpolitik" excuses for Stalinism or Heinz Eulau's "objective" analyses that consistently wound up defending Soviet policy, the moral indignation that contemporary observers like Fischer or later historians have expended on this array of rationalizations of Stalinism is justified. But the moral indignation has, in the hands of some, also been filled with self-righteousness. Fischer was correct in much of what he wrote in the spring of 1945, but less than ten years earlier he had been guilty of having the same "sacred cows" and even having a clearer line—facts that he rationalized in 1945. More important, however, is that moral indignation has sometimes served as a replacement for historical understanding.[8]

To understand the thinking of American liberal intellectuals on foreign policy and on the Soviet Union, it is necessary to step back a little to the Nazi-Soviet Pact and the outbreak of World War II, both of which severely shook the American liberal attitudes both toward foreign policy and toward the Soviet Union. The outbreak of the war and the Nazi blitzkrieg in the spring of 1940, culminating in the fall of France, turned many former opponents of collective security into supporters of all-out U.S. aid to the Allies. *The New Republic* symbolized this change. Between 1940, when the journal abandoned isolationism, and the summer of 1941, when it called for U.S. entrance into the war, a dramatic evolution in attitude had occurred. This evolution aligned *The New Republic* with *The Nation*. To a lesser extent and with more qualifications, Alfred Bingham's *Common Sense* underwent a similar shift from isolationism to support for aid to the Allies. World War II, then, closed the isolationist–collective security debate of the 1930s and created a liberal unity on the basic contours of foreign policy: total support for an antifascist, pro-democratic war.[9]

If the coming of World War II disrupted previous liberal attitudes toward foreign policy in general, the Nazi-Soviet Pact did the same to previous liberal attitudes toward the Soviet Union. Former Soviet fellow travelers like Fischer became bitter opponents. Former sympathizers like Bruce Bliven and Kirchwey condemned the pact and its aftermath and began publishing articles critical of the Soviet Union.[10]

When Germany attacked the Soviet Union, the major voices of liberal opinion endorsed Roosevelt's announcement of extending lend-lease to the Soviet Union. The liberals did *not* argue that the Soviet Union had been transformed into a democracy, much less, as the Communist Party said, that the nature of the war had been transformed from an imperialist to a progressive war. Rather, they argued that the main enemy had always been fascism and that it was vital for the defense of democracy to stop Hitler's invasion of the Soviet Union.

Thus, support for lend-lease to the Soviets after June 22, 1941, and liberal arguments for cooperation with the Soviet Union during the early stages of the war had little to do with the romanticization of Stalin or the Soviet Union. Liberal critics of the Soviet Union, like James Loeb, Lewis Corey, and Fischer argued for aid and cooperation. So did conservatives like Walter Lippmann and moderates like Herbert Agar.

All this is not to deny that a romanticization was beginning to take place. Responding to what he saw as a misplaced liberal romanticization of the Soviet Union, Corey, in *The Unfinished Task*, reminded his readers that the Russian people's fight was being romanticized while people forgot that the Soviet resistance would not have been possible without Britain's heroic withstanding of the Nazi air war in the winter of 1940–41—the very period when Stalin was abetting Hitler's war plans. But for a number of liberals the negative images of the Soviet Union and of Stalin that had developed during the period of the pact were being replaced by positive ones.[11]

But why the need for rehabilitation when, as we have just seen, it was possible to argue for support of the Soviet Union on a "realistic" basis in which national interest predominated, and a critical attitude toward Stalin and the Soviet Union prevailed? Some of the rehabilitation can be explained by the intensity of the liberal desire to defeat fascism and to build an international organization that would create a peaceful world. To do so required Soviet cooperation, and it was very easy to develop a style of thinking that presented Stalin in a positive light. However, this liberal rehabilitation of Stalin cannot be explained simply by focusing on events after the German invasion of the Soviet Union. It was based on both attitudes and ideas that go back to the 1930s and even the 1920s, as well as on factors that had emerged during the war.

For those who looked positively on the Soviet Union during World War II, one of the most common distinctions made was between economic and political democracy. Harold Laski, who was influential in liberal circles, based much of his praise of the Soviet Union on what he saw as its extension of economic democracy—a democracy that was defined both in terms of workers' benefits and in terms of workers' voice in the system of planned production. Henry Wallace, too, stressed this distinction. A staple argument among liberal Russian sympathizers in the 1930s, this emphasis on economic democracy was tempting during the war years because it could point in two positive directions for liberals. First, if the Soviet Union had economic democracy already and if it were moving toward political democracy, then it could comfortably be aligned with the Western political democracies in a democratic war against fascism. In this way, the distinction between economic and political democracy provided a view of the Soviet Union that made it intellectually consistent with the basic liberal interpretation of the war. Second, the distinction provided an argument for the United Nations to become a world organization, one in which collective security, operating effectively against aggression, would permit the Soviet Union to progress to political democracy.[12]

One might have expected that the Nazi-Soviet Pact and the critiques of the Soviet Union that followed would have voided the distinction between economic and political democracy. Indeed, for some liberals, like Fischer, the events surrounding the pact completely nullified the distinction. But for others, the meaning of the pact was less total. For writers like Kirchwey, Bliven, and Lerner, the evolution of the Soviet Union in the late 1930s had made them more appreciative of democracy and civil liberties, but before the pact they had not doubted the sincerity of Stalin's support of collective security. The pact was so shocking to them because it betrayed collective security and gave Hitler the green light to begin his attack on the West. But if the pact led liberals like Kirchwey, Bliven and

Lerner to criticize both Hitler and Stalin, it did not lead them to link the systems or draw the kind of parallel features of totalitarianism that Corey enunciated in *The Unfinished Task*. For these three writers, the pact shattered Stalin's image as antifascist and peace-loving; it made them believe that the dictatorship had become corrupted. Kirchwey opened her pages during the period of the pact to Corey's efforts to rethink Marxism and economic systems, rethinking that found in its way into *The Unfinished Task*. However, although Kirchwey could not escape entirely the kind of thinking on totalitarianism found in Corey's writings and in the non-Communist left journals, there was no fundamental reexamination of her own premises.[13]

Thus, when Hitler attacked Stalin and forced him to the Allied side, it was possible to resurrect the distinction between economic and political democracy. Because one did not have to deny the existing dictatorship and could even be critical of both its structure and its excesses, and because the theory did not require any change in attitude toward the American Communist Party, it was possible for people like Kirchwey, Bliven, and Lerner to cooperate enthusiastically in the UDA with the more critical Loeb, Corey, and Fischer, who had come to reject the distinction between economic and political democracy.

A second idea that contributed to the rehabilitation of Stalin and the Soviet Union was one that might have expected to have been thoroughly destroyed by the pact and its aftermath in Poland and Finland: the idea of the Soviet Union as a nonimperialist power. This had been the view of many Russian sympathizers during the 1930s and was, of course, a key reason why the Nazi-Soviet Pact was so shocking.[14]

The possibility of interpreting Soviet behavior as anti-imperialist in light of its post-pact actions resulted from two different ways of interpreting the pact. If one viewed the Soviet side of the pact as aggressive and interpreted the pact as a land-grabbing agreement in which two powerful nations agreed to divide Poland, then there was no denying Soviet imperialism. However, if one believed the Soviet side of the pact was motivated by security concerns, then it was open to a variety of both positive and negative interpretations. For Frederick L. Schuman, a frequent *New Republic* contributor in the thirties, the pact was a brilliant realpolitik maneuver whereby Stalin protected the Soviet Union by buying time for Germany's inevitable attack. Although Schuman professed not to be condoning, only explaining, the pact, his views amounted to a cynical defense — too cynical for *The New Republic* editors.[15]

There was, however, a way to take Schuman's "security" interpretation and use it negatively as a vehicle for criticizing Stalin and the Soviet Union without accepting an "imperialist" interpretation of the pact. Many liberals believed Stalin had made the pact to protect Soviet interests, *but* that he had chosen the wrong way to achieve this end. Stalin's way was seen as cynical and as setting off World War II. In this view, Stalin had seriously miscalculated the dangers of world war and a Nazi victory. He had dangerously and recklessly believed that one could do business with Hitler. Although he was only trying to create a security ring, and although his and Hitler's ends would ultimately conflict, Stalin had not only exposed the western democracies to attack, but he had revealed himself to be untrustworthy to boot.[16]

This view amounted to a serious critique, but because it saw all of Stalin's duplicitous and mistaken actions as taking place in the context of protecting Soviet security, it did not automatically label the Soviet Union as imperialist. It was a far cry from the Communist claim that the Soviets were marching into Poland for peace and freedom, but because it saw Stalin's actions as stemming not from aggression but from a distorted view of Soviet security, it was compatible with a nonimperialist interpretation of the Soviet Union.

As Hitler's troops pressed further into the Soviet Union, it was easier to seize on this second interpretation of the pact and to analyze the strengths and weaknesses of Soviet foreign policy in terms of a concern for security. For Kirchwey, Lerner, and Bliven, this was the thrust of their analysis. It remained perfectly compatible with their critique of the pact, although admittedly as the war progressed there was increasing amnesia about the pact among some liberals. And it was compatible with a degree of criticism of Soviet foreign policy. Writers like Schuman continued to defend Soviet foreign policy on realpolitik grounds, but Schuman published less frequently in the liberal journals in the forties than he did in the thirties. Heinz Eulau, who worked in the war policy unit of the Department of Justice, and who consistently managed to find a plausible and positive rationale for Soviet foreign policy, did publish regularly in *The New Republic;* and the effusive Soviet enthusiasts Jerome Davis and Anna Louise Strong published several articles in *The New Republic* and *The Nation,* respectively, in 1944. But the key to understanding liberal attitudes toward the foreign policy of the Soviet Union is not to be found in unambiguous champions like Strong. For Kirchwey and Bliven it was not a matter of *always* defending Soviet foreign policy actions. The important thing is that they always interpreted and consequently drew their judgments — negative and positive — from a perspective that focused on security as the basic motive behind Soviet foreign policy.[17]

What this perspective assumed was that the Soviet Union was not, like fascism, fundamentally aggressive, and that when it erred or was too recalcitrant this was due to security concerns that were understandable in the light of the history of capitalist counterrevolutionary activity and nonrecognition in the early postrevolutionary years. And it meant that while approval on the part of the West was not mandated, it was necessary for the West to have an understanding of Soviet security concerns and to respond to them with friendship and aid rather than with hostility and fear. Thus, by differentiating security moves from aggression and imperialism, these liberals opened up the possibility of viewing Soviet desires or claims on Eastern Europe as benign, as not necessarily to be applauded and approved but to be understood and tolerated.[18]

The Nation, The New Republic, and *PM* wrote about the legitimate concern of the Soviet Union in having friendly nations on its borders. They praised the Soviet-Czechoslovakia Treaty as recognizing this concern, and pointed to Eduard Beneš as the kind of democratic statesman who recognized the need for Soviet friendship, and to Stalin as a leader who, in accepting a friendly but nonsocialist Czechoslovakia, did not demand ideological uniformity. In the writings of James Warburg, the Soviet Union's intent not "to tolerate unfriendly governments in neighboring states" was presented as neither aggressive nor expansionist. Its interest in Central Europe resembled our "good neighbor policy" in Latin America. Indeed that analogy was frequently used to describe the kind of relationship that Stalin was seeking in Eastern Europe.[19]

It is easy to dismiss this attitude as a reflection of a liberal pro-Soviet bias. But it is important to remember that the people who set forth the idea of a legitimate security zone for the Soviet Union were not all liberals, and those who were liberals were not necessarily associated historically with a high degree of sympathy for the Soviet Union. The conservative Walter Lippmann argued for the legitimacy of Soviet security needs in Eastern Europe. So did Hiram Motherwell, who was a defender of American capitalism and even of "benign" American imperialism. And Niebuhr, though critical of a number of Soviet actions, developed his analysis from the same "security" framework as Kirchwey.[20]

This does not mean that all liberals agreed that security was the prime motive of Soviet foreign policy. There were liberals, especially on the issue of Poland and the future of Eastern Europe, who did see Soviet overlord-ship of Eastern Europe as illegitimate. Certainly, Fischer and Fry believed it was. Albert Guerard, a frequent reviewer in *The Nation* and *The New Republic*, professed friendship for the Soviet Union but condemned its uni-lateral actions that ran counter to his hopes for a European federation. The UDA became increasingly critical of Soviet foreign policy in 1945. It ex-pressed fears of Soviet ambitions in Eastern Europe and disputed those who were willing to concede the Soviets a permanent sphere of influence there. But it is also important to recognize that Loeb never denied that the So-viets had security needs. It was a matter of how these needs should be fulfilled.[21]

If the belief that Soviet foreign policy was defensive and motivated by security needs was an important aspect of the rehabilitation of Stalin and the Soviet Union following the pact, so too was another liberal belief that sometimes rested uneasily with the idea of the Soviet Union as defen-sive—the basic liberal idea that World War II was a democratic revolu-tionary war against fascism, a war that was going on in countries through-out the world. In this view, a democratic revolutionary struggle was taking place in the occupied countries of Europe. The underground and partisan struggles all involved the participation of an array of political perspec-tives, but the left played an important role. With the Soviets supporting De Gaulle's broad political coalition and the United States resisting the recognition of De Gaulle, it became easy to associate the Russians with the forces of democratic social change and the United States and England with the conservative status quo. The same was true of Spain. And it was true of Italy—at least until the Soviets recognized the Badoglio government—and of Yugoslavia, where the Soviets were first to recognize Tito's Parti-sans, although in this case the British followed suit. Poland was a more complicated situation, but for liberals, the exiled London Polish govern-ment contained too many conservatives and reactionaries to be considered an adequate force for the democratic revolutionary change they sought.[22]

Although the democratic revolution that the liberals sought was not a communist revolution, the events in Europe, as well as in China, seemed to many liberals to indicate that the Soviet Union stood for democratic change. The treaty with Beneš was used as proof that the Soviets were supporting broad democratic forces—not simply communist groups—for social change. The State Department appeasement of Vichy, the contin-ued distancing of the U.S. government from De Gaulle, the British and American toleration of Franco in Spain, the recognition of Badoglio in

Italy, and the British policy in India and in Greece were all used as proof that the Allies were missing the democratic revolutionary boat, that they were trying to check it by buttressing the prewar status quo.[23]

Through his writings in *The Nation* and in the Political Warfare section, which he edited, J. Alvarez Del Vayo probably voiced most strongly the democratic revolutionary quality of the war and how Soviet foreign policy supported the war's revolutionary implications while American and British foreign policy opposed them. Occasionally this perspective could lead to a criticism of Soviet foreign policy: Del Vayo, in response to the Soviet recognition of Badoglio, condemned the Soviet betrayal of this litmus test of the antifascist democratic revolutionary war. But most of the time Del Vayo believed that Russian foreign policy was pro-democratic.[24]

That there were conflicts between an analysis that focused on Russian security and an analysis that focused on the spread of democratic revolutions was not always apparent to writers like Kirchwey who simultaneously embraced both. The former was often accompanied by announcements that the Soviet Union no longer sought world revolution, that it had ceased to be a revolutionary country, and that its interests lay in having the security to rebuild its economy in the postwar period. The latter did not argue that the Soviets were pushing an international communist revolution, but it did argue that the Soviets remained interested in ideology and not simply narrow security needs. The two could be reconciled by arguing that friendly democratic regimes on the Soviet borders were part and parcel of protecting Russian security. But the potential conflict between a "defensive" nonideological analysis and an "offensive" ideological analysis was always there. However, the important point is that both contributed to the rehabilitation of Stalin and the Soviet Union in the eyes of the liberal intellectuals.

However, the prime factor in rehabilitating the Soviet image among liberals was an emotional one brought about by the conjunction of three factors: the liberal interpretation of the war, the liberal total support of the war, and the Soviet defense against Hitler's invasion. Given the "people's war" interpretation and enthusiastic endeavors to create a national morale for all-out support of the war, it is little wonder that the war in Russia should have drawn such attention and sympathy. As the Battle of Britain had at least temporarily rehabilitated Churchill, a longtime object of liberal criticism, so the war in Russia rehabilitated Stalin, a not-so-long object of liberal criticism.

For the liberals, the military defense of the Soviet Union from Hitler's attacking army was a people's defense. The stubbornness of the resistance, the manner in which encircled cities held on in the face of mass suffering, stirred the emotions of the liberal community and many others as well. As the struggle in Spain had symbolized the Popular Front in battle, the struggle in the Soviet Union symbolized the people's war in action. Although not all liberals waxed emotional over Stalin, he could not avoid spillover credit for the fight. It was not just credit for saving the West, although this was frequently cited in liberal circles. More important, in the minds of many liberals (with some notable exceptions) the defense itself served to vindicate the regime. The Russian people simply could not have been coerced into their defense; therefore the defense indicated that the system worked, that it functioned for the people, that Stalin, no matter how much power he had, did not simply rule by force, and that the Soviet Union had a democratic dimension. In this way too, the analysis of the Soviet Union as an economic democracy in which the rights and security of the Russian workers had been enhanced connected with the validation of the system in the people's defense of Stalingrad. In addition, Lerner's and others' sentimentality about the Russian people grew out of the defense and reinforced their belief that the war was a people's war—and this, in turn, led them to sentimentalize the "common man" and the "little people" of all countries.[25]

The liberal sentimentalization of the Russian defense against the German attack was not wrong about the heroic nature of the defense, nor was there anything inherently wrong with being emotionally engaged by it. The problem was that by viewing the defense as symptomatic of the nature of the Soviet system, these liberals were masking the nature of Stalinism. The very dictator who had purged his army in the late thirties, made a deal with Hitler that strengthened the German economy, and cavalierly dismissed British warnings of an imminent attack by Hitler in the spring of 1941 now was the recipient of much liberal praise. The Russian sympathizers of the 1930s had been impressed with Stalin the man of action, the man who "got things done," in contrast to Trotsky the ideologue. The quality of ruthlessness that went with the image of the man of action had not served Stalin well during the period of the pact, when his ruthlessness appeared cynical and deceptive, but now, as Soviet resistance stiffened, it could be appreciated again. His activism was credited with enabling the Soviets to advance industrially and thus be in a position to withstand Hitler's assaults. Like the Americans of the 1830s and 1840s who had admired the "iron will" of Andrew Jackson, many American liberals of the war years admired the iron will of Stalin—a will they believed had rallied the Russian people to their heroic defense.[26]

As in the case of Andrew Jackson, the hard image of Stalin was tempered. Americans had tempered the image of Andrew Jackson with stories of his love of children. In the war years, many liberals tempered the image of Stalin with stories of him as a kindly, gentle man. After meeting the Soviet leader, Margaret Bourke-White wrote of his strength and determination (his unsmiling face of "granite") but then added he had a gentler "second personality" ("genial, cordial, and kindly"). Just as the myth of Jackson prevented Americans from facing the reality of the forces transforming the country, so the myth of Stalin prevented many American liberals from confronting the nature of Stalinism.[27]

Once Stalin was rehabilitated, it was easier to "understand" and defend Soviet foreign policy. We have already seen how the liberal interpretation of the war and the liberal commitment to the New Deal combined to make genuine criticism of Roosevelt take on a ritualistic quality: the criticism was sincere, but since liberals would never consider even becoming critical supporters of the war, there was never any sustaining power behind their criticism. Similarly, for those liberals who were led to defend Soviet foreign policy, the support given that policy made some of their criticism of Stalin and the Soviet Union take on a ritualistic quality.

This is clear from the response of *The Nation* and *The New Republic* to the Soviet execution of two Polish socialist labor leaders, Victor Alter and Henryk Ehrlich, early in 1943. Originally arrested following the Russian invasion of Poland in 1939, Alter and Ehrlich had been tried twice, sentenced to death and later freed before their final arrest in December 1942. Charged with pro-Nazi activities, they were sentenced to death. The executions of two well-known socialist antifascists on such unbelievable charges shocked the socialist and labor world. *The Nation* and *The New Republic* were also distressed and critical but—because of their analysis of the war, of the Soviet relation to the war, and of the nature of Stalin and the Soviet Union—nothing followed from their criticism. They acknowledged the negative side of Stalin and condemned the peremptory executions, but it did not mean that there would be less of a defense of Soviet foreign policy. Indeed, *The Nation* warned against turning the justified criticism of the executions into vehicles for excessive criticism of the Soviet Union. That this refusal to reconsider basic premises was true of others with far more influence and power, like Sidney Hillman, does not minimize the fact that those liberals who had rehabilitated Stalin to the progressive cause lacked moral sensitivity. The same was true with other instances: *The Nation* and *The New Republic* attributed the Soviet refusal to aid the Warsaw uprising to a "liaison" problem; it was a "tragic misunderstanding" and not a matter of "bad faith." Any criticism of the Soviet response was minimal. A few months later, when the Soviet government arrested sixteen Polish leaders who had come to Russia from London to attempt to settle the Polish issue, there was little criticism.[28]

The issue, as with liberal criticism of the New Deal, is not liberal insincerity. The criticism of the murder of Alter and Ehrlich and even the more muted criticism of the arrest of the Polish leaders was genuine. But moral sensitivity is not simply a matter of sincere disapproval but of the consequences that follow from such disapproval. The absence of significant consequences, even if those consequences were only an intellectual change of heart, is what is still upsetting today. When Granville Hicks criticized Lerner in 1945 for his rationalizations of Soviet policy, he connected it with Lerner's pulling his punches on the New Deal. Post–World War II liberal defenders of the New Deal and critics of the Soviet Union have not wanted to see the connection. But both derived from the liberal interpretation of the war and the desire not to reconsider it even in the face of evidence that raised fundamental political and moral questions. The very interpretation that was loaded with a democratic moral perspective provided a fig leaf for a refusal to face moral questions raised by the actions of both the American and Soviet governments.[29]

However, those historians and writers who have focused exclusively on the details of liberal self-deception about the Soviet Union have done an injustice to the American liberal intellectual community of the war years. In the first place, the romanticization of Stalin and the Soviet system was not the sole product of liberals. As Paul Willen demonstrated many years ago, American moderates and conservatives contributed to the distortions. It was *The New York Herald Tribune* that talked of "Uncle Joe's boys," and it was Henry Luce's *Time* that, in January 1943, gave Stalin its "man of the year" award. And it was Luce's March 29, 1943, *Life* issue on the Soviet Union that enhanced the public's positive perception of Stalin far more than the small liberal journals. It was not *The Nation–New Republic–Common Sense–*UDA circle of liberalism that was the driving force behind the Committee for Soviet-American Friendship; it was long-time defenders of the Soviet Union like Corliss Lamont and new-found friends of the Soviet Union like Thomas Lamont.[30]

In the second place, what was characteristic of some liberals was not characteristic of all. Corey strongly criticized Communist totalitarianism, and Loeb's desire for Soviet-American cooperation never prevented him from strongly criticizing Stalinism. In *Common Sense*, Alfred Bingham sought friendship with the Soviet Union, but he never romanticized Stalin or masked the nature of his dictatorship. And there was a clear demarcation between *The Nation's* and *The New Republic's* positive views of the Soviet Union and the more excessive romanticization and defenses. Both journals joined with *Common Sense's* editors, John Dewey, Sidney Hook, Dwight Macdonald, and others to condemn the historical distortions in the movie version of Joseph Davies's starry-eyed *Mission to Moscow*. When Arthur Upham Pope protested to Kirchwey that *The Nation* had been unfair to both the Davies's book and film, she firmly defended *The Nation's* negative view of both. Nothing significant separated Kirchwey from Fischer on the issue of *Mission to Moscow*.[31]

Perhaps the greatest problem in focusing on liberal Soviet apologetics is not the injustice involved in generalizing about liberalism but the way it prevents a serious examination of what was itself a serious discussion of foreign policy during the war years. There was plenty of wishful thinking about foreign policy during the war, but underneath the plethora of proposals and ideas a serious exploration was taking place. Plans for a postwar world abounded. World government advocates like Ely Culbertson competed with advocates of a Western European federation like Clarence Streit. All kinds of books on a world federation or a European federation appeared. Advocates of peace through Big Three or Big Four cooperation contended with those who viewed such a peace as a perpetuation of power politics. Idealists who proclaimed Roosevelt's Atlantic Charter a fulfillment of Wilsonian ideals of self-determination found their hopes dampened by the thinking of power politics and spheres-of-influence advocates, but those idealists kept arguing their cause. Realists, in turn, were suspicious of Wilsonian ideals divorced from a recognition of the reality of power.

Nicholas Spykman, John MacCormac, and other outspoken advocates of power politics in foreign policy hardly found a warm welcome in liberal circles, but their ideas were debated and occasionally not rejected in total. Niebuhr found Culbertson and other world government advocates utopian, but he also found the power politics of Spykman and, from a different political perspective, Schuman, without ideals or morality. Bingham wrote enthusiastically at first about Culbertson's plan but later had doubts. Fischer criticized Culbertson's world government ideas but later advocated a strengthening of the world organization. Those who believed in a United Nations or a federation of similar governments (democracies) argued with those who believed that such limited world or regional organizations would exclude the Soviet Union, among others, and this would not be a step to peace.[32]

By pointing out the different positions, I am not denying Robert Divine's argument that internationalism triumphed during the war. Rather, I am arguing that while there was a consensus on antifascism and the need for some kind of international cooperative system, internationalism among the liberal intellectuals meant different things. Was collective security guaranteed only through world government? or by a resurrected League of Nations? or a new kind of organization somewhere between the League of Nations and world government? Did American participation in world affairs point toward a membership in a solitary world organization or toward membership in one of a series of regional federations or both? Both Wilsonian idealism and a realpolitik big-power peace were forms of internationalism. Was peace to be secured by the latter, the Big Three or Four, or only by a world organization? And what about the rights of small nations? Did true internationalism require their having equal or near equal rights with large nations? Or could the goals of internationalism be achieved only by assuring that the large powers had the predominant power? Even spheres of influence—which almost all liberals opposed— were tricky. What constituted a sphere of influence? It might seem clear enough, but *The New Republic*, while opposing spheres of influence, supported what it called a "concert," which other liberals believed looked remarkably like spheres of influence.[33]

These questions were not, of course, unique to liberals. Nor were they simply interesting theoretical questions. They related to issues that were of immediate and paramount importance. They were issues that Roosevelt had to address. In his study of wartime diplomacy, Lloyd Gardner has shown how the twin themes of Wilsonian internationalism and cooperation and traditional spheres of influence ran through—often colliding—wartime diplomacy. Committed to the former, yet also increasingly believing that it— and world peace—could only be achieved by Big Four or Five postwar control, the Roosevelt administration weaved and vacillated between the two. It was, according to Gardner, only able to reconcile itself to the postwar settlement by considering arrangements that Roosevelt made with Stalin, unlike those Churchill made, non–spheres of influence.[34]

If one understands that the liberal intellectuals, like Roosevelt, were trying to formulate a policy for future world peace and, in the process, again like Roosevelt, exploring the intricacies of what true internationalism and collective security meant, then it becomes possible to understand liberal evaluations of the Soviet Union in another context. To do so is not to seek to mask or obliterate the moral issues raised previously but, rather, to understand historically the context of the debate that had led to different moral evaluations. In attempting to understand this context, it is important to understand the twins goals of the liberal intellectuals: world peace and the worldwide democratic revolution—goals that in the mind of conservative statesmen were not compatible.

Having lived through World War I, the failure of the United States to join the League, the Depression, the rise of fascism, and the coming of World War II, liberals were determined to build a world in which peace would be a permanent reality. In their minds, this required eliminating depressions and economic dislocations. They also believed that it required the elimination of the economic and political conditions that had created the rise of fascism. Their second goal of a worldwide democratic revolution entered here. The defeat of fascism was necessary both for a democratic equitable world and for future world peace.

Although many had not felt this way in the 1920s and 1930s, by the beginning of World War II most liberals attributed the failure to maintain world peace after World War I to isolationism and its result: appeasement. Great Britain and France and finally the Soviet Union had appeased fascism, and the United States had followed an isolationist course that encouraged and contributed to Europe's appeasement. Without the U.S. membership and without any clear power to enforce collective security, the League of Nations had failed. Therefore, the foreign policy goals of liberals during World War II were to create a world organization with a strong mechanism for collective security, and to ensure the ultimate defeat of fascism by the triumph of democratic revolution throughout the world.[35]

Given these positions, it is easy to see why, for many American liberals, Wilsonian ideals of self-determination provided the ideological underpinning of their views on foreign policy. Reiterated in the Atlantic Charter, self-determination, no acquisition of territory, and democratic self-rule provided their fundamental guidelines. These liberals were almost unanimously committed to a second aspect of Wilsonianism: a world organization and collective security. This vision led directly to advocating the destruction of empires, the freedom of colonial nations, and opposition to spheres of influence and big-power hegemony.

This Wilsonian vision remained attractive to most liberals. But the reality of the world situation seemed to a number of liberals not to permit the implementation of Wilson's ideals in their pure form. Sharing many of the same goals but skeptical of their lack of consideration of power relationships in the concrete world of diplomacy, some liberals insisted that whether or not one liked it in the abstract, the reality of power had to be recognized. These writers formulated different plans and placed varying emphasis on the element of power. But central to their thinking was the belief that peace could not be maintained and collective security could not work without the concurrence of the Big Three—the United States, Great Britain, and the Soviet Union. What they agreed on was that, in the immediate postwar period, it was the big powers who would have to check aggression. Most liberals saw this as a transition to an effective world organization. But even within such an organization, they argued that the large powers would be required to play the major role. Implicit—and sometimes explicit—within this kind of thinking was the belief that the large powers had particular needs of their own.[36]

This latter acknowledgment raised the possibility or likelihood of spheres of influence—or, as some preferred to put it, friendly borders. To Wilsonian liberals, such thought, at least when raised in noneuphemistic terms and with a realpolitik theoretical framework behind it, had the suspicious odor of imperialism and an imperialist peace. To the other group, the Wilsonian framework, without any recognition of the reality of power, was unrealistic and thus dangerous. In their minds, collective security divorced from large power concurrence could not work.

Most American liberals may have been Wilsonian in their ideals, but in their analyses of world affairs they were neither pure Wilsonians nor pure realists. They wrestled with the respective analyses as they sought to apply them to world events; sometimes they vacillated and appeared contradictory. *The Nation, The New Republic,* and the UDA could all be said to be Wilsonian in their ideals. They all subscribed to a permanent world organization, collective security, self-determination, and the principles of the Atlantic Charter; they all opposed spheres of influence, colonial empires, and big-power hegemony. Yet world events forced them to temporize. While none took Churchill's position that the Atlantic Charter applied only to Europe and all clamored for more action on Churchill's part on Indian independence, most accepted Kirchwey's temporary detente with British rule rather than Fischer's more strident antiempire stance. But the British Empire was not the hard case for liberals.

The Soviet Union presented the harder case. If one were a consistent Wilsonian, it would have been hard not to have developed a critical perspective on Soviet foreign policy. But that, of course, was the point: although Wilsonian ideals prevailed for most liberals, few were consistently Wilsonian in practice. Liberals—even those critical of the Soviet Union, like Loeb—recognized that world peace required the cooperative participation of the Soviet Union in world affairs. A world organization minus the Soviet Union or even a big power peace minus the Soviet Union could not assure peace and instead was a prelude to a third world war. Thus a constant motif in liberal thought was the need not to isolate the Soviet Union, not to build a new cordon sanitaire around her. If one were to do so, the Soviet Union would adopt a nationalistic isolationist policy that would set the stage for a new war.[37]

Here entered the argument that Soviet foreign policy was defensive. Both *The Nation* and *The New Republic* saw the Soviet policy as responsive, but they did not always approve of the responses. They believed the Soviets acted too unilaterally in Eastern Europe, but they interpreted the unilateralism as Russia's second choice: Russia would have preferred cooperative decisions about postwar Europe and the immediate creation of a genuine collective security system, but, in their absence, it would—as all countries did—look after its own self-interest by unilateral actions. In this manner, many liberals were able to maintain their pro-Soviet and pro-Wilsonian views.[38]

As spheres of influence were carved out in Europe (the outlines of the 1944 Stalin-Churchill division were recognized, though all the details and parameters were not known), the difficulty of holding to both Wilsonianism and a favorable view of Soviet foreign policy increased. Sometimes the latter was achieved by a continued focus on the defensive-responsive nature of Soviet foreign policy. Sometimes, as in the case of *The New Republic*, spheres of influence became "concerts." Sometimes a favorable view was achieved by blaming the Allies; the Soviet unilateral creation of a German committee in order to discuss peace terms in the summer of 1943 was explained as resulting from the American dalliances with reactionary groups in Europe and by the lack of "a common political strategy" for Europe after the war. Sometimes it was achieved by blaming the recalcitrance on other parties involved, particularly in the case of the Polish government-in-exile in London. But sometimes Soviet unilateralism in Eastern Europe, particularly in Romania and sometimes in its handling of Poland, went too far, jeopardizing postwar cooperation, and *The Nation* and *The New Republic* condemned it—usually alongside Great Britain—for irresponsible actions.[39]

The need for permanent postwar cooperation made the creation of a world organization so important. With some exceptions, liberals were enthusiastic about the cooperative spirit they detected at Yalta. As the earlier Bretton Woods agreements seemed to lay the foundation for postwar economic cooperation and prosperity, so, for most liberals, the Yalta agreements generally raised the hopes for postwar political cooperation. Despite serious issues that could have led to unbridgeable differences, I. F. Stone wrote, "the solid ties of a wartime alliance" had held. In some ways, however, the plans for the United Nations were a disappointment. The issue of multi-Soviet votes in the General Assembly proved unimportant in the end, but the secrecy surrounding the issue was disturbing to liberals. The issue of the veto was more significant because it ran counter to their Wilsonian principles of collective security enforced by the majority. The big power veto on actions not taken by themselves was reluctantly accepted by liberals as realistic in two ways: agreement among the United States, Great Britain, and the Soviet Union was essential for collective security; and none of the major powers would enter the world organization without it. Nevertheless, such a veto of even the Security Council considerations of their own actions was embarrassing, since Wilsonianism and the principles of the Atlantic Charter seemingly led away from special privileges for the big powers. But *The New Republic* rationalized the issue on the grounds that aggression by one of the big powers would, by taking it out of the world organization structure, automatically destroy collective security and a world organization; thus the issue was meaningless.[40]

For liberals, what was most disturbing about the United Nations proposals was that they institutionalized, at least temporarily, big power control. But even as they urged greater small nation equality, *The Nation* and *The New Republic* had come to accept that in the immediate postwar period the United States, the Soviet Union, and Great Britain had to be the guarantors of peace. Since their predominance was essential only for a transitional period, Wilsonian principles could still be upheld as the goal. But the fact that they had come to accept big power predominance and with it—although they were not always willing to face it—spheres of influence is a measure of how far liberals had come in adjusting to the power realities of the war.[41]

Having made the adjustment, *The Nation, The New Republic,* and *PM* concluded that the essential element of postwar world peace was cooperation between the Soviet Union and the United States. Unfortunately, as the war drew to a close, there were ominous signs that relations were deteriorating. In February 1945 Stone optimistically described the Yalta decisions as "a new Emancipation Proclamation to free all the peoples of the world from the fear of tyranny and war." But three months later he was worried that the United States was attempting to turn the United Nations into "an anti-Soviet bloc." Lerner warned against talk that war with Russia was inevitable; he insisted that the issues dividing the two countries were not insurmountable. Irving Brant saw continuations of the State Department's wartime reactionary biases creating conflicts that threatened the peace. "The State Dept. is instinctively receptive to anything which comes from semi-fascistic European sources," Brant declared. "It is instinctively suspicious of social revolution." As one group of liberals became increasingly fearful in the late spring and summer of 1945 that an anti-Soviet mentality had permeated Washington and the rest of the country, other liberals were becoming increasingly fearful that the Soviet Union was crushing the hopes for democracy and freedom in Eastern Europe. When the first group looked at the Soviet presence in Poland, it saw Polish reactionary forces resisting needed social change; when the second group looked at the events in Poland, it saw the suppression of the rights of small nations and the Polish people. Both interpretations of Polish events developed out of the liberal interpretation of World War II, but now, rather than unifying liberals around the ideological war of the democratic revolution against fascism, the liberal interpretation was open to increasingly discordant viewpoints. It is against this background that Fischer sent his letter of resignation to Kirchwey.[42]

Fischer was perhaps the most consistent advocate of Wilsonian self-determination and the principles of the Atlantic Charter among the American liberals. Since his disillusionment with the Soviet Union over the Nazi-Soviet Pact, he had developed a deep suspicion of Soviet designs; this combined with his long-standing opposition to imperialism and empire, made him a critic of all big power efforts to control self-determination. Given his Wilsonian principles, then, it is not surprising that he should have worried that fascist aggression in Eastern Europe was being replaced by Soviet expansionism. Unlike some liberals who interpreted the Soviet dissolution of the Comintern as a positive sign, one that pointed away from proselytizing revolution and toward a more cooperative policy with the West, Fischer saw it as a sign of xenophobia in which proletarian internationalism had disappeared and had been replaced by an aggressive nationalism that would seek to carve out its own expansionist sphere of influence. Upset by the secrecy of the Yalta accords, the granting of the big power veto under Soviet pressure, the Ehrlich-Alter affair, and Soviet territorial demands in Eastern Europe, Fischer by the spring of 1945 was ready to break with his *Nation* associates.[43]

Kirchwey had adhered to Wilsonian principles longer than Fischer. An advocate of collective security when Fischer still viewed it as an imperialist ploy to protect one group of capitalists from another, Kirchwey's prime motive, as Sara Alpern has shown, was always antifascism. It permeated her thinking throughout the thirties. Moved by the report of German atrocities (she was one of the first to publicize the Holocaust), Kirchwey's thinking on foreign policy always had in mind the necessity of destroying fascism *and* of preventing its rise. She was convinced that a resurgence of fascism and future wars could be prevented only if the United States and the Soviet Union maintained their friendship. Big power agreement was necessary.[44]

What this meant was that Kirchwey was pulled from two sides on foreign policy issues: by her belief in self-determination and no territorial acquisitions and by her belief in big power harmony and cooperation in the postwar period. What she was running up against, as were liberals in general, was that the latter precluded the former. Big power harmony meant acceptance of spheres of influence—and not only on the part of the Soviet Union. But for Kirchwey to accept spheres of influence in the same manner that Walter Lippmann could would be to betray her Wilsonian principles. The only thing to do was to place Soviet territorial concerns in Eastern Europe in a different category; those concerns she located in Russia's fears of capitalist encirclement dating back to the revolution. Thus, they were of a different variety than Churchill's desire to maintain the empire or return the king to Italy or Greece. Unlike the latter, they had, for Kirchwey, a legitimacy. The unpleasantness of having to accept the Soviet sphere of "friendly neighbors" would be overcome as the Soviets took their place as an equal among the world's powerful nations; equal acceptance would mitigate Soviet fears. A Wilsonian world still might emerge in the future.

Kirchwey was also pulled from a third side: the liberal interpretation of the war. If one returns to Kirchwey's defense against Fischer's criticisms one sees that she associated the democratic revolution in Europe with Soviet influence on the European continent. Kirchwey was not arguing for a communist revolution throughout Europe. In fact, close attention to her editorials, as well as those in *The New Republic*, suggests that she and Bliven were critical of Roosevelt's foreign policy because it failed to support a democratic revolution that would be an alternative to Russian communism and British monarchism. She spoke of the need for Roosevelt to play a role in reducing the harsher aspects of the Soviet and British spheres. She addressed the possibility of a democratic socialist Europe as a balance between Russia and Great Britain. Thus, when she expressed the need for a democratic revolution in Europe and linked the Soviet Union to it, she was arguing not that it was trying to communize Europe, nor that Europe should be communized, but that Soviet foreign policy had stimulated democratic forces in Europe, that it was not the enemy of economic, political and social change, as Churchill was, and that it was compatible with the democratic revolution. A truly democratic revolution would not, of course, permit spheres of influence or big power hegemony. Once more, she was forced to fall back on the temporary nature of Soviet–Eastern European small-state relationships. Unwary of the tragedy to come, she cited the treaty between the Soviet Union and Beneš to indicate the possibility of a non-dominating relationship between the Soviet Union and smaller nations.[45]

The three perspectives Kirchwey embodied—Wilsonian idealism, big power realism, and democratic revolution—can be symbolized in the figures of three men active on *The Nation* throughout the war years. Del Vayo was a close friend of Kirchwey and a leading articulator of the democratic revolution ideology. Also a proponent of this ideology, but only as it was compatible with Wilsonian self-determination and the principles of the Atlantic Charter, Fischer had been a major contributor to *The Nation* for many years. Until his resignation, he represented the counterweight of the Atlantic Charter against Del Vayo's belief that the Soviet role in Eastern Europe was furthering the democratic revolution. Although Del Vayo's role in Kirchwey's personal and intellectual life has often been stressed, if one examines *The Nation's* analyses of Soviet foreign policy, the figure who appears to have had far more influence on its editorial policy than he has been credited with was the "realist" Niebuhr. This should suggest that the intellectually uncomfortable—not to mention morally uncomfortable—way Kirchwey sought to overcome the forces of Wilsonian self-determination, the democratic revolution, and the reality of big power diplomacy was not simply the result of her sympathies for the Soviet Union. Niebuhr was not associated with pro-Soviet liberals but with Loeb of the UDA who was under no illusions about Stalinism and who was trying to keep the UDA on a middle course that maintained cooperative relations with the Soviet Union while at the same time criticizing its intransigence.[46]

When Niebuhr wrote to *The Nation* to describe himself as closer to Kirchwey's position than to Fischer's, he warned liberals against romanticizing Stalin and the Soviet Union. But his own analysis of foreign policy, an analysis that led him throughout the war to criticize world government enthusiasts and to argue that a future peace depended on big power accord, made him more sympathetic to Kirchwey's desire for the United States and Great Britain to continue their wartime cooperation with the Soviet Union in the postwar period. It is thus worth exploring Niebuhr's wartime writings on the Soviet Union in *The Nation*.[47]

In January 1943 Niebuhr wrote that "the logic of facts" had triumphed over the rigid ideology of both communism and capitalism and had made cooperation possible. Hitler's attack upon the Soviet Union and the Japanese attack upon the United States had destroyed the theories of the impossibility of collaboration between capitalism and communism. Like Kirchwey, Niebuhr argued that Germany's defeat required cooperation between the West and the Soviet Union, and so did "a durable peace." The end of illusions about ideological distinctions made cooperation possible because it suggested that neither capitalism nor communism had "the complete answer to the vexatious problem of social and political justice." Niebuhr then went on to point out what the West had in common with Russia and how the Russian dictatorship differed from the Nazi dictatorship:

> The fact is that though communism uses dictatorship brutally, it does not exalt it as an end in itself. Nor does it worship either race or war. Its moral cynicism is only provisional, and it is never morally nihilistic, as the Nazis are. It is, in fact, ultimately utopian in morals, just as is the liberal-democratic world. . . . we should recognize that communism believes in universal standards of justice. . . . We have, on the whole, more liberty and less equality than Russia has. Russia has less liberty and more equality. Whether democracy should be defined primarily in terms of liberty or of equality is a source of unending debate. But history proves fairly conclusively that if we subordinate one too much to the other, we shall end by losing both.

Niebuhr's constant balancing act between polar ideals (already seen in his analysis of civil liberties in wartime America) here provided a rationale for cooperation; in the common failure of both systems to achieve their desired goals, but also in the common striving for "universal standards of justice," lay the grounds for cooperation.[48]

The following week, Niebuhr returned to a theme he had briefly introduced in his previous article: the role of Communist parties throughout the world and the tension between communism as a worldwide revolution-ary movement and the needs of the Soviet Union to live, function, and cooperate in the postwar world. The "international Communist Party," as a revolutionary party, stood in the way of postwar cooperation. As "an instrument of the foreign policy of the Russian state," it was ineffective. Niebuhr wondered why the Russians did not surrender to "the logic of facts" and liquidate the revolutionary Communist parties throughout the world.[49]

In searching for an answer, Niebuhr thought it possible that the Com-munist parties in Europe might help to prevent reactionary developments in the postwar period. However, in Great Britain the Communist Party interfered with the bonds between Great Britain and the Soviet Union that would increase in the postwar period as both sought "the stabilization of Europe." Already thinking in terms of power relations in the postwar world, Niebuhr believed that the British were more certain of Russia "as a partner than us." In any case, they would want "Russia as a counterweight against our superior power."[50]

What stands out in these early 1943 articles was that they were filled with a number of arguments that were staples in Kirchwey's and *The Na-tion's* views of the Soviet Union and Russian foreign policy: the possibility of postwar cooperation despite the differences in economic systems; the need to include the Soviet Union in any "mutual security" plans; the So-viet system as a dictatorship but different from the Nazi dictatorship; the greater interest of Stalin in postwar cooperation than in world revolution; the progressive nature of Russian foreign policy in Europe in contrast to the U.S. State Department; and—with more emphasis perhaps than Kirchwey was prepared to give it at this stage of the war—the need to recognize the existence of big nation power in postwar planning. Even Niebuhr's dis-paragement of the American Communist Party was not absent, as we have seen, from the wartime *Nation*.[51]

In the summer of 1943, Niebuhr published an article on England's post-war role. He focused on two themes about the Soviet Union that were central to Kirchwey's analysis: the Soviet desire to rebuild—an argument that pointed to the defensive and security-minded nature of Soviet foreign policy—and the nonrevolutionary nature of Russia's desires. He described the British attitude toward the working out of postwar problems among the Big Three as "promising" and "in accord with realities." It was obvious to Niebuhr that the Big Three needed "to hold together to form a nucleus for a world organization," and Great Britain was strategically located to be "best able to act as an equilibrator of the partnership." Both were "quasi-European powers," but this was not likely to lead to conflict "because Russia gives no indication of desiring an active part in Continental reconstruction." This brought Niebuhr to the ground he shared with Kirchwey:

> Russia's desire to rebuild its land in peace and security will be the dominant motive of all its policies, and that task will absorb its resources for a long while to come. The devastation in Russia has been underestimated in America. . . . I do not pretend to know . . . what Russia will do about the various radical ferments and revolutions which are bound to break out in Europe. But it is fairly safe to guess that it will not encourage them unless it is obliged to frustrate attempts at a reactionary solution of the Continental problem. One contribution which the Soviets will probably make toward the peace will be to oppose the dismemberment of Germany, a policy ominously favored by certain circles in both Anglo-Saxon countries.[52]

In his 1943 articles Niebuhr had recognized the impediments to a big power system of mutual security, but he had been generally upbeat in considering the prospects. By March of 1944, he had grown more pessimistic. Despite the Moscow and Teheran conferences, he wrote, there were growing signs that there had been "no great advance . . . toward a genuine system of mutual security." If no accord was reached, each side would pursue a spheres-of-influence solution. Such a solution could avoid immediate conflict but not future conflict, as each nation sought to extend its spheres. Unless an accord could be reached that prevented the domination of Europe by either side, a third world war was inevitable. Both the United States and the Soviet Union had justified fears that each was out to dominate the continent; in each case, "the impulse to dominate" was "partly a defensive strategy against the supposed or real peril of domination by the other side." In these circumstances "the vicious cycle of fears" that produced wars needed to be broken; a big power agreement was essential.[53]

In his own manner and with perhaps more cynicism about the Soviet system than Kirchwey, Niebuhr had again emphasized one of her basic points about the Soviet Union: in the absence of a general agreement over Europe that guaranteed "mutual security," the Soviet Union would pursue unilateral plans to try to protect its own security. Just as much as Niebuhr, Kirchwey was skeptical about the success of such plans, for she also saw the cycle of countermeasures that would lead to World War III.

When in 1944 the Dumbarton Oaks Conference announced the initial proposals for the United Nations organization, Niebuhr labeled the Russian demand for a big power veto as "ridiculous" from a juridical point of view. But the political problem was more important: the demand reflected the lack of agreement and the continued "deep chasm of mutual mistrust between the great powers." The same themes that Niebuhr had developed earlier in the year were continued. World peace required "order and justice." Order could only be established by those nations with the greatest power; the order could be made just only if there were "constitutional forms" to prevent large nations from oppressing smaller ones. Finally, compounding the problem of attaining a system that established the beginning of world peace was the "irresponsible idealism" of American liberals and internationalists who believed the United States should only support "a perfect constitutional system." It would be impossible even to begin building a system if the United States should withdraw its power, as "the camp of irresponsible nationalists" had—for "opposite reasons"—been demanding all along.[54]

Niebuhr's concerns about irresponsible idealists only grew as the war reached its conclusion and the Allies staked out their spheres. Writing in *The Nation* in January 1945, Niebuhr saw that Russia and Britain were staking out spheres of influence—spheres that offered no foundation for a permanent peace. But what really concerned Niebuhr was the response of the American liberal community. The pro-Soviet liberals who believed that Russian support of "radical resistance movements [was] ideologically more correct" than Western support of "conservative governments in Europe" were justified in condemning Western policy for "its lack of democratic justice" and for its futility. But the idea that the Russians could unify Europe and bring it "economic health" was mistaken. There was "no hope in a Russian-dominated peace and no justification for a liberalism which gives Russia uncritical support."[55]

On the other hand, Niebuhr was equally upset by liberals who attributed all "international virtue" to the United States and was indignant at "the power politics of Russia and Britain upon the Continent." Such liberals fixed on Russian actions in Poland and British actions in Greece and failed to see "the hidden realities of international politics," one of which was that the United States was equally a threat to "international accord." This more "subtle" threat derived from the fact that the United States had a predominance of economic power whose future use concerned Europe and the Allies and whose present use was not always reassuring. This, combined with the United States' predominant military power and the absence of "political pawns" in Europe, created, in Niebuhr's mind, "a hazard to

America's continuing responsibility in the community of nations." It produced a "mixture of nationalistic and idealistic isolationism which the other nations fear." According to Niebuhr, U.S. geography, its constitutional procedures for ratifying treaties, and the fact that the American people had not "been shaken to the foundations of our national life" contributed to the dangers of isolationism and made the American need for "a system of mutual security" less obvious. Given the uncertainty of U.S. participation "in the peace," other nations were tempted to take "expedient precautions." The situation offered "partial justification" for the Russian "desire for unilateral security" and partial justification for the British desire for continental "vantage-points" to check Russia's exclusive domination.[56]

From Niebuhr's perspective, the outrage of "our internationalist idealists" at the Russian and British actions ignored the fact that those actions were partly in response to fears that the United States would not approve the Dumbarton Oaks agreements. The indignation of Secretary of State Edward Stettinius at Russian actions in Poland and British action in Greece might have the moral strength of the principles of the Atlantic Charter on their side, but Europe saw the statements as the "sentiments of a new isolationism." Having agreed to decisions in Europe at Teheran for domestic political reasons, "we washed our hands" of them. Thus, "the vicious circle [was complete]": "Our policy, or the lack of certainty about our future policy, prompts Europe to action which increases the danger of the American errors of omission. The fear of our isolationism and of the unilateral expression of American economic power drives European powers into unilateral policies of security, which in turn make our isolationism more probable."[57]

Removing the United States from this vicious cycle, Niebuhr said, did not necessitate its sphere of influence; it could not be achieved by "pious criticisms" and "implied threats of withdrawal"; and it did not mean "a new Wilsonian program would save us." It did mean that it was necessary for the United States to have a realistic program of "economic health and political stability" to offer Europe. But this, Niebuhr admitted, was unlikely. It was hard for him to be anything but pessimistic about the prospects. Every nation lacked the "resources for a creative approach to the global problem":

> Britain clings desperately to its imperial and political resources because of its very consciousness of weakness in the economic realm. America exploits its economic power the more obviously because it lacks both political experience and instruments of world political power. Russia is still suffering from

the fear of the capitalistic world, a fear which is partly justified by past events and partly the product of Communist dogma. Its Communist universalism has disintegrated, moreover, into a Russian nationalistic fervor and will to power. We are living in a tragic age in which the available moral and political resources are not sufficient for the task in hand. We can now only hope for an approximation of the needed solution. Even that will elude us if Americans fail to understand their own contribution to the failures and errors of our time. For in that event disappointed American idealists will again play into the hands of American cynics. Already liberal criticism of Britain and Russia have an ominously similar accent to those which the Chicago *Tribune* peddles daily in its columns.[58]

Kirchwey might have objected to some of Niebuhr's comments about the Russian "will to power." But there was nothing in his article that departed drastically from *The Nation*'s analysis of Soviet foreign policy. Soviet unilateral moves were still seen as defensive — or at least partly defensive. American isolationism was still portrayed as the greatest danger. In fact — likely by design — one of *The Nation*'s lead editorials in the same issue as Niebuhr's article reflected Niebuhr's concern and cited his discussion of the American "Pilate-washing" of its hands of Europe's power politics. In the absence of American participation, England, France, and the Soviet Union would attempt to create their spheres of influence and build balance-of-power alliances. The result would not bring peace but would breed war. Insofar as this result sought to "suppress popular movements" it would fail. "With Europe in its present revolutionary state," the result of attempted suppression would be "a state of civil war from which European civilization may never recover."[59]

If the latter point reflected the democratic-ideological interpretation of the war more than Niebuhr's realism, the rest was pure Niebuhr. There were critical comments about America's "shocked disapproval," its "moral aloofness," and "the spiritual isolation from Europe's mess" enjoyed by American "liberal internationalists." There was the same critique of isolationism and the same demand for American participation; if the wording reflected Kirchwey's idealism, the sentiments were the same as Niebuhr's.[60]

In his last article on foreign policy in *The Nation* before Fischer's resignation, Niebuhr sought to defend the Dumbarton Oaks and the Yalta agreements from the criticisms of those who viewed them as having "capitulated to expediency" and "forsaken principle." Niebuhr defended the extension of "the core of world community created by the war partnership of the great powers" against those who attempted to create a "constitution of world authority above and beyond the sovereignty of the great powers."

The latter constitutional approach was, for Niebuhr, abstract, ahistorical, and not reflective of "the main currents of history," which had made some nations stronger and some weaker. This was Niebuhr's old argument about recognizing the necessity of the large powers playing a major role in keeping the postwar peace. It was a position that the liberals of The Nation and The New Republic had come to accept in a temporary and transitional form. Niebuhr saw the need for reforms giving the smaller nations "greater authority" (especially not leaving "military strategy . . . completely in the hands of the great powers"), but he was more concerned with having liberals recognize the necessity of accepting big power predominance and not repeating the mistakes of World War I, when "a constitutional solution . . . was sabotaged by American cynics, nationalists, and realists."[61]

In a revealing passage that would establish why Niebuhr was closer to Kirchwey than to Fischer, he addressed the Soviet threat to the mutual security system he was defending:

> It is true of course that Russia seems particularly intent upon establishing a system of unilateral security and that its hegemony in Eastern Europe may threaten the stability of a mutual system. But even so its policy differs in degree rather than in kind from that of the other great powers. Let those of our critics who insist that we are dealing not with "one world" but with "two worlds" state their alternatives clearly. Do they want to prepare for the next war between Russia and the West? Dumbarton Oaks is different from Munich because Russia is different from Germany. Russia is not driven by the mania of world conquest, though it obviously has residual fears of the Western world. Shall we seek to quiet those fears by efforts to achieve a mutual-security system, or shall we play upon those fears and make another war inevitable? Is it not quite clear that our idealist critics are offering us nothing but another war under the guise of an unattainable purer constitutional system?[62]

When Fischer, one of those idealist critics, resigned from The Nation, Niebuhr's response was to criticize the journal for its oversimplification when it said that the Russians had made mistakes but had "a more rigorous anti-fascist policy than the Americans." He pointed out that Russia was using fascist forces in Hungary and Romania and that if the Soviets destroyed "the independence of Czechoslovakia completely, as now seems likely, and if it refurbishes Marxism as an instrument of policy in the central and western parts of Europe, while holding eastern Europe through pan-Slavism . . . this will present us with problems that transcend the fascist–antifascist category you use."[63]

Although this criticism may have presaged an increasingly critical attitude toward Soviet foreign policy and an increase in his own previous criticism of those liberals who defended all aspects of Soviet foreign policy, it is easy to see why Niebuhr was still closer to *The Nation* than to Fischer. Even while criticizing Soviet foreign policy, he indicated that it resulted from fear—a policy consistent with Kirchwey's defensive and responsive interpretation of Soviet foreign policy. But most of all, for Niebuhr, Fischer must have appeared as an abstract moralist, the kind of "pure" liberal internationalist, who by his moralistic condemnations of Soviet behavior, encouraged the cynical and nationalistic isolationists who were leading the United States down the path to a new war.[64]

This excursion into the similarities and parallels between Kirchwey's and Niebuhr's views on Soviet foreign policy was not made in order to suggest that Kirchwey and Niebuhr did not have differences on the nature of the Soviet foreign policy. Kirchwey was more influenced by, and was one of the leading proponents of, the democratic revolutionary interpretation of World War II. The kind of political rhetoric found in the writings of Del Vayo, with its progressive image of Soviet foreign policy, was frequently used in her editorials and no doubt was a major reason why Kirchwey and Niebuhr took different paths on foreign policy in the postwar period. It would be wrong to think, however, that Niebuhr was not influenced by the democratic revolutionary interpretation of the war; he too spoke of a revolutionary-minded Europe and the advantage that gave Soviet foreign policy. Unless Niebuhr was a complete hypocrite, the praise he heaped on Kirchwey at her honorary dinner on February 27, 1944, suggests that he had more than personal admiration for her. There was also a strong agreement on the major motives behind Soviet foreign policy, on the kind of response that the United States should make, and on the necessity of balancing big power realities with the ideals of Wilsonianism, the Atlantic Charter and a democratic world organization. The parallels are important not for their own sake, but because they suggest a certain consensus about foreign policy by those who did not necessarily share the same evaluation of the Soviet internal regime. They also serve as a warning against reading back into the war years all the battles of the cold war, during which Kirchwey and Niebuhr found themselves in fundamental disagreement.[65]

Finally, these parallels suggest the complications facing—and the resulting complexity in the views of—those writing on foreign policy during the war. The balancing of principles and realities, the efforts to build a world organization based on cooperation among statesmen with self interest—and selfish interests—and suspicions, and the variety of internationalist perspectives all led to attempts at definition and analysis that sometimes were contradictory and always incomplete. That the liberal intellectual community generally held together throughout the war on the issue of foreign policy is remarkable. The tensions were always there, but not until Fry's and Fischer's resignations did they break out into the open.

By the summer of 1945 the scattered signs of disagreement had increased. British actions in Greece, the German settlement, and especially Russian actions in Eastern Europe were creating stresses within those seeking the liberal objectives of the war. By the middle of 1946 the cold war among liberals was under way. The intellectual cold war would turn out to be as disastrous for liberalism and the left as the actual cold war was for humane values throughout the world. The defenders of American policy made valid criticisms of Wallace and of those liberals who continued to indulge Soviet foreign policy, but the haste with which they rushed to judge the moral delinquents prevented them from critically examining American foreign policy. They might chafe at specific actions on the part of the West, but they could not envisage any true third alternative between the Soviet Union and the West.[66]

Moreover, by holding one's attitude toward the Soviet Union as the *only* litmus test of what today would be called "political correctness," the debate—simplistic and crude as it often was—that had begun during the war years was cut short. If one assumed all Soviet actions justified as "security needs" were aggression and all American reactions were legitimate security needs (or vice versa), then any discussion of what constituted, if anything, legitimate security was curtailed. Of course, Wallace contributed to the confusion. Not only did he make foolish and morally blind comments on the internal conditions and foreign policy of the Soviet Union, but his statements were a jumble of often contradictory elements. Wallace spoke for free trade capitalism and postwar cooperation with the Soviet Union and ignored the fact that the Soviet Union was not anxious for free trade in its sphere of influence. He spoke for self-determination, voiced Wilsonian ideals, *and* defended a Big Four peace and the need for Soviet friendly borders—which translated into spheres of influence, a philosophy he opposed. Wallace spoke against imperialism, but urged an expansive capitalism and the penetration of Third World markets, without ever stopping to ask if there might be any conflict between the various positions.

But Wallace was not that different from many of the wartime liberals, Kirchwey and Niebuhr included. Liberals were trying to combine and balance ideas about foreign policy that rested uneasily together. "Moralistic" Wilsonian idealism, big power "realism," and the goal of a "democratic revolution" were not easily reconcilable intellectual and moral frameworks. Both Wilsonian idealism and a democratic revolution seemed increasingly divorced from achievable possibilities; big power realism seemed to validate what had been achieved and to dismiss any other possibilities. When found together, as in the case of Kirchwey, they took on the jumble and confusion of irreconcilable goals. Unfortunately, what replaced the confusion of the war years was a simplistic dichotomy between totalitarianism and "the free world" on the part of the defenders of "the West" and a dubious defense of Soviet actions by many critics of "the West." The consensus over foreign policy that developed in the cold war years was the result of the attenuation of the foreign policy debate of the war years. The many crosscurrents about foreign policy that went on in the midst of a general consensus about the foreign policy goals during the war was frustrating to those who sought clarity and neatness. But the clarity that developed between cold war apologists for the United States and cold war apologists for the Soviet Union in the postwar years was more intellectually sterile and morally blind than the confusion of the war years.

10

Socialists at War

IN SPITE of their differences with Norman Thomas over the domestic Popular Front issues, *The Nation* and *The New Republic* opened their columns to him in the late 1930s. During the war, however, neither journal did. It was not that Thomas lacked outlets beyond the party's newspaper, *The Socialist Call*. But the absence of any Thomas articles in *The Nation* and *The New Republic*, even in the form of a debate, reflects the tension between the editors and the leading spokesperson of the Socialist Party.

Nor did either journal publish articles written by other prominent members of the Socialist Party. The same effort to distance oneself from Thomas and his organization can be seen in the UDA's attitude toward the Socialists. In September 1941, Mary Hillyer of the Thomas-led Keep America Out of War (KAOW) Congress wrote to James Loeb offering to cooperate on activities where KAOW and the UDA held parallel positions. Loeb rejected the offer. After the war began, Hillyer, Thomas, and a number of Socialists joined with such liberals as Oswald Garrison Villard to form the Post War World Council. When the council organized a petition protesting the internment of Japanese Americans, Hillyer requested Loeb's signature. There is no evidence Loeb replied.[1]

It is clear that the pro-war liberal community did not want to have any close relations with the Socialist Party, whose opposition to the war before December 7, 1941, had, in its mind, contributed to the fascist danger. In January 1943 Louis Nelson, the manager-secretary of Local 155 of the Knitgoods Workers' Union, wrote to *The Nation* to express his—and others'—indignation that Thomas had not been invited to attend the UDA-*Nation*-sponsored testimonial dinner for Senator George Norris. Thomas, Nelson said, had fought and would continue to fight for the rights of labor and for a "better world," and the idea of sponsoring a dinner for Norris was to honor a fighter for justice and not "to give prestige to the Union for Democratic Action or to Freda Kirchwey or any other individual." The editors replied that they had decided "quite deliberately" not to invite as "speakers or sponsors . . . men who had been fundamentally opposed to the war and to the whole anti-Axis policy which led up to the war and gives it meaning . . . to the people who organized the dinner the idea of having isolationists and pacifists to take part would have seemed entirely inappropriate."[2]

When the controversy became public in *The Nation*, Loeb quickly assured Thomas that the oversight was inadvertent and that it had been a mistake—not a deliberate exclusion as *The Nation* editors asserted. Loeb's apology rings hollow and can best be explained by his personal regard for Thomas.[3]

The reason for liberal hostility to Thomas was not simply that he was an isolationist in the 1930s but that he had come to symbolize *left* isolationism, that he had remained opposed to the war until Pearl Harbor, and that he had participated on the same platform with Charles Lindbergh and other members of the America First Committee. The pro-war liberals— even as late as 1944, in Niebuhr's reply to Thomas's overtures for liberal presidential support—could not refrain from reminding Thomas of what they deemed his irresponsible political behavior during the two years leading up to U.S. entrance.[4]

Those two years stuck in both the liberals' and Thomas's craw. When the UDA and *The New Republic* published their 1942 voter supplement for a Congress to Win the War, the Socialists felt—with some reason—that they had made a congressman's prewar foreign policy record the key determiner of whether he should be elected. The Socialists chastised the supplement for not criticizing "reactionary interventionists," and Thomas accused the UDA of "blindly" supporting Roosevelt. Frank McCulloch, an ex-Socialist UDA member from Chicago, defended the use of prewar foreign policy issues as an indicator of administration support. In the process, he criticized the Socialists' use of the phrase "totalitarian liberal." Thomas replied by expressing his disappointment in the UDA and its "backward look prompted by its own interventionist stand." He also defended his use of the term "totalitarian liberal" for those who accepted the concentration camps ("humanely run but still concentration camps") for Japanese Americans, opposed efforts to feed Europe's children, and favored "total mobilization." On these scores, he found the UDA on the wrong side.[5]

Unlike Thomas, some liberal ex-isolationists were not excluded. Alfred Bingham, for example, had only modified his isolationist stance toward the war after the fall of France and was still talking of a possible negotiated peace in the fall of 1941. Yet, the UDA invited Bingham to be a member of its goals committee that fall. One of the reasons for the different treatment was that Bingham viewed the war as a worldwide democratic war. Although Thomas favored democratizing the nation's economy, dismantling empires, and supporting a "people's peace," he never interpreted the war in the liberals' particular ideological terms.

Liberal hostility to Thomas and to the Socialist Party was only reinforced when, following Pearl Harbor, the party, under the prodding of Thomas, adopted a position that was tantamount to "critical support." This position was the way Thomas surprisingly was able to keep the party together. The splits and defections that had characterized the Socialist Party in the 1930s would appear to have made inevitable a new schism. While the vast majority of pro-war Socialists had resigned from the party by the fall of 1941, many of those left in the party were pacifists. Others were advocates of "revolutionary socialism" or, at least, no political support for capitalism and its wars. Thomas was torn. Not a total pacifist, he nevertheless had strong pacifist inclinations and a philosophical respect for the pacifist philosophy. Never an advocate of revolutionary socialism, he knew that some of its sympathizers, like Travers Clement, who served as national secretary for a while before the war, and Lillian Symes, a columnist for The Socialist Call, had been willing to submerge their more radical inclinations in order to keep the party together during this difficult period. Thomas was grateful for their cooperation. Although Clement and Symes were engaged in a rethinking of some of the old radical concepts, accepting a position of critical support went against their entire analysis of capitalism and imperialism.[6]

After Pearl Harbor, the National Action Committee (NAC), which was created to speak for the party between meetings of the National Executive Committee (NEC), issued a statement that avoided the term "critical support." But its phrasing suggested that the party accepted military victory. Meeting in January 1942 the NEC issued the party's official position on the war. Despite the desire on the part of a few Socialists like John Lester Lewine to adopt a pro-war position, Thomas recognized that his main problems lay with the pacifists and with the Clement-Symes supporters' desire for the party to go on record as opposed to World War II. Thomas believed that the pacifist opposition to the war was fine as a matter of individual conscience, but he felt that it did not address the political problem of how the party could best function effectively. He knew that the majority of Socialists, including himself, were not pacifists and that certainly the overwhelming majority of the American people were not. In this context, a declaration of opposition to the war would serve neither the party nor the future of socialism. The public would not understand, and its hostility to socialism would be even greater. And despite his intense discouragement at the coming of the war, Thomas believed there was both a need and an opportunity for getting the socialist message across.[7]

Above all, Thomas was determined to hold the party together; small as it was, it could not afford a further loss of members if it was to survive. He was helped in this desire by the fact that all groups within the party agreed on the kind of program that was needed: to protect and expand labor's rights; to protect civil liberties, including the right of conscientious objection in wartime; to fight for civil rights; to fight against colonialism and an imperialistic outcome of the war; to fight for a democratic people's peace; to urge on labor the need for independent political action; and to engage in socialist education.

Thomas recognized that by combining criticism of the capitalist system with an acceptance of a war victory, the party would be giving critical support to the war. Personally, but not publicly, Thomas was willing to accept the position of critical support and at various times during the war he described in personal letters his and the party's position as critical support. But in drafting the NEC's official statement he was determined not to publicly use the divisive phrase, which conjured up remembrances of European socialism's embrace of World War I and thereby created a red flag for the pacifists and for the Clement-Symes supporters. His substitute language was vague; it managed to refer to the war and to accept military victory in such general terms that, while focusing on the specific areas where socialist criticism and action were needed, it could serve as a blanket for all the political and philosophical persuasions within the party. The final version still did not satisfy Clement and Symes. At the January meeting of the NEC, Symes introduced an amendment calling for political nonsupport of the war. The amendment was defeated by a vote of 6 to 5. The defeated amendment was sent to the party for a referendum, which supported Thomas's side. Despite the different perspectives within the party, enough common ground had been found to keep it together.[8]

Nevertheless, important differences remained. Many of the pacifists were deeply upset by the statement; some resigned from the party. Most sought conscientious-objector status and refused to register; they went either to jail, to government conscientious objector camps, or to the civilian public service camps run by the Quakers and other pacifist religious groups. But although a few young revolutionary socialists left the party over the war statement, Clement and Symes remained. Symes wrote her lively column until illness forced her to stop (she died at the young age of fifty in 1944), and Clement, with less time because of Symes's illness, still served on the NEC and wrote or consulted on occasional party pamphlets.[9]

The war was not the only issue dividing Clement and Symes from Thomas and the rest of the Socialist Party leadership. There was also the issue of the party itself: its political direction and what kind of party it should be. Clement and Symes had a different conception of the Socialist Party than Thomas and his closest associates. Clement and Symes were anti-Leninist as far as the idea of a vanguard party went—the whole idea was garbage, Clement said—but they were also opposed to an amorphous mass party. They believed that even at its height before World War I, the Socialist Party had been filled with so many tendencies that were essentially Populist-reformist rather than Socialist that it had been ineffective in crisis situations. A cohesive and ideological Socialist Party, on the other hand, could offer the necessary political leadership for the labor movement.[10]

On the opposite side, Thomas and the leadership of the Socialist Party were attempting both to build the party and to lay the groundwork for a larger radical mass party built along the lines of the Canadian Commonwealth Federation (CCF). Maynard Krueger, the chairman of the party, made a disappointing attempt to begin such a movement, the American Commonwealth Federation (ACF), in Chicago. Judah Drob, the party's representative in Michigan, was active in the Michigan Commonwealth Federation, which had somewhat more promise than the ACF but ultimately never fulfilled the hopes of the Socialists. In the Far West, efforts were made to build American branches of the CCF.[11]

In early 1943, Thomas expressed support for an "organized mass party of workers." At the same time, he saw little hope for it developing in a satisfactory way. He feared that if such a party did arise it would resemble the unsatisfactory American Labor Party (ALP), which, according to the Socialists, was too tied to the Democratic Party, was too supportive of Roosevelt's foreign and domestic policy, and had too many Communist members. In outlining the distinction between a legitimate labor party and one designed to garner votes for the old parties, Bill Becker, the party's labor secretary, stressed that a true labor party needed to have rank-and-file participation and a program, and it needed to be independent of the two old parties. Thomas was also insistent that a labor party would have to permit the Socialist Party to maintain its existence within a mass party.[12]

Thomas's interest in a mass party was so deep that in the summer of 1943 the NEC passed his motion calling for the creation of a new mass party based on the need to offer the American people a clear choice. But the call did not preclude the Socialist Party from running its own candidate in 1944. By late 1943, Thomas had concluded that it would be necessary; otherwise, it would mean "the end of the Socialist Party." It was necessary, he said, for the Socialists to try to get "the big ideal across."[13]

With the decision to run its own candidate in 1944, the Socialist Party began to focus on what this meant in terms of new party formations. While running their own candidate, Socialists continued to talk about the desirability of a mass party combining all progressive groups; during the campaign, Thomas said he wanted a party like the CCF. The final Socialist resolutions on political action adopted in 1944 sought to accommodate differing views, with a strong statement on the necessity of a Socialist presidential campaign and a strong statement of welcome for new political formations. So the debate over the formation of a mass party continued during 1944, but the efforts in Chicago, Michigan, and elsewhere continued to produce little success.[14]

During the debate over the future of the Socialist Party in a mass party, Symes expressed skepticism over whether the CCF could help build an "American mass labor party." Because of the CIO's ties with Roosevelt and of the Canadian CIO's ties with the CCF, Symes was afraid the CCF would support Roosevelt as a "lesser evil." On the other hand, Drob saw Symes's fear as part of her "b.s." and claimed that the CCF was "a socialist party in every sense of the word." Although Symes and Clement shared the party's disdain for the ALP, they were not pleased with the direction in which they believed people like Drob, with Thomas's support, were trying to take the party. Convinced that the party was going in the wrong direction and that the failures and corruptions of socialism required a rethinking, although not an abandoning, of Marxism, Clement and Symes placed a far greater emphasis on "ideological" work than most of the rest of the party. They began a *Perspectives* discussion group among Socialists interested in their concerns.[15]

The party leaders, Thomas and National Secretary Harry Fleischman, were not overly disturbed by this possibility of new party factionalism.

Thomas respected Symes and Clement, although he had little patience with their demand for more philosophy. He described as apt a remark that Clement wanted "Jeffersonian Bolshevism"—a small party that would lead the great masses. When one writer criticized Symes and Clement's idea of a disciplined party, Fleischman replied that they were "too dogmatic and inflexible" but attributed it to their "living in the country," where they had "nothing to do but think." When Clement set forth some of his "Perspectives" on the Socialist Party for discussion, Fleischman indicated he agreed with much of his analysis of the world and of socialism but that it became "fuzzy as all hell" when they began discussing the application to "current problems." [16]

Clement himself found "intellectual lethargy" in the party. Disturbed by the party's response to their initial statement, the *Perspectives* group circulated a discussion bulletin, which showed that one source of the *Perspectives* group's discontent was its feeling that the party reached decisions on the basis of trying to accommodate Thomas. The bulletin cited Thomas's support for Ely Culbertson's world federation plan in the *Socialist Call* followed by an article opposing the plan. In such circumstances, the party, according to the *Perspectives* group, either took no position on the issue or sought a policy that did not "exclude that of Comrade Thomas." [17]

In other parts of the bulletin, the *Perspectives* group sought to distinguish between the Communists' "vanguard party," the present Socialist policy of seeking to be a "leavening" force (having influence), and its own idea of the Socialist Party as a "spearhead party." It also emphasized that the greatest dangers for labor came not from "old-fashioned labor haters" but from the totalitarian trend toward statism. Deeply concerned about labor incorporation into the state and its dependency on the Roosevelt administration, Clement's group sought to build an intellectual foundation for labor's becoming politically independent: "Labor cannot afford to ally itself with a world-wide totalitarian tendency in order to fight 'reaction'. It must establish and maintain its own structural and political independence in order that it can strike out in any direction from which the threat to that independence may come. It is the *labor and progressive dependence on the Roosevelt administrative apparatus* which represents the greatest danger at the moment." [18]

The Socialist Party and Thomas were certainly not oblivious to these dangers, since much of the wartime criticisms coming from all segments of the party focused on state capitalism and the dangers of statism. However, there was a significant difference in their analysis of the direction of capitalism. Thomas and the majority in the Socialist Party spoke frequently about postwar economic crises, but they clearly did not think that they were living in the kind of "revolutionary" period that Clement had envisioned. Indeed, Thomas's sympathy for the Culbertson Plan lay partly in his belief that one was not about to get rid of the nation-state and that it was necessary to come up with at least partial reforms to reduce its dangers. Clement, on the other hand, saw the inadequacies of the Culbertson Plan and the "haphazard" ways in which the party accommodated itself to Thomas's views of it as indicative of the lack of revolutionary seriousness in the party's majority. Convinced that a revolutionary period did exist, the *Perspectives* group believed the party might help define "the direction of the revolution." The party leadership, however, was content to try to "influence" conditions; it could not imagine "directing them." [19]

The disputes between Clement's *Perspectives* group and the party leadership were symptomatic of the uneasy peace that existed within the party. It was as if all sides recognized that ideological and political differences could not be pushed too far or else the entire party would disintegrate. But this recognition did not stop the bickering, for example, between John Lester Lewine, a pro-war Socialist, and Robin Myers, a Clement-oriented New York Socialist leader. *The Socialist Call* featured columns by Lewine alongside those of such antiwar "third camp" socialists as Symes, Andre Martin, and a non-party member, Jim Cork. At one point, Lewine demanded the party repudiate Symes's pamphlet on the Indian revolution. Harry Paxton Howard, who wrote frequently for the *Call*, mostly on foreign policy — and a man who never heard a rumor of a capitalist or Stalinist conspiracy that he did not accept — proved embarrassing for all factions. He upset the Clement-Symes-Cork group with his outspoken attacks on the Indian Congress Party, attacks that challenged both the party's official position on India and Symes's pamphlet. His undifferentiated attacks upon Axis and Allies upset Lewine. And when he spoke to a right-wing isolationist organization in Chicago, despite the advice of the local Chicago members and Fleischman, he upset the entire party. [20]

Although none of these controversies attained anything like the scope and intensity of the bitter controversies of the 1930s, they were constant sources of irritation to Fleischman and to Thomas. Indeed, the entire period was one of intense discouragement for Thomas. In letters, he frequently complained of the dark outlook for the world and of his own mental anguish — only to end on a note reaffirming the need to carry on. There were three main reasons for his feelings of gloom. One of course was the constant quibbling within the party. Another, especially in the first months following the U.S. entrance into the war, was his belief that the Japanese attack had resulted from American policies he had warned against; he was convinced that Roosevelt and Cordell Hull had acted in a duplicitous manner before the attack. The third was his constant need to defend himself from previous supporters outside the party who felt that his tacit critical support of the war had betrayed the pacifist or isolationist cause. Some, like the pacifist anarchist Jo Cantine, poured out their disappointment to him in long letters throughout the war. Many demanded that he begin a peace offensive for a negotiated settlement. And from both the pro-war and antiwar sides came charges of inconsistency—that if he had really believed what he had said previously about the nature of the war and the consequences of U.S. participation, then he should still be against it.[21]

Thomas was most sensitive to the accusation that he had betrayed his pacifism. In response to this charge—sometimes accompanied by bizarre stories (one well-known writer accused Churchill of bombing Pearl Harbor and faking the Japanese attack)—Thomas patiently sought to explain his position. He insisted quite correctly that as much as he admired the pacifist faith and hoped it would prevail in the future, he had not been a pacifist since the mid-thirties. He also argued correctly—something neither Kirchwey and her friends nor many of Thomas's allies and supporters understood—that he had never been an isolationist. He had, he said, been an anti-interventionist, and to his mind there was a big difference. He had never believed that the United States was self-sufficient or entitled to ignore developments throughout the world. What he had insisted at the time—and what he continued to insist—was that before Pearl Harbor the cause of future world peace and world justice could better be served by American noninvolvement in the war. He had never, he said, argued that German and British imperialism were on a par—rather, he had always insisted that Germany's had reached new levels of brutality—but he had argued that this in itself was not a sufficient cause for U.S. entrance.[22]

However, for Thomas, Pearl Harbor had changed everything. For one thing, the United States, whether it liked it or not, was in the war. The question then became whether it could now serve the cause of world peace and world justice by participating in a military victory over fascism or by urging a negotiated settlement. In the spring of 1942 Thomas did not rule out a negotiated settlement in all circumstances. But under the circumstances then existing, he believed that a military victory was preferable to a negotiated peace. Part of these circumstances involved the manner in which the United States entered the war. The Japanese treachery—and despite Thomas's bitter condemnation of Roosevelt and Hull's pre–Pearl Harbor policy, he considered it treachery—had created a climate of public opinion that would not understand a Socialist peace offensive. Moreover, a negotiated settlement in early 1942 would have been advantageous to Hitler; he had the military advantage.[23]

Although Thomas could speak for the Socialist Party on the issue of a negotiated peace, he could not speak for all Socialists. One party member and friend, George Hartmann, a onetime member of the Columbia Teachers College faculty, organized the Peace Now Movement soon after the United States entered the war. Hartmann argued that the terms of his proposed peace offer were antifascist and would be offered to the German and Japanese peoples, but he conceded that it was preferable to negotiate with Hitler (assuming the people could not put themselves in a position to negotiate) than to have the war continue. He acknowledged that the triumph of fascism would be a tremendous setback for both socialism and humanity, but that the carnage of the war was worse.[24]

Pro-war liberals wrote exposés of the fascists involved in Hartmann's Peace Now Movement. Thomas had no reason to doubt Hartmann's own motives, but he also knew from his experience of seeing the America First Committee in operation that it was difficult to keep the reactionary isolationists and pro-fascists out of a loosely organized movement. This was one reason why Thomas kept the Socialist Party at a distance from Hartmann's movement. But the main reason was that Thomas believed that the call for a negotiated peace in 1942 was both morally and politically misguided.[25]

Although Thomas did reject Hartmann's Peace Now Movement, a closer look at the party response to Peace Now reveals that he was not nearly as hostile to it as most party members were. There were some Socialist conscientious objectors and pacifists who supported the movement, but other Socialist pacifists, like Winston Dancis, condemned it. Dancis agreed with Peace Now's objective of "an immediate peace" but disagreed with their efforts to recruit former America Firsters and their willingness to accept support from "former Bundist elements." Moreover, he found the movement's peace terms and war aims vague. Some Socialists were so opposed to Hartmann's endeavors that in 1943 they sought to bring disciplinary charges against him.[26]

By early 1944, with criticism of Peace Now growing and with attempts to smear the Socialist Party by linking it with Peace Now also increasing, the party began to feel the need to clarify its position on Peace Now. After the NEC passed a resolution in January 1944 condemning any negotiated peace with Hitler or Hirohito, Fleischman requested that Hartmann meet with the NAC. Fleischman also urged Hartmann to repudiate any fascists and Coughlinites who had attached themselves to the Peace Now Movement. Explaining the damage that Peace Now's failure to repudiate these elements did to Thomas and the Socialist Party, Fleischman said that if Hartmann were unable to shed the "shady elements" who had been supporting the Peace Now Movement, then he should resign from it. Hartmann's reply was to deny that Peace Now had any "true association" with such elements.[27]

After meeting with Hartmann, the NAC and later the NEC considered what, if any, disciplinary measures should be taken against him. Of the various resolutions considered, Thomas's was the weakest, calling only for Hartmann to bring his organization into line with party policy, to develop better control of the fascist penetration of his organization, or to resign from Peace Now. The matter of disciplining Hartmann ended inconclusively. While it seems clear that Thomas had strategic differences with Hartmann and had grown, perhaps because of his experience with America First, wary of the kind of groups attracted to the Peace Now Movement, it also seems clear that, at least temperamentally, he was closer to Hartmann's position than most on the NEC.[28]

Despite his differences with the NEC over disciplining Hartmann, Thomas did reject Hartmann's movement and made negative responses to many of his admirers' pleas for a peace offensive. Yet, he indicated that there might easily come a time when a peace offensive was called for and that therefore it was important for the Socialist Party to formulate its ideas on peace. But as he thought to formulate his ideas on peace, there was much in world affairs that discouraged him.

From the beginning of the war, Thomas had feared a Big Three–dominated peace. Before the United States entered the war, he had warned that Hitler's imperialism might be followed by Stalin's imperialism; the U.S. entrance made him all the more convinced that there was a danger of exchanging one brutal imperialism for another. The western Allies offered little better. There was no indication that the British were going to dismantle their empire. Thomas and the Socialist Party called for Indian independence and were far more sympathetic to the Congress Party and to

Gandhi than the liberal community, with the exception of Louis Fischer. Taunting the liberals for their lack of real enthusiasm for Indian independence, *The Socialist Call* asked: "Where are the liberals, where are the New Dealers, where is the Wallace cult. . . . At what point do they start fighting a people's war instead of talking one?"[29]

According to Thomas and the Socialists, if British policy continued its defense of colonialism, and if Soviet policy threatened a new imperialism in Eastern Europe, little else in the way of Allied diplomacy offered room for optimism. De Gaulle, so celebrated by the liberal community, was viewed by the Socialists as a conservative autocrat intent upon maintaining the French North African empire. And the United States appeared to Thomas and the Socialists to be endorsing the power politics of their allies. Thomas saw little hope in the Atlantic Charter. The words were noble, but they were inadequate to ensure peace, and in any case, there were few signs that any of the Allies were living up to them. Every sign, he felt, pointed in the direction he had warned of: the imposition of a Big Three imperial peace.[30]

The 1943 Moscow foreign ministers' conference did little to reassure Thomas or the Socialist Party about the goals of Stalin, Churchill, and Roosevelt. The party issued a statement in which it said that Great Britain and the United States "yielded" to Stalin's demands on Poland, "no doubt" in exchange for his recognition of Western Europe as a western sphere of influence. The actions were taken "at the expense of Europe as a whole"; Europe had no voice at the conference; the "antifascist" forces in Germany, Poland, and throughout Europe were not heard.[31]

In their criticisms of the foreign policy of the United States, Thomas, the Socialist Party, and the liberals often overlapped. All criticized the Darlan deal, the dealings with Badoglio, and the general support of reactionary forces in Europe. But the Socialists could not resist deriding the liberals' faith in Henry Wallace and their lack of support for revolution. McAlister Coleman called the Darlan deal "an inauspicious approach" to Wallace's "brave new world of the common man." Sebastian Franck wrote that Secretary of State Hull, rather than Wallace, had won Roosevelt's support. This meant that Wallace made "speeches in praise of the people's revolution and Hull . . . [made] politics to suppress them." Symes condemned the Darlan deal, but chastised the "embattled liberals" who bemoaned the deal, but did not "appeal to the oppressed colonial people of French Africa to rise up against both the French and Axis control."[32]

Thomas had a somewhat different perspective on the State Department's relations with the Vichy government and with Franco. He opposed the breaking of diplomatic relations on the grounds that it was an ineffective way to fight fascism and that it might lead both governments to throw their full military support to Hitler. It is not clear whether his position represented the views of most party members (at one point he seemed to be asking others in the party for persuasive pragmatic reasons why breaking relations with Franco could be effective). Although his position led him to appear to take a softer line on Vichy and Franco than the liberals, his position was not the result of softness. Rather, it was based on what he thought was an effective way of fighting fascism and restoring democracy. What he believed needed to be done in Spain was not the withdrawal of American diplomatic recognition but the beginning of American support for Spanish democrats. Admittedly, he was vague on how this could be achieved; in this case at least, the liberals' demand for the withdrawal of recognition had greater specificity. In any case, it was a difference over how best for the U.S. government to oppose the Franco regime; here the goals of the liberals and Thomas were the same.[33]

There was also similar talk about the need for a democratic revolution in Europe. Here divergences between the Socialists and the liberals appear. The liberal call for a democratic revolution in Europe — and elsewhere — flowed from their belief that the war was a democratic, antifascist war. The failure of Allied policy to live up to the liberal belief was at the root of their frustration. But insofar as it did live up to the belief, it was fulfilling the democratic goals of the war and, in this way, furthering democratic revolution. This was not true for the Socialists. For them, democratic revolution was the alternative to Allied policy. It was not that the Allies failed to live up to the idealistic goals of the war by their practice of power politics and, in the case of Great Britain and the United States, their alliance with reactionary forces. Rather, for the Socialists it was that the Allies were fulfilling their imperial goals at the expense of the peoples of the world.[34]

For the Socialists, the only idealistic goal was that of the people's democratic revolution which for them meant a democratic socialist revolution. The regular columnists for *The Socialist Call* were clearest about this. In their columns Andre Martin, Louis Clair, Sebastian Franck, and Jim Cork repeatedly argued for a "third camp" or "third front" position. The third front was the people's front against fascism *and* against an imperial peace imposed by the capitalist powers and Stalin; it was a front that centered on the underground revolutionary forces throughout Europe. These writers insisted that the democratic third force existed. They combated the Van-sittart argument on the inherent aggressiveness and guilt of all Germans by insisting that a democratic Germany existed inside the closed fascist regime. Hitler had placed large parts of the democratic force in concentration camps, they wrote, but he had not destroyed it. Sharing the same hopes and assumptions as Paul Hagen, although not his faith in the programs of the liberal community, they seized on any signs of internal German discontent. At the end of the war, the Socialists cited the Buchenwald Manifesto, a democratic socialist manifesto from a group of former inmates of Buchenwald, to show that the democratic Germany had not been eliminated. The same was true of Italy, where strikes and general unrest at the time of the Allied invasion were cited to indicate the democratic revolutionary impulse. In France, the French underground and a revolution of the colonial peoples, not De Gaulle, offered the only hope.[35]

The third camp writers spoke eloquently against a vindictive peace. They believed that threats of harsh retaliation played into the hands of the fascists and discouraged democratic uprisings. When it became clear that the Allies would win the war, the emphasis of the third camp shifted from the idea of a democratic socialist revolution as an alternative to fascism and an Allied imperial victory to the idea of a democratic socialist revolution as an alternative to Stalinist imperialism and American and British capitalist imperialism. Unlike Kirchwey and Lerner, they saw nothing progressive in the Soviet Union; unlike Niebuhr and Lerner, they did not believe that Soviet aggression could be explained by the need for security. And unlike all the liberals, they did not believe that a Roosevelt who lived up to his ideals would change the nature of American capitalism.[36]

Thomas's ideas on foreign policy during World War II fit partly into the third camp position. He too was searching for a democratic socialist alternative to fascism, Stalinism, and capitalism. He too spoke out frequently against Vansittartism and a vindictive peace. He too had no faith in Stalin, Churchill, or Roosevelt; they all played the power politics game at the expense of the people. Like the third campers, Thomas wrote positively of a democratic socialist federated Europe. But there were differences of emphasis between Thomas and the third camp writers in *The Socialist Call.* Although he had little faith in Roosevelt, he was far more likely to make appeals to him or to the leaders of the Allies to change their policies. The immediate effect of these appeals seemed to make him more of a socialist reformer and less of a socialist revolutionary than those in the third camp. Some of his Socialist critics argued that there was a contradiction between his analysis of capitalist imperialism and his continued efforts to modify its policies—as if one could really change the essential nature of capitalist foreign policy. They queried him as to why he used the phrase "our war" when referring to the United States, as if there were common ground between himself and the capitalist state.[37]

One should not mistake the third camp position as "the worse, the better" argument; its advocates were not claiming that the worse things were under capitalism, the better it would be for the revolution. All had witnessed too much of fascism to have any such confidence. Rather, the argument was over the building of a socialist movement. His critics were charging that Thomas spent too much time trying to influence capitalist policy rather than on building the radical alternative to it. Thomas, however, was not prepared to draw such sharp lines. He believed that capitalism could not solve the fundamental economic problems of full production and full employment or the social goals of justice and equality, but he did not believe that it was impervious to change or that the changes were unimportant in terms of people's lives.

Thus Thomas sought ways to influence U.S. foreign policy and the postwar peace. His creation of the Post War World Council was an effort both to broaden the base of change beyond the Socialist Party and to provide a vehicle in which he could speak as an individual and not as the leader of the Socialist Party. Thomas felt that he had a public presence that could have a positive influence, and he wanted to have somewhat more freedom than that granted an "official spokesperson of a party." For example, although he had doubts about Culbertson's world federation plan, Thomas did not condemn it as a vehicle for big power imperialist domination, as many socialists and liberals did. He had particular respect for Culbertson's idea of an international police force based on a quota system as a substitute for national armies. Thomas believed that force was not the answer to the world's problems and that any world federation had to emphasize cooperation and voluntary compliance, but as long as force would be used in the world, Culbertson's idea held promise. Thomas realized that many in the Socialist Party did not share his endorsement of this particular feature of Culbertson's plan, and so when he set his conditions for running for president in 1944 he did not insist that the party endorse the concept of an international police force. But he did insist that he had the personal right to support it without the party repudiating him.[38]

One of Thomas's biggest endeavors in foreign policy during World War II was not outside the party; rather it became party policy and part of the

1944 presidential campaign. In rejecting the pleas of former supporters to begin a peace offensive in 1942, Thomas had said that he was not permanently ruling out a peace offensive. When in late 1942 Roosevelt and Churchill announced at Casablanca the policy of unconditional surrender, they articulated Thomas's worst fears of a vindictive, draconian peace based on Vansittartist principles. A statement by the British Labour Party containing Vansittartist phrases, the refusal of Roosevelt to present any clear war aims for Germany, and the mixed messages coming out of the Soviet Union were all foreboding. Unconditional surrender appeared to offer nothing but death and destruction and a vindictive peace that would prepare the way for a vengeful resurgence of fascism and for Stalinist domination of much of Europe. In Asia, it promised the continuation of "white man's imperialism." Neither the cause of humanity nor the cause of democratic socialism, linked as they were in Thomas's mind, could benefit from unconditional surrender.[39]

Thomas began his assault on the doctrine of unconditional surrender from the moment it was announced. *The Socialist Call* writers joined in. They stressed its damage to the democratic revolutionary forces in all countries: if there was no hope of avoiding a harsh imposed peace through unconditional surrender, how could anyone be persuaded not to fight to the bitter end?[40]

With such questions in mind, Thomas frequently began to pose the alternative of a "people's peace." To liberals, the two were linked; unconditional surrender translated into the eradication of fascism and thus was consistent with a people's peace and with democratic revolution. But Thomas saw the contradiction between calling for a democratic revolution and then calling for unconditional surrender. The presupposition to a democratic revolution was that terms of surrender were conditional—that a democratic regime would not have imposed upon it the same terms as the fascist regime. The contradiction between calling for unconditional surrender and a democratic revolution convinced him that the Allied powers had no interest in the latter.[41]

By 1944 Thomas had begun to mull over the idea of a peace offensive. The policy of unconditional surrender had played a large role in pushing him in this direction. In addition, the failure of his and others' efforts to feed the starving children of Europe convinced him that the idea of liberals being able to persuade the administration to accept liberal and democratic war aims was utopian. Indeed, his efforts to feed the children had been met with rebuff in many liberal quarters. With the prospects for democratic socialism so small and with the prospects of a brutally harsh peace so great, Thomas began to believe that the time was "ripe for a political peace offensive." Although he was giving the idea some thought, it was not clear at first where his thinking was taking him.[42]

There was still what might be called the "Hartmann problem." Hartmann's Peace Now Movement ran the risk of alienating groups inside and outside the party and thus damaging any Thomas initiative for a political peace offensive. If he had any hope of success with the public, Thomas had to avoid becoming a victim of guilt by association. There had been no change in his attitude toward those urging him to support the Peace Now Movement. He continued to insist that a Hitler victory would be catastrophic, that any idea of negotiating with Hitler would be rejected by the American people, and that the individual pacifist psychology subscribed to by many in the Peace Now Movement was equally unacceptable to the public and therefore could not furnish the basis for a political peace offensive. However, it was not clear exactly how he could formulate a peace offensive that could avoid what he criticized Hartmann for: urging negotiations with the present rulers of Germany and Japan. Thomas rejected this both on the grounds that the maintenance of the rulers in power would simply momentarily delay a new world war and on the practical grounds of public opinion. In the absence of a revolution in Germany or Japan, how could these previous criticisms, which had seemed so telling, be overcome?[43]

With these nagging thoughts in mind and with the road closed to a new mass party after the failure of any CCF-style party to develop in the United States, Thomas prepared to challenge the American people with the "big ideal" in the 1944 campaign. By the spring of 1944 he was ready to offer a political peace offensive as an alternative to unconditional surrender. In early May he sent a confidential memo to a number of socialists and pacifists in which he expressed the need for a such peace offensive. He drew the pessimistic picture of postwar Europe that he had drawn so frequently: a brutalized and Balkanized Europe controlled by rival imperialists. He expressed his fears of the growing power of Soviet imperialism and of the reactionary colonialism of Great Britain, and his worry that a democratic revolution could not occur under these conditions. Affirming the hopelessness of looking toward liberal influence as a way of changing American willingness to subscribe to a Big Three, power-politics peace, Thomas laid down his own conditions for peace: the relinquishment of conquered territories, the surrender of colonial empires, disarmament, and the replacement of the existing Axis governments.[44]

On the key issue of whom to negotiate with, Thomas acknowledged his uncertainty. He believed that democratic revolution was unlikely, but he also knew that leaving the defeated governments in place was morally wrong and politically untenable. He also saw little hope for a revolution that would create an alternative for negotiations. He acknowledged that he was "puzzled" about this point and hoped his correspondents would help him in their comments.[45]

In the replies to his memo, several of Thomas's correspondents urged him to clarify his position on this issue. Clement said that the only way to avoid confusion was to call upon the German people and the people of the conquered nations to make peace over the heads of their leaders. Only Oswald Garrison Villard was concerned with the timing—the fact that a peace offensive would be perceived as undercutting American troops in the impending invasion. Bertram Wolfe did urge him to present his ideas as a way to shorten—not stop—the war by helping to create a democratic revolution. With these generally supportive replies, Thomas was ready to go public.[46]

When Thomas publicly set forth his plans for a political peace offensive, the phrasing had changed little from his original memo. But in articulating his ideas, he laid greater stress on the conditions calling for the replacement of the present fascist rulers. He also, perhaps picking up on Clement's suggestion (although he had used the phrase before), began to speak more frequently of a "people's peace." To critics who said his terms were being offered to Hitler, he responded that they were being offered to the German people.[47]

Thomas's political peace offensive made no dent in either Allied policy or public opinion. He was never able to persuade any significant group that the policy of unconditional surrender extended Hitler's domination or that his conditions could serve as a vehicle for shortening that rule. The liberal community continued its enthusiasm for unconditional surrender. If anything, the peace offensive only served to further marginalize Thomas and the Socialist Party.

Thomas's futile efforts to make a political peace offensive a key issue in the election of 1944 symbolizes the difficulty he had in maintaining the Socialist Party's relevance during the war. In a political world in which public opinion was divided among those who believed the war should be fought on a military basis alone, those who yearned for an isolationist "fortress America" and criticized any signs that wartime cooperation would extend into peacetime; and those who, like the liberals, believed that wartime decisions had to take into account the ideological nature of the war but brooked no criticism that was not made within a pro-administration context, it was hard for the Socialists to gain a hearing. To oppose all three tendencies; to favor international cooperation but not the New Deal, to distrust those with whom the United States would cooperate, as well as the United States's motives, but not to support fortress America were combinations that brought little public support.

If the public was little inclined to listen to Thomas's foreign policy message in 1944, it was less interested in his domestic message. Thomas still argued, as he had in the 1930s, that a full production economy was impossible under capitalism. When he spoke of a democratic revolution, it was clear that it was socialism, not reformed capitalism, that he was advocating. Thomas took care to distinguish socialism from simple nationalization and from the communist total state. He never suggested in his campaign that socialism would be unaccompanied by reform, but there was a line that differentiated him from the liberal critics of capitalism and the liberal advocates of a full production economy. And that line was socialism.[48]

Finally, Thomas was handicapped in the election by the absence of any significant institutional base outside the small Socialist Party. This was especially true in the labor movement. There were Socialists in the union movement, but a number of them were supporters of the Social Democratic Federation (SDF), which supported Roosevelt, and not the Socialist Party. Both the CIO and AFL leadership backed Roosevelt, and it was difficult for the Socialists to win political support within the two key labor organizations.

Without significant labor support and cut off from the main body of intellectuals by his stand on the war and the administration, Thomas did his best to carry his Socialist message. But every effort proved unsuccessful. Thomas could not even gain the confidence of opponents of the war. Radical pacifists like Dwight Macdonald considered Thomas's critical support of the war unsubstantially different from outright support. In a devastating and, I believe (as he later did) an unfair critique of Thomas, Macdonald ridiculed his criticism of the war as a sham and dismissed his socialism as too tepid. For Macdonald, Thomas represented no threat to the government warriors and the capitalist war state. Thomas's socialism, he said, was the socialism of the respectable: it offended no one; it threatened no one. Macdonald's opinion was inconsequential in terms of votes, but it was the final straw in a disastrous campaign.[49]

The lack of public support or influence does not mean, of course, that Thomas and the Socialist Party were wrong about foreign policy. In fact, in their fundamental analysis of what was occurring among the Big Three, they were basically correct. The process by which the Big Three arrived at their agreements was undoubtedly more complex than the Socialists granted, but a Big Three, power-politics peace was indeed the result. Thomas and the Socialists recognized that within the Soviet sphere of influence democratic forces were not being unleashed. They recognized that British policy was based on the protection of its empire and of its own European sphere; that Great Britain, as it had done in Greece, would suppress revolutionary forces that threatened its sphere; and finally that the United States policy might speak of the Atlantic Charter but that the charter was meaningless. American policy was based on order and stability, not democracy and justice. It buttressed conservative and reactionary forces throughout Europe. The liberals also believed that this was too often true, but, unlike the liberals, the Socialists did not blame it simply on the State Department. Thomas specifically criticized the liberals for shielding Roosevelt from legitimate criticisms by always blaming bad policy on the State Department.[50]

Liberals and Socialists could agree on Badoglio or disagree on De Gaulle, but these are not the most important areas to look at in trying to understand the key differences between the two groups on foreign policy. What fundamentally divided the Socialists and the liberal community was their respective position on the war: total support versus critical support. As a result, the liberals constantly looked for signs of cooperation among the Allies. The major diplomatic conferences were evaluated, usually positively, as advances in Big Three cooperation. The liberals were concerned about the Big Three's traditional spheres-of-influence approach, but they saw nothing inevitable in the Allies carving out of respective spheres. For the liberals, cooperation competed with spheres in an undetermined contest.

For the Socialists, there was no contest. They did not believe that Stalin preferred genuine collective security and only opted for the spheres approach when the Western Allies did not move toward collective security. The Socialists did not believe that Roosevelt had any firm set of principles that were embodied in the Atlantic Charter or that he looked toward a democratic world organization. Instead, they saw from the very start of the war that power politics had prevailed among all the Allies. Unlike the liberals, who saw the Dumbarton Oaks agreements as signs of progress toward a genuine collective security, the Socialists saw them as ratifying a big power peace and strongly criticized them.

Nor did Thomas and the Socialist Party see Yalta as a sign of progress in postwar cooperation. They believed that Roosevelt and Churchill had sold out to Stalin on Eastern Europe, that Poland in particular had been betrayed, and that the statements about self-government and free elections were meaningless given the military and political reality of Stalin's control. Great Britain and the United States had been willing to grant the Soviet Union its sphere of influence because they were interested in their own spheres.[51]

Much of Thomas's and the Socialist Party's criticism of Yalta and Dumbarton Oaks applied to the final United Nations Charter. Thomas, however, was able to lead the party in the direction of supporting congressional passage of the charter. For this, he was criticized by a number of Socialists and others who did not understand how, given his criticisms of the plans all along, he could now support passage. Thomas answered by arguing that all his previous criticisms still held but that he believed that the establishment of the United Nations would make it easier to win the kind of reforms that would be necessary to make it a meaningful organization. Defeat would only encourage nationalistic isolationism. His Socialist critics had a point; given his diagnosis of the world there seemed to be little chance that the United Nations could either be a source of international reform or be reformed itself.[52]

Thomas's pessimism on international affairs was constantly reinforced by his growing opposition to and fear of Stalinist Russia. Throughout the war as he sought to answer the criticism that he and the party were too anti-Soviet, Thomas emphasized that he still favored constructive U.S. relations with the Soviet Union. When he was charged late in the war with aiding a war fever against the Soviet Union, he vehemently denied it. Just as he did not favor breaking diplomatic relations with Franco, he did not think that peace would be served by failing to deal diplomatically with the Soviet Union. And he never believed that strong criticism translated into a demand for war — or else he would have been advocating war against the British and French empires.[53]

But there was no denying his strong criticism. Thomas saw in the Soviet Union dictatorship, mounting privileges for rulers, the absorption of unions into the state, and the suppression of opposition. He wrote frequently that his earlier hopes for the Soviet Union had been aborted and that he was reluctantly forced to view Stalinism along with fascism as a modern form of totalitarianism. He distinguished it from fascism in terms of its treatment of racial minorities and in terms of its philosophic roots, but he believed that in the total state domination of life, the two systems bore terrifying similarities.[54]

The Soviet execution of the Polish socialists Victor Alter and Henryk Ehrlich in 1943 symbolized for Thomas, as it did for most Socialists, the essence of Stalinism. While the liberal community had condemned the executions, some, like *The Nation*, had added the proviso that they hoped the executions would not lead to any excessive criticism of the Soviet Union. But there were no provisos among the Socialists. What Stalin did to Alter and Ehrlich, to the workers and peasants of the Soviet Union, to all potential institutional checks and individual critics, and what he had done to build up a privileged class of party bureaucrats, explain why Thomas and the Socialists opposed the Soviet Union. But what they feared was not simply its system but its system backed by military power. Thomas believed that the Soviet Union was emerging out of World War II as the most powerful force in Europe. It had achieved this status, he felt, partly through its own inner dynamics: Stalin's total militarized state. But he also believed it had achieved it through British and American appeasement.[55]

It is here that Thomas's and many of the Socialists' critique of the Soviet Union became simplistic in its analysis. Thomas and the Socialists had developed a damning moral assessment of the Soviet Union. In the midst of the wartime celebratory attitude toward Stalin and the Soviet Union, they had refused to put on moral blinders. But perhaps because the moral critique was so devastating, there was a tendency to assume that Soviet predominance in Eastern Europe had only been successful because of Allied capitulation and appeasement. They never sufficiently addressed the fact that Soviet predominance was the result of the military developments of the war and that U.S. policy in particular had played little role in creating the situation. The Socialists were correct in seeing Yalta as big power politics and as a spheres-of-influence settlement, but they ignored that the outlines of the settlement had been established by the military events of the war and not by Western capitulation to the Soviet Union. And they ignored the give-and-take that had occurred; in order to gain his goal of a world organization, Roosevelt had conceded on other issues — issues that because of the military situation he had little control over. In supporting, despite his criticisms, the passage of the United Nations Charter, Thomas refused to address the question of the price that had to be paid to achieve it.

My point here is not to defend Yalta against the Socialist critique;

rather, I am suggesting that in their rightful moral indignation over Stalinism, as well as over British and American imperial policy, the Socialists often simplified the context in which decisions were made. They always tended to reach for the most perfidious explanation of American foreign policy. Harry Paxton Howard was the most notorious in this respect, but Thomas was not free from conspiracy theories. There was a strong case to be made against American Far East policy without endorsing the kind of conspiracies that later filled the World War II revisionist literature. In his desire to defend his prewar policy, Thomas seized on every wartime effort to portray Roosevelt as having manipulated Japan into an attack. Unlike the later revisionists, Thomas did not use this to excuse Japan; in the face of Roosevelt's provocations, he said, Japan had a choice. Yet, his willingness to accept every secondhand story of Roosevelt's perfidy could only feed the conspiracy mill and so contribute to a debate that led away from a more valid critique of American Far East foreign policy.[56]

The tendency to sometimes let overblown rhetoric serve as critical analysis could also be found in the Socialist critique of New Deal domestic policy. Nevertheless, despite the unnecessary exaggeration, the Socialists had a penetrating critique of domestic wartime developments. On one level, the Socialist critique resembled the liberal critique: too many dollar-a-year men, too many business-oriented decisions. But the Socialists were not content simply to attribute these actions to Roosevelt's unwillingness to apply his liberal beliefs or to his political need for wartime unity. They believed his policies were more systemic to capitalism. Thomas and other Socialist writers were concerned about the growth of state power: with its growth came the tendency to absorb all countervailing institutions within the state. It was in this light that they feared the various efforts to restrict labor's right to strike and to "draft labor." The Socialists spoke for that part of the labor movement which opposed labor's no-strike pledge. Although Thomas and the official Socialist policy had little sympathy for John L. Lewis the person, there was a great deal of sympathy for Lewis's actions and even more for the striking miners during the war. The veteran Socialist newspaperman MacAlister Coleman wrote frequently and sympathetically of the miners' cause. From his position as national labor secretary of the Socialist Party, William Becker sought to encourage the minority opposition to the no-strike pledge.[57]

Congress's response to the miners' strikes, culminating in the Smith-Connolly Act, was viewed by Socialists as part of capitalism's attempts to permanently control unions. Probably the Socialists exaggerated Roosevelt's role in the bill's passage (it passed over his veto), but they were convinced that his opposition had not been genuine. They pointed to the workings of the War Labor Board to indicate the direction in which New Deal labor policy was heading; in league with big business, they believed, the board also took part in crushing an independent labor movement. The Socialists also viewed Roosevelt's National Service Act as part of capitalism's effort to conscript workers and to destroy an independent labor movement. The act, like Smith-Connolly and Congress's unsuccessful efforts to go beyond Smith-Connolly in Austin-Wadsworth, was viewed as part of the trend toward statism—a trend in which Democrats and Republicans, whatever their minor differences on particular pieces of legislation, participated.[58]

When Roosevelt, and then Truman, expressed support for postwar peacetime military conscription, Thomas and the Socialists were convinced that the danger of a totalitarian state had increased tremendously. To Thomas, the idea that the state could conscript anyone ran counter to his democratic socialist and civil liberties ideals. The fact that the proposal was for military conscription only worsened his fears and sometimes led to a rhetoric that conjured up images of capitalist plots. But the concerns that lay behind the exaggerated language were genuine. Tentatively and sometimes simplistically, the Socialists were broaching an analysis of capitalism that saw the driving force of capitalism during the war years as moving toward some variety of state capitalism with a tamed and incorporated labor movement and a militarized economy—and not backward toward laissez-faire and antistatism. The Socialists played their part in combatting the resurgence of classical economics. Drob and Clement wrote a pamphlet to answer Frederick Hayek's *Road to Serfdom,* and frequent articles in *The Socialist Call* criticized Hayek and the American intellectuals who were rediscovering the virtues of nineteenth-century liberalism. The Socialists, however, unlike the liberals, did not believe the greatest fear was the dismantling of the New Deal state; they did not view the new breed of businessmen as wedded to a nineteenth-century philosophy. Rather, the greatest fear was the transformation of the New Deal into a full-blown state capitalism, which could ultimately lead to totalitarianism.[59]

It was for this reason that Thomas and the Socialists did not greet the Beveridge Plan with the kind of unambiguous enthusiasm found among liberals. On one level their criticisms were pragmatic: the plan only addressed social security and full employment and not income distribution and inequality; it ignored that full employment without socialism was an impossibility. But the plan also created the fear of a modern form of the Bismarckian state—controlled public works and social security designed to stabilize capitalism and maintain the existing property relations. Thus, while the Socialists believed that the Beveridge Plan had proposals on health and social security that were positive, they feared that in the absence of socialism these features could become means of control rather than means of emancipation. It was with similar fears that the Socialists greeted the Murray Full Employment Bill in 1945. For the Socialists, the Murray Bill presented some of the same problems as the Beveridge Plan. They did not oppose the idea of public works per se, but they did not believe they offered a solution to unemployment. Only socialism could create a full production economy. And, as with the Beveridge Plan, they believed the Murray Bill did not address the issue of income distribution.[60]

Given this analysis, it was natural that the Socialist Party proposed an alternative bill. But the lack of a congressional sponsor proved to be a handicap. An even greater problem was the widespread liberal and labor support for the Murray Bill. If the Socialists were perceived by the labor movement as completely rejecting the bill, then their influence in the labor movement would be further reduced. Ultimately they adopted a position of arguing that support for both the by-now watered-down Murray Bill and the Socialist Bill were compatible. Following the defeat of the Murray Bill in 1945, both bills were introduced in Congress in early 1946. The Murray Bill passed and the Socialist Full Production Authority Act went nowhere. The Socialists' struggle for their bill, however, reveals their political predicament. They sought to offer an alternative to the Democratic and Republican parties and to the capitalist system, but they—and especially Thomas—were opposed to the philosophy of radical parties that eschewed all reform under capitalism. Thomas believed such an approach would make the party irrelevant to labor and to the public in general. Full employment was a key Socialist issue, since the inability of capitalism to solve the problem of unemployment was central to the entire Socialist position. Yet they had to fight the battle for full employment on a terrain where the capitalist reformers had the advantage. There was no hope of gaining their program unless capitalist reform was tried first. And once it was tried, the initial issue of postwar employment disappeared in the arms economy that the Socialists had warned against.[61]

The areas where the Socialist Party could establish a clear alternative position—without making the kind of gestures they had to make to the Murray Bill—were in those areas where conservatives and liberals were united or where liberal opposition to the existing New Deal policy was weak and scattered. One of those areas was the internment of Japanese Americans. When Thomas heard from Ann Ray, a Socialist organizer, and Hugh Macbeth, a West Coast lawyer, about government plans for the evacuation and internment of Japanese Americans, he immediately went into action. The party began a campaign to publicize the issue, and throughout the war the issue was constantly used as a touchstone in its criticism of the New Deal. Thomas also immediately urged the American Civil Liberties Union to take a strong stand against the government's order. The southern California ACLU was reluctant and the national ACLU hesitated to take the kind of strong stand Thomas wished. The ACLU was prepared to challenge the government on the issue of racial discrimination but not on the evacuation order itself, because that had been done under military authority in wartime. Thomas was acutely aware of the racial issue, but he also felt that the basic order itself was a violation of civil liberties. At one time he considered resigning from the ACLU because he felt its willingness to challenge the government in wartime was too weak.[62]

Throughout the war, Thomas stayed in touch with a number of the interned Japanese Americans. Through his and other columns in *The Socialist Call* the issue was kept in the forefront. Some liberals, like Reinhold Niebuhr, agreed with Thomas from the beginning and joined with him in a letter of protest to Roosevelt. Others like Carey McWilliams criticized the orders, then supported them (though criticizing camp conditions), and then turned more critical again. By 1944 the liberal voice against internment was heard more frequently, but by then victory in the war was assured.

What is most impressive is not the liberal support for internment but the liberal silence about it. Thomas could not even persuade Margaret Anderson of *Common Ground*, a journal dedicated to racial tolerance and understanding, to take the kind of unambiguous opposition he favored. With the liberal voice silent and the Communist voice supporting the policy, Thomas and the Socialists were among the few outspoken in their opposition. Thomas constantly reminded his listeners and readers that the internment of Japanese Americans represented the largest single violation of civil liberties during wartime in American history and "the most completely totalitarian act ever committed by an American President."[63]

Thomas was not afraid to take on other unpopular causes during the war. He supported Winfred Lynn's refusal to serve in a segregated army, and also Alton Levy, a party member who was court-martialed and sentenced to prison for challenging the army's segregation rules. The Socialist Party was the major publicizer of the Odell Waller case. A black sharecropper, Waller, who had been exploited and attacked by a Virginia landowner, killed the landowner in self-defense. The Socialist Party joined in all the appeals and kept the case in the public's attention until Waller's execution in July 1942. Liberals did join in support of Waller and Lynn, but there was nothing in the liberal press, for example, that matched *The Socialist Call*'s efforts to help Waller. In addition, the party supported the March on Washington Movement, campaigned for integrated housing in Detroit, and backed a strong and permanent Fair Employment Practices Commission (FEPC).[64]

The most unpopular types of cases Thomas became involved in were those dealing with conscientious objectors. The cases involved men who based their status on religious and on political grounds and men whose consciences allowed for a variety of responses to their own internment—from total noncooperation to a willingness to perform certain tasks. Throughout the war—and after—in this complicated and often emotional milieu, Thomas kept up a steady barrage of activity: writing letters supporting those applying for conscientious-objector status, campaigns to publicize those denied their conscientious objector's rights, letters to government officials demanding investigations of conditions in the camps and in prison.[65]

As with the case of the internment of Japanese Americans, there was virtual silence in the liberal intellectual community on the conscientious-objector issue—as if it would prove an embarrassment to support the rights of those who were unwilling to serve militarily in the democratic antifascist war. No prominent liberal called the conscientious objectors traitors or demanded harsh punishments; but there were numerous violations of the civil liberties of the conscientious objectors, and one cannot find any outpouring of liberal protest or liberal activity on their behalf. For that, one has to turn to the pages of Dwight Macdonald's radical *Politics*, to *The Socialist Call*, and to the activities of people like Macdonald, Thomas and Thomas's brother Evan.

There was one final issue of World War II on which Thomas and the Socialists stood apart from the majority of liberals: the dropping of the atomic bomb. Scattered religious leaders, pacifists, and independent radicals like Macdonald condemned the dropping of the bomb. But neither *The Nation* nor *The New Republic* nor UDA as an organization raised the moral issue of the dropping of the bomb. To Thomas it was an appalling decision, a reprehensible, if fitting, end to a war that he had concluded was the cruelest in history. Neither bomb could be excused, he believed, although the second one was worse because the United States had not given Japan sufficient opportunity to surrender. After the bombs were dropped, Thomas shared with the liberals the belief in the necessity for international control, although he was less inclined than they to share atomic secrets with the Soviet Union before such an agreement. Viewing the Soviet Union as more aggressive than Kirchwey did, he saw little reason to share the secrets without an international accord, but there was some common ground between the two in their opposition to a militaristic and nationalistic solution to the problem. At the time of the dropping of the bomb itself, however, there was a large moral divide.[66]

Was that divide unbridgeable? Was there room and were there opportunities for cooperation between the Socialists and liberals? When one considers the liberal critique of U.S. foreign and domestic policy during World War II, one finds areas of overlap: criticism of appeasement of reactionaries and criticism of the Badoglio and Darlan deals. The Socialists and most liberals opposed Vansittartism and a draconian peace. There was similar criticism of the American Military Government in Germany for its too great reliance on ex-fascists and for its antifraternization policy. There were similar fears of a big power spheres-of-influence peace. Both groups criticized big business influence in Washington, the lack of postwar economic planning, and the failure of the administration to combat the Dies committee. And there were similar causes: the fight against the poll tax, the fight for a more effective control of inflation, the fight for an open refugee policy, and opposition to peacetime military conscription.[67]

There were, of course, differences in the areas of civil liberties. And there were differences in regard to labor. The Socialists and the UDA shared similar concerns about the power of the Communist Party within the labor movement, and *The Nation* and *The New Republic* certainly looked positively on noncommunist progressive labor leaders like Walter Reuther. But the UDA was closer to the labor leaders and usually operated through them, while the Socialists sought to work through the rank and file. Issues like the no-strike pledge separated the Socialists from leaders like Walter Reuther. The Socialists in Michigan remained close to Victor Reuther, but, as Drob put it, although the Socialists would probably vote for Walter Reuther in the end, they were not going to blindly accept his position on issues and they were working with "militant pressure groups."[68]

The Socialists' efforts to combat what they believed was the conservative antilabor policy of the Communists reflected their combative stance

toward the American Communist Party. Although the interradical bitterness may have put Socialist polemics on a different level of rhetoric
than liberal criticism, there was nothing in the Socialist critique of the
American Communist Party that was not also voiced by liberals during the
war. Both condemned the Communist Party's subservience to the Soviet
Union, its enthusiasm for "progressive" capitalism, and its national unity
embrace of Mayor Frank Hague of Jersey City. As we have seen, the liberals
generally supported the "right wing" against the Communist side in the
American Labor Party's internal disputes. The Socialists criticized both
groups for supporting Roosevelt, but they shared the right wing's criticism
of Communist tactics within the organization. There were, of course, differences over Sidney Hillman's PAC committees. The liberals supported
and participated in them, believing that they held promise. Thomas, on
the other hand, called the CIO-PAC a "company union" designed to tie
labor to an antilabor administration and steer it away from independent
labor action.[69]

Certainly the issue of the Soviet Union separated Thomas and the Socialists from *The Nation–New Republic* editors and most of their writers,
but it was not the Soviet Union that created the insurmountable barrier
to joint Socialist-liberal cooperation. The key issue was how both sides
viewed the war and how they viewed the New Deal. Surveying liberal
opinion on immediate issues can easily lead one to conclude that they had
adopted a position of critical support of both the war and the New Deal.
But this would be misleading. Having defined the war ideologically as an
international civil war between democracy and fascism and having interpreted Roosevelt and the New Deal as representative of the American expression of the worldwide democratic revolution, the liberals' individual
criticisms bore few consequences as far as changing their basic orientation
toward the war or the New Deal. The criticisms were reasons to be disappointed, frustrated, or to feel betrayed—but not reasons to break with the
administration. However, when the Socialists criticized the New Deal,
their criticisms did not take place within the context of support for the
New Deal. Instead, the faults of the New Deal, according to the Socialists,
reflected the workings of the capitalist system and the New Deal priorities
within that system.

Socialists believed that business power was bound to be reflected in the
political state and that an administration that was not—and never had
been—motivated to transform the system could not help reflecting business priorities, especially in a war crisis. Thomas did not share the tradi-

tional Marxist belief that the political state was simply a mirror or an executive of the capitalist class. As one who believed that worthwhile reforms were possible and necessary within capitalism, Thomas recognized that all New Deal actions were not predetermined by the business class. But neither did he or his fellow Socialists write with any faith that a group of "liberals" in Washington—Wallace, Eleanor Roosevelt, Leon Henderson, and Chester Bowles—could redirect the New Deal if only the liberal intellectuals could bring a little more lobbying pressure or have a little more influence. In the business-ridden atmosphere of wartime Washington, Thomas's and the Socialists' analysis of capitalism and the New Deal exploded into florid overstatements of Roosevelt's perfidy. Nonetheless, by developing a line of criticism that had at least the consequences of seeking to move labor away from the New Deal and toward a position of independent labor action and of seeking to develop a mass progressive party outside the Democratic and Republican options, Thomas and the Socialists developed a more substantial and politically serious critique than those who, as Thomas said, would stick "thick and thin" with Roosevelt no matter what he did.[70]

11

The Breakup of the
Liberal Community

IN NOVEMBER 1946 as James Loeb was deeply involved in organizing
the January 4, 1947, conference that established the Americans for Democratic Action (ADA), he received Bruce Bliven's letter of resignation from
the UDA. Bliven wrote that he had no fundamental differences with the
organization, but that he had requested that all editors of *The New Republic*
resign from all outside political organizations. Loeb's reply indicated his
personal regret; nobody, he said, had been better to work with during the
war than Bliven.[1]

While Bliven was breaking with the UDA, Chester Bowles was debating his prospective relationship with the proposed new organization of
"non-Communist liberals." Loeb had assiduously courted Bowles, along
with a list of other prominent labor leaders and liberal politicians including Eleanor Roosevelt, Leon Henderson, Wilson Wyatt, Hubert Hum-
phrey, Phillip Murray, William Green, James Carey, and Walter Reuther.
Bowles had agreed to speak at the opening meeting, but he became reluctant to associate himself too deeply with the new organization. There were
rumors from England, where Bowles was visiting, that he would not attend
the conference. He kept his commitment to attend but decided against
joining — although he did agree to head an ADA committee to make a
report on the economy. With political ambitions in Connecticut, it was
clear that Bowles was hesitant to get caught in the political crossfire developing among liberals, especially between the UDA members and those
closely connected with NC-PAC.[2]

The crossfire quickly developed into a conflict between the ADA and

234

Henry Wallace's newly formed Progressive Citizens of America (PCA). In *The New Republic,* Wallace wrote that as far as he knew Mrs. Roosevelt was not a member of the ADA. When questioned he defended his claim by saying that Bowles had told him that he and Mrs. Roosevelt "were keeping aloof from the ADA." However, Bowles assured Loeb that this was not so, that he had never told Wallace that Mrs. Roosevelt was disenchanted. He also told Loeb that he felt positively toward the ADA but had decided not to join any formal political organizations.[3]

Also in January 1947, Lillie Shultz, director of The Nation Associates, Inc., wrote to Carey McWilliams about a confidential meeting that she and Freda Kirchwey, Max Lerner, Ray Walsh of the PCA, and a few others had held with Mrs. Roosevelt. Shultz told McWilliams that she (Shultz), Lerner, and Kirchwey were not going to join either the ADA or the PCA. She also described Mrs. Roosevelt's positions on foreign policy as similar to theirs. At one point Shultz indicated that Mrs. Roosevelt had a softer line on working with Communists than Lerner, who, perhaps taking his lead from his friend Harold Laski's position in the British Labour Party, had said that liberal organizations should exclude Communists from both leadership and membership. According to Shultz, Mrs. Roosevelt had said that it was important only to exclude them from leadership, thus leaving open the door to liberal-Communist programmatic cooperation—a cooperation that Loeb and his fellow UDA liberals opposed.[4]

Whether or not Shultz correctly transmitted to McWilliams Mrs. Roosevelt's sentiments, the issue of liberal-Communist cooperation had become paramount in the liberal community. By 1947 Loeb's old friends James and Phyllis Warburg had already resigned from the UDA over the issue. Phyllis Warburg wrote Loeb that she had no objection to the UDA's exclusionary policies but believed that in the fight for programs, such as the struggle for the Murray Full Employment Bill, different political ideologies could cooperate if they agreed on the program. She was afraid that liberals would become more concerned with enforcing political litmus tests than with the pressing social issues. Following the formation of ADA, a number of Loeb's correspondents shared similar concerns.[5]

Throughout the war, Loeb, Bliven, Kirchwey, Lerner and the Warburgs had cooperated with each other. It was Loeb, Bliven, Kirchwey, and John Lewis from *PM* who had raised the need to reform the NC-PAC after the 1944 elections. All had admired liberal politicians like Henderson, Bowles, and, of course, Henry Wallace. They had participated in the CIO-PAC and the NC-PAC, both of which had Communist and fellow traveler members.

Loeb was more philosophically opposed to working with Communists and fellow travelers than Kirchwey, Bliven, or Lerner; but all had supported the UDA's exclusionary policy. Now—in 1946—they were being pulled between the people who would form Wallace's PCA and those who joined the ADA.

What had happened to cause the change? It would be easy, and not entirely incorrect, to answer "Wallace," since Wallace's break with the Truman administration over foreign policy placed the issue of the Soviet Union and liberal-Communist cooperation squarely on the liberal table. However, Wallace was in some ways the final factor. In early 1946 there were no signs of a break with Wallace—even though the UDA had become more critical of Soviet policy, and Loeb would soon publish a letter in *The New Republic* opposing any united-front activity with the Communist Party. In February 1946 Loeb urged Wallace to coordinate his speaking trips with UDA centers of strength. The organization was critical of Wallace's September Madison Square Garden speech, but during that fall Loeb clearly tried to keep a door open to Wallace. In sending Wallace a copy of the UDA board's response to his speech, Loeb urged him to meet with a few of the board members, particularly Reinhold Niebuhr. Saying that it was impossible to overemphasize "the impact of recent events upon the progressive movement," Loeb thought it would be "extremely valuable" to learn more about Wallace's thinking. In a letter to Wallace in late September, Loeb expressed his sorrow at Wallace's leaving the government and said it had been a "privilege" to work with him on the full employment campaign. He told Wallace that he was searching for answers to the "foreign policy problem" and that his answers would not be based on support Wallace received from "the extreme left" or on the attacks on him from "the extreme right." He expressed the hope "that a way can be found in which democratic liberals will be able to work side by side with you in pursuit of common aims." Reiterating his hopes in early October, Loeb again encouraged Wallace to have "a good talk" with Niebuhr: "In my opinion you are the two men of greatest personal integrity and genuine progressivism that I know in American life. Surely there must be a way in which he and you can agree on a program for American liberals."[6]

In the fall of 1946, when he was already preparing for the January conference and a new non-Communist organization, Loeb sent Wallace a critical comment on his foreign policy positions from Jennie Lee, a left-wing British Labour Party member. Loeb included a note saying that he was one of Wallace's "friendliest critics." Whether the note represented Loeb's true feelings or not — there are other signs of some bitterness toward Wallace — or was written with some hope that he might lead Wallace back on course is impossible to say. What it does suggest is that Wallace's speech did not precipitate Loeb's and the UDA's decision to form a new organization. The plans were already under way.[7]

The plans for a new organization were under way precisely because of the political questions generated by the Soviet Union, the concerns which had caused Fischer to resign from *The Nation* in the spring of 1945 and which during the summer of that year had increasingly dissolved the wartime ties binding the liberal intellectual community. Alexander Uhl, I. F. Stone, Saul Padover and Lerner at *PM* grew more despairing of an American foreign policy, which, they believed, was tied to British imperialism and motivated by hostility to the Soviet Union. Kirchwey and Bliven shared most of their concerns. But Loeb, Alfred Bingham, and the other editors at *Common Sense,* as well as Fischer, viewed the world from the opposite, if equally pessimistic, viewpoint. To them, Russian imperialism was the main, though not the sole, cause of the threatened postwar peace, and liberals who misunderstood this had political and moral blinders. Lerner may have agreed with Loeb that Communists should be excluded from liberal organizations, but he felt that Loeb and his associates were becoming too fixated on the evils of the Soviet Union. Loeb may have agreed with Lerner that the United States was not blameless in the breakdown of the wartime alliance, but he had little tolerance for liberals who continued to interpret Russian moves as defensive responses to the West's attempt to build a new anti-Soviet bloc.[8]

With liberals divided and apparently on the defensive in the face of resurging conservatism, it is easy to understand, why by the early spring of 1946 Loeb was talking about the need to call a national UDA conference in order to set a course for liberalism in the postwar period. He, along with Niebuhr as national chairman of the UDA, believed that this was necessary for several reasons, which included, but went beyond, the Russian/Communist issue. For one thing, the death of Roosevelt and the ascension of Truman had created a new relationship between liberals and the administration. Many of the old New Dealers were being shunted aside; those remaining, like Bowles, were feeling increasingly isolated. The spirit of liberal support of and cooperation with Truman that had initially marked Truman's assumption of the presidency had collapsed. In 1946 Truman's actions against labor increasingly isolated him from the liberal community. Not only did the UDA liberals oppose some of Truman's policies, they also did not have the contacts and entrees with the Truman administration they had with the Roosevelt administration. Those contacts had given them the illusion of influence and the feeling that the Roosevelt administration could be relied on. Thus, it was necessary, they believed, to develop a new organizational momentum.[9]

There was a sense in which the UDA felt itself floundering. Recently returned from the service and appointed executive director of the UDA New York City with the goal of reinvigorating that key chapter, Joseph Lash voiced the sense of drift: "When Franklin D. Roosevelt was alive we had a sense of direction, almost of destiny, as a people. . . . Since President Roosevelt's death we have lost our sense of direction." The growth of the UDA during the latter part of the war had not been extensive. Lash thought the problem was the lack of a cohesive ideological framework in which to operate and develop a program. He wrote Loeb a long memo criticizing the day-to-day unsystematic approach, but Loeb defended the UDA's proposed program for 1946 against Lash's criticisms and emphasized that he thought that there was little to be gained from trying to create a systematic ideological approach. Still, the UDA was not making progress in the new postwar political climate. Although it played a major role in the eventual passage of the Murray Full Employment Bill in 1946, it was clear that the watering down of the bill meant that Congress was still conservative. The UDA's hopes of contributing to a political redirection of Congress had proved unsuccessful, and by the beginning of 1946 it was time for some political stock-taking. This became all the more necessary as it became apparent that the Republicans were going to make gains in the 1946 congressional elections.[10]

The sense of political floundering cannot be divorced from the partial shattering of liberal hopes about World War II. In 1944 Kirchwey had written after the liberation of Paris that the war was but a "fragment of an unfinished revolution," and Lerner spoke about the inevitability of the European democratic revolution that could not be "thwarted." Although Kirchwey continued to hope for a democratic revolution, and her associate J. Alvarez Del Vayo never abandoned his belief in its inevitability, by 1945 the world looked different. The liberals still believed in the need for a democratic revolution to counter the fascist revolution, but with fascism defeated without a democratic revolution and with the Allies quarreling among themselves, the old hopes were dimmed. Now Kirchwey wrote of the world as a "fragment of one world." And in a quote that, compared to its early wartime editorials, suggests the contrast between the earlier high expectations for a democratic revolution and what the world looked like at the end of the war, *The New Republic* wrote in August 1945:

> But the war was a defensive one. By means of it we have avoided exchanging a highly unsatisfactory human society for something much worse. But the war is the end only of this intolerable retrogression. It has not in itself been cre-ative of anything better. It is only one episode in a world-wide pilgrimage which must go on from where we were. Humanity, like a weary traveler on a muddy road in a stormy night, has with immense effort extricated itself from a swamp into which it had wandered. Now it has to plod on from the point which the misstep occurred . . . We have simply won the chance to do better in the future than we have done in the past. The struggles and toils of arriv-ing at a decent civilization are still ahead. Something of this feeling tempers jubilation at the prospect of victory.

There was nothing in this tempered message that admitted defeat or called for a passive acceptance of things as they were; but its tone suggests that there would have been a reassessment of liberal strategy even without the immediate issue of liberal-Communist relations.[11]

But the most important element in Loeb's efforts to call a UDA na-tional conference was the change in international relations. Although the UDA continued to support cooperative relations with the Soviet Union, and to define its position as one that criticized equally Soviet aggression, British imperialism, and American errors, it was clear that between the end of the war and 1946 its main target was the Soviet Union. According to the UDA, it was the main aggressor and precipitator of the international tensions. The organization was also upset at the British policy toward Pal-estine and its continued role in Greece, but they also were active in de-fending the new Labour government. To those liberal and left critics who constantly chastised the Labour Party, Loeb issued a reminder that it was that party which freed India.[12]

At home the UDA criticized the military backing of Chiang Kai-shek, the admittance of Argentina into the United Nations, and the continued appeasement of Franco's Spain. But these were criticisms of mistakes and blunders and did not express a fundamental disagreement with the foreign policy of the U.S. capitalist system. With regard to the Soviet Union, how-ever, the UDA saw the Soviet actions in Eastern Europe as indicative of the aggressive intent of Stalin and the Soviet system. At this stage, the UDA still believed the Soviets could change. It urged a continued effort on the part of the West to negotiate firmly, but fairly, with the Soviet Union, and when in 1946 it briefly appeared as if Stalin were holding open the possibility for more cooperative relations, the UDA quickly encouraged Truman to respond positively. But beneath these continued calls for cooperative efforts, there was growing pessimism about the future prospects of cooperative U.S.-Soviet relations. This pessimism flowed from their analysis of Stalin and the Soviet Union and manifested itself in an increased support for Secretary of State James Byrnes's firm stance in negotiations.[13]

The UDA's growing criticism of the Soviet Union was matched by that of American public opinion. Thus, the issue was both a moral and a political one. On the moral side, if the Soviet Union was an aggressor whose domination destroyed the kind of independent trade union and liberal and socialist opposition that the UDA supported—not to mention the domination over the people in general—what was the common ground for cooperating with American Communist Party members who were dedicated to furthering Soviet goals? And what was the common ground for cooperating with the party's fellow travelers who cynically or naïvely supported it? By 1946 Loeb concluded that cooperation had become morally untenable for democratic liberals.[14]

But equally important were the political problems. In a growing climate of public anticommunism, cooperation was creating problems. The Dies committee and the Republican Party had red-baited Sidney Hillman and his PAC organizations in the 1944 election. An earlier target of the Dies committee, the UDA did not want to contribute to red-baiting, nor did it want liberals tarred with pro-Sovietism because they might be fearful of making legitimate criticisms of Communist-controlled organizations. Loeb had concluded that the NC-PAC and the Independent Citizens Committee of the Arts, Sciences and Professions (ICC)—unlike the CIO-PAC—were Communist-dominated. Although the CIO-PAC might have Communist participation, it was controlled by the non-Communists in the labor movement; but this was not true of NC-PAC and the ICC, Loeb believed. These were run by party members or those whose politics were indistinguishable from the party.[15]

That Loeb had been giving considerable thought to the problem of liberal-Communist relations is shown by his letter, solicited by Bliven, published in The New Republic in April 1946. Loeb wrote that American liberals were faced with three decisions. First, they needed to decide whether the present international conflicts were "due *exclusively* to the

imperialistic, capitalistic, power-mad warmongering of the Western democracies aimed at the destruction of the peace-loving workers' democracy
of the Soviet Union" or whether they were products of both sides seeking
"unilateral advantage and security" and thus creating "distrust and tension." Second, liberals had to decide if "economic security" was the "*sole*"
goal of progressivism or whether "human freedom" was a "co-equal dynamic of progressivism."[16]

Loeb assumed that "democratic progressives" would choose the second
alternative on both questions. In that case, he went on, they were faced
with a third strategic decision: "whether or not they can or should work
within the same political organizations with those who have decided for the
other alternatives, namely the Communists." Loeb argued that united-
front organizations inevitably become Communist fronts, that liberals
simply would not "group themselves into a disciplined semi-conspiratorial
caucus" as the Communists did in order to control organizations. Moreover, practically, united fronts might win short-term successes, but not
overall success. He cited the defeat of a united Socialist-Communist ticket
in Hungary and the victory of the non-united-front British Labour Party
to indicate that united fronts could not "win political power through
democratic means." If "the American progressive movement is to survive
and grow," he concluded, it needed to answer the third question with a
negative.[17]

Loeb's letter was debated in subsequent letters columns of *The New
Republic,* an indication that the united-front issue had touched a nerve in
the liberal community. In Loeb's letter he had referred to the resolutions
passed by the April Win-the-Peace Conference as illustrating pro-Soviet
bias. Held in Washington, the conference played an important role in
bringing the issue to a head. In a confidential memo written by an anony-
mous attendee and circulated to select people, the organizers of the conference were accused of being Communists and fellow travelers. The writer
of the memo described the "one-sided" nature of the conference, where
British and American imperialism was condemned but Russian actions in
Eastern Europe were ignored, and where political conditions were placed
on support for a loan to England that would make it practically unworkable
while blanket support was given to a loan to the Soviet Union. Detailing
the conference's plans for the future, the writer of the memo concluded:
"It is increasingly clear that an effort is being made to form, within Congress and throughout the nation, an organization that, although designed
to appeal to liberals and progressives, has as its basic purpose complete

apology for the Soviet Union and consistent opposition to the policies of the Western democracies, without regard to the inherent merits of the issues that confront American progressives or their counterparts throughout the world." [18]

The Win-the-Peace Conference helped push Loeb into action. The idea of a national convention of the UDA was shunted aside as Loeb began to develop the idea of a conference of non-Communist liberal politicians, labor leaders and leading liberal intellectuals. Working with Niebuhr, Alfred Baker Lewis, Arthur Schlesinger Jr. and others, Loeb had decided by the early fall of 1946 that an "off-the-record" conference of about fifty leading liberals would be most productive. New impetus was given to his plans by the Conference of Progressives in Chicago at the end of September. Sponsored by the NC-PAC, the ICC, and the CIO-PAC, it had a broader base of speakers than the earlier Win-the-Peace Conference. Its speakers included Phillip Murray, president of the CIO; Jack Kroll, the head of the CIO-PAC; Harold Ickes, secretary of the interior; James Patton of the National Farmers Union; Walter White of the NAACP; and Senator Claude Pepper. Coming on the heels of Wallace's Madison Square Garden speech and resignation from the cabinet, the conference appeared to offer a major challenge to Loeb and the UDA. Most of the speeches themselves represented mainline liberal themes, and with the possible exception of Claude Pepper's speech on foreign policy (with its tribute to the "martyr" Wallace), expressed sentiments that were acceptable to the UDA. In fact, Murray's speech criticized specifically the domestic role of the American Communist Party, and Ickes's speech had strong criticism of Soviet foreign policy. [19]

But Loeb was disturbed by the sponsorship of the conference and the reports on the Communist nature of the organizers and resolutions. He particularly resented the manipulation of the Roosevelt name. Calls for a return to the foreign policy of Roosevelt were interpreted by Loeb to be criticisms of Truman's and Byrnes's strong stand against the Soviet Union; there was evidence, he said, that Roosevelt would have adopted the same policy as Truman. Equally disturbing was the amount of CIO participation. Loeb sent a lengthy memo to Murray outlining the concerns about the Communist nature of the conference, in hopes of winning Murray's support for his plans for a new non-Communist liberal organization. In presenting his arguments, Loeb carefully distinguished between the CIO-PAC, for which he had high praise, and the NC-PAC and ICC, which were too greatly influenced by Communists and fellow travelers. Loeb probably knew that Murray had become increasingly disenchanted with the Communist role in the CIO. In any case, his arguments apparently worked. Although he himself was tied up in negotiations, Murray designated two prominent CIO national officials to represent him at the January meeting. Together with promises for attendance from Mrs. Roosevelt and other prominent New Dealers, Murray's response made Loeb feel that the conference would be one of the most important developments in history of liberalism.[20]

It was this developing debate over liberal-Communist cooperation and U.S.-Soviet relations that made Wallace's Madison Square Garden speech, his resignation from the cabinet, and the publication of his hitherto confidential July letter to President Truman on U.S. and Soviet foreign policy so important. Wallace's actions quickly made him a hero to those who held the United States and Great Britain largely responsible for the deterioration of relations with the Soviet Union. When Wallace was forced to resign from the cabinet, *The New Republic* said that he had now "raised the banner of the Peace Party and has enlisted for the long campaign," and that it was "the duty of every progressive American . . . to enlist behind him." Kirchwey used Wallace's speech to mount a progressive call to action, a move toward a progressive "realignment within the two old parties." The heart of Wallace's speech, she wrote, was its call for a "democratic foreign policy" based on Roosevelt's conception of "a close alliance of the three great powers" and a rejection of the "ruthless struggle" between East and West rival blocs with the United States using a "schoolyard-bully technique in dealing with Russia." *PM* writers consistently praised Wallace and criticized Truman. The editors called Wallace's position "close to our own editorial position," and Saul Padover said it "hit the bull's-eye." Lerner described Truman's actions as "lame and shabby" and "one of the sorriest performances in the history of the Presidential office." Wallace, on the other hand, had solidified his leadership of the "liberal forces."[21]

But to Loeb and the UDA, who a few months earlier had been praising him and looking forward to cooperative efforts with him, Wallace's position on foreign policy was too one-sided. They shared his hopes for better Soviet relations but believed that his apparent readiness to accept two spheres of influence and to ignore and excuse antidemocratic developments within the Soviet sphere were morally wrong and politically disastrous. Because of its past relations with Wallace and because it knew it was an explosive issue, the UDA carefully considered his speech before issuing a statement. Although not criticizing it entirely, the thrust of its analysis was critical of what it saw as Wallace's pro-Russian biases. "Mr. Wallace," the UDA's statement on his speech read, "has pointed out certain aspects of American policy which seem to increase and encourage Russia's sense of insecurity, but he has said little of those policies of the Soviet Union which breed insecurity." Loeb wrote one correspondent that Wallace had badly damaged "the whole liberal movement," but that the UDA had concluded that not much was "to be gained by name-calling."[22]

Wallace was quickly removed from his wartime pedestal within the liberal community by an important segment of that community. Undoubtedly the issues raised by Loeb in his April letter and the increasingly differing liberal opinion on U.S.-Soviet relations (as witnessed in the Alsop brothers–Max Lerner debate in *The New Republic*) would have continued and grown even without the issue of Henry Wallace. But there is no question that the Wallace issue presented a focus for the rancorous debates over those issues.[23]

By January 1947 everyone recognized that a split had taken place in the liberal community. The NC-PAC and ICC had formed the Progressive Citizens of America at the end of December 1946, and the ADA was formed at the January conference. Writing in *The New Republic*, Helen Fuller emphasized the weakening of the liberal forces by the split. Kirchwey in *The Nation* picked up on this. She believed that the commonality of much of the domestic program pointed toward the need for and possibility of unity. Prospects for unity were "dimmed," she said, by "genuine Communist sympathizers" in the PCA and by the tendency of the ADA to equate communism with fascism. The latter, she wrote, "distorts the meaning of history and the plain lesson of present-day realities." But she hoped that leaders like Mrs. Roosevelt could lead the way toward unity and away from "factional infighting." Lerner chided Wallace's PCA for including Communists in a liberal organization, but like Kirchwey, he chided equally the ADA for its equation of communism and fascism. In his new position as editor of *The New Republic*, Wallace denied that he and Mrs. Roosevelt were in "warring camps." Both, he said, were speaking in their respective organizations about unity in the progressive ranks.[24]

The denial of fundamental differences and the urging of unity tended to reflect the views of those liberal intellectuals who, like Lerner, Kirchwey, and Bliven, wanted to avoid making the choice between the two organizations. We have seen the political reasons for some politicians like Bowles to avoid joining either organization, although Bowles became quickly aligned in practice, if not in membership, with the ADA. While most liberals who abstained from joining either the ADA or the PCA wished to avoid choosing sides, there were some like James Patton of the National Farmers Union whose rejection was based on apparent disgust with all liberal organizations. Tom Amlie shared Patton's disgust. No friend of the Communists (he referred to party members as "C.P. stooges" and criticized Hillman for trying to build a liberal movement through a NC-PAC staffed with fellow travelers and probable Communists), Amlie after the war thought that liberals were mistaken when they blamed everything on the Communists. The ADA, he said, was "full of socialists and trade unionists who have been fighting the commies so long that they have lost sight of the real enemy." But the PCA had the same NC-PAC Communist leadership that had played a disastrous role in the 1946 elections. Although a number of liberals abstained for Kirchwey's and Lerner's "ecumenical reasons," few were prepared to follow Amlie's condemnation of both sides. Most, instead, chose sides.[25]

To Loeb and the founders of ADA it was not a matter of weakening the liberal forces through division; on the contrary, they saw themselves as strengthening the liberal forces by their clear-cut refusal to cooperate with Communists. In a letter to *The New Republic*, Loeb said that the liberal progressive forces had been on the decline since the death of Roosevelt and that the formation of the ADA represented the beginning of the counterattack against reaction. What needed emphasizing, he declared, were not stories of disunity; rather, "the historic importance of the ADA" was that it was "the organization of a broader coalition of liberal-labor leadership than has been attained in this generation."[26]

But in order to achieve this coalition and to develop a democratic momentum, it had been necessary to face the issue of liberal-Communist cooperation. Insisting that the ADA did not seek to aid the red-baiters or to be "Russophobes," Loeb argued for the principled necessity of taking this position:

> This meeting . . . was . . . a declaration of liberal independence from the stifling and paralyzing influence of the Communists and their apologists in America. The ADA is fully aware that rejection of any alliance with Communists gives no automatic assurance of affirmative success in the grave struggles ahead. It was recognized, however, that this step was an essential prerequisite to the aggressive fight for democracy that we propose to wage. No movement that maintains a double standard on the issue of human liberty

can lay claim to the American liberal tradition. The ADA's unequivocal rejection of any ties with the Communists reflects more than expedient awareness of the political kiss of death which they bestow; it expresses the painfully acquired conviction of American progressives that there can be no organizational compatibility between Communists and liberals, regardless of any coincidental agreement on specific issues.[27]

Loeb denied that the ADA's rejection of a Popular Front strategy reflected "an inflexible and doctrinaire 'anti-Sovietism.'" The ADA, he said, presented "no blueprint for American-Soviet relations"; it viewed Russia neither as "the perennial villain of the international show" nor "as the fixed point of international virtue." There was room in the organization "for honest differences of opinion on the strategic details of diplomatic negotiations in the quest for an enduring peace." The ADA rejected "both Soviet orthodoxy and American jingoism." Finally, he wrote, "it denies that all Russian actions are a product of American and British sins, and it emphatically contends that the methods of the police state are abhorrent to progressives, whether practised in Eastern Europe or in Franco Spain."[28]

Having spent the better part of his letter explaining the ADA's perspective on the Soviet Union and liberal-Communist relations, Loeb then said the press had "understandably exaggerated" the "split" among the liberals and the ADA's relations with liberals who favored "collaboration with Communists" and with "pro-Communist groups." The convention, he argued, had not been negative; it had been "affirmative and pro-democratic." The ADA had developed "a positive and militant credo"; it sought "new frontiers of opportunity and social reform in America." It had simply had to resolve "the Communist issue swiftly and decisively so that liberals may be free to organize their lines and fight the battle against reaction without artificial cries of 'unity' and disingenuous charges of 'Red-baiting.'"[29]

No doubt the ADA's program was positive, as Loeb stressed in his letter to *The New Republic* and Bob Bendiner wrote in *The Nation;* the organization had not been formed simply because Loeb and the leaders of the UDA had decided that in the wake of Soviet expansionism liberalism had "to clean house." Loeb and Niebuhr had genuinely come to feel that liberalism in the postwar period needed a "new beginning" and a new momentum. But if it is simplistic to see anticommunism as the entire mission of ADA, it would be foolish to deny that the issue was central to its origins. Without the new climate of opinion created by the breakdown of the wartime alliance and the Soviet domination of Eastern Europe, the UDA would not have thought the issue of liberal-Communist relations so paramount. As an organization it had already excluded Communists, but with the new, international relations and the new more antagonistic line of the American Communists, the issue became at once a moral and a political issue for the UDA and then for the ADA.[30]

And so the wartime unity among liberals came to an end, shattered by the issue of Stalinism. Bliven and Loeb, the closest of political collaborators during the war, no longer worked together. Del Vayo and Norman Angell, the editor of *Free World*, a journal dedicated to furthering the ideals of the United Nations, no longer coexisted on the editorial board. What had the wartime experience meant? Had liberals learned anything?

Apparently, despite high-sounding words, they had not learned the difference between grassroots and leader-directed organizations. In her comments on the newly organized PCA, Fuller commented that its test would be, not in its founding conference or its announced program, but in how well it could become a genuine grassroots organization on the local level. The chairpersons of PCA rushed to assure *The New Republic* readers that the organizing conference reflected grassroots organizers and that this direction would continue. But the PCA turned out to be a Wallace-directed organization; Wallace and his advisers ran and shaped the organization ideologically and politically. Perhaps there was no difference between the ideology and politics of its leaders and those it attracted, but the directions came from above. Just as the PACs had been Hillman's organizations in 1944, so the PCA was Wallace's.[31]

The ADA was no different. Just as the UDA was directed by its leaders toward placing great emphasis on attracting influential members, so the ADA started as an organization of influential members. Its very beginnings were "managed" from the top. Loeb planned the resolutions to be introduced at the founding convention and assigned the persons to introduce them. He even picked persons to make comments at stages where he felt the meetings would lag. Every detail was planned. It was an inauspicious beginning for an organization that wanted to make new departures. Less than a year after its founding, one member was complaining to Niebuhr about the lack of grassroots democracy within the ADA.[32]

Perhaps Loeb's belief that American liberalism had been in decline only since the death of President Roosevelt prevented any great organizational or ideological rethinking. It was clear in the quarreling over who spoke for Roosevelt that the dependency on and liberal enchantment with

Roosevelt continued. The UDA claims may have had some validity in terms of what Roosevelt actually would have done about relations with the Soviet Union; on the other hand, the PCA claims may have had some validity in Roosevelt's hopes for the postwar world. But both set of claims also suggest that neither Loeb and his supporters nor Wallace and his supporters were willing to go beyond Roosevelt's name to examine the myth that liberalism was in a healthy condition up to his death. Nowhere was the liberal mythologizing of Roosevelt more apparent than in *The New Republic*'s 1946 memorial appraisal. Philip Murray's article was entitled "He Was Indispensable"; Wallace's was entitled "He Led the Common Man." Arthur M. Schlesinger Jr. recognized FDR's "conservative conception" of the war ("it was for him a war of survival, not a war of revolution") but believed that he "left us the fighting spirit and broad democratic faith." Lash, the UDA's New York City leader, echoed these sentiments in the chapter's newsletter: "And never, either in war or peace, did FDR depart from his forward-looking conception of the role of the Democratic Party."[33]

All sides, of course, claimed they were charting new directions, but the figure of Roosevelt continued to hang over their efforts. In his opening editorial for *The New Republic*, Wallace, calling Roosevelt "a progressive first and a Democrat second," appealed to the Roosevelt heritage—not "to look backward," but "to look ahead." Looking ahead, however, meant looking ahead without Roosevelt. No one was more anxious than Loeb to develop a dynamic progressive movement. Like Kirchwey and Bliven during the war, Loeb was concerned that liberalism had grown overly dependent on Roosevelt. But to follow through seriously on what this implied about the failure to build an independent liberal-left would have forced the UDA to reexamine its strategy of operating through influential members and depending on them. This Loeb and the UDA were unwilling to do. Two years later Loeb acknowledged to critics of the ADA's decision to support the Truman Doctrine and both military and economic aid to Turkey and Greece that one of the reasons the ADA decided to support them was that aid to Greece had been developed by two liberal New Dealers, Paul Porter and Mark Etheridge, who were close to the ADA. For an organization that claimed to be part of building a dynamic new liberal movement this was a pretty thin thread to rely on for making policy decisions.[34]

But this is not so different from the way the liberal community acted during the war. The apotheosis of Wallace during the war was part and parcel of the liberal reliance on "some good men" to spread the liberal message and to guide Roosevelt to follow his best instincts. The unwillingness of the liberals to face clearly Roosevelt's responsibility for the wartime policies they opposed was part of the same process of relying on "liberal persons" and the liberal professions of those persons.

Any such analysis would have forced liberals to reexamine the entire Roosevelt legacy. It was far easier to grab hold of the presumed liberal legacy of Roosevelt and to stake out one's territory on that basis. Thus, when Wallace broke with Truman and began organizing what would eventually lead to the Progressive Party, Wallace and his followers claimed that he was the heir of Roosevelt's New Deal legacy. The ADA denied this; but when many of the ADA liberals raised the possibility of a break with Truman in 1948, they justified it not only by citing his political precariousness but by claiming he had departed from Roosevelt's liberal legacy.[35]

In practice the ADA carried on very much like the UDA had before: it looked to Washington. And so did the labor movement. The New Deal had been vital in building the labor movement in the 1930s. Hillman's vision of consumer capitalism with a high-wage economy and a strong labor movement had won enough support in the New Deal's middle phase to convince the government to help create a milieu in which labor, using its own militant tactics, could grow. The nod of approval given to labor by the government, accompanied by the institutional agencies relating to labor relations, encouraged labor to increasingly look toward Washington. This trend was strengthened by the plethora of wartime government agencies connected with labor and the economy. When the New Deal approved the "maintenance of union membership" plan during the war, it was a mixed blessing. Perhaps vital for sustaining membership in the conservative antiunion climate of the war, it also accentuated the trend of looking to Washington for protection rather than outward to a mass union movement built on one's own. In the postwar period both the ADA and the union movement chose getting a hearing in the halls of power in the nation's capital over building mass activist movements. Loeb's hopes for a new liberal-labor dynamic relationship were no doubt genuine, but it was headed in the same direction as it was during the war: toward Washington.[36]

As Loeb hoped, the ADA did become more influential than the UDA, and it attracted wider support among politicians. However, this only emphasized its increased emphasis on practicality, its diminished expectations. Although Loeb and Niebuhr had not shared completely in the heady wartime optimism of many of their fellow liberals about the democratic revolution, they nonetheless had expectations that went beyond the administration's agenda. They hoped to steer the administration toward their agenda, not accept, with only minor modifications, the administration's agenda. At the end of the war, they had accepted the badly compromised Murray Full Employment Bill, a far cry from their literature of a full production economy. They did it because it appeared to be the practical course — a sign of things to come.

In April 1947 Charles Bolte, the head of the liberal American Veterans Committee, wrote an article for *The Nation* on the March ADA convention in Washington. The article was positive, portraying the ADA as a democratic organization in which members made decisions "on the basis of facts and arguments" and not on "orders from above." He denied that the organization was "obsessively anti-Communist" and pointed to its far greater attention to the dangers from reaction. Bolte commented on the majority of the convention's support of military and economic aid to Greece and Turkey:

> Was this a by-product of the A.D.A.'s "anti-communism"? After serious consideration (and after opposing and voting against the policy), I am sure it was not. Rather, I believe it was a vestigial remnant of old-fashioned "practical" thinking on the part of the majority. The argument — chiefly and ably articulated by Franklin D. Roosevelt, Jr., and Marquis Childs — ran like this: the United Nations is the only hope; we must strengthen it; cooperation between the United States and the Soviet Union is the only basis for that strengthening; such cooperation cannot flow from weakness; therefore we must stem Soviet expansion; therefore we must hold our noses and aid Greece and Turkey. The argument overlooks the fact that by pursuing a unilateral policy you inevitably undercut any multilateral policy; yet I believe it was advanced in good faith (which may be the death of us yet).[37]

It is tempting here to trace how "holding one's nose" set the stage for a long liberal capitulation to a foreign policy that wasn't the death of "us" but led to the death of many. But for the purpose of this study, it is important to notice the obeisance to the argument of practicality. The bane of the insider game and what Amlie had warned against, it led increasingly to what later came to be called "anticipatory surrender." It was implicit during the war in the liberals' refusal to break with the Roosevelt administration. This refusal resulted from the liberals linking the New Deal with the worldwide democratic revolution. But once the promise of that revolution grew dimmer and more distant, and once the New Deal, with its willingness to allow liberal rhetoric to define the meaning of the war, was over, the implications of the insider Washington game would play themselves out in the tortured relationship between the ADA and the Truman administration.

In 1948 the issue in the liberal efforts to dump Truman was more practical than programmatic. The ADA liberals bantered around the name of Eisenhower—not without some trepidation. The mere fact that they were considering a political unknown, a person with no claims to a liberal ideological perspective, suggests that electability, not liberal ideology, was the issue. This was possible, of course, because liberal ideology had become less important, or rather, it had changed so that even the wartime calls for a full production economy within a reformed capitalism seemed utopian. But electability and the declining importance of ideology were not the only factors in the liberal willingness to consider Eisenhower a possible candidate in 1948. The idea also assumed that the power of the liberal intellectual community was such that it could be a major influence on policy. This wartime illusion is part of the intellectual baggage that continues to burden the liberal intellectual community. The "fantasy of access and influence," as Katha Pollitt has characterized it, did not begin in the war years, but the war years fed it.[38]

It is true that Loeb, Niebuhr, and the founders of the ADA retained a positive attitude toward democratic socialism in Europe. In 1946 the UDA urged Truman to support the British government's approval of the nationalization of German industry. And in 1947 the ADA looked favorably on a democratic socialist Europe. In an October 1947 letter to Niebuhr, Loeb described the American liberals as "blood brothers" to "the Socialists of Europe." The ADA also retained its strong ties with the British Labour Party through its London office and *London Letter.* But except to ultraconservatives, German socialism and, after the decline of the Keep Left group, British socialism posed no major threat, since both were supportive of American initiatives to build a strong Western military alliance. With its mixture of New Dealism and European democratic socialism as an alternative to Marxism and laissez-faire capitalism, Schlesinger's *Vital Center* (1949) may have seemed vital to him and his fellow ADA liberals, but compared to the hopes for a democratic revolution—a revolution that was also thought of as an alternative to unbridled capitalism and Soviet communism—Schlesinger's "vital center" was fairly tepid.[39]

The liberals who did not participate in the consensus politics of the 1950s, particularly those around *The Nation,* were also distanced from the highs hopes of the war years. Whatever belief they still maintained in the possibility of some kind of worldwide democratic revolution seemed far removed from the reality of McCarthyism. Absorbed in a defense against reaction and McCarthyism, there were few in the circle who could retain much of the wartime optimism.

If there was no rethinking of the Roosevelt legacy or of how to build a dynamic liberal movement, there was also very little rethinking about the people. For liberals on both sides of the PCA-ADA debate, "the people" still were right. Although Wallace, in taking the job as editor of *The New Republic* in late 1946, recognized the defeats progressives had suffered, he still proclaimed that the American people would always reject a Democratic Party that was not "militantly progressive." The belief that the majority of people were liberal or progressive formed the basis for Lerner's analysis of the congressional elections of 1946. "A clearcut choice between liberal decency and reaction," he said, would result in a liberal victory. Responding to Wallace's 1946 Madison Square Garden speech, the editors of *The New Republic* wrote: "We live in a progressive world. . . . In voicing our progressive spirit, Wallace stands as a world leader . . . President Truman is being subjected to immense pressure in the name of national unity to destroy the Wallace spirit, and, with it, the last hold of the Democratic Party on national power. . . . If unity with Senator Vandenberg means world disunity, the American people will choose Wallace."

Loeb and the ADA shared the same underlying perspective on "the people." In one of their first press releases, ADA's co-chairs Leon Henderson and Wilson Wyatt announced their efforts to lead American progressives with the words, "knowing the great body of Americans to be progressive." If the majority of the American people were liberal, the issue was proper leadership—how to persuade, not how to educate. Just as the progressive educators forgot about the necessity of educating the people because they thought the only enemy was reaction, so the liberals paid more attention to persuading Washington than they did to working with the people—the majority of whom, if both sides were correct, already had liberal values.[40]

Four years later the anticommunist, anti-McCarthy liberals would suddenly discover that the majority of the American people did not share their liberal values, and they would seek the protection of the "liberal" elites against the people. The remnants of Popular Front liberalism would complain that McCarthy was misleading the people (which he was), as they bewilderingly tried to understand what could have happened to their romanticized people.

A major problem was that wartime liberals often evoked instead of analyzed; they evoked "the people" without concretely analyzing the term. Even when they had begun the analytical process—as in the liberals' 1930s/wartime redefinition of America as a pluralistic, diverse nation—too often they had been content with the rhetoric of redefinition. Here they had been successful. I am convinced that insofar as nations can be said to have a conception of themselves, the United States emerged out of World War II with a liberal self-image—as a pluralistic nation of all races and religions sharing in the values of freedom and democracy. However, this was not a reality: there were many Americans who did not share this conception and certainly did not share the values it proclaimed. What is important is that most Americans proclaimed these values *and* failed to practice or support them. The liberals had made an important contribution in the redefinition of America; but perhaps because they continued to romanticize the liberalism of the people, they were not prepared to confront the distance between rhetoric and reality.

This was not the only victory for liberal rhetoric or the only time that liberal rhetoric did not always wind up serving liberal ends. The very rhetoric of freedom and democracy that Kirchwey had trumpeted during the war became the rhetoric of her conservative opponents during the cold war; the division of the world into an antithesis between fascism and democracy needed only the word fascism changed to communism to serve conservative ends. The international civil war between fascism and democracy became the international civil war between communism and democracy. The language used to describe fascist conspiracies in Latin America directed by Franco became the language used for Communist conspiracies in North America directed by Stalin. While it is doubtful that the post–World War II conservatives consciously expropriated Kirchwey and Bliven for their anti-Soviet purposes, the acceptance of the latter's rhetoric as the meaning of the war provided an image of American reality and ideals that was easily available for a variety of purposes far different from theirs.

This brief exploration into the fate of the liberal rhetoric of freedom and democracy in the postwar world has admittedly been designed to suggest how abstract the liberal intellectual world of the war years was. Although, like Norman Thomas, I have a deep admiration for the pacifist values, and although I have a great deal of political sympathy for the third camp position, I still believe that World War II deserved "critical support" or whatever term one wants to apply to support for victory combined with a substantive and consequential criticism of capitalism and the Roosevelt administration. But it was not "the good war"; no war is good. Nor was it an international civil war of democracy versus fascism, although there were incipient democratic forces that neither Stalin nor the West wished or allowed to manifest themselves. By perpetuating an ideological picture of the war that had little to do with political reality, liberals distorted their politics. It made their criticisms of the Roosevelt administration superficial; as deeply as they felt betrayed, the liberals would not break with him. It led them to take nonliberal positions on civil liberties, to defend the no-strike pledge even when they thought they were pro-labor, and to tacitly accept the internment of Japanese Americans. It led them to romanticize the people and Wallace, whom they believed spoke for the people, and in doing so it increased their reliance on "liberal persons" rather than on movement-building.

But if the liberal aspirations and hopes were abstract and their resulting politics often illusory, there was a nobility to their dreams. The noble abstractions helped them further the redefinition of America, which—even if the result was often ambiguous and if it sometimes fostered a widespread hypocrisy, particularly over race—was important in efforts to develop an egalitarian America. The ideas of freedom, democracy, greater equality, and a full production economy were not wrong. With them, the liberal support for the war became abstract; without them the war might have become mired in cynical realism. For all my criticism of the liberal performance, I would not want anyone to think that the conservative alternative or the "realistic" liberalism of the postwar years offered superior values or politics.

If I defend the nobility of the abstractions, I also need to end on two negative notes. First, there was an alternative to the liberal pro-war position—the Socialist position of critical support. There were abstractions in that position too; undoubtedly the third camp Socialists exaggerated the possibilities of revolution in Europe. But at least these abstractions did not lead them to support either the Roosevelt administration or Stalin. There is much to criticize in the Socialist critical support position, but with all its simplifications it offered a better perspective on the domestic and international world. If the liberals had looked to the Socialist left, instead of contributing to its and Thomas's marginalization, they might have served to reduce some of the simplistic conspiracy thinking of the Socialists.

They would not have solved the problem of political influence and they might have had no more—and perhaps less—political power in Washington. But they might have helped start the development of an independent left mass movement, which, after all, was the only thing that would have made their criticisms of the Roosevelt administration have political consequences—and was the only thing that could concretize their noble abstractions.

But the liberals would not look to the Socialist left. To them, its critical support position breathed the air of opposition. Nothing less than total support was acceptable. The argument here is not that this was a great missed opportunity for the left; I am not presenting any simplistic argument about how the liberal-left could have built a successful movement. But I am arguing that the liberals' total support of the war blinded them to potential democratic allies and reinforced their ties to an administration that either did not share their values or felt that it was impossible to share them during the war.

The final note of criticism involves more a sense of the world that the war was producing. Lewis Mumford, who in the late 1930s helped generate the spirit of total war and unambiguous support for the war, later came to feel that in the process of fighting the war, American values had become brutalized, that in the massive saturation bombing that culminated in the dropping of the atomic bomb, the United States had come to accept the totalitarian logic of the fascists. I do not want to suggest that the liberal community lost all sense of humane values and all sense of the relation of means to ends. On issues like the dropping of the atomic bomb the absence of criticism revealed an insensitivity; on other issues, such as the plight of the Jewish refugees, liberals were the conscience of the nation.[41]

What I am suggesting is that the liberal intellectual community showed no sign of a sustained sense of the tragedy of the war. I suppose that to have taken a tragic vision of the war—which to my mind is compatible with critical support—would have been to most liberals too negative an attitude. Niebuhr had a pessimistic view of human nature and wrote about the inability of the liberal mind to understand the nature of evil, but he also connected the pessimistic view of human nature with a politics that emphasized the "realistic" limits of social change. Thus, his view fed into the New Deal as much as Kirchwey's more utopian beliefs in the democratic revolutionary nature of the war. Neither presented a tragic view of the world in 1945. Not even the chastened view of *The New Republic*, with its image of a plodding liberal reform, was truly tragic. A truly tragic view pointed away from the New Deal, away from conservatism and reactionary politics, and away from Stalinism—and toward democratic socialism. Writing at the end of the European war, Jim Cork, an ex-Lovestoneite who, through his friendship with Travers Clement, had been brought close to the Socialist Party, set down this tragic view in his column for *The Socialist Call*: "It will be a slow and weary way back from the sorrows and hatreds engendered by this war to a state of things where a civilized being can draw a free breath. Above all, it is necessary to recapture the feeling, now all but lost, of the sanctity of human life, of the inviolable worth of the individual. Never was a pain-racked and warped and twisted world in greater need of the ideals of a democratic and egalitarian socialism."[42]

Notes

The following abbreviations are used for periodicals in the notes:

CC   *Christian Century*
C&C   *Christianity and Crisis*
CG   *Common Ground*
CS   *Common Sense*
FW   *Free World*
N   *The Nation*
NL   *The New Leader*
NR   *The New Republic*
PR   *Partisan Review*
SC   *Socialist Call*

The following abbreviations are used for manuscript collections:

AB   Alfred Bingham Papers, Manuscripts and Archives, Yale University Library
ADA   Americans for Democratic Action Papers, State Historical Society of Wisconsin, Madison
CB   Chester Bowles Papers, Manuscripts and Archives, Yale University Library
DM   Dwight Macdonald Papers, Sterling Library, Yale University
FK   Freda Kirchwey Papers, Schlesinger Library, Radcliffe College
LF   Louis Fischer Papers, Seeley G. Mudd Manuscript Library, Department of Rare Books and Special Collections, Princeton University
MC   Malcolm Cowley Papers, Newberry Library, Chicago
MJ   Matthew Josephson Papers, Beinecke Library, Yale University
ML   Max Lerner Papers, Manuscripts and Archives, Yale University Library

NT   Norman Thomas Papers, Manuscript and Archives Division, The New York Public Library, Astor, Lenox and Tilden Foundation

RB   Robert Bendiner Papers, State Historical Society of Wisconsin, Madison

RN   Reinhold Niebuhr Papers, Library of Congress, Washington, D.C.

SP   Socialist Party Papers, Rare Book, Manuscript, and Special Collections Library, Duke University

TA   Thomas Amlie Papers, State Historical Society of Wisconsin, Madison

The following persons' names are abbreviated in the footnotes:

HA	Herbert Agar
GA	Gehrta Amlie
TA	Thomas Amlie
RB	Roger Baldwin
CaB	Carl Becker
WiB	William Becker
WB	William Benton
VB	Victor Bernstein
AB	Alfred Bingham
BB	Bruce Bliven
CB	Chester Bowles
IB	Irving Brant
SC	Stuart Chase
TC	Travers Clement
MaC	McAlister Coleman
LC	Lewis Corey
MC	Malcolm Cowley
EC	Ely Culbertson
AD	J. Alvarez Del Vayo
CD	Carl Dreher
JD	Judah Drob
HE	Heinz Eulau
LF	Louis Fischer
HaF	Harry Fleischman
VF	Varian Fry
HF	Helen Fuller
AH	Alvin Hansen
SH	Seymour Harris
GH	George Hartmann
MJ	Matthew Josephson

DK	J. Donald Kingsley
FK	Freda Kirchwey
MK	Maynard Krueger
HL	Harold Laski
ML	Max Lerner
JLL	John Lester Lewine
AL	Alfred Baker Lewis
JL	James Loeb
DM	Dwight Macdonald
AM	Archibald MacLeish
JM	James McGill
CM	Carey McWilliams
RN	Reinhold Niebuhr
NP	Nathalie Panek
JP	James Patton
DP	David Petegorsky
NR	Nathan Robertson
SR	Selden Rodman
FDR	Franklin D. Roosevelt
GS	Gaetano Salvemini
FS	Frederick L. Schuman
CS	Claire Sifton
PS	Paul Sifton
IS	I. F. Stone
LS	Lillian Symes
NT	Norman Thomas
AU	Alexander Uhl
JV	Jerry Voorhis
HW	Henry Wallace
JW	James Wechsler
AW	Aubrey Williams
DW	David Williams
HoW	Howard Y. Williams
WZ	William Zeuch

INTRODUCTION

1. ML, *PM*, March 28, 1944. On Mayor Hague, see *N*, July 17, 1943, 58–59; *NR*, July 19, 1943, 61.

CHAPTER 1

1. FK, "Let France Clean House," N, September 2, 1944, 255–56.

2. For an excellent history of the Office of War Information, see Allan M. Winkler, The Politics of Propaganda: The Office of War Information, 1942–1945 (New Haven, 1978). On how words "do" things, see Daniel Rodgers, Contested Truths: Keywords in American Politics (New York, 1987), 3–16.

3. For an analysis that focuses on World War II propaganda as simply a device to maintain the morale of the troops, see Paul Fussell, Wartime: Understanding and Behavior in the Second World War (New York, 1989), 129–80. For liberal expressions of the importance of propaganda, see "Propaganda and the War," CS, February 1942, 54–55; "What Is Wrong with American Propaganda" (Round Table #5), FW, March 1942, 132–43. See also AM, "Words Are Not Enough," N, March 13, 1943, 368–72.

4. In a recent important study, Steven Biel writes: "If intellectuals saw the necessity of fighting the Second World War, they did not view it as a clear-cut conflict between fascism and democracy." See Biel, Independent Intellectuals in the United States, 1910–1945 (New York, 1992), 225. On the fear of losing the war, see, e.g., "We Can Lose the War," N, February 14, 1942, 179–80; AD, "Leaders, Not Ghosts," N, February 7, 1942, 160–63; George Soule, "The Lessons of Last Time," NR, February 2, 1942, 170; NR editorials, February 23, 1942, 255–56; March 9, 1942, 320.

5. On military advice, see, e.g., articles by Donald Mitchell in N on January 24, 1942; March 28, 1942; Max Werner, "The Offensive Is Possible," NR, March 23, 1942, 387–88. See also editorials in N on January 24, 1942, 81–82; March 7, 1942, 271–72; March 14, 1942, 297–98; May 9, 1942, 531–32. On foot-dragging and slackness, see, e.g., "Still Muddling Through," N, December 12, 1942, 638; "FDR Gives Marching Orders," NR, January 19, 1942, 70–71. For warnings against slacking off even though the war production had increased and the military news was better, see, e.g., articles by IS in N on April 24 and July 17, 1943, and editorials in NR on May 25, 1942, 715; November 30, 1942, 695.

6. Richard Rovere, "A Warning to Liberals," CS, August 1942, 266–68. FK, "The People's Revolution," N, May 16, 1942, 561–62.

7. Mary McAuliffe, Crisis on the Left: Cold War Politics and American Liberals, 1947–1954 (Amherst, 1978), 5–6; William O'Neill, A Better World: Stalinism and the American Intellectuals (New York, 1982), 138.

8. See "The SEP Again," NR, February 28, 1944, 261. In an important work that was published after the manuscript for this book was completed, Michael Denning argues for the wartime continuity of the political Popular Front. See Denning, The Cultural Front: The Laboring of American Culture in the Twentieth Century (London, 1997). I agree with Denning that there was continuity in the cultural Popular Front and in what I call the Popular Front sensibility. For my criticism of

Denning's fusion of the cultural and the political Popular Front, see *New Politics* 7 (Winter 1999).

9. Daniel Aaron, *Writers on the Left: Episodes in American Literary Communism* (New York, 1961), 376–77; MJ to Robert Lynd, November 7, 1939, MJ Papers; Lynd to MJ, November 11, 1939, MJ Papers; MC to MJ, November 2, 1939, MC Papers; Unsigned [MC] to ML, November 26, 1939, MC Papers.

10. RN, letter, *N*, April 10, 1943, 537; *NR*, October 16, 1944, 479–80. On advice to Moscow to drop the American Communist Party, see RN, "Russia and the West," *N*, January 23, 1943, 126–27; T.R.B. in *NR*, June 22, 1942, 859; November 23, 1942, 677. On Browder, see *N*, March 28, 1942, 355; *NR*, May 25, 1942, 716.

11. *NR*, May 29, 1944, 728. On the liberal response to the transformation of the Communist Party to a "political association," see FK, "Stalin's Choice," *N*, January 22, 1944, 89–90; *NR*, January 17, 1944, 69; Granville Hicks, review of Earl Browder's *Teheran*, *NR*, July 17, 1944, 79–80; Harold Lavine, *PM*, March 26–28, 1944.

12. ML, *PM*, May 22, 1943; January 13, 1944; FK, "A New Popular Front?" *N*, December 2, 1944, 677–78.

13. Editorials in *N* on July 31, 1943, 114; September 11, 1943, 283; April 15, 1944, 435; Richard Rovere, letter, *N*, September 11, 1943, 306; FK, "American Labor Pains," *N*, April 8, 1944, 409–10; editorials in *NR* on August 9, 1943, 181; September 27, 1943, 409; April 10, 1944, 484; April 17, 1944, 516; May 29, 1944, 728; Eugene Connolly, letter and editors' reply, *PM*, July 30, 1943; JW, *PM*, July 25, 1943; John P. Lewis, *PM*, February 13, 1944. For an extremely harsh critique of the role of Hillman and the Communists in the American Labor Party, see Will Herberg, "The Stillborn Party," *CS*, May 1944, 161–64. See also UDA, Release, "Statement on the Union for Democratic Action Urging Support of Right Wing in Labor Party Primaries," August 9, 1942, TA Papers.

14. JL to Andrew Brown, October 27, 1942, R-F 15-277, ADA Papers.

15. "Propaganda and the War," *CS*, February 1942, 54–55; "Willkie Speaks Out," *NR*, October 19, 1942, 482–83; AM, "The Moral Front," *N*, December 4, 1943, 660–63; VB, "A People's War," *PM*, June 13, 1943; "Fifth Year of the War," *NR*, August 30, 1943, 271–72.

16. "What Liberals Must Do," *NR*, September 7, 1942, 271–72; Robert Lynd, "The Structure of Power," *NR*, November 9, 1942, 597–98; "Mr. Jones and Mr. Smith," *CS*, November 1942, 378–79; BB, "The Hang-Back Boys," *NR*, March 6, 1944, 307.

17. HA, *A Time for Greatness* (Boston, 1942), 132–52. See the editorials in *CS* on January 1942, 18–19; February 1942, 54–55; March 1942, 90–91.

18. "Declaration" *FW*, July 1942; Louis Dolivet, "Political War," *FW*, January 1942, 365–68; editorials in *FW* on January 1942, 317–20; February 1942, 5–6; AD, "Political War," *N*, September 26, 1942, 263.

19. "Deadwood at the Top," *NR*, March 2, 1942, 285–86; FK, "Hitler Underground," *N*, August 12, 1944, 173; AM, "The Moral Front," *N*, December 4, 1943, 660–63; LF, review of MS's *Make This the Last War*, *N*, January 16, 1943, 96–97; "The Moral Crisis of the War," *NR*, February 8, 1943, 165; AD, "How to Use a Revolution," *N*, August 7, 1943, 143–44; AD, "Crisis in Confidence," *N*, December 5, 1942, 615; "The President's Message," *N*, September 25, 1943, 539–40; VB, "The Enemy Is Fascism," *PM*, January 28, 1944.

20. AD, "As Simple as That," *N*, January 23, 1943, 129–30; "Propaganda and the War," *CS*, February 1942, 54; "What Is Wrong with American Propaganda," *FW*, March 1942, 132–43.

21. "Our Revolution or Theirs?" *CS*, June 1942, 198–99.

22. BB, "F.D.R. in '44," *NR*, January 17, 1944, 75; Pearl Buck, "Make It Freedom's War," *NR*, December 21, 1942, 824–25; BB, "Where Do We Go From Here?" *NR*, December 21, 1942, 813–15.

23. MS, "Is It a People's War?" *NR*, November 16, 1942, 633–35; MS, "The Planners Look Backward," *NR*, November 23, 1942, 664–66; MS, "The Warning," *NR*, November 30, 1942, 704–8.

24. Henry Luce, "The American Century," *Life*, February 17, 1941, in John K. Jessup, ed., *The Ideas of Henry Luce* (New York, 1969), 105–20. FK, "Luce Thinking—II," *N*, February 28, 1942, 245–46. Kirchwey developed the same theme in a speech on Bastille day in 1944: the civil war in Europe, the struggle between tyrants and free people, the existence of the counterrevolution and the revolution, and the failure of the United States to recognize the reality of these developments. See Kirchwey, speech delivered at Hunter College, July 14, 1944, FK Papers. Immediately after Pearl Harbor, Seldon Rodman wrote to his co-editor at *CS*, Alfred Bingham: "I think it is very important that we stress and even overstress the revolutionary character of this war." SR to AB, December 11, 1941, AB Papers.

25. FK, *N*, February 28, 1942, 245–46.

26. Ibid.

27. For a forceful challenge to the democratic nature of World War II, see Julius Jacobson, "The USSR and the Nature of World War II," *New Politics* 6 (Summer 1996): 176–90.

28. ML to editor of *The Wall Street Journal*, n.d. [c. August 1942], ML Papers.

29. ML, "In the Wake of Liberation," *NR*, June 19, 1944, 807–8.

30. "War and Revolution," *NR*, August 9, 1943, 179–80; "American and European Reaction," *NR*, September 27, 1943, 411.

31. T.R.B., *NR*, June 21, 1943, 828.

CHAPTER 2

1. Charles W. Eliot, "Winning the Peace That Follows," speech delivered at the City College of New York, February 4, 1942, AB Papers.

2. JV, *Beyond Victory* (New York, 1944); DK and DP, *Strategy for Democracy* (New York, 1942), 5.

3. CaB, *How New Will the Better World Be?* (New York, 1944). See also CaB to ML, March 11, 1942, ML Papers.

4. DP to SR, November 30, 1942, AB Papers.

5. ML, *Ideas for the Ice Age: Studies in a Revolutionary Era* (New York, 1941), 5–6.

6. Ibid., 6–7.

7. Ibid., 5–9, 18. See also ML, "Enigma of FDR," *PM*, April 14, 1943.

8. CD, *The Coming Showdown* (Boston, 1942), 310–11, 398.

9. DK and DP, *Strategy for Democracy*, 4–5, 30.

10. Frank A. Warren, *Liberals and Communism: The "Red Decade" Revisited* (Bloomington, 1966); Warren, "Alfred Bingham and the Paradox of Liberalism," *The Historian*, February 1966, 252–67; Donald L. Miller, *The New American Radicalism* (Port Washington, NY, 1979); AB, *The Techniques of Democracy* (New York, 1942).

11. Warren, "Alfred Bingham and the Paradox of Liberalism," 252–67; AB, *The Techniques of Democracy*, 312–13.

12. In a series of articles in *N* in 1940, Corey reevaluated Marxism in ways that foreshadowed *The Unfinished Task*. See LC, "Marxism Reconsidered," *N*, February 17, 1940, 245–48; February 24, 1940, 272–75; March 2, 1940, 305–7.

13. LC, *The Unfinished Task: Economic Reconstruction for Democracy* (New York, 1942), vii–viii, 118–24; ML, *Ideas for the Ice Age*, 182.

14. HA, *A Time for Greatness*, 3–39, 155–83.

15. Winkler, *The Politics of Propaganda*, 73–111; James Warburg, *Foreign Policy Begins at Home* (New York, 1944), v–ix, 24; James Warburg, *The Long Road Home: The Autobiography of a Maverick* (New York, 1964).

16. Warburg, *Foreign Policy Begins at Home*, 27, 53.

17. AB, *Techniques of Democracy*, 7–14, 18–258, 313–14.

18. RN, *The Children of Light and the Children of Darkness* (New York, 1944); RN, review of AB's *Techniques of Democracy*, *N*, December 5, 1942, 626–27; ML, *Ideas for the Ice Age*, 9.

19. CD, *The Coming Showdown*, 341–52, 400.

20. LC, *The Unfinished Task*, 257–90.

21. DK and DP, *Strategy for Democracy*, 6, 10–12, 302–4.

22. Ibid., 314–17; AB, *Techniques of Democracy*, 285–87.

23. HA, *A Time for Greatness*, 125–26.

24. Ibid., 131–37; ML, *Ideas for the Ice Age*, 398–99; Pearl Buck, *American Unity and Asia* (New York, 1942), 11–42; JV, *Beyond Victory*, 190–213.

25. DK and DP, *Strategy for Democracy*, 31–32.

26. HA, *A Time for Greatness*, 137–39, 146, 151; ML, *Ideas for the Ice Age*, 53–57; MS, *Make This the Last War* (New York, 1943), ix.

27. HW, "The Price of Free World Victory," in Wallace, *The Century of the*

Common Man (New York, 1943), 16. G. A. Borgese, *Common Cause* (New York, 1943), 2.

28. Hiram Motherwell, *The Peace We Fight For* (New York, 1943), ix–x, 3–54, 196–224.

29. JV, *Beyond Victory*, 41–60, 168–69, 213–35; Warburg, *Foreign Policy Begins at Home*, 51–60, 254–90; Motherwell, *The Peace We Fight For*, 165–224.

30. See editorials in *N* on January 10, 1942, 26–27; January 30, 1942, 24–25; AD, "American Progressives—Your Hour," *N*, November 7, 1942, 475; Max Werner, "Global Strategy," *NR*, January 12, 1942, 40–41; articles by MS in *NR* on February 2, 1942; March 16, 1942, 353–54; April 20, 1942, 530–31; November 2, 1942; "For a Supreme War Council," *NR*, July 6, 1942, 3–4; FS, "The Need for Global Strategy," *NR*, August 10, 1942, 162–64;

31. DK and DP, *Strategy for Democracy*, 283–84.

32. Ibid., 283, 285–87, 292–93.

33. MS, *Make This the Last War*, 270–71.

34. Ibid., 283.

35. FK, "The Taste of Defeat," *N*, July 11, 1942, 25; AD, "American Progressives—Your Hour," *N*, November 7, 1942, 475; MS, "Toward World Organization," *NR*, February 2, 1942, 136–37; MS, "Wanted: United Nations," *NR*, April 20, 1942, 530–31; MS, "Freedom's Crisis," *NR*, July 6, 1942, 10–13; MS, "The Crisis of the U.N.," *NR*, November 2, 1942, 565–67; Max Werner, "The Power of Unified Strategy," *NR*, November 2, 1942, 568–70. See also editorials in *NR* on July 6, 1942, 3–4; November 2, 1942, 561–62; February 1, 1943, 136.

36. IS, "Will America Go Socialist?" *N*, August 11, 1945, 124–25.

37. For liberal reaction to the 1942 congressional elections, see Robert Bendiner, "Dunderhead Election," *N*, November 14, 1942, 497–98; IS, "Prospects for the New Year," *N*, January 2, 1943, 7–8; "Picking Up the Pieces," *NR*, November 16, 1942, 626–28.

38. BB, ML, and George Soule, "America and a World Economy," *NR*, November 29, 1943, 766–68; "The American Peace Plan," *NR*, September 4, 1944, 263–64; "The World after the War IV: Prosperity: The Key to Peace," *NR*, February 12, 1945, 216–17; Richard Lee Strout, "Four Post-War Essentials," *NR*, August 23, 1943, 244–45.

39. AH, *America's Role in the World Economy* (New York, 1945); AH, "Our Coming Prosperity," *CS*, June 1942, 186–89; TA, "Jobs for All," Special Supplement, *N*, November 27, 1943, 625–52; "Economy Security and World Peace" (speeches at Nation Associates Conference, October 7–8, 1944), *N*, October 21, 1944, 491–95; AH, "Planning Full Employment," *N*, October 21, 1944, 492; JP, "A Plan for Prosperity," *NR*, November 6, 1943, 586–88; articles by SH in *NR* on January 15, 1945; January 22, 1945; March 19, 1945; HW, "Jobs for All," *NR*, January 29, 1945, 138–40; articles by AH in *NR*, February 19 and 26, 1945; March 5, 1945; ML, *PM*, March 29, 1944; IS, *PM*, February 23, 1944; LC, "Mix-

ture for a Mixed Economy," *CS*, February 1944, 65–69; Robert Nathan, "A Plan for Free Enterprise," *CS*, March 1944, 103–5; SC, "Exploring Full Employment," *CS*, March 1944, 108–10; SC, *The Road We Are Traveling* (New York, 1942); SC, *Goals for America* (New York, 1942); JV, *Beyond Victory*, 68–118; CB, "War Effort Versus the Post-War World," speech, March 21, 1942; CB, "The Role of Government after the War," address, May 8, 1944; CB, address, San Francisco, August 25, 1944; CB, address, New Orleans, November 24, 1944; CB, *A Plan to Prevent Depression* [n.d.], all in CB Papers; HW, *Sixty Million Jobs* (New York, 1945).

40. On the connection between American economic postwar prosperity and world peace, see editorials in *NR* on November 20, 1944, 648; February 12, 1945, 216–17; June 25, 1945, 862–63. See also IS, "Planning and Socialism," *N*, October 21, 1944, 493; IS, "Only Full Employment Will Keep the Peace," *PM*, April 29, 1945.

41. LC, *The Unfinished Task*, 177–97, 231–56; CD, *The Coming Showdown*, 93–94; AB to TA, December 9, 1943, TA Papers. On the battle against cartels, see, e.g., the articles by IS in *N* on April 4, 1942, 387–88; April 18, 1942, 451–52; editorials in *N* on January 23, 1943, 113–14; November 25, 1944, 632; January 20, 1945, 60–61; "Cartels: the Menace of Worldwide Monopoly," Special Supplement, *NR*, March 27, 1943, 427–47; IS, *PM*, April 26–27, 1943; February 6–7, 1944.

42. DK and DP, *Strategy for Democracy*, 169–91; HA, *A Time for Greatness*, 33–36, 172, 181.

43. Editorials in *N* on December 12, 1942, 636–37; December 19, 1942, 669–70; March 20, 1943, 401–2; June 12, 1943, 824–25. "A Beveridge Plan for America," *NR*, December 21, 1942, 810–11; ML, "Charter for a New America," *NR*, March 22, 1943, 369–72; BB, "When We Rebuild America," *NR*, April 12, 1943, 473–74; BB, ML, and Soule, "Charter for America," Special Section, *NR*, April 19, 1943, 523–42; JP, "A Plan for Prosperity," *NR*, November 6, 1944, 586–88; "Prosperity," Special Section, *NR*, November 27, 1944, 707–26; HE, Mordecai Ezekiel, AH, JL, and Soule, "The Road to Freedom: Full Employment," Special Section, *NR*, September 24, 1945, 395–415. On PM and the National Resources Planning Board's Economic Bill of Rights, see *PM*, November 15, 1942; Selwyn James, *PM*, December 2, 1942.

44. On the UDA support of the Murray Bill, see Chapter 6. IS, "The New Reservationists," *N*, September 22, 1945, 274–75. See the editorials in *N* on December 23, 1944, 761–62; June 16, 1945, 664–65; August 25, 1945, 169–70. AH, "Beveridge on Full Employment," *NR*, February 19, 1945, 250–54; SH, "The Way to Full Employment," *NR*, June 4, 1945, 783–86; Soule, "The Full Employment Bill," *NR*, August 6, 1945, 154–56; HE et al., "The Road to Freedom: Full Employment," Special Section, *NR*, September 24, 1945, 395–415; "Peace in Progress," *CS*, February 1945, 19–22; IS, *PM*, June 4, 1945; August 17, 1945; VB, "Business and Employment," *PM*, August 27, 1945.

45. Warburg, *Foreign Policy Begins at Home*, v–ix, 51–60; JV, *Beyond Victory*, 88–118; HW, *The Century of the Common Man*, 56–68; HW, "Address at Dinner of Business Men for Roosevelt," November 2, 1944, CB Papers; HW to CB, April 26, 1944, CB Papers; AH, review of HW's *Sixty Million Jobs*, *NR*, September 17, 1945, 353–55; CB, "War Effort Versus the Post-War World," speech, March 21, 1942, CB Papers; CB, "Price Control Today and Business after the War," speech, April 24, 1944, CB Papers. One can look at Bowles's phrase "free enterprise" cynically. Bingham complimented Bowles for making "a fairly extreme view sound respectable" but wondered "whether you aren't a little too flattering to the dear old 'free enterprise' system." AB to CB, September 12, 1944, CB Papers. Bowles replied that he shared Bingham's "feeling on those paragraphs about 'free enterprise'" but included them because "it becomes far easier to get people to accept the other ideas." See CB to AB, October 11, 1944, CB Papers. However, if one interprets Bowles as an antimonopolist (though not anti–big business), Keynesian-influenced advocate of consumer capitalism, one is justified in viewing this phrase about "unleashing free enterprise" not simply as an ex-advertiser's manipulative cliché designed to minimize conservative opposition but also as an expression of what he genuinely expected to be the result of a government-aided capitalism. See CB to WB, June 28, 1944; CB to HW, January 26, 1945, CB Papers. In any case, when Bowles entertained the possibilities of postwar progress, he saw it as being made "along truly democratic, liberal, capitalistic lines." See CB to Eric Johnston, May 8, 1946, CB Papers. And during the war he had praise for the work of the CED. See CB to WB, September 9 and December 9, 1944, CB Papers.

46. DK and DP, *Strategy for Democracy*, 320. Alan Brinkley's *The End of Reform* was published after my book was completed. He and I are essentially in agreement about where the New Deal ended up in 1945 (though not where it started in 1933). He sees the move away from structural change among New Dealers and toward consumer capitalism as beginning in the mid-thirties. Although I have questions about how he defines structural change, I do not disagree that among New Dealers a consumer capitalism that involved little structural change was developing in these years. But for the liberals I have studied, structural change was always thought to be necessary to achieve full employment. The "democratic revolution" required changes in power relations, in government control, and in institutional relations. Although I admire Brinkley's work, I have occasional questions about how he uses liberal intellectuals who supported the New Deal (as distinct from liberal New Deal administrators) during the war to buttress his case. Thus, at one point he footnotes I. F. Stone as one of the liberals who believed that "postwar abundance" would depend more on "how government dealt with 'aggregate demand' than on the basis of how successfully it controlled corporate behavior." But Stone's point in this and other articles he was writing on postwar prosperity and planning was exactly the opposite: the need to control corporate behavior in order to have a full employment economy. Despite such reservations, I believe that *The*

End of Reform is a vital book in understanding the history of liberalism. See Alan Brinkley, *The End of Reform* (New York, 1995), 231; IS, "On Reconversion," *N*, August 12, 1944, 175–76; IS, "'Backward Area,'" *N*, July 29, 1944, 117–18; IS, "Planning and Socialism," *N*, October 21, 1944, 493.

47. HL, "Plan or Perish," *N*, December 5, 1945, 651.

CHAPTER 3

1. FK, "Mr. Hull Should Resign," *N*, January 3, 1942, 1–2. See also "St. Pierre and Miquelon," *NR*, January 5, 1942, 3; IS, "Aid and Comfort to the Enemy," *N*, January 3, 1942, 6–7.

2. Ibid., 1–2.

3. George Soule, "Roosevelt in 1943," *NR*, September 6, 1943, 326–27; "Backstairs Diplomacy," *N*, July 31, 1943, 115. See also "Lost Victory," *CS*, September 1943, 328–29.

4. James MacGregor Burns, *Roosevelt: The Soldier of Freedom, 1940–1945* (New York, 1970), 286–87; Robert Bendiner, *The Riddle of the State Department* (New York, 1942), 63–98. See also Robert Dallek, *Franklin D. Roosevelt and American Foreign Policy 1932–1945* (New York, 1979), 362–63.

5. FK, "Free and So-called Free," *N*, January 24, 1942, 832–83; FK, "Laval Takes Over," *N*, April 25, 1943, 477–79; LF, "Laval and Roosevelt," *N*, April 25, 1942, 486–87.

6. Material on the UDA role in the anti–State Department campaign can be found in R-F 15-275, ADA Papers. See also Frank Kingdon, "Dear Friend," August 19, 1942, R-F 13-220, ADA Papers; Bendiner, "Who Is the State Department?" *N*, July 25, 1942, 66–69; August 1, 1942, 87–90; August 8, 1942, 107–11; August 15, 1942, 126–29; Bendiner, *The Riddle of the State Department*.

7. On Stone, see, e.g., articles in *N* on March 21, 1942; April 11, 1942; April 18, 1942; May 2, 1942; May 9, 1942; November 7, 1942; July 17, 1943; DM, "Jesse Jones, Reluctant Dragon," *N*, February 7, 1942, 157–60; February 14, 1942, 187–90; articles by MS in *NR* on January 19, 1942; March 30, 1942; April 6, 1942; BB, "Rubber," *NR*, July 13, 1942, 41–43; IS, *PM*, November 8 and December 7, 1942; JW, *PM*, August 21 and 24, 1942.

8. William Dodd, Robert Morss Lovett, Goodwin Watson, Malcolm Cowley, Roy Parmelee, and John Kenneth Galbraith were all either denied appointments, withdrew their nominations, or were let go because of conservative pressure from within and without government agencies. For an example of liberal displeasure with the New Deal response, see IS, "Dies and the Backbone Shortage," *N*, February 13, 1943, 223–24.

9. MC, "The End of the New Deal," *NR*, May 31, 1943, 729–32.

10. "Martin Dies," Special Supplement, *N*, October 3, 1942, 309–28; FK,

"What Dies Is Up To," Special Supplement, *N*, October 3, 1942, 310; FK, "What's Wrong with Martin Dies," *PM*, October 1, 1942. Material on the UDA-sponsored anti-Dies meeting can be found in R-F 4-55, ADA Papers. See also MC to AM, April 12, 1942, MC Papers.

11. "Mr. Jones and Mr. Smith," *CS*, November 1942, 379; IS, "Capital Notes," *N*, January 23, 1943, 115.

12. IS, "What F.D.R. Forgot," *N*, January 8, 1944, 34–35; Stephen Fraser, *Labor Will Rule: Sidney Hillman and the Rise of American Labor* (New York, 1991), 259–88.

13. "The Double Fight," *NR*, December 28, 1942, 844–45.

14. AB to CB, September 12, 1944, CB Papers; "It's Roosevelt Again!" *NR*, November 13, 1944, 612. Earlier, Bingham had written Bowles that only the latter's prospective large role in "postwar economic policy" would make him "cast a fervent vote for him [Roosevelt] where I otherwise would scarcely bother to vote." AB to CB, August 2, 1944, CB Papers. For Bingham's postelection discouragement, see AB to CB, November 27, 1944, CB Papers.

15. "Why F.D.R.?" *N*, October 28, 1944, 503; "First in War, First in Peace," *N*, November 4, 1944, 548.

16. "The New Deal Must Go On," *NR*, January 3, 1944, 6–7.

17. *N*, October 2, 1943, 366.

18. *N*, August 21, 1935, 202.

19. UDA, Release, n.d. [1941]; RN et al., "An Open Letter to the President," August 4, 1941, R-F 9-138, ADA Papers.

20. Burns, *Roosevelt*, 285–95; Warburg, *Foreign Policy Begins at Home*, 190–91; Walter Langer, *Our Vichy Gamble* (New York, 1947), 225–26.

21. Burns, *Roosevelt*, 295–98; editorial, *NL*, November 21, 1942, 1, 7; editorial, *NL*, November 14, 1942, 8. On *PM*, see Crawford, December 1, 1942; AU, December 2, 1942; MS (*PM*) December 3, 1942.

22. "Who Will Lead France?" *NR*, November 23, 1942, 659–60.

23. "Liberals, Be Strong!" *NR*, November 30, 1942, 698–99. Perhaps because he wrote for both *PM* and *The New Republic*, Max Lerner straddled the fence. See ML to BB, November 19, 1942, ML Papers.

24. FK, "America's First Quisling," *N*, November 21, 1942, 529–30.

25. Burns, *Roosevelt*, 285–98; IS, "Fighting the Fighting French," *N*, November 28, 1942, 565; "Liberals, Be Strong!" 699; FK, "Darlan and American Liberals," *N*, November 28, 1942, 559–60; AU, *PM*, April 11, 1943. On Uhl's repeating the litany of appeasement, see AU, *PM*, February 6 and 11, 1944.

26. Burns, *Roosevelt*, 286–87, 297–98; Langer, *Our Vichy Gamble*, 316; William Leahy, *I Was There* (London, 1950), 17.

27. FK, "Darlan and American Liberals," 559–60.

28. Burns, *Roosevelt*, 319–23; Warburg, *Foreign Policy Begins at Home*, 192; FK, "What Next in Africa?" *N*, January 23, 1943, 111–13; editorials in *NR*, January 4,

1943, 7–8; January 25, 1943, 102–3; February 1, 1943, 131–132; VF, "Giraud and the Future of France," *NR*, January 11, 1943, 43–46.

29. "Trying to Just Say Peyrouton," *NR*, February 8, 1943, 165–66; *N*, January 30, 1943, 146; IS, "Moral Issue for Mr. Hull," *N*, January 30, 1943, 151–52; IS, *PM*, March 16, 1943; AU, *PM*, April 1, 1943. On the UDA, see Dorothy Norman to Mr. and Mrs. Lewisohn, February 18, 1943, R-F 13-226, ADA Papers; JL to ML, March 6, 1943, R-F 9-142, ADA Papers; "Peyrouton: Incident or Precedent?" March 31, 1943, R-F 16-311, ADA Papers. See RN, "The Politics of North Africa," *C&C*, February 22, 1943, 2.

30. Burns, *Roosevelt*, 319–23; FK, "The Meaning of Algiers," *N*, June 12, 1943, 823–24; editorials in *NR* on January 18, 1943, 68–69; April 5, 1943, 427; May 3, 1943, 582–83; June 14, 1943, 782–83; June 26, 1944, 834–35; ML, *PM*, May 29, 1944.

31. FK, "Coalition Against De Gaulle," *N*, July 3, 1943, 5; editorials in *N* on July 10, 1943, 30; *N*, September 18, 1943, 310; March 11, 1944, 296–97; "North African Politics," *NR*, July 19, 1943, 62–63; FK, "There Stands De Gaulle," *N*, April 15, 1944, 438–39; FK, "Dialogue in Limbo," *N*, June 17, 1944, 693–96. In August 1943 I. F. Stone reported that the North African and French policies were as much Roosevelt's as they were the State Department's, but the full meaning of his report was never incorporated into the liberals' perspective. See IS, "How Washington Reacted," *N*, August 7, 1943, 147.

32. Burns, *Roosevelt*, 384, 391–94; Warburg, *Foreign Policy Begins at Home*, 197–200, 202; *N*, July 31, 1943, 113; IS, "How Washington Reacted," *N*, August 7, 1943, 146–47; "Italy after Mussolini," *NR*, August 2, 1943, 126–27.

33. Articles by GS in *N* on January 30, 1943; November 27, 1943; January 1, 1944; and in *NR* on August 9, 1943; August 16, 1943; September 20, 1943; November 8, 1943; November 15, 1943; December 27, 1943; GS and George La Piana, *What To Do with Italy?* (New York, 1943); AD, "How to Use a Revolution," *N*, August 7, 1943, 143–44; Count Sforza, "Badoglio—and after," *NR*, August 9, 1943, 189–90.

34. R-F 14-245, ADA Papers.

35. "Italy after Mussolini," *NR*, August 2, 1943, 126–27.

36. Burns, *Roosevelt*, 390–94; Warburg, *Foreign Policy Begins at Home*, 197–202, 221–22; editorials in *N*, August 14, 1943, 172–73; April 22, 1944, 464; FK, "Stalin and Badoglio," *N*, March 25, 1944, 351–52; "Italy after Mussolini," *NR*, August 2, 1943, 126–27.

37. "The Allies and Italian Politics," *NR*, October 4, 1943, 439; "Expediency Plus Caution," *N*, October 9, 1943, 397.

38. *N*, April 8, 1944, 405; GS, "Reviving a Corpse in Italy," *NR*, May 8, 1944, 623–25; AU, *PM*, March 15, 1944; *N*, June 17, 1944, 697; *N*, July 1, 1944, 3; "Badoglio Is Out," *NR*, June 19, 1944, 800; GS, "Friends, Romans, Monarchists!" *N*, August 19, 1944, 211–12; GS, "'Purifying' Italy," *N*, August 26, 1944, 238–39;

AU, *PM*, February 6, 1944; AU, *PM*, April 11, 1944. See also Warburg, *Foreign Policy Begins at Home*, 202; Hannah to MJ, n.d. [1943], MJ Papers.

39. On the policy of expediency, see "Politics in Italy," *NR*, February 7, 1944, 167–68. On the influence of Great Britain and Churchill, see GS, "'Purely an Italian Affair,'" *N*, December 30, 1944, 799–800. See also "Mr. Churchill Reports," *N*, March 4, 1944, 268–69.

40. AU, *PM*, September 6, 1942; FK to LF, December 19, 1944, LF Papers; FK, "The Puppet Axis," *N*, March 21, 1942, 330–31; AD, "Three Years of Franco," *N*, April 4, 1942, 391–92; AD, "Spain's Mounting Crisis," *N*, November 20, 1943, 576–79; "Will the Blue Legion Change Color?" *NR*, November 1, 1943, 604; AU, *PM*, January 7, 1944.

41. Editorials by FK in *N* on February 5, 1944, 149; May 13, 1944, 556–58; December 16, 1944, 731; January 13, 1945, 33; June 30, 1945, 711–12; FK to Dear Friends, December 5, 1944, TA Papers; FK, address, Madison Square Garden, January 2, 1945, FK Papers; AD, "Negrin's Fight for Unity," *N*, August 11, 1945, 122–23; editorials in *NR* on September 20, 1943, 377; October 9, 1944, 447–48; April 30, 1945, 573; VB, *PM*, October 14, 1942; January 27, 1944; articles by AU in *PM* on October 14, 1942; January 27, 1943; June 22, 1945; JW, *PM*, January 18, 1945; JW, *PM*, January 21, 1945.

42. On Roosevelt's expression of regret to Bowers, see Claude Bowers, *My Mission to Spain* (New York, 1954), 418.

43. FK, "Interventions — Old and New," *N*, March 7, 1942, 273.

44. Ibid., 273–74.

45. Henry Ehrmann, "Washington's Plan for Germany," *NR*, May 3, 1943, 585–87; "Thinking About Germany," *NR*, August 2, 1943, 124–25; "War and Revolution," *NR*, August 9, 1943, 179–80; FK, "How to Keep the Peace," *N*, September 16, 1944, 312–14.

46. Lord Robert Vansittart, *Lessons of My Life* (New York, 1943); Vansittart, *Bones of Contention* (New York, 1945). For criticism of Vansittartism, see Fritz Sternberg, "Germany, Economic Heart of Europe," *N*, February 12, 1944, 187–89; Erika Mann and Sternberg, exchange of letters, *N*, March 11, 1943, 318–19; LF, "Does Europe Need Germany?" *N*, March 18, 1943, 333–37; MC, *NR*, October 25, 1943, 586–88; HE, *NR*, February 28, 1944, 290–94; "Germany's Place in the Peace," *CS*, June 1944, 223. For letters defending Vansittart, see, e.g., Harold Clausen, *N*, March 25, 1944, 375–76; *NR*, August 14, 1944, 189.

47. Paul Hagen, *Will Germany Crack?* (New York, 1942). JW, *PM*, April 13, 1943; Hagen, letter, *N*, January 16, 1943, 105; Hagen, *PM*, June 20, 1943; Hagen, letter, *N*, October 14, 1944, 447; Hagen, review, *NR*, October 9, 1944, 465–66; Hagen, "Our Allies Inside Germany," *CS*, September 1942, 294–98; Hagen, "Germany — the Wrong Solution," *CS*, April 1945, 23–25. UDA support for Hagen can be found in R-F 1-1, 1-2, 1-3, ADA Papers. On *The New Leader* controversy, see Ann Caples to JL, January 9, 1945, R-F 16-289, ADA Papers, as well as

other material in this folder. Gerhard Seger and Rudolf Katz, "Under False Colors," *NL*, January 6, 1945; James Luther Adams et al., letter, *NL*, January 27, 1945, 14–15; Seger and Katz, reply, *NL*, January 27, 1945, 14–15.

48. Articles and reviews by RN in *N* on April 4, 1942; November 28, 1942; January 1, 1944; November 4, 1944; editorials by RN in *C&C* on January 10, 1944; March 20, 1944; "The Peace Settlement in Europe," *C&C*, June 26, 1944, 6–7; "Germany's Place in the Peace," *CS*, June 1944, 223; "A Policy for Germany," *CS*, October 1944, 371. On the Rex Stout–Sidney Hertzberg controversy, see "The Shame of American Writers," *CS*, May 1944, 187; "American Writers on Germany," *CS*, June 1944, 206–12; letters in May 1944 section of AB Papers. On Lerner's view of the controversy, see ML, *PM*, April 26 and 27, 1944. The Hagen-Niebuhr-inspired manifesto can be found in *C&C*, May 15, 1944, 3–4.

49. "A Plan for Germany," *N*, October 7, 1944, 395–97; editorials in *NR* on April 24, 1944, 551–53; October 2, 1944, 415–16; January 8, 1945, 40–41; ML, *PM*, May 9, 1944. As the war reached its end, the calls for thorough denazification became more urgent. See a series of articles by IS in *PM* in February and April 1945.

50. "A Plan for Germany," *N*, October 7, 1944, 395–97. See also *N*, May 13, 1944, 555; "The Carthaginians," *NR*, October 2, 1944, 415–16. For expressions of the German peoples' communal responsibility and guilt, see ML, *PM*, March 4, 1945; June 17, 1945; VB, *PM*, April 25, 1945; May 6, 1945.

51. ML, "Germany without Illusions," *NR*, October 30, 1944, 553–54. For the writings of Thompson and Brailsford on Germany, see Dorothy Thompson, *Listen, Hans* (Boston, 1942); H. N. Brailsford, *Our Settlement with Germany* (London, 1944); Brailsford, *Germans and Nazis* (London, 1944); Brailsford, "What to Do with Germany," *NR*, July 10, 1944, 36–38. For CS, see "A Policy for Germany," *CS*, October 1944, 371; Hagen, "Germany—the Wrong Solution," *CS*, April 1945, 23–25.

52. ML, "Germany without Illusions," 554–55. In an article the following year praising the Yalta Statement on German policy, Lerner referred to "the hasty and irresponsible" attacks on the Morgenthau Plan. See ML, *PM*, February 18, 1945.

53. ML, "Germany without Illusions," 555–56. A year and a half earlier, Lerner believed the goal was "a democratic revolution in Germany." ML, *PM*, April 30, 1943. By 1944 he was no longer speaking of a democratic revolution. The theme of a Big Three–imposed solution built on "pooled" approaches, rather than a democratic revolution, was at the center of his analysis. See ML, *PM*, March 7, 1944. After a trip to Europe, Lerner was even more pessimistic about the future of German democracy. See ML, *PM*, March 4, 5, and 26, 1945.

54. "Germany in the Peace," *NR*, October 30, 1944, 551–52. See also "The Carthaginians," *NR*, October 2, 1944, 415–16.

55. HE, "A Diagnosis of Germany," *NR*, December 25, 1944, 858–59.

56. "Hard or Durable Peace," *NR*, December 30, 1944, 789; "Policy in Ger-

many," *NR*, July 16, 1945, 62–64. For criticism of the Morgenthau Plan, see the articles by HE in *NR* on October 8, 15, and 22, 1945. See also "A Policy for Germany," 371. For Guerard's change, see his review of Vansittart's *Bones of Contention, NR*, August 4, 1945, 111–12.

57. On the liberal defense of their criticism of the New Deal, "Who Shall Make the Peace?" *NR*, December 14, 1942, 779–80; George Soule, "Liberals and the State Department," *NR*, December 14, 1942, 788–89; NR, *PM*, October 6, 1943. Robertson said that much of the criticism came from Roosevelt's "best friends" and from "people who have faith in Franklin D. Roosevelt, the man who has done so much to make a better America."

58. On the internment of Japanese Americans, see, e.g., Charles Inglehart, "Citizens Behind Barbed Wire," *N*, June 6, 1942, 649–51; John Larison, "'Jap Crow' Experiment," *N*, April 10, 1943, 517–19; articles by CM in *N* on May 29, 1944; June 12, 1944; December 30, 1944; Richard Lee Strout, "The War and Civil Liberties," *NR*, March 16, 1942, 355–57; CM, "Japanese Out of California," *NR*, April 6, 1942, 456–57; Ted Nakashimo, "Concentration Camps: U.S.A. Style," *NR*, June 15, 1942, 822–23; Dillon S. Myer, "The WRA Says 'Thirty,'" *NR*, June 25, 1945, 867–68; editorials in *NR* on March 30, 1942, 413; June 15, 1942, 815–16; January 18, 1943, 72; July 19, 1943, 63; Harold Lavine, *PM*, January 21, 1944; April 28, 1944; CM, *PM*, May 21, 1944. On the report of the ACLU, see "Civil Liberties and War," *NR*, June 22, 1942, 848–49. On Bingham and Niebuhr, see AB et al. to FDR, April 23, 1942, R-F 7-108, ADA Papers. See also RN, "Evacuation of Japanese Citizens," *C&C*, May 18, 1942, 2–5.

59. *The New Republic* wrote that the War Relocation Authority was turning a "disagreeable necessity" into something that might be "constructive and useful." See "Democracy and the Nisei," *NR*, August 10, 1942, 158. In 1942 Carey McWilliams wrote a strange article, not consistent with his more critical articles, on the internment. He denied that the assembly center at Santa Anita was a "concentration camp," despite being surrounded by barbed wire, spotlights, and prison guards. He presented all the government's rationalizations for internment sympathetically, and he saw no reason why the "relocation projects" could not, if run fairly, "reflect great credit as a nation." CM, *Harper's*, September 1942, 359–69. On the JACL, see Roger Daniels, *Concentration Camps, U.S.A.: Japanese Americans and World War II* (New York, 1971), 79–81, 104–29; RB, Letter, *NR*, April 24, 1944, 562.

60. FK, "Curb the Fascist Press!" *N*, March 28, 1942, 357–58; MS, "Hitler's Guerillas Over Here," *NR*, April 13, 1942, 481–83; editorials in *NR* on April 27, 1942, 559–60; June 15, 1942, 815–16; Kenneth Crawford, *PM*, August 3, 1942; John P. Lewis, *PM*, August 6, 1942; "Coughlin Speaks Same Old Poison," *PM*, September 25, 1942. The liberals' applause of the administration's efforts to curb the fascist press meant applauding FDR's own lack of commitment to civil liberties. On Roosevelt's role in the internment of Japanese Americans and his lack of com-

mitment to civil liberties, see Daniels, *Concentration Camps*, 72–73; Burns, *Roosevelt*, 213–17, 266–68, 463–64; Dallek, *Franklin D. Roosevelt*, 334–36. Dallek finds FDR's "hypocrisy" on civil liberties "striking."

61. RN, "The Limits of Liberty," *N*, January 24, 1942, 86–88.

62. RB, letter, *N*, February 7, 1942, 175; RB and editors, exchange, *N*, April 11, 1942, 444; RB, letter, *N*, April 25, 1942, 499; James Rosenberg, "Words Are Triggers," *N*, May 2, 1942, 511–12; Arthur Garfield Hays, "Indictments Pull Triggers," *N*, May 9, 1942, 543–45; Rosenberg, letter, *N*, May 9, 1942, 555; Alan Brown, letter, *N*, May 16, 1942, 582; David Weintraub, letter, *N*, May 16, 1942, 582; John Haynes Holmes, letter, *N*, May 23, 1942, 611; NT to FK, April 3, 1942, FK Papers; Holmes to FK, April 13, 1942, FK Papers. On the sedition and conspiracy trials, see *N*, January 2, 1943, 2–3; JW, "Sedition and Circuses," *N*, May 6, 1944, 530–31; *N*, December 9, 1944, 702; "Charged with Sedition," *NR*, January 17, 1943, 68; Edwin Lahey, "Fascism's Day in Court," *NR*, June 5, 1944, 759–60; VB, *PM*, January 9, 1944; John P. Lewis, *PM*, May 16, 1944; ML, *PM*, May 22–24, 1944.

63. For liberal expressions of horror and criticisms of the administration, see, e.g., VF, "Our Consuls in Europe," *N*, May 2, 1942, 507–9; Philip Bernstein, "The Jews of Europe," *N*, part 1, January 2, 1943, 8–11, and part 2, January 9, 1943, 48–51; editorials by FK in *N* on March 13, 1943; June 5, 1943; August 26, 1944; IS, "For the Jews—Life or Death?" *N*, June 10, 1944, 670–71; VF, "The Massacre of the Jews," *NR*, December 21, 1942, 816–19; Bernstein, "What Hope for the Jews?" *NR*, April 26, 1943, 554–56; "The Jews of Europe: How to Help Them," Special Section, *NR*, August 30, 1943, 299–315; John P. Lewis, *PM*, December 2, 1942; AU, *PM*, April 25, 1943; ML, *PM*, July 22, 1943; March 31, 1944; October 2, 1945; "9-Pt. Program for Freeing Enslaved Jews . . . ," *PM*, July 26, 1943; VB, *PM*, January 30, 1944; JW, *PM*, January 31, 1944; Richard Yaffe, *PM*, May 17, 1944; "1700 Profs," *PM*, May 17, 1944; IS, *PM*, September 27 and October 1, 1945. For *NL*, see Jonathan Stout, *NL*, December 2, 1944. For a critique of *NL* on this point, see DM, "The Jews, *The New Leader,* and Old Judge Hull," *Politics*, January 1945, 23–25. For the story of Varian Fry's rescue work, see VF, *Surrender on Demand* (New York, 1945).

64. BB, "F.D.R. in '44," *NR*, January 17, 1944, 75.

65. On civil rights, see, e.g., Alvin White, "Four Freedoms (Jim Crow)," *N*, February 21, 1942, 213–14; Horace Cayton, "Fighting for White Folks," *N*, September 26, 1942, 267–70; Suzanne LaFollette, "Jim Crow and Casey Jones," *N*, December 19, 1942, 675–77; JW, "Pigeonhole for Negro Equality," *N*, January 23, 1942, 121–22; DM, "The Novel Case of Winfred Lynn," *N*, February 20, 1943, 268–70; Cayton, "The Negro's Challenge," *N*, July 3, 1943, 10–12; IS, "Grist for Goebbels," *N*, December 25, 1943, 750–51; DM, "The Supreme Court's New Moot Suit," *N*, July 1, 1944, 13–14; Henry Lee Moon, "What the Negro Hopes For," *N*, October 21, 1944, 486–87; IS, "Jim Crow Flies High," *N*, June 23,

1945; editorials in N on March 21, 1942, 329; May 27, 1944, 612–13; August 12, 1944, 172–73; Clark Foreman, "Race Tension in the South," *NR*, September 21, 1943, 340–42; articles by Thomas Sancton in *NR* on January 4, 1943; January 11, 1943, 50–51; January 18, 1943; December 20, 1943; John Beecher, "8802 Blues," *NR*, February 22, 1943, 248–50; "The Negro: His Future in America," Special Supplement, *NR*, October 18, 1943, 535–50; Lucille Milner, "Jim Crow in the Army," *NR*, March 13, 1944, 339–42; Lillian Smith, "Addressed to White Liberals," *NR*, September 18, 1944, 331–33; Ida Fox, "Trying to Wreck the FEPC," *NR*, February 19, 1945, 260–61; editorials in *NR* on November 2, 1942, 560–61; January 25, 1943, 101–2; February 22, 1943, 240–41; August 14, 1944, 176; September 25, 1944, 360–61; July 23, 1945, 92; Pearl Buck, "Freedom, East and West," *CS*, September 1942, 291–94; Shirley Graham, "Negroes Are Fighting for Freedom," *CS*, February 1943, 45–50; Pauli Murray, "Negroes Are Fed Up," *CS*, August 1943, 274–76; Arnold Beichman, *PM*, July 29, 1942; John P. Lewis, *PM*, October 5, 1942; ML, *PM*, June 25, 1943; July 15, 1943; IS, *PM*, April 28, 1944; May 17 and 19, 1944; IB, *PM*, February 26, 27, 1945. On wartime race riots, see, e.g., "Defeat at Detroit," *N*, July 3, 1943, 4; Sancton, "The Race Riots," *NR*, July 5, 1943, 9–13; Walter White, "Behind the Harlem Riot," *NR*, August 16, 1943, 220–22.

66. See the editorials in N on May 23, 1942, 587; June 6, 1942, 643–44; June 13, 1942, 672; June 27, 1942, 727; July 11, 1942, 24; "The Waller Case" *NR*, June 1, 1942, 752; "The Waller Case" *NR*, June 15, 1942, 813; Sancton, "The Waller Case," *NR*, July 13, 1942, 45–47; Francis McConnell et al. to FDR, and WA and Laurence Hosie to TA, June 11, 1942, TA Papers. The UDA activities on the March on Washington petition drive can be found in R-F 3-47 and R-F 10-159, ADA Papers.

67. For liberal criticisms of John L. Lewis, see "John L's Show," *N*, May 15, 1943, 688–89; editorials in *NR*, May 3, 1943, 579–80; May 10, 1943, 622–23; May 24, 1943, 688; June 7, 1943, 748–49; JW, *PM*, March 25, 1943; April 30, 1943; AU, *PM*, May 2, 1943. For liberal support of labor, see IS, "All-Out Against Labor," *N*, March 28, 1942, 358–60; FK, "Labor on the Spot," *N*, January 15, 1944, 61–62. For liberal support of the no-strike pledge, see, e.g., editorials in *N* on January 8, 1944, 31–32; June 3, 1944, 638. *The New Republic* argued that labor needed to focus on "long-run interests" that were best served by labor participation in government agencies. See "War Thoughts on Labor," *NR*, January 25, 1943, 103–4. For liberal views on wage increases, see "Should Wages be Frozen?" *N*, July 18, 1942, 13–14; editorials in *NR* on July 6, 1942, 7–9; April 19, 1943, 495–96; December 20, 1943, 869. With the cost of living rising, *The New Republic* became more agreeable to wage increases. See editorials in *NR* on April 10, 1944, 487–88; March 5, 1945, 316–17. For liberal views on the Labor Draft (National Service Act), see "The Five-Point Plan," *N*, January 22, 1944, 88; "National Service Again," *N*, January 13, 1945, 31–32. *The New Republic* opposed the recommended National Service Act, although it did not rule out passage of some kind of a na-

tional service act. See *NR* editorials on January 29, 1945, 135–36; February 12, 1945, 212–13. Lerner wrote that he could only support the National Service Act as part of Roosevelt's Five-Point economic/tax program and as a manpower method, but not alone or as method to control strikes — strikes which, he said, *PM* also opposed, but which had their roots in genuine grievances and could only be controlled by a policy of equal sacrifices. See ML, *PM*, January 12, 1944. Stone, unlike Lerner, was unambiguously against the National Service Act. See IS articles in *N* on January 22, 1944; January 29, 1944; February 5, 1944, 150–51.

68. NT to RN, September 15, 1941, R-F 7-120, ADA Papers; JL to NT, September 18, 1941, R-F 7-120, ADA Papers.

69. Editorial, *CC*, August 15, 1945; "Atomic Atrocity," *CC*, August 29, 1945; SR to AB, August 22, 1945, AB Papers. On Niebuhr's thoughts on the dropping of the atomic bomb, see RN to James Conant, March 12, 1946, RN Papers. On liberal response to the dropping of the atomic bomb, see FK, "One World or None," *N*, August 18, 1945, 149–50; FK, "Notes on the War's End," *N*, August 25, 1945, 170–71; "The Atomic Bomb," *NR*, August 13, 1945, 173–74; BB, "The Bomb and the Future," *NR*, August 20, 1945, 210–12; "Atomic and Human Energy," *NR*, August 27, 1945, 240–41; IB, *PM*, August 7, 1945; AU, *PM*, August 10, 1945; ML, *PM*, August 21, 1945. In his 1970 interview for the Truman Library, Loeb questioned Truman's decision to drop the atom bomb. But at the time, the UDA release only urged public release of information on the peaceful uses of atomic energy and the need to "cooperate or die" in terms of its control. Oral History Interview with JL, June 26–27, 1970, The Harry S. Truman Library, 74–76, 219; UDA, Release, August 9, 1945, R-F 1-10, ADA Papers.

70. Paul Boller, "Hiroshima and the American Left: August 1945," *International Social Science Review,* 57 (Winter 1982): 13–28. For discussions of the future control of the bomb and of the peaceful use of atomic energy, see editorials in *NR* on October 29, 1945, 555–56; November 26, 1945, 691–92; December 31, 1945, 885; FK, "One World or None," *N*, August 18, 1945, 149–50; "The Challenge of the Atomic Bomb," Special Supplement, *N*, December 22, 1945, 701–20; IS, *PM*, August 8, 1945; NR, *PM*, August 13, 1945; ML, *PM*, August 19, 1945; AU, *PM*, October 18, 1945; UDA, Release, October 29, 1945, R-F 13-228, ADA Papers. Niebuhr, who favored sharing the bomb with Russia, discussed control in the context of the deterioration of U.S.-Soviet relations. See RN, "The Atomic Issue," *C&C*, October 15, 1945, 5–7. On saturation bombing, see "A Revolting Necessity," *N*, March 18, 1944, 323–24; *N*, March 24, 1945, 318; "The Bombing of Berlin," *NR*, December 6, 1943, 795; ML, *PM*, March 9, 1944. For AB's criticism of the saturation bombing, see AB, "Lynch Law or Justice?" *CS*, January 1944, 20–21.

71. For a full discussion of Roosevelt's dropping of Wallace, see Torbjörn Sirevag, *The Eclipse of the New Deal and the Fall of Vice-President Wallace, 1944* (New York, 1985). See also Burns, *Roosevelt*, 503–6.

72. On the role of Hillman in the dropping of Wallace, see Sirevag, *Eclipse of*

the New Deal, 194–96; Fraser, *Labor Will Rule,* 531–34. Hillman once told William Benton that his enemies respected him because they knew that they could trust him. Perhaps Wallace would have been better off as an enemy. See WB, memo to Paul Hoffman, Ralph Flanders, and Chester Davis, November 6, 1944, CB Papers.

73. NT, SC, August 4, 1944; RN, SC, September 8, 1944; "The Basic Issues of 44," CS, November 1944, 411; ML, speech over CBS, November 5, 1944, ML Papers; "Why Roosevelt?" N, October 21, 1944, 503–4; "The Home Stretch," NR, November 6, 1944, 579–80; "Willkie as Candidate," NR, October 4, 1943, 442–43. Even after defending CS's moral approach to issues against the "practicality" of NR (which, he said, opted for Big Power cooperation at the expense of 200,000 Poles crushed in the Warsaw uprising), Bingham's close friend and co-editor Seldon Rodman said that CS should support the "erring incumbent" and that Sidney Hertzberg should keep "his mouth shut" about Norman Thomas even if it meant losing Hertzberg for the magazine. See SR to AB, September 1, 1944, AB Papers.

74. BB, "Franklin D. Roosevelt," NR, April 23, 1945, 548; FK, "End of an Era," N, April 21, 1945, 429–30. See also IS, PM, April 13, 1945; ML, PM April 15, 1945; JW, PM, April 16, 1945.

CHAPTER 4

1. M. S. Venkataramani, "Norman Thomas, Arkansas Sharecroppers, and the Roosevelt Administration Agricultural Policies, 1933–1937," *Mississippi Valley Historical Review,* September 1960, 225–46; Frank A. Warren, *An Alternative Vision: The Socialist Party in the 1930s* (Bloomington, 1974), 128; David Conrad, *The Forgotten Farmers: The Story of Sharecroppers in the New Deal* (Urbana, 1965); Sirevag, *The Eclipse of the New Deal,* 51–53.

2. IS, "Production Politics," N, January 10, 1942, 27.

3. When Roosevelt eliminated the Wallace-led Board of Economic Warfare in 1943, *The Nation* wrote that he may have become the "stepchild" of the Roosevelt administration, but for the workers and small farmers he was "the authentic voice of the New Deal." See N, August 7, 1943, 142–43. During the vice presidency fight in 1944, Kirchwey called him the "the one remaining symbol of democratic reform in the Roosevelt Administration." See FK, "The People Want Wallace," N, July 22, 1944, 89. In January 1945 *The Nation* described Wallace as "the man on whom liberal hopes for the future are pinned." See N, January 6, 1945, 2.

4. HW, "The Price of Free World Victory," in *The Century of the Common Man,* ed. Russell Lord (New York, 1942), 10–12, 19–20.

5. Ibid., 16–26.

6. Ibid., 10, 14–15, 26.

7. Ibid., 15.

8. FK, "The People's Revolution," *N*, May 16, 1942, 561–62; "A Fine Speech," *NR*, May 18, 1942, 652; "The People's Revolution," *NR*, May 25, 1942, 725–27; "Common People March," *PM*, May 10, 1942; AU, *PM*, May 14, 1942. Major George Eliot, a writer on military strategy, compared it to the Gettysburg Address. See HW, "The Price of a Free World Victory," 32–33.

9. HW, *The Century of the Common Man*, 73.

10. Ibid., 73–83.

11. *N*, March 13, 1943, 363.

12. See HW, *The Century of the Common Man*, 23–31, 35–68, 83–87; HW, *Democracy Reborn*, ed. Russell Lord (New York, 1944), 238–45, 249–53, 263–73. The best critique of the contradictory themes in Wallace's views remains DM, "The (American) People's Century," *PR*, July–August 1942, 294–310.

13. *N*, April 3, 1943, 470; Manuel Seoane, "Wallace in Chile," *N*, May 1, 1943, 634–35; HW, "America Tomorrow," in HW, *Democracy Reborn*, 238–45; "Wallace Again Makes History with Words," *PM*, November 9, 1942; John P. Lewis, *PM*, November 9, 1942; "Wallace Sees Jobs for All an Answer to Communism," *PM*, May 17, 1943. *PM* writers hailed Wallace's November speech. Kenneth Crawford declared that "Vice-President Henry A. Wallace again has proved himself the most daring and imaginative, yet down-to-earth planner and interpreter of the Common Man's Century." And Lewis, who believed that Wallace spoke for the administration, wrote, "Wallace's voice is a voice of evangelism with a message of the faith and challenge of democracy, going out to a world plagued with the gospel of cynicism and resignation that is Fascism." See Crawford, *PM*, November 10, 1942; Lewis, *PM*, November 12, 1942.

14. IS, "The Anti-Wallace Plot," *N*, December 19, 1942, 671–672; *N*, January 2, 1943, 1; T.R.B., *NR*, April 26, 1943, 565.

15. "Who Shall Make the Peace?" *NR*, December 14, 1942, 779–80; T.R.B., *NR*, April 26, 1943, 565; *N*, January 30, 1943, 147; IS, "Why Wallace Spoke Out," *N*, July 10, 1942, 34–36; "All Support for Wallace," *N*, July 17, 1943, 60–61; HF, "The Jones-Wallace Feud," *NR*, July 12, 1943, 43–44; *NR*, *PM*, June 30, 1943; VB, *PM*, July 6, 1943.

16. "Mr. Wallace Walks the Plank," *NR*, July 26, 1943, 93–95. See also IS, *PM*, July 16, 1943.

17. *N*, July 24, 1943, 86; IS, "Wallace Betrayed," *N*, July 24, 1943, 89–90.

18. John P. Lewis, "Should Wallace Resign?" *PM*, July 18, 1943; ML, "Wallace and Roosevelt," July 19, 1943.

19. HW, "America Tomorrow," in *Democracy Reborn*, 240–41.

20. Ibid., 238; "Wallace Speaks Out," *NR*, August 2, 1943, 127–28; *N*, August 7, 1943, 142–43. See also JW, *PM*, July 26, 1943; ML, "Wallace at Detroit," *PM*, July 27, 1943.

21. "Wallace's World—and Hull's," *NR*, September 20, 1943, 378–80; JW, "Wallace Haunts the Press," *PM*, February 13, 1944; "Henry Wallace and '44,"

NR, February 21, 1944, 229; Russell Lord, "Henry Wallace of Iowa," *NR*, May 29, 1944, 737; HW, *Democracy Reborn*, 196–200; AD, "Wallace in Chungking," *N*, June 17, 1944, 707–8; editorials in *NR* on May 29, 1944, 729; June 19, 1944, 800.

22. LF, untitled speech, Liberal Party, May 20, 1944, LF Papers.

23. IS, "The Plot Against Wallace," *N*, July 1, 1944, 7–8; *N*, July 15, 1944, 58–59; JL to Robert Hannegan, July 13, 1944, R-F 8-125, ADA Papers; RN to FDR, July 12, 1944, R-F 3-47, ADA Papers; RN to HW, n.d. [c. July 1944], R-F 16-288, ADA Papers.

24. "Keep Vice President Wallace," *NR*, July 17, 1944, 62–63; T.R.B., *NR*, July 17, 1944, 76; FK, "The People Want Wallace," *N*, July 22, 1944, 89.

25. IS, "The Plot Against Wallace," 8; IS, "Henry Wallace—a Great American," *N*, July 22, 1944, 91–92.

26. IS, "Henry Wallace—a Great American," 91; FK, "The Battle of Chicago," *N*, July 29, 1944, 118–20.

27. "Democrats Face the Future," *NR*, July 31, 1944, 117–18. See also HF, "Throwing Wallace to the Wolves," *NR*, July 31, 1944, 121–22.

28. "Wallace Fights On," *NR*, August 7, 1944, 150; FK, "Campaign Notes," *N*, September 30, 1944, 369–70.

29. CB to AB, February 17, 1945, AB Papers.

30. ML, *PM*, January 31, 1945; IS, articles in *PM* on January 23–26, 1945; January 28–29, 1945; February 2, 1945.

31. IS, "Toward Imperialism," *N*, December 30, 1944, 791–92; "Wallace's World—or Jones's," *NR*, February 5, 1945, 167; IS, "Wallace: Second Round," *N*, February 10, 1945, 146–47; TA to William Evjue, January 24, 1945, TA Papers.

32. JL to Henry Kaiser, December 29, 1944, R-F 16-289, ADA Papers; JL to HoW, February 6, 1945, R-F 5-87, ADA Papers; TA to JM, January 24, 1945, TA Papers. The Wallace testimonial pamphlet is in R-F 6-93, ADA Papers. The speeches at Wallace's testimonial dinner are found in R-F 6-92, ADA Papers. John William Ward, *Andrew Jackson: Symbol for an Age*, New York, 1955.

33. PS, "Henry Agard Wallace," in *Public Men in and out of Office*, ed. John Salter (Chapel Hill, 1946), 91–92.

34. Ibid., 92–93.

35. Ibid., 94–95.

36. Ibid., 98–99.

37. Ibid., 100–101, 104.

38. *N*, March 10, 1945, 262; Sirevag, *The Eclipse of the New Deal*, 164–72. Elizabeth Donahue, *PM*, March 2, 1945.

39. HW, *Sixty Million Jobs*.

40. Ibid. In an interview with James Wechsler in early 1946, Wallace said, "I've never changed my basic feeling that business—especially small business—has a real identity of interest with labor and the farmer. If you don't believe that you

can't believe in this system. That's what I was saying last year and nothing has changed my mind." JW, *PM*, February 10, 1946. Fraser, *Labor Will Rule.*

41. For the hope of a democratic socialist Europe, see ML, *PM*, April 1, 1945.

CHAPTER 5

1. James W. Davidson and Mark H. Lytle, *After the Fact: The Art of Historical Detection*, 3d ed. (New York, 1992), 2: 228–51.

2. William Stott, *Documentary Expression and Thirties America* (New York, 1973).

3. Ibid., 46–73, 145–237; John Dewey, *Liberalism and Social Action* (New York, 1935), 62.

4. Harvey Swados, ed., *The American Writer and the Great Depression* (Indianapolis, 1966), xvi. See also Charles Alexander, *Nationalism in American Thought, 1930–1945* (Chicago, 1969).

5. Jerre Mangione, *The Dream and the Deal: The Federal Writers' Project, 1935–1943* (Boston, 1972), 49–50; Stott, *Documentary Expression.* Stott writes: "Like a great deal of thirties literature, the documentary book began as a way of calling attention to America's failures and ended by celebrating its successes" (237).

6. Warren, *Liberals and Communism*, 103–26; Maurice Isserman, *Which Side Were You On?: The American Communist Party during the Second World War* (Middletown, 1982), 1–17; Richard Pells, *Radical Visions and American Dreams* (New York, 1973), 292–329; Granville Hicks, *Only One Storm* (New York, 1942); Hicks, *Small Town* (New York, 1946). In "The Culture of the Thirties," Warren Susman has connected Hicks's Communist experience with his sense of community in small-town America. See Susman, *Culture as History* (New York, 1984), 174.

7. Stott, *Documentary Expression*, 235–36.

8. In the "Ballad for Americans," the narrator asks "the people" who "carried through" America's development, "who are you?" The answer is "Well I'm everybody who's nobody. I'm the nobody who's everybody. . . . Well I'm an engineer, musician, street cleaner, carpenter, teacher. . . . How about a farmer? Also! Office clerk. . . . Yes sir! Mechanic? That's right! Housewife? Certainly! Factory worker? You said it! Stenographer? Yes, Ma'am! Beauty specialist? Absolutely! Bartender? Positively! Truck Driver?. . . . Definitely! Miner. . . . Ditch digger. All of them. I am the etceteras. And the 'and so forths' that do the work."

9. Gunnar Myrdal, *An American Dilemma* (New York, 1944); David W. Southern, *Gunnar Myrdal and Black-White Relations* (Baton Rouge, 1987), 1–99; Walter A. Jackson, *Gunnar Myrdal and America's Conscience* (Chapel Hill, 1990), 135–273.

10. George Mayberry, review of CM's *Brothers Under the Skins*, NR, June 21,

1943, 836; Saunders Redding, review of Myrdal's *An American Dilemma*, NR, March 20, 1944, 386; Pearl Buck, *American Unity and Asia* (New York, 1942), 31. Buck's book was influential among liberals. Herbert Agar wrote that she might "turn out to be the Tom Paine of our world-wide civil war," and used her book to emphasize that the war must become a war of "freedom for all." See HA, PM, July 24, 1942.

11. Langston Hughes, "My America," in *What the Negro Wants*, ed. Rayford W. Logan (Chapel Hill, 1944), 300.

12. "Statement of Purpose," CG, winter 1942, 2.

13. Edward Grusd, "Some Questions for America," CG, winter 1944, 36; Louis Adamic, *A Nation of Nations* (New York, 1945), 1–13; Jacob Riis, *How the Other Half Lives* (New York, 1890).

14. Adamic, *A Nation of Nations*, 12; Edward Saveth, review, N, December 15, 1945, 666; Eric Goldman, review, NR, November 19, 1945, 680–81.

15. Warren, *Liberals and Communism*, 63–88. On the extension of political democracy to include economic democracy, see DK and DP, *Strategy for Democracy*, 3–32, 298–320; HL, *Reflections on the Revolution of Our Time* (New York, 1943), 179–229, 346–419; MS, *Make This the Last War*, 344–53. In Wallace's November 1942 speech at the Congress of American-Soviet Friendship, he defined five types of democracy: political, economic, ethnic, educational, and democracy between the sexes. He found American racial practices working against ethnic democracy. See HW, "Russia" and "America Tomorrow" in HW, *Democracy Reborn*, 196–200, 238–45.

16. DK and DP, *Strategy for Democracy*, 314–17; MS, *Make This the Last War*, 15–23, 116–18, 327–53.

17. DK and DP, *Strategy for Democracy*, 298–320; MS, *Make This the Last War*, 333–44; HL, *Reflections*, 346–419; RN, *The Children of Light*, 92–118.

18. DK and DP, *Strategy for Democracy*, 277–97; MS, *Make This the Last War*.

19. After listening to Robeson sing, a PM writer wrote that what made him "so convincing and moving" was "his social convictions and their deep-felt sincerity." Henry Simon, PM, July 13, 1943.

20. On the Communist record, see Isserman, *Which Side Were You On?* 123–24, 143–45; Irving Howe and Lewis Coser, *The American Communist Party* (Boston, 1957), 417–19.

21. Katrina McCormick to SR, n.d. [March 1942], AB Papers; AB to McCormick, April 1, 1942, AB Papers.

22. Alexander Pekelis, "Group Sanctions Against Racism," NR, October 29, 1945, 571.

23. For articles and editorial dealing with women and the war, see "Women in War Work," NR, May 4, 1942, 593; "Equal Pay for Women," NR, December 21, 1942, 809–10; "Working Mothers," NR, February 22, 1943, 238; Gene Dickson, "Housewife-War Worker," NR, October 18, 1943, 518–19; Dickson, review of

Elizabeth Hawes's *Why Women Cry, NR,* December 20, 1943, 892; Susan B. Anthony II, "Working at the Navy Yard," *NR,* May 1, 1944, 597–99; Edith Stern, "America's Pampered Husbands," *N,* July 10, 1943, 40–42. See also Lerner's support for drafting women, ML, *PM,* July 14, 1943.

24. "Equal Rights for Women," *NR,* August 21, 1944, 207; "Mr. Wallace and Equal Rights," *NR,* February 7, 1944, 165; T.R.B., *NR,* May 14, 1945, 676; *N,* April 10, 1943, 507. On the view of women New Dealers, see Susan Ware, *Beyond Suffrage* (Cambridge, 1981), 14, 77–79. On the National Farmers Union and the UDA role in opposing the ERA, see Gladys Edwards to Congressman Zebulon Weaver, March 9, 1945, R-F 15-268, ADA Papers; CS to Weaver, March 17, 1945, R-F 15-268, ADA Papers. Sifton's letter expressing the UDA's reasons for opposing the ERA is practically word for word the same letter that Edwards, the director of education for the National Farmers Union, sent Weaver. In its September 29, 1944, *Congressional Newsletter,* the UDA proudly proclaimed: "ANOTHER VICTORY: EQUAL RIGHTS AMENDMENT shelved until after the election." See R-F 13-47, ADA Papers.

25. Olga Robinson to SC, June 7, 1944, AB Papers.

26. FK, "The President's Pledge," *N,* February 20, 1943, 257–58.

27. RN, *The Children of Light.* For two examples of his balance of realpolitik and idealism, see RN, review of FS's *Design for Power, N,* January 10, 1942; RN, review of Wendell Willkie's *One World, N,* April 24, 1943, 604–6.

CHAPTER 6

All references to manuscript sources in this chapter are to the ADA Papers, State Historical Society of Wisconsin, Madison, unless otherwise noted. Reel-Folder and the identifying numbers appear as R-F with the numbers following.

1. Materials on the formation of the UDA can be found in R-F 3-47 and R-F 9-137. See also AB to AL, October 17, 1940; AL, A Suggested Program; AB to Murray Gross, December 13, 1940; AB, revision of conference statement; Warder W. Norton to Originating Committee, January 20, 1941; AB to Norton, January 27, 1941, in AB Papers.

2. RN and FK, "Dear Friend," n.d. [c. fall 1941], R-F 13-213; UDA, "General Principles," n.d. [1941], R-F 16-281. For Niebuhr's role in the founding of the UDA, see Richard Fox, *Reinhold Niebuhr* (New York, 1985), 197–201.

3. *A Program for Americans,* 3–5, 9–10, n.d. [1941], R-F 16-311.

4. Ibid., 10–12.

5. JL to Jacob Potofsky, December 18, 1941, R-F 3-47; JL to Louis Walinsky, June 13, 1941, R-F 9-137.

6. R-F 15-266 and 15–272; Phone interview with Ira Marienhoff, February 1994.

7. UDA, Release, June 11, 1941, R-F 14-245; UDA, Release, n.d., R-F 9-138; UDA, Release, June 25, 1941, R-F 13-228; RN, "Turn of War . . . ," *UDA Bulletin,* August 1941, 2, R-F 16-306; UDA Speakers Information Letter #1, August 5, 1941, 3, R-F 9-139; memorandum to New York Branches, October 23, 1941, R-F 4-70.

8. JL, untitled, July 20, 1942, R-F 13-228; JL to ML, March 6, 1943, R-F 9-142; JL to Johannes Steel, March 6, 1943, R-F 9-142; JL to Dear Member, November 4, 1946, R-F 12-189; "Niebuhr Reports on Germany" *UDA Bulletin,* November 1946, R-F 12-189; Barbara Rehm to JL, November 7, 1946, R-F 7-98; NP to Barbara Rehm, November 14, 1946, R-F 7-98; JL to L. P. Chambers, November 30, 1946, R-F 4-67; Henry D. Chapman to JL, December 7, 1946, R-F 5-75; Edward Winston to UDA, December 17, 1946, R-F 5-83; RN, "The Fight for Germany," *Life,* October 21, 1946, 65–72; NP to JL, July 19, 1946, R-F 9-125.

9. Material on the December conference can be found in R-F 1-25, 1-28, 1-29, and 8-121. Material on the January 1942 conference, which ratified the program of the December conference and reorganized UDA can be found in R-F 13-231.

10. R-F 1-29.

11. Ibid.

12. Ibid.

13. *N,* January 17, 1942, 51. See also FK, "The People's Revolution," *N,* May 16, 1942, 561–62. See also n.d., R-F 2-36; Louis Adamic et al. to FDR, December 29, 1941, R-F 2-47.

14. JL to Eduard Heimann, March 30, 1942, R-F 3-47; phone interview with Ira Marienhoff, February 1994.

15. "Democratic Action Union Asks Ending of Minneapolis Trial," *Weekly,* November 15, 1941, R-F 14-245.

16. *What's Doing in the UDA,* March 1943, 2, ML Papers. Letters, UDA releases and statements pertaining to civil rights can be found in R-F 3-47, 9-138, 10-158, 10-159, and 10-162.

17. UDA, Statement on Aliens, December 21, 1941, conference, R-F 1-28. JL to Editor, *New York Post,* June 20, 1941, R-F 3-47; John Childs to Senator James Mead, June 9, 1943, R-F 1-13; Monroe Sweetland, "Open Letter to the President and Secretary of State," n.d. [August 1943], R-F 8-121. On the conference on inflation, see the material in R-F 2-38. Material on the UDA-sponsored conference on taxation and on the UDA opposition to the sales tax can be found in R-F 16-281. On Standard Oil, I.G. Farben, and the rubber bottleneck, see letters and memos in R-F 15-262 and unsigned letter to Frank [Kingdon], February 4, 1942, R-F 15-16. On the UDA and labor, see the letters and statements in R-F 3-47 and R-F 4-62. See also UDA Action Leaflet No. 1, "The Enemy Is Hitler—Not Labor," n.d. [1941], R-F 9-138.

18. RN to Sumner Welles, March 26, 1942, R-F 4-60; Eduard Heimann et al. to Stimson, n.d. [c. March 1943], R-F 15-276; "An Open Letter to the President" August 4, 1941, R-F 4-70; UDA, Release, n.d. [c. 1941], R-F 9-138.

19. Many letters and releases pertaining to the UDA and the Dies committee can be found in R-F 4-55. See also Kingdon to Congressman Joseph Starnes, June 25, 1942, R-F 1-4; UDA, Release, "UDA Asks All Congressmen . . . ," July 7, 1942, TA Papers; JL, statement, May 28, 1942, R-F 1-11; "The Case Against Martin Dies," meeting, July 28, 1942, R-F 13-228; *What's Doing in the UDA*, August 3, 1942, R-F 16-310; "What Is the UDA," n.d. [fall 1942], R-F 9-131.

20. For the wrangles over the publication of Heimann's pamphlet on foreign policy, see R-F 7-102.

21. *N*, January 9, 1943, 38. Kirchwey's and Loeb's activities in arranging the Norris testimonial dinner and in organizing the committee can be found in R-F 13-225.

22. On the liberal reaction to the election losses, see articles in *NR*, November 16, 1942: "Picking Up the Pieces," 626–28; Thomas H. Eliot, "The Meaning of the Elections," 630–32; and Samuel Grafton, "The Meaning of the Elections," 632–33; also Robert Bendiner, "Dunderhead Election," *N*, November 14, 1942, 497–98. In a letter to Tom Amlie, Loeb wrote: "I tried to get together about four or five key individuals for lunch and found a veritable ground swell of interest in political activity. Most of the people were shocked at the election results, and, I hope, shocked into activity . . . there were about thirty-five people present including such prominent CIO people as John Brophy . . . Walter Reuther, etc." JL to TA, November 27, 1942, R-F 2-34.

23. The list of invitees, attendees and Loeb's invitation letters to the Pittsburgh conference are found in R-F 2-34. On the discussions at the conference, see "Summary of Discussions at the Pittsburgh Conference on Political Action," December 13, 1942, R-F 2-34; Special Conference, Report of Sessions, December 13, 1942, R-F 2-34.

24. "The Norris Committee," n.d. [December 1942], R-F 13-225; Paul Porter, "Possible Directors of Norris Committee," n.d. [c. December 1942], R-F 13-225; "Review of Developments on Norris Committee," n.d. [c. January 1943], R-F 13-225; JL to Dear Friend, January 4, 1943, R-F 5-87; JL to Dear Board Member, February 9, 1943, R-F 5-87; "The UDA and the Norris Committee," *UDA Bulletin*, February 1943, R-F 16-306; JL to TA, December 24, 1942; TA to JM, 1943 [c. January]; TA to JM, February 4 and 7, 1943; TA to JL, March 2, 1943; JL to TA, March 19, 1943; JL to TA, April 20, 1943, in TA Papers.

25. Fraser, *Labor Will Rule*, 503–4; JL, "The Rising Tide of Progressivism," *NR*, August 9, 1943, 185–87; "Brief Statement of Work of Past Year," April 13, 1944, R-F 3-47. On the liberal coverage of PAC, see, e.g., HF, "Labor and Politics," *NR*, January 24, 1944, 111–13; Bendiner, "Labor's Fourteen Million Votes," *N*, January 1, 1944, 7–10. Bendiner did not like Hillman's intrusion into the American

Labor Party quarrels. For a history of the CIO-PAC, see James C. Foster, *The Union Politic* (Columbia, 1975).

26. UDA material on the forty-hour week and the Little Steel Formula can be found in R-F 4-62. Heimann, *The United Nations*, n.d. [1943], R-F 7-102; Heimann et al. to Henry Stimson, n.d. [c. March 1943], R-F 15-276; Town Hall Meeting, "Peyrouton: Incident or Precedent?" March 31, 1943, R-F 16-311; Dorothy Norman to Dear Mr. and Mrs. Lewisohn, February 18, 1943, R-F 13-226; UDA, Release, Statement on Italy, June 24, 1943, R-F 14-245.

27. Fraser, *Labor Will Rule*, 510–11; Sidney Hillman to ML, July 13, 1944, ML Papers; National Citizens Political Action Committee Officers and Members, n.d., R-F 9-149; JL to PS and CS, July 13, 1944, R-F 8-125; JL to George Outland, March 27, 1944, R-F 3-47; *NR* Supplement, "A Congress to Win the War and Peace," *NR*, May 8, 1944, 643–56.

28. RN to FDR, July 12, 1944, R-F 3-47; Burns, *Roosevelt*, 506; JL to CS, July 18, 1944, R-F 8-125. See also JL to CS, July 24, 1944, R-F 8-125.

29. JL, letter, *NR*, February 21, 1944, 245; RN, letter, *NR*, February 21, 1944, 245.

30. RN, letter, *NR*, February 21, 1944, 245; JL, "The Next Congress: I," *NR*, October 9, 1944, 449–52; JL, "The Next Congress: II," *NR*, October 16, 1944, 487–90.

31. JL, letter, *NR*, February 21, 1944, 245; JL, "A Letter to Wendell Willkie," *NR*, July 17, 1944, 67.

32. JL, "August Stock-Taking," *NR*, August 14, 1944, 179. Bruce Bliven also saw optimistic signs for liberalism "after Chicago." See BB, "The Liberals after Chicago," *NR*, August 7, 1944, 152–54.

33. *N*, July 31, 1943, 114; ML, *PM*, March 25, 1943; March 5, 1944; July 11, 1944; editors, *PM*, April 6, 1944.

34. The UDA did its best in the campaign to assure that there would not be a loss of liberal and labor support. See HoW to Jim [McGill], October 29, 1944, TA Papers; James Warburg, *The Republican Party and U.S. Foreign Party* (New York, 1944), R-F 16-311. On UDA cooperation with NC-PAC, see JL to PS and CS, July 13, 1944, R-F 8-125. Freda Kirchwey invited Tom Amlie to join the NC-PAC in a letter containing effusive praise for NC-PAC, and Bliven defended NC-PAC against its conservative critics. See FK to TA, September 5, 1944, TA Papers; "The Meaning of PAC," *NR*, August 14, 1944, 174–75.

35. JL to Morris Cooke, July 11, 1944, R-F 8-125.

36. JL to PM, November 14, 1944, R-F 8-125.

37. JL to Mrs. FDR, November 15, 1944, R-F 8-125. See also JL to Hon. Gifford Pinchot, December 7, 1944, RF 3-47; JL to HW, November 14, 1944, R-F 16-288; JL to Mrs. FDR, December 12, 1944, R-F 8-125; JL to TA, November 18, 1944, TA Papers.

38. FK, "A New Popular Front?" *N*, December 2, 1944, 677–78; "The Role of

the PAC's," *NR*, November 13, 1944, 612; "Progressives Must Organize," *NR*, November 27, 1944, 678–79; JL, "Post-Election Stock-Taking," *NR*, November 20, 1944, 649–52.

39. JP and JL, "The Challenge to Progressives," Special Section, *NR*, February 5, 1945, 187.

40. Ibid., 187–88.

41. Ibid., 197.

42. Ibid., 197–98.

43. Ibid., 198–99.

44. Ibid., 199.

45. Ibid., 200–205.

46. Ibid., 205–6.

47. Joseph Gaer, *The First Round* (New York, 1944), xiv, 228–29.

48. Material on the UDA dinner for Wallace can be found in R-F 6-91, 6-93, 12-203, 16-289. On the Wallace rally, the UDA efforts to win his confirmation, and its response to his victory, see R-F 6-91, 6-92, 16-290. On the moving of the national office to Washington, see JL to HoW, February 6, 1945, R-F 7-106, 14-245. On Aubrey Williams's defeat, see unsigned to Mr. ————," April 17, 1945, R-F 5-87.

49. UDA, memorandum, March 8, 1945, R-F 4-47; Mortimer Hays to Hon. Edward Stettinius, February 23, 1945, R-F 5-86; Foreign Policy Committee of UDA, draft response to Yalta, n.d., R-F 5-86; Foreign Policy Committee of the UDA, "Statement," June 11, 1945, R-F 5-83; UDA, *From the Garden of Eden to Dumbarton Oaks*, n.d. [April 1945], R-F 11-179; UDA Foreign Policy Statement, *UDA Bulletin*, November 1945, R-F 12-194; UDA, release on Representative Governments for Poland and Greece, March 12, 1945, R-F 14-245; "Statement for Consideration at Foreign Policy Committee Meeting," October 8, 1945, R-F 5-86.

50. HoW to Trio, May 12, 1945, TA Papers.

51. For the abundant material on the UDA's efforts for the Murray Full Employment Bill in 1945, see R-F 1-1, 2-40, 4-47, 4-58, 5-71, 5-86-87, 6-91-94, 7-109, 8-125, 9-125, 11-185, 11-187, 11-189, 12-189, 12-194, 13-213, 13-233, 14-240-241, 14-244-246, 15-263, 15-268, 16-284, 16-286, 16-288, 16-307. On Loeb's differences in style with Sifton, see JL to CS, July 18, 1944, R-F 8-125. On Loeb's unsuccessful attempt to get Truman to speak at a UDA-sponsored full employment dinner, see JL to PS, June 21, 1945, R-F 8-125.

52. On the UDA fight for the Murray Bill in 1946, see R-F 6-91, 6-93. On the UDA's endorsement of the final bill, see JL to Truman, February 8, 1946, R-F 6-91. On the UDA's praise of Truman, see JL to Truman, November 1, 1945, R-F 6-91; JL to Truman, December 29, 1945, R-F 6-91; JL to John Tucker, June 5, 1945, R-F 4-47; UDA, Release, letter to Truman, April 25, 1945, R-F 14-245. On China, see UDA, Release, November 14, 1945, R-F 13-228. On American occupation policy in Germany, see Hays to Stimson, April 9, 1945, R-F 1-2;

"UDA Protests Use of German Industrialists," *UDA Bulletin*, May 1945, R-F 7-117. On the UDA position on U.S.-Soviet relations, see "Foreign Policy Statement," [adopted National Board of UDA, October 28, 1945], *UDA Bulletin*, November 1945, R-F 12-194; UDA, Release, "The Foreign Policy of the UDA," [c. June 9], 1946, R-F 5-83. The release of the June foreign policy statement coincided with a UDA blitz of journalists, labor leaders, and politicians. See the material in R-F 5-83.

53. William Dodds to JL, June 12, 1945, R-F 4-56; JL to Dodds, June 18, 1945, R-F 4-56.

54. Charles Forcey, *Crossroads of Liberalism* (New York, 1961), 241–46, 250–63. In 1939 Bingham encouraged Amlie to become a propagandist for the New Deal, partly because he saw CS being most effective as an "unofficial organ of really intelligent New Dealers." He hoped it would get "some of the reputation for inside dope that the New Republic had I understand in the Wilson administration." AB to TA, April 5, 1939, AB Papers.

CHAPTER 7

All references to manuscript collections in this chapter are to the Thomas Amlie Papers at the State Historical Society of Wisconsin, Madison, unless otherwise noted.

1. Donald L. Miller, *The New American Radicalism*, 68, 74–75, 85–89, 112–41; AB to TA, April 5, 1939, AB Papers; TA, "Dialectics Adrift," *CS*, July 1934, 13–16; Robert Whitcomb and SR, "Amlie: New Party Builder," *CS*, May 1936, 17–20. A short biography of Amlie accompanies the collection of his papers at the Wisconsin Historical Society.

2. Miller, *New American Radicalism*, 85–89, 137–42; Donald McCoy, *Angry Voices* (Port Washington, 197); TA, "The Collapse of Capitalism," *CS*, October 1933, 6–9; TA, "The American Commonwealth Federation," *CS*, August 1935, 6–7; TA, "How Radical Is the New Deal?" *CS*, August 1936, 21–24; TA, "How the American Mind Works," *CS*, March 1937, 11–12; TA, "The 'Human Rights' Amendment," *CS*, May 1937, 19–21; TA, "The Answer to Fascism," *CS*, August 1937, 8–10; TA, "Two More Years," *CS*, November 1938, 8–11; TA, "How to Win the Election," *CS*, June 1940, 3–7.

3. TA, "The Answer to Fascism"; TA, "Amlie Takes the Stand," *CS*, March 1939, 22–24; AB to TA, April 5, 1939, AB Papers; biography with TA Papers.

4. On Spain, see TA to Olin Clark, November 28, 1940. On Amlie's split with Phil LaFollette, see letter to Evjue, July 24, 1941. By mid-1941 both Phil and Bob LaFollette were opposing Amlie. See TA to JM, July 24, 1941; TA to Scott, November 16, 1942.

5. TA to AW, July 11, 1941; TA to Mayor F. L. LaGuardia, August 5, 1941; TA, analysis of election, n.d. [1941]; TA to Lawrence Smith, August 17, 1941; TA to FDR, September 4, 1941; TA to P. J. Amlie, October 21, 1942; TA to Scott, November 16, 1942.

6. See TA to Niles, September 6, 1941; TA to AW, January 5, 1942; TA to Paul Porter, January 15, 1942; Casey to HoW, December 17, 1942; M. H. McIntyre to HoW, December 18, 1942; HoW to TA, December 21, 1942; TA to Casey, January 23, 1943; TA to JM, n.d. [c. January 1943].

7. TA to Hans Amlie, January 30, 1941; TA to Felix Fraser, January 30, 1941; TA to HoW, January 27, 1941; TA to Greverus, November 11, 1941; TA to JM, September 14, 1945; TA to AW, October 24, 1959.

8. JL to TA, January 22, 1942.

9. TA to JM, January 27, 1942; TA to JL, January 27, 1942. On the "opinion formers," see TA to Hon. John Gutknecht, August 10, 1942; TA to Hillman, 1945 [c. February]; TA to Charles Ervin, July 10, 1949.

10. For examples of Williams's reports, see HoW to JL, May 10, 1942; HoW to TA, May 16, 1942; HoW to TA, June 22, 1942. For Amlie's political reports to Loeb, see three letters from TA to JL, June 30, 1942. On Amlie's interest in Wisconsin politics, see TA to Paul Alfonsi, March 25, 1942; TA to W. C. Sullivan, October 12, 1942; TA to Sam [Sigman], May 23, 1944. On Evjue, see TA to AW, May 19, 1942.

11. "A Congress to Win the War," Special Supplement, *NR*, May 18, 1942. R-F 1-4 of the ADA Papers contains a large number of letters pertaining to Amlie's work for the UDA in general and on *The New Republic* supplement in particular. See also materials and letters in the R-F 10-161, 14-241, 14-242. Amlie's work can be followed in March–June 1942 correspondence with Loeb, Bliven, Lewis Murphy, Frank Trager, and Frank McCulloch.

12. See, e.g., TA to JL, September 11, 1942; TA to JM, September 14, 1942.

13. TA to JM, September 14, 1942; TA to JL, September 24, 1942; TA to JM, September 26, 1942; TA, "Memo: The Congressional Elections of 1942," September 26, 1942.

14. Unsigned [prob. TA] to Dear Congressman, n.d. [c. May 1942]; Unsigned, undated, UDA demand for investigation of State Department leak to the *Chicago Tribune*, R-F 10-161 ADA Papers; UDA, release, July 7 [1942].

15. TA to JL, September 11, 1942; TA to JM, September 14, 1942; TA to HoW, September 28, 1942; TA to Sponsors of Washington Office, October 26, 1942.

16. In early 1943 Amlie was disappointed in labor's rejection of the Norris committee but felt the CIO leadership wanted "to do the decent thing in the long range fight for democracy." TA to JM, February 7, 1943. But soon he became more skeptical of labor's initial interest in the committee. He wrote Howard Williams that "these laborites are only interested in buying up what is left of Norris' reputation at bargain counter rates and then using it in their own short range program

which is essentially one of defensive warfare." TA to HoW, February 28, 1943. See also TA to JM, February 28, 1943; TA to JL, March 2, 1943.

17. TA to JM, October 1, 1944. See also TA to JL, September 26, 1942; TA to JM, February 4, 1943; TA to Ervin, July 25, 1943.

18. TA, "Jobs for All," *N*, November 27, 1943, 625–52. On Bingham's differences with Amlie, see AB to TA, December 9, 1943; AB to WB, December 9, 1943, AB Papers.

19. TA, "Jobs for All," 625–31.

20. Ibid., 631–38.

21. Ibid., 638–44.

22. Ibid., 646–48.

23. Ibid., 648–52.

24. Ibid., 628, 652.

25. TA to WZ, December 8, 1943; TA to Fred Hamlin, September 24, 1945; TA to Brand, November 12, 1945. In early 1941 Amlie described his views as following "rather closely the ideas of Mr. Laski." TA to AW, February 11, 1942. See also TA to R. C. Jacobson, April 11, 1941; TA to WZ, March 19, 1942.

26. TA to Robert Parrish, April 11, 1941; TA to Benjamin Cohen, July 8, 1945; TA to John Coffee, November 29, 1945.

27. "A Congress to Win the War and the Peace," Special Section, *NR*, May 8, 1944, 643–58; TA to AW, December 3, 1942; TA to Hillman, Memorandum in Re Congressional Elections, November 8, 1944.

28. See, e.g., TA to JM, September 14, 1945; TA to Mr. and Mrs. Norman Kuhne, November 15, 1948; TA to HoW, November 7, 1949; TA to WZ, January 4, 1951; GA to TA, June 2, 1949.

29. TA to FK, April 10, 1945; TA to FK, August 15, 1945; TA, "The Good Life in Our Times," draft of supplement, n.d.; TA to JM, March 21, 1945. Amlie's letters do not contain many comments on Wallace before 1945. He was supportive of the UDA's efforts for Wallace's confirmation as secretary of commerce. See TA to JM, January 24, 1945; TA to JM, February 9, 1945; TA to Evjue, January 24, 1945. And when Roosevelt died Amlie wrote to his wife that Roosevelt had done "a great wrong" in rejecting Wallace as vice president. See TA to GA, April 13, 1945. But even before the publication of Wallace's *Sixty Million Jobs*, Amlie was dismissing it ("it will merely be a sort of a vague MURRAY BILL which is quite meaningless from the standpoint of full employment"). In contrast, he called Beveridge's *Full Employment in a Free Society* an important book that "will render irrelevant, anything that Wallace might be likely to write." See TA to Mr. [Bernard] Smith, March 6, 1945. Amlie had sought to have the *Reader's Digest* let him answer Hayek. See TA to DeWitt Wallace, April 20, 1945. On Amlie's claim that Wallace's *Reader's Digest* answer to Hayek had been written by William Hard, and for his other criticisms of Wallace ("a well meaning religious man who has surrounded himself with a bunch of politicians who think they are smart."), see TA to GA, May 12, 1945.

30. TA to JM, August 11, 1945. On Spain, see TA to Olin Clark, November 28, 1940. In one of his first comments on what was emerging in the postwar period, Amlie wrote McGill that the people had not been prepared for the development of the Soviet Union as the dominant world power in Europe, Africa, and Asia. Having accepted the geopolitical thinking of Sir Halford Mackinder, Amlie said that he had recognized that "the power is control of the 'Heartland' or Russia would dominate the 'World Island' Europe and Asia and possibly Africa." But, he went on, "it would be a lot easier if there were more of the followers of Trotsky in Russia and less of the chauvinistic Pan-Slavism that is in the process of emerging. . . . I hate to see Europe destroyed in the process; first by our stupidity in trying to reconstitute the status quo in Europe and second by Stalin's need of security and consequent fear of a united Europe, even a united socialist Europe." See TA to JM, April 3, 1944.

31. TA to Ginzburg, November 28, 1945; TA to JM, November 28, 1945; TA to Coffee, November 29, 1945. In his November 26, 1945, letter to McGill, Amlie conceded the division of the world to the United States and the Soviet Union. He offered only "responsible" authority as a bulwark against world catastrophe. As long as the United States was a capitalist nation, he saw little hope that it would act responsibly.

32. In May 1945 Amlie wrote to his wife that he was working on an article that proposed a democratic socialist Europe. He said that the alternatives were an "independent socialist Europe or a Communist Europe." TA to GA, May 12, 1945. Amlie developed his ideas of an independent democratic socialist Europe in a long letter to Benjamin Cohen of the State Department and in the article that he was unable to get published. See TA to Cohen, July 8, 1945; TA, "Europe's Alternatives Are Democratic Socialism or Communism," n.p., 1945. On Amlie's urging Niebuhr to go to Europe, see TA to RN, n.d. [1945]; TA to FK, June 6, 1945. Part of Niebuhr's reply to Amlie is found in TA to FK, June 18, 1945.

33. Amlie's criticism of the anticommunism of the ADA did not reflect any latent Popular Frontism. See Amlie's criticism of the Communists in TA to HoW, n.d. [1940]; TA to GA, May 30, 1945; TA to JM, April 26, 1946; TA to HoW, June 15, 1946; TA to JM, July 29, 1946. For Amlie's criticism of the UDA, the ADA, and the PCA, see TA to Howard [McMurray], October 10, 1947; TA to Nathan Levine, February 4, 1947; TA to Hippelhauser, April 21, 1947. On Schlesinger, see TA to Robert McGill, April 1, 1947. On Amlie's support for Wallace's foreign policy ideas, see TA to Hippelhauser, June 17, 1947. For a critique of the ADA's foreign policy position, praise of Wallace's position, and rejection of both the anticommunist ADA and the procommunist PCA, see TA to McGill, November 10, 1947.

34. TA to United Press Association, June 20, 1945; TA to FK, August 15, 1945; TA to GA, July 5, 1945; TA to Hamlin, September 24, 1945. See also TA to Brand, July 3, 1945.

35. John Bernard to TA, June 2, 1942; TA to JL, June 15, 1942; TA to Coffee,

June 14, 1942. On McCarthy and McCarthyism, see TA to Dear Friend, March 27, 1952; TA to Birkhead, February 8, 1951; TA to Eloise Jessup, n.d. [c. November 1953]; Old Time Progressive [TA] to Evjue, Editor, *The Capital Times*, February 22, 1956; February 18, 1957.

36. On the idea of Wallace taking over the Socialist Party, see TA to HW, n.d. [1947 or 1948]; TA to McGill, December 24, 1947. Amlie wrote to his son about his daughter-in-law: "Polly told me that she considered her own career to be as important as your career. There is no use in going into the absurdity of this statement." TA to Tom, August 15, 1954. On his wife's exhaustion and his treatment of her, see unsigned [GA] to TA, n.d. On Amlie's apparent affair with Evelyn Brand, see correspondence between Amlie and Brand from August 1946 until October 1948.

CHAPTER 8

1. "Britain's Peril" *N*, June 1, 1940, 667–68; FK, "Help Britain Win!" *N*, August 10, 1940, 105–6; FK, "British Morale," *N*, September 21, 1940, 233; FK, "S.O.S. from Britain," *N*, December 7, 1940, 549–50; "Britain Alone," *NR*, June 24, 1940, 842–43; "Destroyers for Britain," *NR*, August 12, 1940, 207; BB, "Not Enough Jitters," *NR*, August 12, 1940, 208–9; "Can Britain Hold Out?" *NR*, September 16, 1940, 371.

2. FS, "The Perfidy of Albion," *NR*, April 20, 1938, 321–23; Quincy Howe, *England Expects Every American to Do His Duty* (New York, 1937); Warren, *Liberals and Communism*, 153.

3. H. N. Brailsford, "Churchill in Command," *NR*, June 10, 1940, 787–88; "Two Worlds at Grips," *N*, May 18, 1940, 642.

4. "A Program for America," n.d. [1941], R-F 16-311, ADA Papers; FK, "Churchill's Vote," *N*, February 7, 1942, 153–54.

5. RN, review of Phillip Guedalla's *Mr. Churchill*, *N*, January 31, 1942, 122; HL, *Where Do We Go From Here?* (New York, 1940), 75, 139.

6. RN, review, *N*, January 31, 1942, 122.

7. Ibid.

8. ML, "The Pilgrimage of Winston Churchill," *NR*, January 5, 1942, 9.

9. Ibid., 12; FK, "New Leaders for Old," *N*, February 21, 1942, 210–11. See also BB, "Mr. Churchill's Untotal War," *NR*, September 28, 1942, 370–72; Frances Gunther, "Victory or Victorianism," *CS*, February 1942. 51–53.

10. Ibid. See also ML, *PM*, March 23, 1943.

11. Ibid.; "Haggling Over India," *N*, March 14, 1942, 300–301; editorials in *NR* on February 16, 1942, 220; April 27, 1942, 558; May 18, 1942, 656–57; MS, "The Future of the United Nations," *NR*, April 27, 1942, 561–63. See also LF, draft of letter to Churchill, n.d., LF Papers.

12. *N*, March 21, 1942, 326; *N*, April 4, 1942, 381–82; editorials in *NR* on March 23, 1942, 379; April 6, 1942, 449; April 13, 1942, 478–79.

13. *N*, April 4, 1942, 381–82; "Hope for India," *NR*, April 6, 1942, 443; "Cripps Must Not Fail," *NR*, April 13, 1942, 478–79; HA, *PM*, July 29, 1942.

14. FK, "India's Zero Hour," *N*, April 11, 1942, 414–15.

15. Ibid., 414.

16. "What Next in India?" *N*, April 18, 1942, 447–48; "Courting Disaster in India," *NR*, April 20, 1942, 524.

17. Krishnalal Shridharani, "What Cripps Faces in India," *N*, March 28, 1942, 365–67; LF, "What Gandhi Wants," *N*, August 15, 1942, 121–22; LF, "Gandhi's Rejected Offer," *N*, August 22, 1942.

18. LF, "Why Cripps Failed," *N*, September 19, 1942, 230–34; LF, "Why Cripps Failed: II," *N*, September 26, 1942, 255–59. See also LF to AM, October 14, 1942, LF Papers.

19. FK, "Churchill's Speech," *N*, September 19, 1942, 224–25; LF to FK, September 19, 1942, LF Papers; FK to LF, September 28, 1942, LF Papers.

20. Graham Spry to FK, n.d. [c. fall 1942], LF Papers; Spry, "A British Reply to Louis Fischer," *N*, November 14, 1942, 501–4; Kingsley Martin, "Talking of India," *N*, September 21, 1942, 538, 543–45.

21. FK to LF, November 5, 1942, LF Papers; LF to FK, November 19, 1942, FK Papers; FK to LF, November 24, 1942, FK Papers. See also Bob [Bendiner] to FK, n.d. [November 1942], FK Papers; LF to FK, November 30, 1942, LF Papers; LF, "Gandhi, Cripps, and Churchill," *N*, December 5, 1942, 619–21.

22. H. N. Brailsford, "What Happened at Delhi," *NR*, June 1, 1942, 760–61; Brailsford, *Subject India* (New York, 1943), 76–77.

23. Brailsford, *Subject India*, 39–89, 57–65, 73–83.

24. FK, "On the Diplomatic Front," *N*, October 17, 1942, 365–66.

25. "Defending the Empire?" *N*, October 31, 1942, 433.

26. Ibid., 433–34.

27. Ibid., 434.

28. George Orwell, "My Country Right or Left, 1940–1943," in *The Collected Essays, Journalism, and Letters of George Orwell*, ed. Sonia Orwell and Ian Angus (New York, 1968), 306–15; Cripps, Telegram to RN, April 10, 1942, R-F 14-245, ADA Papers; JL to Smith, November 4, 1944, R-F 15-270, ADA Papers. For responses to Gandhi's civil disobedience campaign and the British reaction to it, see editorials in *N*, July 25, 1942, 63–64; August 8, 1942, 102; August 15, 1942, 123; FK, "Churchill's Speech," *N*, September 19, 1942, 224–25; FK, "The Indian Dilemma," *N*, August 22, 1942, 144; editorials in *NR* on May 11, 1942, 619–20; June 29, 1942, 877; LF, "Gandhi's Rejected Offer," *N*, August 22, 1942, 145–47. *PM* writers were especially critical of Gandhi's nonviolent campaign and the All-India Congress. See HA, *PM*, July 22, 1942; July 31, 1942; AU, *PM*, August 7, 1942. *PM* did publish excerpts from Fischer's sympathetic portrait of Gandhi in *N*. See LF, *PM*, August 23, 1942.

29. LF to FDR, August 7, 1942, LF Papers; LF, "The Riddle of India," 1943, LF Papers; LF, "Open Letter to Winston Churchill," *N*, June 5, 1943, 797; Rustum Vambery, "Open Letter to Louis Fischer," *N*, June 26, 1943, 902–3; LF, "Britain and India," *N*, July 3, 1943, 25; *N*, July 3, 1943, 3; LF, letter, *N*, October 9, 1943, 418; IS, "The Indian Skeleton at Atlantic City," *N*, December 11, 1943, 686–87; LF, "Gandhi's New Strategy," *N*, July 29, 1944, 123–25; editorials in *NR* on August 17, 1942, 191–92; August 24, 1942, 215; August 31, 1942, 246–47; October 12, 1942, 449–50. See also MS, "Is It a People's War?" *NR*, November 16, 1942, 633–34; Kate Mitchell, review, *NR*, February 22, 1943, 258–60; Mitchell, "An Indian Government Is Possible," *NR*, August 30, 1943, 275–77; Frances Gunther, review, *NR*, January 10, 1944, 60–61; ML, *PM*, April 11, 1944.

30. VB, *PM*, May 25, 1944; Kuh, *PM*, May 29, 1944; editorials in *N* on October 2, 1943, 367–68; March 4, 1944, 268–69; June 3, 1944, 640; editorials in *NR* on May 18, 1942, 656–57; June 5, 1944, 754–55; June 26, 1944, 835–36.

31. "Churchill as Peace Leader," *NR*, April 12, 1943, 462–63; RN, "Great Britain's Post-War Role," *N*, July 10, 1943, 39–40; ML, *PM*, May 15, 1945.

32. Editorials in *N* on March 4, 1944, 268–69; January 27, 1945, 88–89; editorials in *NR* on December 18, 1944, 819–21; January 22, 1945, 101; January 29, 1945, 133. See also Michael Clark, "Greek Politics and Puppets," *N*, December 23, 1944, 765–67; Constantine Poulos, "Rule Britannia," *N*, December 23, 1944, 772–74.

33. "No, Mr. Churchill!" *NR*, June 5, 1944, 755; ML, *PM*, May 15, 1945.

34. Editorials in *N* on March 4, 1944, 268–69; June 3, 1944, 640; June 10, 1944, 680–81.

35. Mallory Browne, "British Tories Look Ahead," *N*, January 1, 1944, 11–12; Keith Hutchison, "Britain's Tories Steal a March," *N*, October 14, 1944, 427–28; editorials in *NR* on May 18, 1942, 656–57; April 3, 1944, 452; June 5, 1944, 751.

36. "Mr. Churchill Protests Too Much," *N*, January 27, 1945, 89.

37. HL, "London on D-Day," *N*, June 17, 1944, 703–4; ML, *PM*, May 15, 1945.

38. On the Josiah Wedgwood dinner, see material in R-F 16-296, ADA Papers. On the hopes for delegations of British trade unionists to tour the United States, see Harold Siegel to Robert Watt, August 18, 1941, R-F 1-18; Siegel to Paul Porter, August 18, 1941, R-F 1-18; JL, Memorandum on British Labor Project, n.d. [c. summer 1941], R-F 1-18. On the Jennie Lee tour, see material in R-F 7-115. On the Martin dinner, see material in R-F 9-132. On Jennie Lee's request for help for the displaced hungry in Austria, see material in R-F 9-130. See also Thomas F. Power to JL, April 2, 1946, R-F 5-81; JL to Lee, April 5, 1946, R-F 5-83. On the solicitation of greetings, see RN et al. to Herbert Morrison, April 23, 1941, R-F 5-83; RN et al. to HL, n.d. [c. April 23, 1941], R-F 5-83. All ADA Papers. On the Gordon-Walker tour, see note 52 below.

39. On Niebuhr's trip to England, see Fox, *Richard Niebuhr*, 217–18. On the Lerner-Laski correspondence, see, e.g., HL to ML, June 17, 1940; October 29,

1941; April 12, 1942; January 2, 1944; October 20, 1945, ML Papers. On Benton, see WB, Eric Johnston, and HL, "The Economic System — Today *and* Tomorrow," The University of Chicago Round Table, August 15, 1943, CB Papers. On the impact of the Beveridge Report, see TA to JM, March 21, 1945, TA Papers; editorials in *N* on December 12, 1942, 636–37; June 12, 1943, 824–25; Richard Lee Strout, "Britain Plans for a New World," *NR*, November 2, 1942, 570–72; Strout, "The Beveridge Report," *NR*, December 14, 1942, 784–86; editorials in *NR* on December 14, 1942, 775; December 21, 1942, 810–11; April 3, 1944, 452; Soule, "Postwar Britain at Home," *NR*, March 12, 1945, 352–54.

40. MS, "Challenge to Action," *NR*, December 7, 1942, 733–35; Wintringham, "Britain Is Not Amused," *N*, January 16, 1943, 84–85; FK, "The People's Revolution," *N*, May 16, 1942, 562; "British Labor Marks Time," *N*, June 26, 1943, 880; FK, "Britain Between the Acts I," *N*, October 9, 1943, 398–400; FK, "Britain Between the Acts IV," *N*, November 20, 1943, 581–83. For a list of *Free World* international headquarters, see its March 1942 issue.

41. Editorials in *N* on November 28, 1942, 561–62; June 26, 1943, 880; November 4, 1944, 560–61; editorials in *NR* on June 8, 1942, 780; October 26, 1942, 531; November 30, 1942, 696; LF to FK, November 30, 1942, LF Papers; ML to BB, September 11, 1942, ML Papers.

42. On Wintringham, see his *Peoples' War* (Harmondsworth, 1942) and *The Politics of Victory* (London, 1941). For Richard Acland's comments on the Commonwealth's program, see his *Forward March* (London, 1941); *How It Can Be Done* (London, n.d.); *Questions and Answers* (London, 1942); *What It Will Be Like* (London, 1942); and *The Winning of the Peace* (London, 1942).

43. Articles by Wintringham in *N* on June 27, 1942; December 5, 1942; April 17, 1943. Correspondence between JL and Acland, JL and Wintringham, JL and R. G. W. MacKay, and Commonwealth material is found in R-F 5-83, ADA Papers. Patricia Strauss, "British Labor's Dilemma," *N*, December 23, 1944, 763–65. Loeb called the results of the British 1945 election "the most significant political event in our time." See JL to Mortimer Hays, August 6, 1945, R-F 5-83, ADA Papers.

44. Warren, *Liberals and Communism*, 6–62; Pells, *Radical Visions and American Dreams* (New York, 1973), 43–150, 292–329.

45. HL, *Where Do We Go From Here?*, 47–48, 119–28, 136–92; HL, *Reflections on the Revolution of our Time*, 285–345.

46. HL, *Reflections*, 38–89, 157–73, 179–229, 246–53, 285–349. See also, HL, "Winston Churchill in War and Peace," *N*, 723–26.

47. E. F. M. Durbin, *The Politics of Democratic Socialism* (London, 1940); LC, *The Unfinished Task* (New York, 1942); IS, "Will America Go Socialist?" *N*, August 11, 1945, 124–25.

48. See, e.g., G. D. H. Cole, *Europe, Russia and the Future* (London, 1942); Cole et al., *Plan for Britain* (London, 1943); Cole, *Great Britain in the Post-War World*

(London, 1945); Cole et al., *Victory or Vested Interest?* (London, 1942); Durbin, *Politics of Democratic Socialism* (London, 1940) and *What Have We to Defend?* (London, 1942); HL, *Where Do We Go From Here?* (London, 1940); HL et al., *Programme for Victory* (London, 1941); HL, *Reflections* (London, 1943) and *Faith, Reason and Civilization* (London, 1944); Francis Williams, *Democracy's Last Battle* (London, 1941), *Ten Angels Swearing* (London, 1941), and *War by Revolution* (London, 1940).

49. Warren, *Liberals and Communism*, 6–62, 103–126; Pells, *Radical Visions and American Dreams*, 292–329; Miller, *New American Radicalism*, 137–61; Arthur Garfield Hays, *Democracy Works* (New York, 1939); John Chamberlain, *American Stakes* (New York, 1940); AB, *Man's Estate* (New York, 1939); George Counts, *The Prospects of American Democracy* (New York, 1938). On the Socialist Party, see Warren, *An Alternative Vision*, 50, 77–108.

50. On Randolph's efforts to found a "New Party," see Paula F. Pfeffer, *A. Philip Randolph, Pioneer of the Civil Rights Movement* (Baton Rouge, 1990), 125–31. Corey was the research director. See "Ideas for a New Party," *Antioch Review* 6 (Fall 1946): 449–72.

51. HL, *Reflections*, 346–53.

52. "The British Election," *NR*, August 6, 1945, 147–49; "Revolution by Ballot," *N*, August 4, 1945, 101–2; AU, *PM*, July 27, 1945. On the Gordon-Walker speaking tour, see the material in R-F 7-98, 9-129, 9-130, ADA Papers. On Great Britain and Palestine, see the JL-DW correspondence in R-F 4-63 as well as JL to DW, July 18, 1946, R-F 9-130; RN to Ernest Bevin, June 12, 1946, R-F 12-193; UDA, Release, n.d. [June 1946], R-F 14-245; *UDA Bulletin*, June 1946, R-F 16-306; *U.D.A. London Letter*, August 15, 1946, R-F 16-308, ADA Papers. On liberal disappointment with the Labour Party, see IS, *PM*, August 22, 1945; JS, *PM*, August 23, 1945; ML, *PM*, February 28, 1946; October 3, 1946; October 20, 1947.

53. JL to RN and Hays, n.d. [c. summer 1945], R-F 9-125, ADA Papers. Letters between Loeb and Duffy, between Loeb and David Williams and UDA work in England can be found in R-F 4-63, 9-129, 9-130, ADA Papers. The UDA *London Letter* beginning in July 1946 can be found in R-F 16-308, ADA Papers.

54. See correspondence between JL and DW in R-F 4-63, on the following dates: September 19, 1946; November 16, 1946; November 21, 1946; November 26, 1946; November 27, 1946; November 29, 1946; December 8, 1946; Jennie Lee to JL, September 19, 1946, R-F 9-130; *U.D.A. London Letter*, December 1, 1946, R-F 16-308, ADA Papers. See also material on the parliamentary "rebellion" in R-F 9-130, ADA Papers.

55. *NL*, January 25, 1947, 1, 19; ML, *PM*, January 23, 1947. For the *Tribune* group's critique of Wallace, see *U.D.A. London Letter*, April 18, 1947, R-F 16-308; Lee, "Comment on Wallace," April 29, 1947, R-F 16-288, ADA Papers. It is true that Michael Foot of the *Tribune* group wrote enthusiastically about one of Wallace's speeches in Great Britain. A reading of his letter, however, indicates that his

enthusiasm was based on the help he felt Wallace offered for an independent British foreign policy—a policy independent of both the American and Soviet blocs and capable of assisting "in the preventing the fatal division of the world into two hostile blocs." See Foot, letter, *NR*, April 28, 1947, 3, 47. At this stage, Foot did not realize just how much Wallace's own formulation accepted the two-bloc division of the world.

56. On the Keep Left group in the Labour Party, see *U.D.A. London Letter*, May 16, 1947, R-F 16-308, ADA Papers; Geoffrey Bing et al., *Keep Left* (London, 1947).

CHAPTER 9

1. LF, letter, *N*, June 2, 1945, 631.
2. Editors' reply, *N*, June 2, 1945, 631–32.
3. Ibid., 632.
4. LF, letter, *N*, June 23, 1945, 706, 708.
5. Ibid.
6. Hicks, review, *NR*, April 16, 1945, 514, 516; "Mr. Hicks and the Liberals," *NR*, April 23, 1945, 544–45; VF, letter, *NR*, April 16, 1945, 507; editors' reply, *NR*, April 16, 1945, 507–8; "The Fischer-*Nation* Debate," *N*, June 30, 1945, 728; Eugene Messner, letter, *NR*, April 23, 1945, 558; Hans Neisser, letter, *NR*, April 30, 1945, 590; editors' reply, *NR*, April 30, 1945, 590; VF, letter, *NR*, May 21, 1945, 710–11; editors' reply, *NR*, May 21, 1945, 711. See also Kenneth Crawford, "The Double Talk of the Liberals," *CS*, May 1945, 6–9; VF, "The Irresponsibles," *CS*, July 1945, 5–6.
7. "The Fischer-*Nation* Debate," 728.
8. Articles by Maurice Hindus in *PM* on July 9, 1943; July 22, 1943; July 25, 1943; Hindus, *Mother Russia* (London, 1944); ML, articles in *PM* on November 26, 1943; March 2, 1944; April 17, 1944; AD, articles in *N* on December 2, 1944; March 17, 1945; December 22, 1945; FS, "The Polish Frontier," *NR*, January 31, 1944, 138–41; FS, "Might and Right at San Francisco," *N*, April 28, 1945, 479–81; HE, articles in *NR* on October 18, 1943; September 25, 1944; February 5, 1945; March 19, 1945; July 23, 1945.
9. Warren, *Liberals and Communism*, 193–215; Miller, *New American Radicalism*, 162–98; "For a Declaration of War," *NR*, August 25, 1941, 235–38; "Russia and the War," *CS*, August 1941, 240–41; "The Aim Is Peace," *CS*, September 1941, 272–73.
10. Warren, *Liberals and Communism*, 193–215; LF to Vernon, August 25, 1939, LF Papers.
11. LC, *The Unfinished Task*, 121; Ralph Ingersoll, *PM*, January 26, 1942; ML, *PM*, April 3, 1944.

12. HW, "Russia," in *Democracy Reborn*, 196–200. See also Warburg, *Foreign Policy Begins at Home*, 83; "Must We Fight Another War?" *NR*, December 21, 1942, 812. At the conclusion of the Moscow Conference, Alfred Bingham showed his greatest wartime optimism about postwar relations with the Soviet Union. He wrote that the American definition of democracy differed from Russia's and that we needed to accept other political forms than our own, as well to get over "our fascination with free enterprise." See AB, "Turning Point," *CS*, December 1943, 444–45.

13. Warren, 194–215; Sara Alpern, *Freda Kirchwey* (Cambridge, 1987), 126–27; LC, *The Unfinished Task*, 102–24.

14. FK, "The Red Star Rises," *N*, February 27, 1943, 293–94; "Russia in the Alliance," *NR*, June 22, 1942, 843–44; "The Soviet-Czech Treaty," *NR*, December 27, 1943, 900; "The Great Pravda Mystery," *NR*, January 31, 1944, 135–36.

15. FS, "Machiavelli in Moscow," *NR*, November 29, 1939, 158–60; "Power Politics and People," *NR*, November 29, 1939, 155.

16. FK, "Moscow-Berlin Axis," *N*, October 7, 1939, 365–66; "Stalin's Munich," *NR*, August 30, 1939, 88–89.

17. On Soviet security motives, see, e.g., FK, "The Red Star Rises," 293–94; editorials in *NR*, September 1943, 320, December 27, 1943, 900. For Strong, see *N*, August 12, 1944; August 19, 1944; September 2, 1944; October 21, 1944; February 3, 1945. For Davis, see *NR*, September 4, 1944; November 6, 1944; January 1, 1945; March 5, 1945.

18. Bates, "Need We Fear Russia?" *N*, January 17, 1942, 60–62; FK, "The Red Star Rises," 293–94; FK, "Russia and the West," *N*, June 23, 1945, 684–86; "What Russia Wants," *NR*, October 11, 1943, 474–75; IB, *The Road to Peace and Freedom* (Indianapolis, 1943), 169–99.

19. Blair Bolles, "The Return of Eduard Benes," *N*, March 20, 1943, 408–10; editorials in *NR* on December 27, 1943, 900; January 17, 1944, 72; February 21, 1944, 230–31; HE, "Russia and the Balkans," *NR*, April 3, 1944; ML, *PM*, January 6, 1944; Joachim Joesten, *PM*, February 13, 1944; "The British Bloc in Europe," *NR*, November 27, 1944, 679–80; Warburg, *Foreign Policy Begins at Home*, 277. In early 1944 Lerner distinguished between old colonialist/imperialist spheres of influence and spheres of influence within "a United Nations framework." The Soviet Union was pointing toward this new kind of "federal regionalism," and Lerner saw signs—though still inadequate—of the United States moving toward a similar kind of liberal regionalism in western Europe. See ML, *PM*, February 8, 1944.

20. Walter Lippmann, *U.S. Foreign Policy* (Boston, 1943), 136–52; Motherwell, *The Peace We Fight For*, 165–208; RN, "Great Britain's Post-War Role," *N*, July 10, 1943, 39–40.

21. Albert Guerard, review, *N*, September 15, 1945, 260–61; Guerard, "For a Federated Europe," *NR*, September 6, 1943, 330–33; "Foreign Policy Statement," *UDA Bulletin*, November 1945, R-F 12-194, ADA Papers.

22. FK, "The Moscow Conference," *N*, October 30, 1943, 489–90; FK, "The Meaning of Moscow," *N*, November 13, 1943, 545–46; FK, "Fragments of One World," *N*, May 19, 1945, 560–61; AD, "Goodbye to the Revolution," *N*, July 15, 1944, 65–68; ML, *PM*, April 27, 1943; VB, *PM*, May 8, 1944; VB, *PM*, May 15, 1944; IS, *PM*, May 14, 1945; Kuh, *PM*, May 16, 1945; IS, *PM*, May 17, 1945.

23. FK, "Year's End," *N*, December 25, 1943, 749–50.

24. Articles by AD in *N* on April 24, 1943; June 3, 1944; December 2, 1944; FK, "Stalin and Badoglio," *N*, March 25, 1944, 351–52.

25. Alexander Werth, "Russia Behind the Lines," *N*, April 18, 1942, 454–57; John Scott, review, *N*, July 4, 1942, 15; Bates, review, *NR*, July 13, 1942, 58–59; MS, "Is It a People's War?" *NR*, November 16, 1942, 633; IS, *PM*, February 1, 1945. Lerner wrote about Stalin following the will of his people, and Ralph Ingersoll attributed the victories of the Red Army to "morale and morale alone." See ML, *PM*, March 2, 1944; Ingersoll, *PM*, January 26, 1942. See also ML, *PM*, April 3, 1944.

26. Joesten, "Why Stalin Acts Like That," *N*, April 1, 1944, 389–90. In an article on the Red Army, Lerner wrote: "And Stalin has shown the cold will and the steel patience of his name." ML, *PM*, March 2, 1944.

27. "Four Men Reshape the World," *NR*, December 13, 1943, 835–37; Margaret Bourke-White, *Shooting the Russian War* (New York, 1942), 217.

28. *N*, March 13, 1943, 362; *N*, April 10, 1943, 507; Max Danish, letter, *N*, March 27, 1943, 466–67; editorials in *NR* on March 15, 1943, 336–37; April 12, 1943, 460–61. In *PM*, Alexander Uhl reported on Ehrlich and Alter with apparent sympathy for the CIO's criticisms of the executions, but many *PM* readers supported the Soviet case. See AU, *PM*, March 18, 1943; "The Ehrlich-Alter Case," *PM*, March 24, 1943. One of the more insensitive responses was by Joachim Joesten in *PM*. In his hands, murder became a "sad" affair in which all the demonstrations and protests could not restore Ehrlich and Alter "to life" but did great "harm to American-Russian relations." Joesten, *PM*, February 15, 1944. On the Warsaw uprising, see editorials in *N* on August 26, 1944, 226; October 14, 1944, 423. See also "From Warsaw to Paris," *NR*, September 11, 1944, 295–96. On the arrest of the sixteen Polish leaders, see BB, "Golden Gate Round-up," *NR*, May 14, 1945, 665–67; IS, "Anti-Russian Undertow," *N*, May 12, 1945, 534–35. *The New Republic* wrote in July 1945 that despite the arrest of the 16 Polish leaders, Russia had emerged from the San Francisco conference as "the winner in terms of moral prestige." And it found the charges against the leaders were true and the trials "fair." See "Plus and Minus at San Francisco," *NR*, July 2, 1945, 3–4; "Solution in Poland," *NR*, July 2, 1945, 6–7. See also ML, *PM*, May 7, 1945; June 22, 1945.

29. Hicks, review of Lerner's *Public Journal*, *NR*, April 16, 1945, 514, 516.

30. Paul Willen, "Who 'Collaborated' with Russia?" *Antioch Review* 14, no. 3 (September 1954): 259–83. *New York Herald Tribune*, January 26, 1945; *Time*, January 4, 1943; *Life*, March 29, 1943.

31. "Russia's Dead Idealism," *CS*, February 1945, 39; Margaret Marshall, review

of Joseph E. Davies's *Mission to Moscow*, *N*, January 31, 1942, 118–19; *N*, May 8, 1943, 651; Manny Farber, review of *Mission to Moscow*, *NR*, May 10, 1943, 636; George Counts, Harry Gideonse, and Sidney Hook, statement on *Mission to Moscow*, n.d. [1943], AB Papers; FK to Pope, July 12, 1943; October 26, 1943, FK Papers.

32. RN, review of FS's *Design for Power*, *N*, January 10, 1942, 42–44; FS and RN, exchange, *N*, January 24, 1942, 103; RN, review of John MacCormac's *America and World Mastery*, *N*, February 21, 1942, 230; RN, review of Lionel Gelber's *Peace by Power*, *N*, April 25, 1942, 495; LF, "Peace—the Culbertson System," *N*, April 24, 1943, 582–86; EC, "My Plan a la Fischer," *N*, May 22, 1943, 727–30; LF, letter, *N*, May 29, 1943, 788; EC, letter, *N*, June 12, 1943, 846; MC, review of Nicholas John Spykman's *America's Strategy in World Politics*, *NR*, April 20, 1942, 546–47; Eunice Clark, "The Culbertson Plan," *CS*, February 1943, 42–45.

33. Robert Divine, *Second Chance* (New York, 1967); editorials in *NR* on October 25, 1943, 559–60; January 10, 1944, 38–39; September 18, 1944, 326; LF, "The Big-Power Peace," *N*, September 16, 1944, 315–17; LF, "The Partitioning of Peace," *CS*, April 1945, 5–8.

34. Lloyd C. Gardner, *Spheres of Influence* (Chicago, 1993).

35. Warburg, *Foreign Policy Begins at Home*, 85–102, 254–90; Divine, *Second Chance*, 6–28.

36. FK, "Total Insecurity," 381, *N*, April 1, 1944, 381; "Have We Lost the Peace?" *N*, June 10, 1944, 669; FK, "How to Keep the Peace," *N*, September 16, 1944, 312–14.

37. "Approaches to Russia," *N*, March 27, 1943, 436–37; ML, *PM*, March 16, 1943, March 31, 1943. In an exchange with Max Eastman, Lerner said that Wendell Willkie, Henry Wallace, and Joseph Davies were "realists" because they knew that the war and the peace could not be won without U.S.-Soviet cooperation. See ML, *PM*, July 1, 1943.

38. Editorials in *NR* June 22, 1942, 843–44; February 22, 1943, 235–36; January 24, 1944, 103–4; January 31, 135–36; BB, "The Chance for World Peace," *NR*, April 3, 1944, 458–60; ML, "Dualism in the United Nations," *PM*, April 10, 1944; "Strategic Frontiers and Collective Security," *N*, March 13, 1943, 354–65. For Kirchwey, Russian unilateralism occurred not only because of the absence of collective security per se but because of the absence of a joint Allied "clear-cut anti-fascist policy." See "First Test of Yalta," *N*, March 24, 1945, 319–20.

39. Editorials in *N* on August 7, 1943, 142; August 28, 1943, 229–31; January 15, 1944, 59–60; January 29, 1944, 114; January 27, 1945, 86; March 24, 1945, 319–20; Kuh, "Two Wars or One?" *N*, August 28, 1943, 240–41; editorials in *NR* on August 9, 1943, 183; January 8, 1945, 35–37; IS, *PM*, June 14, 1945. The criticism of Soviet unilateralism in Poland applied to its tactics and not to its Western border demands; the Curzon line was defended as reasonable, and those who questioned it were seen as disrupting Allied unity. See "Senatorial Trouble-

Maker," N, March 17, 1945, 292–93. At one point, *The Nation* sought to distinguish "the mischievous attacks of the professional Russophobes" from the legitimate concerns of the "average American" that the "independence of Poland and the political rights of all democratic groups in Poland be respected." This left open the question of defining "democratic groups." See "Hour of Decision," N, April 28, 1945, 473. In early 1944 Lerner criticized the Russian creation of "sixteen autonomous republics" as being indefensible ("even the friends of Russia cannot defend her"); it was "a dangerous game of power politics within a United Nations framework." See ML, PM, February 2, 1944. By the spring of 1945, Bliven had concluded that the Russians were only interested in collective security "if it coincide[d] with what they feel is Russia's interest." Russia's demands had become "horse trading." See BB, "San Francisco: Now or Never," NR, May 7, 1945, 634.

40. On Bretton Woods, see IB, PM, March 16, 1945; IS, PM, April 18, 1945; IS, PM, April 19, 1945; UDA, Release, June 27, 1945, R-F 1-17, ADA Papers. On Yalta, see IS, PM, February 13, 1945; "More Perfect Union," N, February 17, 1945, 169–70; IS, "This Is What We Voted For," N, February 17, 1945, 174–75; "The Crimean Conference," NR, February 19, 1945, 243–44. On the United Nations, see "Great-Power Hegemony," N, October 21, 1944, 451–52; editorials in NR on October 23, 1944, 510–11; February 26, 1945, 278–80; March 12, 1945, 350–51; UDA, *From the Garden of Eden*, R-F 11-179, ADA Papers; ML, PM, April 2, 1945. Stone argued that if the Soviets had not insisted on a big-power veto, the U.S. Senate would have, and that therefore those who attacked the veto were anti-Soviet. See IS, "It's Not Clockwork," N, March 17, 1945, 295–97. For liberal criticism of Yalta, see "The Curse of Realism," CS, March 1945, 3–4; Bertram Wolfe, "Poland: Acid Test of a People's Peace," CS, March 1945, 5–12; LF, "The Partitioning of Peace," CS, April 1945, 5–8; Maurice Goldbloom, "The Fruit of Yalta," CS, August 1945, 3–4.

41. "Great-Power Hegemony," N, October 21, 1944, 451–52; FK, "Yalta and San Francisco," N, March 3, 1945, 201; "Mr. Roosevelt's Peace Plan," NR, June 26, 1944, 835–36; "World Security: The San Francisco Conference," Special Section, NR, April 30, 1945, 603–17. I. F. Stone argued that big-power unity, better understanding, and "the willingness of the peoples of the major powers to see each other's point of view and make the necessary adjustments and compromises" were essential if the United Nations was to prove successful. See IS, "It's Not Clockwork," 297. Lerner believed that the commitments that could make a world organization work had to come from the Great Powers. Those who did not recognize this were "living in a dream." It was necessary for Great Power common action to "come first": "If it breaks, everything breaks. If it holds, our world holds." Ultimately, however, Lerner believed that the Great Power alliance needed to be "incorporated within the structure of a new world community." See ML, PM, April 26, 1945.

42. IS, PM, February 13, 1945; ML, PM, April 2, 1945; May 1, 1945; IS, PM,

May 4, 1945; AU, PM, May 14, 1945; "Lerner Warns Against Ganging Up on U.S.S.R.," PM, May 21, 1945; "Lerner Warns Soviet War Would Be 'Greatest Crime,'" PM, May 29, 1945; IB, PM, June 1, 1945; IS, PM, June 14, 1945; ML, PM, June 22, 1945; AU, PM, July 13, 1945.

43. LF, "Russia and the Peace," N, June 12, 1943, 835–36; LF, "Washington Jitters," N, October 2, 1944, 453–54.

44. "Murder of a People," N, December 19, 1942, 668–69; FK, "Rescue Hungary's Jews," N, August 26, 1944, 229. Kirchwey was also convinced that the Soviet Union took the necessary steps to get rid of fascism in Europe, whereas the United States temporized too often with fascist sympathizers. See "Let's Finish the War," N, June 9, 1945, 635–36. On the theme of Russian policy, in contrast to the West's policy, being designed to "smash fascist power," see also FK, "Russia and the West," N, June 23, 1945, 684–86. Alpern, Freda Kirchwey, 118, 127, 141–44, 150, 164–65, 177.

45. FK, "Russia and the West," 684–86; "Have We a Foreign Policy?" NR, February 21, 1944, 231–32. In 1943 The New Republic said that Europe needed a "middle ground between a reactionary capitalism and an irresponsible communism." See "What Russia Wants," NR, October 11, 1943, 474. At the beginning of 1945, The New Republic saw Roosevelt's role as using "a veto on behalf of the decent sentiments of mankind when the common ruthlessness" of Soviet communism and British imperialism required action. See "The World after the War," NR, January 1, 1945, 4. In May 1945 Stone criticized Truman for not continuing Roosevelt's role of mediating between the Soviet Union and Great Britain. See IS, "Trieste and San Francisco," N, May 26, 1945, 590. A month later, however, he saw indications that Truman intended to play Roosevelt's "middle role." See IS, "Truman and the State Department," N, June 9, 1945, 637–39.

46. In 1944 Niebuhr criticized Harold Laski for his "idolization" of Russia. See RN, review, N, June 17, 1944, 710–11. Some have speculated that Del Vayo had an excessive influence on Kirchwey because they had a lengthy love affair. Alpern, who has researched the relevant papers and conducted many interviews, concluded that there was no evidence that their relationship was other than platonic. See Alpern, Freda Kirchwey, 277. There is another point to be made about their relationship, however. Although it is clear that Kirchwey admired Del Vayo's experience in the Spanish Republican government and his antifascism, it does not necessarily follow that the influence ran in only one direction—from Del Vayo to Kirchwey. In using Del Vayo, Fischer, and Niebuhr to symbolize three different foreign policy perspectives that motivated Kirchwey, I am not suggesting such a one-dimensional approach to personal influences.

47. "The Fischer-Nation Debate," N, June 30, 1945, 728.

48. RN, "Russia and the West," N, January 16, 1943, 82–83.

49. RN, "Russia and the West II," N, January 23, 1943, 124–25.

50. Ibid.

51. For Niebuhr's criticism of the American Communist Party, see RN, letter, *N*, April 10, 1943, 537.

52. RN, "Great Britain's Post-War Role," *N*, July 10, 1943, 39. Despite its criticisms of Churchill, *The Nation* also believed that in the absence of a strong British postwar influence in Europe the world could easily be divided into a Russian and an American sphere of influence with a resulting increase in the possibility of a new world conflict. See "Smuts Thinks Aloud," *N*, December 18, 1943, 720. See also RN, "Letter from Britain," *C&C*, July 12, 1943, 2.

53. RN, "World War Three Ahead?" *N*, March 25, 1944, 356–57.

54. RN, "The Basis of World Order," *N*, October 21, 1944, 489.

55. RN, "Will America Hold Out," *N*, January 13, 1945, 42.

56. Ibid., 42–43. On his fear of "a new isolationism," see also RN, "Editorial Notes," *C&C*, January 8, 1945, 2; RN, "Editorial Notes," *C&C*, February 19, 1945, 2.

57. RN, "Will America Hold Out," 43.

58. Ibid.

59. "We're in to Stay," *N*, January 13, 1945, 32–33.

60. Ibid. Kirchwey wrote: "The eradication of that covert isolationism is the most critical problem which American liberals face today. The full participation of the United States with England and Russia in a responsible concern for the future of Europe is not only the sole hope for the survival of Europe's forces of liberation and for the utter defeat of fascism; it is the sole hope for the survival of our own democracy. . . . And our full participation in the common action of the United Nations is not only the sole guaranty of rebirth of freedom in Italy, Greece, and Poland but the sole guaranty of the postwar freedom and security of all peoples throughout the world."

61. RN, "Is This 'Peace in Our Time'?" *N*, April 7, 1945, 382–84. As early as 1942, in a comment on an "excellent article" by Del Vayo, Niebuhr asserted that it was inevitable that the Big Four "dominate the peace," but that "constitutional commitments" of these four powers needed to be extended to other powers "as much as possible." See RN to FK, June 19, 1942, FK Papers.

62. Ibid., 383.

63. "The Fischer-*Nation* Debate," *N*, June 30, 1945, 728.

64. Niebuhr and Fischer did not disagree only on the Soviet Union. Niebuhr had accepted the plans for the United Nations as imperfect, but realistic. Unlike Niebuhr and Kirchwey who argued that the imperfections could be corrected, Fischer thought "differently." He condemned the entire enterprise as a "big-power peace" and suggested that there needed to be a crusade by "democratic internationalists in all countries" for a democratic world organization and against the proposed "camouflage" of spheres of influence. "The real battle for peace," he wrote, "begins when the diplomats finish." See LF, "The Big-Power Peace," *N*, September 16, 1944, 315–17.

65. RN, address, February 27, 1944, FK Papers.

66. It is true that the ADA presented itself as an alternative to those who acted as if the war with the Soviet Union was inevitable and to those who believed the conflict with Russia derived from American imperialism. But the ease with which the organization moved to support the Truman Doctrine and the fact that ADA members by the fall were speaking of Wallace's PCA position as treasonous, suggest that it was quickly becoming an organization whose framework was determined by the foreign policy of the two quarreling camps. See Wilson Wyatt, speech, April 8, 1947, R-F 5-83; Unsigned [Ethel Epstein] to Leo Mayer, September 9, 1947, R-F 4-68, ADA Papers.

CHAPTER 10

1. JL to Hillyer, September 22 and 23, 1941, R-F 3-47; Hillyer to JL, April 24, 1942, R-F 7-108, ADA Papers.

2. Louis Nelson, letter and editors' reply, N, January 30, 1943, 178–79.

3. JL to NT, January 4, 1943, SP Papers.

4. Niebuhr chided Thomas saying that if "Americans and the democratic forces" had followed the Socialist position before Pearl Harbor, "Hitler would be making the peace today." RN to NT, CS, September 8, 1944.

5. SC, May 29, 1942; NT, "How Not to Serve Democracy," SC, May 29, 1942; LS, SC, July 31, 1942; Frank McCulloch to Mary Hillyer, November 20, 1942, NT Papers; NT to McCulloch, November 27, 1942, NT Papers.

6. On the decline of the Socialist Party over the war issue, see Warren, An Alternative Vision, 158–61.

7. National Action Committee, "Socialist Statement on the War," SC, December 20, 1941. For Thomas's views on the war and the Socialist Party, see NT to Ken Cuthbertson, January 2, 1942, SP Papers.

8. NEC, "Statement on the War," SC, January 11, 1942; NT, statement, SC, January 17, 1942. The opposition to the term "critical support" is seen in a letter from Willard Uphaus, a leading Wisconsin Socialist. See Uphaus to NEC, December 16, 1941, SP Papers. Symes Amendment to the NEC Statement on the War, n.d. [c. December 1941 or January 1942], SP Papers; NT, Resolution on Symes Amendment, n.d. [c. December 1941 or January 1942], SP Papers.

9. On pacifist criticism of the NEC Statement on the War, see Harold Flincker and George Kingsley, statement, January 21, 1942, NT Papers; Philip Isely to TC, January 30, 1942, SP Papers. For a revolutionary socialist critique of Thomas, the pacifists, and the Symes-Clement Amendment, see Dan Roberts, Resolution on War, May 23, 1942, SP Papers. See also Robert Pearsall to HaF, June 22, 1942; Mary R. Schneider to Barshop, February 27, 1942, SP Papers.

10. In early 1943 Clement apparently prepared a statement containing his criticisms of the party's orientation. See HaF to TC, February 14, 1943, SP Papers.

11. Frequent motions and resolutions reflect the party's interest in a mass party, as do Thomas's letters throughout the war. See, e.g., NT, motion, NEC, July 23–25; NAC Minutes, January 4, 1944; MK, memorandum to NEC, January 1944; SP Resolution, February 1944; NEC Minutes, February 18–20, 1944; NT to Barshop, January 18, 1943, NT Papers; NT to JD, September 16, 1943, NT Papers.

12. NT to MK, February 1, 1943, SP Papers; WiB, "A Statement on Labor Political Action," [1943], SP Papers.

13. NEC Meeting, July 23–25, 1943, SP Papers; NEC Minutes, "Political Perspectives," November 19–21, SP Papers.

14. NT to Dear Comrade, December 6, 1944; HaF to Overholt, January 29, 1944; NEC, Discussion of Campaign and Third Party Situation, n.d. [February 1944]; "Resolution on Political Action in 1944," February 1944; Resolution on Socialist Non-Electoral Activity, February 1944, SP Papers.

15. NAC Minutes, December 7, 1943, SP Papers; LS articles in SC on January 21 and 28, 1944; TC et al. to Dear Comrade (with report to 1944 Convention), July 1944, SP Papers; TC to MK, August 28, 1943, SP Papers; JD to Harry, Al, Bob and Bill, December 17, 1943; JD to WiB, August 24 and October 4, 1944, SP Papers.

16. NT to MK, December 31, 1942, SP Papers; HaF to Munson, March 25, 1943, SP Papers; HaF to Sheehan, May 13, 1943, SP Papers.

17. *Perspectives* No. 1 [c. late 1943 or early 1944], SP Papers.

18. Ibid.

19. NT to EC, June 17, 1942; NT to CB, June 10, 1942; NT to CB, July 21, 1942; NT to William B. Lloyd, July 27, 1942, NT Papers; *Perspectives* No. 1.

20. JLL to HaF, December 27, 1942; JLL, "Notes on 'India's Revolution' by Lillian Symes," n.d. [c. December 1942]; JLL to HaF, January 8, 1943; HaF to JLL, January 9, 1942, SP Papers. For Symes's answers to Lewine's criticisms, see LS, reply to JLL memo., n.d. [1943], SP Papers. On Howard, see Harry P. Howard, letter, SC, October 2, 1942; Jim Cork, SC, October 30, 1942; New York Executive Committee Minutes, September 14, 1942, SP Papers; Lillian Muniz to Howard, June 27, 1944; HaF to Howard, June 28, 1944; NAC Minutes, August 29, 1944, SP Papers.

21. On Thomas's views of American-Japanese pre–Pearl Harbor relations, see NT, "What About American Morale?" Radio Broadcast, March 15, 1942, SP Papers. On Thomas and his antiwar and pacifist critics, see NT to Harold Flincker and George Kingsley, January 21, 1942; NT to Mayer, December 8, 1942, NT Papers. See also the long correspondence between Anna Graves and Thomas on the following dates: January 21, 23, and 25, 1942; February 6, 1942; August 2 and 5, 1942, NT Papers. On Jo Cantine, see correspondence between her and Thomas on March 21, 1942; April 2, 4, 1942; May 15, 1942; June 9 and 23, 1942, NT Papers. Cantine was persistent in urging Thomas to begin a "peace offensive" and a "negotiated peace drive." See her letters of September 24 and 27, 1942; January 23, 1943; April 13, 1943; May 21 and 26, 1943; August 18, 1943, NT Papers.

22. Graves to NT, April 2, 1943; NT to Editor, *Chicago Sun*, December 14, 1944, NT Papers; NT, *We Have A Destiny* (New York, 1944); Villard, review, SC, July 7, 1944.

23. See NT to Cantine on April 2, 1942. See also NT to Cantine, September 29, 1942; January 26, 1943, NT Papers.

24. The Peace Now Movement, Newsletter No. 8, January 6, 1944; GH, "America Faces the Great Decision . . ." December 30, 1943; GH, *A Plea for Immediate Peace By Negotiation* (New York, 1942), SP Papers.

25. For a pro-war liberal attack on Hartmann, see M. M. Marberry, *PM*, January 26, 1944. For the Socialist Party position on Hartmann's call for negotiations now, see Socialist Party, "Resolution on Negotiated Peace," January 1944, SP Papers.

26. Lazarus to Dancis, June 7, 1944; Arthur Calhoun to SP, U.S.A., February 1, 1944; Calhoun to HaF, February 4, 1944; Flincker to Dancis, February 29, 1944; Dancis to Glenn Miller, February 14, 1944; Meyer Miller to the NAC, January 28, 1944; Pierson Ostrow to Comrades, May 1, 1942; Ostrow to Socialist Party of Mass., n.d. [1944], SP Papers. For the Party's opposition to the Peace Now Movement, see SC, February 4, 1944.

27. NAC Minutes, January 4, 1944; "Resolution on Negotiated Peace," n.d. [January 1944]; HaF to GH, January 24, 1944; GH to HaF, January 26, 1944; HaF to GH, January 28, 1944; GH, "How to Abolish Anti-Semitism," January 28, 1944; GH to HaF, January 30, 1944, SP Papers.

28. NAC Minutes, February 29, 1944; NAC Sub-Committee Minutes, meeting with GH, February 27, 1944; HaF to Dear Comrades, March 8, 1944; TC to HaF, March 14, 1944; NT to Members of the NEC, March 1944; NAC Minutes, April 4, 1944, SP Papers.

29. For Thomas's fear of any kind of imperial peace, see NT columns in SC on April 18, 1942; July 30, 1943; September 22, 1943; October 15, 1943. For an expression early in the war of the fear of a Soviet-dominated sphere of influence, see LS, SC, March 7, 1942. On British imperialism, see SC, November 20, 1942. On India see, LS, *India's Revolution* (New York, 1943); SC, March 7 and April 25, 1942; Jim Cork, SC, August 7, 21, and 28, 1942; NT, SC, August 21, 1942; LS, SC, August 28, 1942; Proposed Platform on India, National Convention, June 1944; NT, "What About American Morale?" Radio Broadcast, March 15, 1942; NEC, Resolution on India, April 10–12, 1942; NT to FDR, August 11, 1942; NT, "India and our Honor," n.d. [c. August 1942]; Socialist Party, release, August 13, 1942, SP Papers; SC, August 21, 1942. The Socialists welcomed the Cripps mission, but were more sympathetic to the Indian rejection of it than were the liberals. On the Cripps mission, see SC, April 4, 11, and 18, 1942; NT, SC, May 1, 1942. On Gandhi and Nehru, see SC, July 31 and August 28, 1942; LS, SC, September 4, 1942; SC, February 26, 1943; Socialist Party Publicity Bureau, release, August 7, 1942; Socialist Party, release, August 9, 1942; HaF and NT to Jawaharlal

Nehru, September 2, 1942; Socialist Party Publicity Bureau, release, February 19, 1943; Socialist Party, Local New York, release, February 26, 1943, SP Papers.

30. NT, SC, October 15, 1943; Andre Martin, SC, June 4 and July 2, 1943; editorials in SC on November 19, 1943; January 29, 1945; July 23, 1945.

31. Socialist Party, news release, November 22, 1943, SP Papers.

32. On the Darlan deal, see NT, SC, December 4, 1942. On Badoglio and dealing with Italian fascists, see SC, August 6, 1943; Martin, SC, August 13, 1943; LS, SC, September 24, 1943; Roy Curtis, SC, August 13 and September 24, 1943; "Italy's Future," n.d. [1943], SP Papers. On the criticism of the liberals, see MaC, SC, January 1, 1943; Franck, SC, February 5, 1943; LS, SC, November 27, 1942.

33. On Thomas's views on diplomatic relations with the Vichy government and Franco, see NT, SC, May 1, 1942; NT to Harry Laidler, December 26, 1944, SP Papers; NT to *New York Times*, January 4, 1945, SP Papers; NT to Cordell Hull, September 1, 1942, NT Papers; NT to FDR, November 17, 1942, NT Papers.

34. The "new world"—the democratic revolution—needed to have "the form of socialism," proclaimed an editorial in *The Socialist Call*. Reformed capitalism via the New Deal was not enough. See SC, December 25, 1942.

35. Louis Clair was the pseudonym of Lewis Coser. Sebastian Franck was the pseudonym of Henry Jacoby. Jacoby also wrote under the name Andre Martin, and occasionally Coser and Jacoby used Martin when they wrote pieces together. Coser to author, March 2, 1944. On the democratic "hidden" Germany and the German underground, see Maurice Goldbloom, review of Paul Hagen, *Will Germany Crack?* SC, July 24, 1942; Martin, SC, July 16, 1943; Martin, SC, April 21, 1944; SC, January 8, 1945; "The Manifesto of Socialists in Buchenwald," SC, July 7, 1945. On antifascist resistance in occupied Europe, see Martin, SC, January 29, 1943; Al Hamilton, SC, April 2, 1943; Martin, SC, April 9, 1943; LS, SC, August 24, 1943; Curtis, SC, October 1, 1943. For the third camp position, see Louis Rose, SC, August 7, 1942; Martin, SC, December 18, 1942; Martin, SC, February 12, 1943. On Vansittartism, see SC, October 2, 1942. The Socialists associated writers like Rex Stout with Vansittartism. See SC, October 27, 1944; NT, letter to Rex Stout, SC, November 24, 1944. See also Socialist Party, Release, November 11, 1944, SP Papers; John Haynes Holmes, *If We Hate, We Shall Fail* (New York, 1942), SP Papers. On the general proposition that "no people, as a people, is responsible for this war," see Socialist Party Publicity Bureau, release, February 24, 1943, SP Papers. On the third camp criticisms of Hagen and the American Friends of German Freedom's "lesser evil" politics, see Franck, SC, July 9, 1943. On the need for Socialists to "defend the coming European revolution" from capitalist interference, see Foreign Affairs Committee, "Defend the Coming European Revolution!" [1942], SP Papers. In this statement the committee asked: "If a Wilkie [sic] and a deGaulle are too much for the American government, what treatment will a revolutionary socialist movement have to expect in Europe?"

36. Louis Clair, SC, May 14, 1943; Martin, SC, August 27, 1943. The view of

the Soviet Union as imperialist had been set forth following the Nazi-Soviet Pact by Lillian Symes. See LS, *Communism—World Revolution to Red Imperialism* (Chicago, n.d. [late 1939 or early 1940]), SP Papers.

37. Early in the war, some antiwar Socialists objected to Thomas referring to "our war" in his radio broadcasts. Their argument was that he had a right to use that kind of language when speaking as an individual but not when speaking or writing "under Party or *Call* auspices." For this controversy, see NT to Albert Hamilton, July 19, 1942; HaF to MK, July 30, 1942, SP Papers. For the kind of activity his critics had in mind (seeing Hull, appealing to Roosevelt on India), see NT, SC, September 4, 1942.

38. The Socialist Party and Thomas's ideas on postwar peace included a democratic socialist Europe, independence for colonial people, defeat of Soviet totalitarian ambitions (which they saw as counterrevolutionary and nationalistic), the prevention of American capitalism's desires for military and economic control over the world's peoples, and American aid for a postwar starving Europe. See NEC, "Socialist Statement on Peace and Postwar Plans," April 25–27, 1943, SP Papers. On Thomas and the Culbertson Plan, see NT to EC, June 17, 1942; NT to William B. Lloyd Jr., July 27, 1942, NT Papers. For Socialist criticism of the Culbertson Plan, see Curtis, SC, February 19, 1943. On Thomas's insistence on his right to support parts of the Culbertson plan, see NT to Dear Comrades, 1944 [c. spring], SP Papers.

39. For criticism of the Casablanca Conference, see SC, February 12, 1943. For criticisms of Vansittartism in the British Labour Party, see LS, SC, July 2, 1943; NEC, letter to British Labour Party, SC, August 20, 1943.

40. See, e.g., NT, SC, June 25, 1943; Martin, SC, March 24 and August 4, 1944; NT, release of speech, July 24, 1944, SP Papers; NT to *New York Times,* May 14, 1945, NT Papers.

41. Even before the policy of unconditional surrender was announced, Thomas had talked of the need for both clearer war aims and a "people's peace." See NT, SC, May 22, 1942. See also NT, "The Alternatives to 'Unconditional Surrender,'" SC, December 3, 1943.

42. On efforts to feed the children of Europe, see Hamilton to NT, February 15, 1943; NEC Minutes, July 24, 1943; NEC Resolution on Refugee and Food Problem, n.d. [July 1943], SP Papers. On talk of a peace offensive, see NT, SC, September 17, 1943; NT, SC, February 4 and 11, 1944. For the comment on the time being ripe, see NT to Overholt, August 6, 1943, NT Papers.

43. NT to GH, September 8, 1943; NT to R. F. Graesser, March 3, 1944; NT to Simon, September 21, 1943; NT to GH, March 23, 1944, NT Papers. In March 1944, Thomas wrote that the issue was not "unconditional surrender" versus a "negotiated peace"; rather, it was negotiations "on what basis and with whom and when." See NT, SC, March 3, 1944. During the period from late summer 1943 to the spring of 1944, Thomas was receiving letters from antiwar people urging him and the Socialist Party to support the Peace Now Movement. See Bessie

Simon to NT, September 20, 1943; Henry Pinkham to NT, October 10, 1943, NT Papers.

44. NT, confidential memorandum, May 1, 1944, SP Papers.

45. Ibid.

46. Villard to NT, May 3, 1944; Wolfe to NT, May 2, 1944; TC to NT, May 12, 1944, NT Papers.

47. NT, SC, May 5, 1944; NT, SC, May 26, 1944; "Resolution on Negotiated Peace," n.d. [c. June 1944]; NT to FDR, July 24, 1944, SP Papers. In a letter to the *New York Times* answering Algernon Lee's criticism of his position on "unconditional surrender," Thomas strongly denied he was for a negotiated peace with the Nazis. He was talking about a peace between peoples, he said, not one based on Big Three power politics. See NT to Editor, *New York Times*, February 21, 1944, SP Papers.

48. NT, SC, October 6 and November 3, 1944. For Thomas's "case for socialism," see NT, *The Truth About Socialism* (New York, 1943), SP Papers.

49. DM, "Thomas for President?" *Politics*, October 1944, 278–81. One young member of the Young People's Socialist League (YPSL) was so upset by Macdonald's criticism that he suggested that Macdonald "go fornicate behind some volumes of Lenin instead of spending your time trying to hinder the Socialist movement." See Irwin Suall, letter, *Politics*, November 1944, 318.

50. For Thomas's criticism of the liberals' focusing their critique on the State Department and not Roosevelt, see NT, SC, September 3, 1943. See also LS, SC, September 10, 1943.

51. See NT column, editorial, Phil Heller article, and news stories in SC, February 19, 1945; MaC, SC, March 5, 1945; NT, SC, March 5, 1945; "The Yalta Decisions," April 9, 1945. Maynard Krueger and Harry Fleischman charged that Yalta betrayed the Atlantic Charter and set the stage for World War III. See Socialist Party, release, February 16, 1945, SP Papers.

52. For Socialist criticism of the San Francisco conference and the United Nations, see "Socialist Statement on San Francisco Conference," SC, April 23, 1945; Martin, SC, April 23, 1945. On Thomas's support for ratification of the United Nations Charter, see NT, SC, July 16, 1945. See also SC, July 2, 1945. On Socialist criticism of Thomas's and the party's position on the UN Charter, see Cork, SC, August 6, 1945; TC, letter, SC, July 30, 1945.

53. Thomas's 1945 pamphlet *Russia: Promise and Performance* was his effort to explain his criticism of the Soviet Union, as well as to set forth the prospects for avoiding war with it. See also NT to WiB, July 2, 1945, NT Papers. Thomas denied that he wanted war with Russia in reply to criticism by Max Lerner. See NT, SC, June 18, 1945.

54. NT to Mrs. J. C. Coons, October 1, 1945, SP Papers; NT, *Russia: Promise and Performance* (New York, 1945).

55. SC, March 12 and 26, 1943; Socialist Party, release, March 4, 1943; Socialist Party, Local New York, March 5, 1943, SP Papers. Fleischman explained the

executions as resulting from the opposition of a "militant, revolutionary, democratic Socialism" to Stalin's totalitarian and imperialist ambitions in Europe after the war. See release, April 23, 1943, SP Papers. The Socialists criticized the tepid response of *The Nation* to the murder of Alter and Ehrlich. See SC, March 26, 1943. See also NT, SC, October 20, 1944. On the fear of Soviet power, see NT, SC, February 5 and June 25, 1945.

56. NT, SC, July 7, 1944; NT, release, June 26, 1944, SP Papers; NT to Cordell Hull, June 26, 1944, NT Papers; NT, SC, September 10, 1945. For Howard's writing on Pearl Harbor, see Howard, SC, January 10 and February 28, 1942. Howard was hardly a reliable writer. During one interparty controversy he accused the Chinese writer Lin Yutang of being "a Moscow fellow traveler"—at a time when Lin was formulating his anticommunist view of Chinese politics in *Between Laughter and Tears*. See Howard to NAC, June 17, 1942, SP Papers.

57. On criticisms of dollar-a-year men, see Hamilton, SC, April 11, 1942. Like the liberals, the Socialists zeroed in on Standard Oil's ties with Nazism. See Hamilton, SC, April 4, 1942. On Lewis and the miners, see articles in SC by MaC on October 23, 1942; April 2, 1943; May 21, 1943; June 4, 1943; December 3, 1943. See also JD, SC, May 14, 1943; Louis Nelson, SC, May 21, 1943; NT, SC, May 21, 1943; HaF, SC, May 21, 1943; SC, November 26, 1943. There were differences among Socialists over Lewis. See Alvaine Hamilton to HaF, June 7, 1943, SP Papers. For Socialist criticisms of the no-strike pledge, see WiB, SC, May 8, 1942; WiB, SC, July 28, 1944; JD, SC, July 28, 1944. On the need for the Socialist Party to take greater advantage of labor grassroots militancy, to defend labor against the antilabor trend in the country and the New Deal, and to steer the rank and file away from its leaders' effort to tie it to the war and the state, see Louis Clair, L. S. Rose, and Sebastian Franck, memo, n.d. [1943], SP Papers. The issues confronting labor in World War II are analyzed perceptively in Nelson Lichtenstein, *Labor's War at Home* (Cambridge, 1982).

58. On the Labor Draft, see SC, April 25, 1942; Barshop, SC, May 1, 1942; SC , April 2 and 16 1943; NT, SC, April 23, 1943; SC, June 25 and July 9, 1943; Robin Myers, SC, July 9, 1943; NT, SC, January 21 and 28, 1944; WiB, SC, January 21, 1944; NEC, Resolution on Labor Draft, April 10–12, 1942. The Socialist critique of the National Service Act and other attempts to draft labor can be seen as part of a general critique of the government's power to conscript its citizens. See, e.g., NT, SC, September 17, 1943. Becker was also concerned that the wartime "maintenance of membership" agreement (which was generally seen as offering protection for unions) would make the unions too dependent on government. See WiB, SC, May 29, 1942. For criticism of the War Labor Board, see, e.g., WiB, SC, April 16, 1943.

59. See, e.g., NT, *Conscription: A Test of the Peace* (New York, 1944), SP Papers; NT to Cong. Andrew May, January 10, 1945, NT Papers; SC, September 22 and 29, 1944; NT, SC, November 17, 1944; JD and TC, *Democracy Is Not Doomed* (New York, 1945). For other Socialist critiques of Hayek, see TC, SC, May 7, 1945;

MaC, SC, May 7, 1945. For the Socialist fear of how the war economy could lead to statism and a kind of totalitarian state capitalism, see "Socialist Statement on the War," n.d., SP Papers. For a Socialist program for democratizing and socializing the economy in order to combat the totalitarian dangers to freedom and economic standards in the wartime economy, see "An Economic Program for War-Time," n.d., SP Papers.

60. Barshop, SC, December 11, 1942; Aaron Levenstein, SC, December 18, 1942; SC, December 18, 1942; LS, SC, January 1, 1943; Raymond Hofses, SC, May 7, 1943; Frank Marquart, SC, March 12, 1945. For Thomas's fear of the Murray Bill's possibility of state control, see NT to F. D. Atherton, January 10, 1945, NT Papers.

61. Material on the Socialist Party Full-Production Bill and the Murray Bill can be found in December 1944–January 1945, SP Papers. See also "Socialists to Push Own Unemployment Bill," SC, March 12, 1945; Levenstein, SC, July 30, 1945. In addition, the Socialist efforts to develop, circulate and to find sponsors for their full employment bill can be followed in the numerous letters between March 1945 and January 1946 in the SP Papers. Material on the Socialist Party regarding its bill and the Murray Bill can be found between September and November 1945, SP Papers. Initially the Socialists had emphasized that their full employment bill was a substitute for—not an amendment to—the Murray Bill. NT to HaF, July 18, 1945, SP Papers.

62. Thomas corresponded with Ann Ray about the internment during the first half of 1942 and again in January 1943. He corresponded with Hugh Macbeth throughout 1942. Macbeth, in turn, corresponded with FDR, Paul McNutt, and Gen. DeWitt. Thomas corresponded with John McCloy in October 1942 and with Dillon Myer in January 1943. Thomas was in correspondence with such religious leaders and pacifists as Paul Hutchinson of the *Christian Century,* John Nevin Sayre, and John Haynes Holmes about the internment. He also encouraged fellow Socialists like Travers Clement, Al Hamilton, and Howard Penly to become involved. In addition, he had frequent correspondence with Caleb Foote, who was writing a pamphlet for the Fellowship of Reconciliation during the summer of 1942. This extensive correspondence can be found in the NT Papers. In addition, Thomas and the Socialists publicly exposed the plight of the internees and protested the internment. The NEC passed a protest resolution. See NEC, Resolution on Japanese Evacuation, April 10–12, 1942, SP Papers. See also MK, memo to National Action Committee, n.d. [c. summer 1942]; NEC, Resolution on Racism, n.d. [July 1943], SP Papers. Thomas published a pamphlet on the internment in which he challenged the legal premises of the action. See NT, *Democracy and Japanese Americans* (New York, 1942). And the *Socialist Call* printed frequent critiques of the action—critiques that raised the civil liberties issues and that held the president accountable. See, e.g., TC, SC, February 21, 1942; "Let's Not Hound Them," SC, February 21, 1942; NT, SC, March 7, 1942; "Persecution in a Democracy," SC, March 14, 1942.

63. Among the Japanese Americans Thomas corresponded with were Sam Hohri, Mike Masaoka, Hideo Hashimoto, and Kiyoshi Hamanaka. Most of the letters written between the spring of 1942 and the fall of 1943 are located in the NT Papers. On Thomas's answer to the Communist position on the internment of Japanese Americans, see NT to Editor, *San Francisco Chronicle*, September 16, 1942, NT Papers. On Thomas and Margaret Anderson, see NT to Anderson, January 15, 1943; Anderson to Kiyoshi Okamoto, March 2, 1943; NT to Ina Sugihara, March 3, 1943; Anderson to NT, March 23, 1943; Anderson to NT, December 27, 1943. At one point in their correspondence, it appeared that Anderson was ready to join in unambiguous opposition. But she always fell back on focusing on improvements in camp conditions combined with recommendations that the internees not be disruptive, a position that Thomas did not oppose but that he felt was compatible with principled opposition. At one point Anderson expressed worry over the Nisei's "tendency to regard democracy as something outside themselves — something that failed and will have to remedy its failure — the remedy to come to them as something of a gift perhaps, not something they too have to work for." The quotation on "the most totalitarian act" is in NT, SC, November 17, 1944. See also NT, SC, August 21, 1942.

64. On the Lynn Case, see Lynn to NT, September 29, 1942; NT to L. M. Ervin, June 3, 1943; Wilfred H. Kerr to NT, October 27, 1944, NT Papers; LS, SC, September 24, 1943; Layle Lane to HaF, June 3, 1944; Lane to Dear Friend, April 16, 1943; Ervin to Dear Friends, May 28, 1943; Robin Myers to Members of the Central Executive Committee, July 14, 1943, SP Papers. Articles and editorials on the Waller Case can be found regularly in SC between December 1941 and July 1942. See also NT to Gov. Colgate Darden, June 8, 1942, NT Papers; March on Washington, release, July 20, 1942; Negro Rights Committee, "Report on Washington Delegation on the Waller Case," July 2, 1942, SP Papers. On the Alton Levy case, see almost weekly articles between September 1943 and January 1944. See also John McCloy to NT, September 28, 1943; Levy to NT, December 30, 1943, NT Papers; Untitled, August 16, 1943; Levy, letters, July 28–August 16, 1943, SP Papers. On the March on Washington Movement, see SC, June 19, 1942; Jack Sessions, SC, June 26, 1942; Pauli Murray, SC, June 26, 1942; Lane, SC, July 16, 1943; Bob Marshall to HaF, April 16, 1943; NEC, Minutes, July 24, 1943; "Eight Point Program," March on Washington Movement, n.d., SP Papers. Judah Drob published several articles on the Detroit Socialists' struggle for integrated housing in SC between March 1942 and May 1943. On the FEPC, see articles in SC on June 25, 1943; September 24, 1943; November 5, 1943; January 7, 1944; March 10, 1944. See also TC and Samuel Friedman to FDR, October 30, 1943; NT to Hon. Mary T. Norton, June 20, 1944.

65. On the efforts of the Socialist Party to publicize the conscientious-objector situation through the SC, see NT, March 14, 1942; Seymour Etkin, May 15, 1942; Etkin, September 4, 1942; NT, December 11, 1942; Bob Marshall, January 8, 1943; Philip Isely, April 2, 1943; NEC Resolution, May 7, 1943; Washington Call Bu-

reau, October 29, 1943; NT, February 18, 1944; "The Forgotten Fighters," December 22, 1944. The NT Papers contain his voluminous correspondence about conscientious objectors—their cases and the conditions in the prisons and camps. There are many letters to officials, including President Roosevelt, Francis Biddle, Lewis Hershey, John McCloy, and James Bennett—the latter over prison conditions including an important case in Missouri in 1943–44. There is correspondence involving the conscientious-objector work of his brother, Evan, and letters to leading pacifists like A.J. Muste and Clarence Pickett. Most of all, there is the correspondence with the conscientious objectors themselves and those seeking conscientious-objector status. In the SP Papers, see NEC, Statement on Conscientious Objectors, October 20, 1942; NEC, Resolution on Conscientious Objectors, December 28, 1942; Dancis to Muste and Evan Thomas, April 11, 1943; NEC Minutes, Resolution on C.O.'s on Strike in Danbury and Lewisburg, November 19–21, 1943.

66. NT, SC, August 20, 1945; "Atomic Era," SC, August 13, 1945; "Socialize Atomic Energy," SC, October 1, 1945. For the Socialist program of international control, see Aaron Levenstein, *The Atomic Age* (New York, 1946). See editorial, CC, August 15, 1945; "Atomic Atrocity," CC, August 29, 1945; DM, "The Bomb," *Politics*, September 1945, 257–60.

67. On the poll tax, see, e.g., Resolution on the Poll Tax, SC, July 3, 1942; Statement on Poll Tax, n.d. [1944], SP Papers; HaF to NT, February 18, 1942, NT Papers. On the Dies committee, see, e.g., SC, April 25, 1942; NT, *Martin Dies and Socialism* (New York, 1943), SP Papers.

68. For Socialist concerns and criticisms of the Communists in the labor unions, see Sheehan to HaF, January 28, 1942; Bob to WiB, April 16, 1943; JD to WiB, September 8, 1945, SP Papers.

69. NT, Open Letter to Sidney Hillman, SC, October 6, 1944. For the Socialist position on the American Labor Party, see "Statement on Labor Party," n.d. [1943], SP Papers. At one point, Fleischman wrote to Drob that he was badly misinformed in thinking that the ALP was moving closer to independent political action. Both wings had endorsed Roosevelt, he reported, and the right wing had "doubled in spades everything the Communists say about Roosevelt." HaF to JD, March 13, 1944; JD to HaF, March 15, 1944, SP Papers.

70. NT to JD, May 7, 1942, NT Papers.

CHAPTER 11

All references to papers in this chapter are to the ADA Papers unless otherwise noted.

1. In R-F 10-165, BB to JL, November 29, 1946; BB to Gentlemen, November 29, 1946; JL to BB, December 6, 1946.

2. The Loeb-Bowles negotiations can be found in R-F 2-30, R-F 4-63, R-F 9-

125, and in the following letters in the CB Papers: JL to CB, October 21, 1946; JL to CB, December 9, 1946.

3. HW, "The Enemy Is Not Each Other," *NR*, January 27, 1947, 23; JL to CB, January 25, 1947; CB to JL, February 1, 1947, CB Papers. See also David Ginsburg to CB, January 23, 1947.

4. Lillie Schulz to CM, February 24, 1947, FK Papers; CM to Schulz, February 18, 1947, FK Papers.

5. On the Warburgs' resignations see the following letters in R-F 4-47: RN to Mrs. James Warburg, April 12, 1946; JL to Mrs. James Warburg, April 25, 1946; Phyllis Warburg to JL, May 14, 1946; JL to Mrs. James Warburg, June 3, 1946. See also Shad Polier to Lash, March 26, 1947, R-F 11-171; Lillie S. Mayer to Eduard Lindemann, April 11, 1947, R-F 11-171.

6. JL to HW, February 25, 1946, R-F 10-153; "Union for Democratic Action Statement on Henry Wallace," September 24, 1946, R-F 13-212; JL to HW, September 27, 1946, R-F 5-83; JL to HW, September 21, 1946, R-F 16-18; JL to HW, October 2, 1946, R-F 16-288.

7. JL to HW, October 23, 1946, R-F 9-125. See also JL to BB, October 29, 1946, R-F 10-165. Some of Lee's comments on Wallace are contained in a letter, Lee to JL, September 19, 1946, R-F 9-130. But it is not clear if this is the "confidential letter" from Lee he mentioned in his note to Wallace. Loeb's private annoyance at Wallace is expressed in a letter to David Williams at the time Bowles was threatening to withdraw from the January 1947 conference: "I lived in this world for several years with Henry Wallace doing us all kinds of dirty tricks simply because Beanie Baldwin or somebody of that school of post-progressivism urged him to. I said nothing during that whole period, but if Chester Bowles, whatever his convictions, is going to make his decisions in the Wallace manner, I can assure him that it will be public property." See JL to DW, December 17, 1946, R-F 4-63. And in a letter to Joe Lash in late 1946, Loeb described Wallace as "punch-drunk, hitting out wildly in all directions." JL to Lash, November 5, 1946, R-F 12-189. Material on the UDA's response to the Wallace speech and resignation can be found in R-F 16-288. Plans for a "National Conference of Democratic Progressives" had begun in the spring and summer of 1946. See "Confidential Memorandum," July 1, 1946, RN Papers; JL to Murray Gross, May 4, 1946, R-F 10-153.

8. On *PM* see ML, October 3, 1945; March 5 and 15, 1946; June 11, 1946; September 2, 1946; AU, October 21 and 29, 1945; Saul Padover, May 30, 1946; October 18, 1946; *PM*, July 24, 1946; IS, *PM*, September 29, 1946. See "Paris Post-Mortem," *NR*, June 3, 1946, 788–89; *N*, May 25, 1946, 613; "Post Mortem on Paris," *N*, June 1, 1946, 644–45. On *CS*, see "Russia's Dead Idealism," *CS*, February 1945, 39. Louis Fischer described the Soviet Union as "immoral, dictatorial, and imperialistic." See LF to Jerome Davis, February 1, 1947, LF Papers. See also LF, "The Partitioning of Peace," *CS*, April 1945, 5–8. In an April 1946 Town Meeting of the Air debate, Lerner and Fischer represented the two sides of the emerging

debate on U.S.-Soviet relations. Both agreed that Russia was expansionist, but they disagreed on the causes. Whereas Fischer saw Soviet expansionism flowing inevitably from the dictatorship and from Russian nationalism, Lerner denied its inevitability. He believed that the United Nations and greater Big Three cooperation would remove the sources of Russian imperialism. See "What Are the Real Issues Behind the Russian-Iranian Dispute?" *Town Meeting*, April 11, 1946, LF Papers. See also LF to ML, October 30, 1947, ML Papers.

9. For the feeling of liberals being shunted aside or feeling out of place in Washington, see Henry Zon, "The Melody is Gone," *N*, October 12, 1946, 404–5. On Truman and labor, see "Truman's Blunder," *NR*, June 3, 1946, 787–88; HF, "Has Truman Lost Labor?" *NR*, June 10, 1946, 826–28; "Truman v. Labor," *NR*, June 10, 1946, 820; "The Labor Crisis," *N*, June 1, 1946, 641–43. In *PM*, Lerner wrote that Truman had asked Congress "for a blank check which would give him a dictator's life-and-death power over American labor." See ML, *PM*, May 28, 1946.

10. Lash, untitled report, n.d. [c. 1946], R-F 9-139. On Lash's belief on the need for a more "comprehensive political documentation," see Lash to JL, April 8, 1946, RN Papers. For Loeb's reply to Lash's desire for a more comprehensive ideological framework, see JL to Lash, April 16, 1946, R-F 12-189. See also Lash to RB, October 25, 1946, R-F 13-210.

11. FK, "Fragments of One World," *N*, May 19, 1945, 560–61; "The Perils of Victory," *NR*, August 20, 1945, 204. On the earlier sentiments, see FK, "The Peace Plans," *N*, September 2, 1944, 256; ML, "In the Wake of Liberation," *NR*, June 6, 1944. On Kirchwey's continued hopes and support for a democratic revolution in Europe, see FK, "Out of the Ashes," *N*, April 7, 1945, 377.

12. On the UDA, the British government and Palestine, see JL to Rabbi Stephen Wise, July 13, 1946, R-F 4-47; UDA, release, n.d. [c. June 1946], R-F 13-228; "Britain, Palestine and the Loan," *UDA Bulletin*, June 1946, R-F 16-306. On Niebuhr's dissatisfaction with Britain's policy on Palestine, see RN, "Palestine: British-American Dilemma," *N*, August 31, 1946, 238–39. For the UDA defense of the British Labour Party, see Untitled Speech [almost certainly by JL], May 11, 1946, R-F 9-125; JL to JV, April 23, 1946, R-F 7-95; "Democratic Liberals Must Stand Together," *UDA Bulletin*, March 1946, R-F 16-306.

13. On the UDA and United States's policy toward the Soviet Union, see, e.g., Hans Simon, statement, February 14, 1946, R-F 14-245 and material in R-F 2-30, 5-83, 5-86. On the UDA's efforts to have Truman respond positively to Stalin's "conciliatory remarks," see UDA, release, September 30, 1946, R-F 13-212.

14. In commenting on the Popular Front quality of the Win-the-Peace Conference sponsors, JL wrote Joe Lash: "Politically this sort of thing is suicidal, as witness France yesterday. Morally it is bankrupt." JL to Lash, May 7, 1946, R-F 12-189, ADA Papers.

15. JL to RN, June 10, 1946, R-F 9-144.

16. BB to JL, April 9, 1946, R-F 12-189; JL, "Progressives and Communists," *NR*, May 13, 1946, 699.

17. JL, "Progressives and Communists," 699. A month later, Loeb published a more extended critique of the Communist Party and of the idea of liberal-Communist cooperation. See JL, "Communists Are Greater Threat to Liberals Than to Rightists," *St. Louis Post Dispatch*, June 16, 1946, R-F 10-154.

18. For the confidential memo on the Win-the-Peace Conference, see memorandum on the Win-the-Peace Conference held April 5, 6, and 7, 1946, R-F 4-58.

19. Material on the plans leading up to the January conference and the creation of UDA can be found in R-F 1-2, 2-30, 7-98, 7-105, 7-119, 8-123, 9-125, 9-135, 9-146, 12-189, 13-222, 14-245. Material on the Chicago Conference of Progressives, including the conference speeches, can be found in R-F 2-30 and 2-31. In a long memo to Eleanor Roosevelt, Loeb outlined the inadequacies of the Chicago conference, particularly its sponsorship by NC-PAC and the ICC. See JL to Mrs. FDR, October 10, 1946, R-F 9-135. Murray, speech, September 28, 1946, R-F 2-31; Pepper, speech, September 28, 1946, R-F 2-31; Ickes, speech, September 28, 1946, R-F 2-31.

20. It would appear that Frank McCulloch of the Chicago UDA and Douglas Anderson, national secretary treasurer of the United Railroad Workers, sent reports to Loeb. See unsigned and untitled report on the conference, R-F 1-31; Unsigned to Murray [draft], October 10, 1946, R-F 9-125; On Murray sending representatives to Loeb's Conference, see JL to Ellery Foster, December 17, 1946, R-F 2-30; JL to David Dubinsky, November 14, 1946, R-F 2-30.

21. "After the Wallace Dismissal: 1. Crisis in Foreign Policy," *NR*, September 30, 1946, 395; FK, "The Challenge of Henry Wallace," *N*, September 28, 1946, 337–339; *PM*, September 13, 1946; Padover, *PM*, September 15, 1946; ML, *PM*, September 16, 1946.

22. "UDA Statement on Henry Wallace," September 24, 1946, R-F 9-147; JL to Louis Burgess, November 18, 1946, R-F 9-150. For the UDA general consideration and response to the Wallace speech, See Minutes of National Board, September 24, 1946, R-F 9-146; NP, statement, September 19, 1946, R-F 10-151; JL to HW, September 27, 1946, R-F 5-83.

23. See J. and S. Alsop, "Liberals and Russia: Why Not Be Russia-Obsessed?" *NR*, October 14, 1946, 481–82; ML, "A Positive Plan for Peace," *NR*, October 14, 1946, 482–83. See also J. Alsop to ML, April 16, 1946; ML to J. Alsop, April 23, 1946; J. Alsop to ML, April 25, 1946, ML Papers.

24. On the formation of the PCA and ADA, see "PCA for Progress," *NR*, January 6, 1947, 8; HF, "The Liberals—Split As Usual," *NR*, January 13, 1947, 26–27; HW, "The Enemy Is Not Each Other," *NR*, January 27, 1947, 22–23; *N*, January 4, 1947, 1; *N*, January 11, 1947, 29–30; FK, "Mugwumps in Action," *N*, January 18, 1947, 61–62; ML, "The Long March," *PM*, January 9, 1947. Lash made unsuccessful efforts to persuade Lerner to have *PM* take a more positive view

toward ADA (it had "potentialities for political effectiveness"), see Lash to JL, January 8, 1947, R-F 12-189. Material on the formation and early statements of ADA can be found in R-F 12-205; 14–245; 16–288; 16–291.

25. JP to CB, January 28, 1947; JP to CB, February 14, 1947, CB Papers. For Amlie's criticisms of the Communists, see TA to HoW, n.d. [1940]; TA to GA, May 30, 1945; TA to JM, April 26, 1946; TA to HoW, June 15, 1946; TA to JM, July 29, 1946, TA Papers. For his criticism of postwar liberalism, the ADA, and the PCA, see TA to Howard [McMurray], October 10, 1947; TA to Nathan Levine, February 4, 1947, TA Papers. In April 1947 Amlie wrote Richard Hippelhauser a long, withering analysis of the role the Communist Party had played during and after the war and of the failure of the ADA to provide a better alternative. TA to Hippelhauser, April 21, 1947, TA Papers.

26. JL, letter, *NR*, January 27, 1947, 3, 46.

27. Ibid., 46. See also JL, letter, February 3, 1947, 45. For a similar belief that the liberals had to get the Communists "out of their hair," see J. Alsop to ML, April 16, 1946, ML Papers.

28. Ibid.

29. Ibid.

30. Bendiner, "Revolt of the Middle," *N*, January 18, 1947, 65–66.

31. HF, "The Liberals — Split As Usual," *NR*, January 13, 1947, 26–27; Jo Davidson and Frank Kingdon, letter, *NR*, January 27, 1947, 45.

32. On the managed orchestration of the conference, see JL to Lash, December 17, 1946, R-F 12-189 and material in R-F 2-30. Given the organizers of the conference, the kind of statements that might emerge from it were predictable. But the fact that in mid-December Arthur Schlesinger Jr. was already drafting press releases for an organizing conference three weeks away suggests how tightly the organizers wished to control its orientation. See AMS Jr, "Draft Press Release," December 13, 1946, R-F 14-245. A confidential "Preliminary and Provisional Statement of Principles" was also being worked on in November; November 15, 1946, R-F 9-135. For the complaint to Niebuhr, see RCJ [no full name given] to RN, February 8, 1948, RN Papers.

33. *NR*, April 15, 1946, 521–60; Lash, "The Roosevelt Heritage," *Our Town*, n.d. [c. May 1946], R-F 12-189. On the resentment of the Wallaceites' appeal to the memory of Roosevelt, see JL, "The Communists: Problem Children of the Left," n.d. [1946], R-F 9-139.

34. HW, "Jobs Peace Freedom," *NR*, December 16, 1946, 785. On Loeb's acknowledgement that Mark Ethridge and Paul Porter played a role in gaining ADA support for military and economic aid to Greece and Turkey, see Charles Bolte to Wilson Wyatt et al., April 23, 1947, R-F 7-99; JL to State AVC Chairman, Indiana, April 25, 1947, R-F 7-99; JL to Co-Chairman of the Williams College Spring Conference of 1947, April 25, 1947, R-F 7-99. On the UDA support for the Truman Doctrine, see Wyatt, speech, April 8, 1947, R-F 5-83; David Lloyd to Wyatt

and Henderson, April 10, 1947, R-F 5-83; JL to All ADA Chapters, April 19, 1947, R-F 7-99; ADA, release, April 19, 1947, R-F 7-99.

35. One Wallace supporter wrote to Bowles that the New Deal had been "scuttled" and "shunted off into corners." Eddie to CB, n.d. [March 1948], CB Papers. On the other hand, Loeb saw himself and his associates as the inheritors of the New Deal. In debating with Lash on the direction UDA should take in 1946, Loeb referred to themselves as "we New Dealers." JL to Lash, April 6, 1946, R-F 9-125. On the resentment of the manipulation of Roosevelt's name, see memorandum on the Win-the-Peace Conference, April 5–7, 1946, R-F 4-58. In one of its first releases, the ADA announced its founding conference had agreed on the principle that "the New Deal program must be expanded." See ADA, release, January 4, 1947, R-F 12-205.

36. On Hillman's vision and the New Deal, see Fraser, *Labor Will Rule*. On the labor movement during World War II, see Lichtenstein, *Labor's War at Home*. On the trend of labor looking toward Washington, conversations with Richard Greenwald, 1994–95. On Loeb's hopes for a new liberal-labor dynamic alliance in ADA, see JL to Frank McAllister, December 3, 1946, R-F 1-2 and the following letters in R-F 2-30: JL to Milton Murray, November 26, 1946; JL to Walter Reuther, November 26, 1946; JL to David Niles, November 29, 1946. The draft report on the Chicago Conference of Progressives that was sent to Philip Murray affirmed the need for a stronger alliance of liberals and labor. See Unsigned to Murray, October 10, 1946, R-F 9-125.

37. Bolte, "A Democratic Assembly," N, April 12, 1947, 424.

38. Katha Pollitt, "We Were Wrong: Why I'm Not Voting for Clinton," N, October 7, 1996, 9.

39. On the nationalization of German industry, see RN to James Byrnes, October 23, 1946, R-F 9-125; UDA, release, October 28, 1946, R-F 14-245; National Office UDA to UDA Member, December 16, 1946, R-F 2-30. On support of "something like socialist democracy in distinction to our laissez faire democracy," see "Notes on Foreign Policy," n.d. [c. 1947], R-F 13-222. The "blood brothers" quotation is in JL to RN, October 22, 1947, R-F 13-222.

40. HW, "Job Peace Freedom," NR, December 16, 1946, 785; ML, PM, April 16, 1946; "Wallace—a World Leader," NR, September 23, 1946, 341; ADA, release, January 17, 1947, R-F 14-245. See also ML, PM, May 15, 1946. When a UDA writer (probably Lash) wrote that the UDA had to make the Democratic Party "more truly representative of the popular will," it was clear that the popular will was assumed to be progressive. See Untitled Report n.d. [1945 or 1946], R-F 9-139. On the progressive educators and the people, see Lawrence Cremin, *The Transformation of the School* (New York, 1961), 314–27, 350.

41. Lewis Mumford, *Values for Survival* (New York, 1946), 78–130.

42. Cork, SC, May 7, 1945.

Index